P9-BHX-470

GENDER
GENRE
AND
RELIGION
FEMINIST REFLECTIONS

EDITED BY
MORNY JOY AND
EVA K. NEUMAIER-DARGYAY

Many feminists today are challenging the outmoded aspects of both the conventions and the study of religion in radical ways. Canadian feminists are no exception.

Gender, Genre and Religion is the outcome of a research network of leading women scholars organized to survey the contribution of Canadian women working in the field of religious studies and, further, to "plot the path forward." This collection of their essays covers most of the major religious traditions and offers exciting suggestions as to how religious traditions will change as women take on more central roles.

Feminist theories have been used by all contributors as a springboard to show that the assumptions of unified monolithic religions and their respective canons is a fabrication created by a scholarship based on male privilege. Using gender and genre as analytical tools, the essays reflect a diversity of approaches and open up new ways of reading sacred texts. Superb essays by Pamela Dickey Young, Winnie Tomm, Morny Joy and Marsha Hewitt, among others, honour the first generation of feminist theologians and situate the current generation, showing how they have learned from and gone beyond their predecessors.

The sensitive and original essays in *Gender, Genre and Religion* will be of interest to feminist scholars and to anyone teaching women and religion courses.

Morny Joy is Associate Professor in the Department of Religious Studies, University of Calgary. She has published many articles on women and religion, feminist theory and contemporary continental philosophy.

Eva Neumaier-Dargyay is Professor and Acting Chair of Comparative Studies in Literature, Film and Religion at the University of Alberta. She has published four single-authored books and one co-authored one on various subjects of Tibetan religion and culture.

GENDER GENRE AND RELIGION

FEMINIST REFLECTIONS

EDITED BY
MORNY JOY AND
EVA K. NEUMAIER-DARGYAY

Essays by

Mary Gerhart

Norma Baumel Joseph

Monique Dumais

Doreen Spence

Eva K. Neumaier-Dargyay

Francine Michaud

Marilyn J. Legge

Marsha Hewitt

Eileen Schuller

Pamela Dickey Young

Naomi R. Goldenberg

Sheila McDonough

Katherine K. Young

Fan Pen Chen

Winnie Tomm

Morny Joy

Published by
Wilfrid Laurier University Press
for
The Calgary Institute for the Humanities

Canadian Cataloguing in Publication Data

Main entry under title:

Gender, genre and religion : feminist reflections

Revised papers originally presented at the
seminar Plotting the paths forward : the future
of women and religious studies convened by the
Calgary Institute for the Humanities in Sept. 1991.
Includes bibliographical references and index.
ISBN 0-88920-253-2

1. Women and religion – Congresses.   2. Feminist
theology – Canada – Congresses.   I. Joy, Morny.
II. Neumaier-Dargyay, E. K. (Eva K.), 1937-
III. Gerhart, Mary.   IV. Calgary Institute for
the Humanities.

BL458.G45 1995   291′.082   C95-930903-9

Copyright © 1995

Wilfrid Laurier University Press
Waterloo, Ontario, Canada
N2L 3C5

Cover design by Leslie Macredie

Printed in the United States of America

Chapter 15, "The Negative Power of 'the Feminine': Herbert Marcuse, Mary Daly and Gynocentric Feminism," by Marsha Hewitt, is reprinted by permission from *Critical Theory of Religion* by Marsha Hewitt, copyright © 1995 Augsburg Fortress.

Gender, Genre and Religion: Feminist Reflections has been produced from a manuscript supplied in camera-ready form by The Calgary Institute for the Humanities

All rights reserved. No part of this work covered by the copyrights hereon may be reproduced or used in any form or by any means—graphic, electronic or mechanical—without the prior written permission of the publisher. Any request for photocopying, recording, taping or reproducing in information storage and retrieval systems of any part of this book shall be directed in writing to the Canadian Reprography Collective, 214 King Street West, Suite 312, Toronto, Ontario M5V 3S6.

TABLE OF CONTENTS

AUGUSTANA UNIVERSITY COLLEGE
LIBRARY

FOREWORD

Established in 1976, the Calgary Institute for the Humanities has as its aim the fostering of advanced study and research in all areas of the humanities. Apart from supporting work in the traditional humanities disciplines such as philosophy, history and ancient and modern languages and literatures, it also promotes research into the philosophical and historical aspects of the sciences, social sciences, fine arts and the various professional disciplines.

The Institute's programs in support of advanced study provide scholars with time to carry out their work. In addition, the Institute sponsors formal and informal gatherings among people who share common interests, in order to promote intellectual dialogue and discussion. Recently, the Institute has moved to foster the application of humanistic knowledge to contemporary social problems.

In keeping with its commitment to sponsor intellectual interaction across disciplines and to focus on issues affecting contemporary society, the Institute convened the seminar *Plotting the Paths Forward: The Future of Women and Religious Studies* in September 1991. The chapters included in this volume arise from papers that were presented and discussed at that seminar. They have since been reconsidered and revised to accommodate the new insights the authors achieved by sharing their ideas with one another. The book is not only a history of feminist scholarship of women and religion in Canada, but a valuable suggestion as to how religious traditions will change as women take on more central roles.

We wish to record our thanks to the Social Sciences and Humanities Research Council of Canada, The University of Calgary Research Grant Committee, the Department of Religious Studies, and the Faculties of Humanities and General Studies at the University of Calgary for their financial support.

Jane H. Kelley
Director
The Calgary Institute
for the Humanities

PREFACE

This book is the outcome of a research network of invited women scholars organized with the intention of surveying the contribution of women
working in the field of Religious Studies. The collection of essays, covering most of the major religious traditions, and which are published for the
first time in this volume, reflects the current situation after twenty years
of feminist scholarship in Canada concerned with women and religion.
Feminist theories have been used by all contributors as a springboard
permitting them to show that the assumption of unified monolithic religions and their respective canons is a fabrication created by scholarship
based on a male perspective. Participants first met in September 1991, on
the invitation of the Calgary Institute for the Humanities, University of
Calgary.[1] This gathering marked the seventeenth anniversary of the first
courses offered in *Women and Religion* at Concordia University, Montreal, in the academic year 1974-75. As well as being a time for assessment, it was also an opportunity to look to the future—to the pathways
that are opening up to innovative and constructive ways of studying how
the concepts of "genre" and "gender" affect the role and status of women
in religion.

There are acknowledgements to the many people who have contributed to this project. Firstly, Dr. Harold Coward, the former Director
of the Calgary Institute for the Humanities provided the strong encour-
agement needed to get such a research project underway. Without the
careful attention to detail of Gerry Dyer, the Institute Administrator, and
Cindy Atkinson, Institute Secretary, the research network would not have
been the success that it was. A special tribute is due to John King's
acumen at copyediting. Connie Fiell-Mahoney, Joan Eadie, Evelyn
Siegfried and Polly Luke have also all made vital contributions at various
stages of the preparation of the manuscript. To all of these people, thank
you.

Morny Joy
Eva K. Neumaier-Dargyay

1 The research grants received from the Social Sciences and Humanities Research
   Council and from the University of Calgary are gratefully acknowledged.

ABOUT THE AUTHORS

Norma Baumel Joseph is a member of the faculty in the Department of Religion at Concordia University, Montreal. For the past eighteen years she has been teaching, lecturing and publishing on women and Judaism, Jewish law and ethics and women and religion. She has lobbied for Jewish women's rights in a variety of contexts, forming local and international groups to further those goals. Norma appeared in and was consultant to the film *Half the Kingdom*. "Mostly, I love teaching, especially teaching women. There is so much on our agenda, we have so much to do; but first we must learn, reflect and study. And then we must share, empower and act."

Fan Pen Chen was born in Taiwan. She grew up in Taiwan, Libya and the US. She received her BA from Yale University and completed her MA, MPhil and PhD in Chinese literature at Columbia University. Having taught at the University of Calgary and the University of Alberta, Fan is currently an Assistant Professor at the Department of East Asian Studies at SUNY-Albany. Her numerous articles in both English and Chinese deal with the treatment of female personae in a wide range of genres of Chinese literature from the eighth to the nineteenth centuries.

Pamela Dickey Young is Associate Professor of Theology and Religious Studies and Dean of Women at Queen's University. She is the author of *Feminist Theology/Christian Theology* (Fortress, 1990) and of many scholarly articles. In 1991-92 she was the President of the Canadian Theological Society. Her current research interests include feminism and religious pluralism and feminist christology. Among recent articles she has published are: "Diversity in Feminist Christology," *Studies in Religion/Sciences Religieuses*, 21/1 (1992): 81-90; "Theology and Commitment," *Toronto Journal of Theology*, 9, 2 (Fall 1993): 169-176; "*Ubi Christus Ibi Ecclesia*: Some Christological Themes Relevant in Formulating New Ecclesiologies," in *New Wine: The Challenge of the Emerging Ecclesiologies to Church Renewal*, ed. H.S. Wilson and Nyambura Njoroge (Geneva: World Alliance of Reformed Churches, 1994), 63-74; *Christ in a Post-Christian World: How Can We Believe in Jesus Christ When Those Around Us Believe Differently Or Not At All?* (Minneapolis: Fortress, Spring 1995); "Beyond Moral Influence to an Atoning Life," *Theology Today* (forthcoming).

Monique Dumais teaches in Theology and in Ethics at the Université du Québec à Rimouski. After studies in Rimouski, her birthplace, she attended Harvard Divinity School and Union Theological Seminary in New York City, where she obtained a PhD in Theology in 1977. Her research is mainly focused on Women and Religion, Women and the Church in Quebec and also on Ethics in Feminist discourses. In 1976, she founded, with three other women, a Christian feminist collective in Quebec called *L'autre parole*. She has published many articles and books on her topics of research with Editions Paulines: *Les femmes dans la Bible* (1985); *Expériences et Interpellations* (1985); *Souffles de femmes* (1989); and with Marie-Andrée Roy, *Lectures féministes de la religion* (1989) and *Les droits des femmes* (1992).

Mary Gerhart is Professor of Religious Studies at Hobart and William Smith Colleges. The author of *The Question of Belief in Literary Criticism: An Introduction to the Hermeneutical Theory of Paul Ricoeur* (1979), she has co-authored *Metaphoric Process: The Creation of Scientific and Religious Understanding* (with A.M. Russell, 1984) and co-edited *Morphologies of Faith* (with Anthony C. Yu, 1992). Her most recent book is *Genre Choices: Gender Questions* (University of Oklahoma, 1992), a study of the reciprocal ways in which genre and gender shape each other. She has served as editorial chair of *Religious Studies Review* and is on the editorial boards of several other journals.

Naomi R. Goldenberg is Professor of Psychology of Religion and former director of Women's Studies at the University of Ottawa. She attended Princeton University and the C.G. Jung Institute in Zurich, and received her doctorate in Religious Studies from Yale University. She is the author of *Resurrecting the Body: Feminism, Religion and Psychoanalysis* (New York: Crossroad, 1993); *The End of God: Important Directions for a Feminist Critique of Religion in the Work of Sigmund Freud and Carl Jung* (Ottawa: University of Ottawa Press, 1982); and *Changing of the Gods: Feminism and the End of Traditional Religions* (Boston: Beacon Press, 1979).

Marsha Hewitt is Associate Professor of Social Ethics and Contemporary Theology at Trinity College and teaches in The Centre for the Study of Religion, University of Toronto. Her publications include *From Theology to Social Theory: Juan Luis Segundo and the Theology of Liberation* (Peter Lang, 1990). *Toward a Feminist Critical Theory of Religion* (Fortress Press, 1995). She is editor of the series, *Feminist Critical Studies in Religion and Culture* (Peter Lang). Her recent articles include: "Cyborgs, Drag Queens and Goddesses"; and "Illusions of Freedom: Some Regressive Implications of Postmodernism."

Morny Joy is Associate Professor of Religious Studies at the University of Calgary. She received her PhD in Philosophy of Religion from McGill University. Her recent publications include "Divine Reservations," in *Derrida and Negative Theology* (SUNY, 1992) and "Feminism and the Self," *Theory and Psychology* 3/3 (1993), and "God and Gender: Some Reflections on Women's Explorations of the Divine," in *Religion and Gender*, (Blackwells, 1994). Morny is currently President of the Canadian Society for the Study of Religion.

Marilyn J. Legge is McDougald Professor of Systematic Theology at St. Andrew's College, Saskatoon. Her publications include *The Grace of Difference: A Canadian Feminist Theological Ethic* (Atlanta: Scholars Press, 1992) and "Liberation Ecclesiology: The Church in Solidarity," in Cadorette et al., *Liberation Theology: An Introductory Reader* (Maryknoll, NY: Orbis Books, 1992). Her commitment to healing and justice is expressed through a diversity of networks, friendships and feminist activities.

Francine Michaud is Assistant Professor in the History Department, University of Calgary. She studied at the Université d'Aix-Marseilles and the Centre of Medieval Studies in Toronto, before obtaining her PhD from Laval University. Her area of interest is social and religious history in the High Middle Ages. Her dissertation on wills in Marseilles at the end of the thirteenth century has been published by the Pontifical Institute of Medieval Studies, Toronto, in 1994.

Sheila McDonough was born in Calgary, and received her doctorate from the Institute of Islamic Studies in McGill University. She taught for three years in the Kinnaird College for Women in Lahore, Pakistan, and for one year in the Selly Oak Colleges in Birmingham, England. Since graduating, she has been teaching World Religions, Islam, and Women and Religion among other subjects at Concordia University, Montreal. She was one of the professors who introduced Women's Studies into the curriculum at Concordia in the early seventies. She is the author of *Muslim Ethics and Modernity* (Waterloo, ON: Wilfrid Laurier University Press, 1984) and *Gandhi's Response to Islam* (New Delhi: D.K. Printworld, 1994).

Eva Neumaier-Dargyay is Professor and Acting Chair of Comparative Studies in Literature, Film, and Religion at the University of Alberta. She received her Dr. phil. and Dr. phil. habil. from the Ludwig-Maximilians University at Munich, Germany (1966 and 1976) in the area of Tibetan and Indian Languages and Literatures. Her research comprises the study and interpretation of Tibetan texts from a feminist and psychoanalytic perspective, and historical, anthropological and sociological studies of Tibetan civilization. She has published four single-authored books and one co-authored book on various subjects of Tibetan religion and culture besides many articles in scholarly journals.

Eileen Schuller did her studies at the University of Alberta, the University of Toronto and Harvard University where she obtained a PhD in 1984 in Near Eastern Languages and Civilizations. She has taught in Edmonton, Atlantic School of Theology in Halifax and presently is Associate Professor of Religious Studies at McMaster University, Hamilton. Her publications include books on *Non-Canonical Psalms from Qumran: A Pseudepigraphic Collection* (Scholars Press, 1986) and

Post-Exilic Prophecy (Michael Glazier Press, 1988) and articles on "Women in the Apocrypha," in C. Newsom and S. Ringe, eds., *The Women's Bible Commentary* (Westminster/John Knox Press, 1991) and "Women of the Bible in Biblical Retellings of the Second Temple Period," in P. Day, ed., *Gender and Difference* (Fortress Press, 1989). She is editing a number of hymnic and psalmic manuscripts from the Dead Sea Scrolls for *Discoveries in the Judaean Desert*, and has been Associate Editor of the Apocryphra section for the *Harper Collins Study Bible*.

Doreen Spence, who is a Cree from Northern Alberta, has been in the nursing profession for the past 35 years. She dedicates the majority of her time to performing volunteer work in the Native and non-Native communities, her emphasis always being on Aboriginal Issues and concerns. Doreen's work in the field of human rights and the protection of fundamental freedoms for her people is unsurpassed in terms of historical and social content, clarity and effectiveness of presentation and in-depth knowledge of various indigenous cultures. She is the President of the Plains Indians Cultural Survival School Society, a position which she has held for over a decade. Doreen was nominated for the Woman of Distinction Award in 1989 and 1993, as well as for the Lamp of Learning Award through the Calgary Board of Education in May of 1993. She received an international award at the New Zealand Spiritual Elders Conference in 1992 along with the Dalai Lama, and also received the Chief David Crowchild Award in 1992.

Winnie Tomm is Associate Professor and Coordinator of the Women's Studies Program at the University of Alberta. Currently she is completing the revisions on a manuscript on spirituality and feminism, supported by a SSHRC grant. She edited *The Effect of Feminist Approaches to Research Methodologies* (Waterloo, ON: Wilfrid Laurier University Press, 1989), and co-edited, with Gordon Hamilton, *Gender Bias and Scholarship: The Pervasive Prejudice* (Waterloo, ON: Wilfrid Laurier University Press, 1988) supported by the Calgary Institute for the Humanities. She has published articles and chapters on feminist spirituality, ethics and epistemology.

Katherine K. Young publishes in the field of Hinduism, especially South Indian Hinduism and Gender and Hinduism as well as comparative studies in Gender and Religion. She has recently edited a book entitled *Hermeneutical Paths to the Sacred Worlds of India* (1994) and is currently finishing two books: *Spiritually Walking a Hindu Way* and *New Perspectives on Women in Hinduism*. She has written the theoretical introductions for three books: *Women in World Religions, Religion and Women*, and *Today's Woman in World Religions* edited by Arvind Sharma. As well she coedits with Sharma the *Annual Review of Women in World Religions*.

I

INTRODUCTION

INTRODUCTION

There are many feminists who believe that religion is such an area of conservatism in its structures and practices that no woman of any integrity could remain either an adherent or a student of its traditions. Yet many feminists today are challenging the outmoded aspects of both the conventions and the study of religion in radical ways. These women feel that to leave religion in the hands of the fathers will merely perpetuate a system that discriminates against women.

But what is the voice of feminism in Religious Studies in Canada? It is obvious that there has been a development in Religious Studies in general from the early historical surveys which attempted to remedy the virtual exclusion of women from any significant place or respect as scholars within both Western and Eastern religious traditions. Detailed descriptions of the misogyny of the learned fathers, patriarchs, monks, gurus etc. provided the initial shock-wave that sent many women searching in other directions to provide alternate answers to this apparently endemic bias. Some totally abandoned the traditional structures, others believed there were ways of reclaiming the core message of a tradition that allowed for the inclusion of women in its structures without compromising the heritage. Arguments were prolonged and often acrimonious. More recently, the grounds of debate have shifted to a concern with questions of "essentialism" (that women have an innate feminine nature) versus "constructivism" (that those characteristics regarded as indicative of the feminine gender are culturally dependent). Such a controversy has several ramifications that find different forms of expression in matters regarding religion. Whether one regards "woman" as having an essential nature or whether one posits woman's nature as a product of socio-cultural forces, indeed affects the stance one adopts regarding the viability of Goddess worship, public intervention regarding standards of equal opportunity, or even the advisability of challenging the symbolic structures that have for the most part operated in a masculine key. Are these changes to be sought (in religion as elsewhere) because women intrinsically have an individual right to their own form of self-determination or because, as human beings, they automatically share equally whatever goods and services are appropriate to that common estate? This dispute for a time seemed to be at an impasse, with proponents of each side vigorously defending the legitimacy and superiority of their view of women's new situation.

Mary Gerhart, in her opening essay, helps to delineate a way beyond such an implacable confrontation. She suggests that juxtaposing gender and genre opens possibilities for a fresh reading which allows for multifaceted studies of women in religion that need not adhere scrupulously to any one rigid definition of "woman." Gerhart's approach is cognizant of the pluralistic nature of religious studies and of the supreme importance

3

of context in any study. As her exemplar of two paradigms often seen to be in conflict, Gerhart advances Anglo-American feminism, with its pragmatic emphasis, and French feminism, with its psychoanalytically related forays into the post-structural dimensions of language and symbolic formations. Gerhart's view is that, from a hermeneutical position, these two options need not be antithetical, but can be mutually informative.

Such an assertion can only be entertained if one is willing to accept that both the terms "genre" and "gender" lend themselves to manifold applications. "Genre" has been traditionally understood as a literary classification alluding to a specific style of work with its appropriate form and conventions. Gerhart demonstrates how Mieke Bal employs the notion of code, a variant of genre, as an interpretive tool to further differentiate the strengths and weaknesses of biblical texts and their accustomed readings. The diverse perspectives provided by the various types of code — theological, anthropological, literary critical, and thematic, for example — alert the reader to the polyphonic possibilities of the interplay of gender with genre. They also demonstrate, however, the inherent limitation of any genre that would claim universalist application. Given this complexity in the various structures available by which we can choose to decipher texts, what becomes of those seeming sacrosanct divisions of gender — "masculine" and "feminine"?

Such categories as "gender," "race" and "class," no longer fit into tidy ideologically sound definitions. Gender, as Gerhart argues, "is far richer and more useful as a social-historical-political construct than as a biological index." This move allows that gender is not a hard and fast designation, but more of a continuum that allows for other sexual identifications such as "androgynous, bisexual, homosexual, heterosexual, transsexual, as well as those who become eunuchs, celibates, transvestites, and berdache."

"Genre" and "gender," then, are both mobile frames of reference that allow for different permutations and combinations, depending on the situation. Thus, the employment of a notion of gender may well reflect the task at hand as well as the selection of an appropriate genre to convey the message. In this light, it may be entirely effective to adopt pragmatically an essentialist or universalist understanding of "woman" when engaged in a debate regarding issues of justice with such modernist institutions as those of church, state or university. On other occasions, however, it may be just as appropriate to undermine universalist masculine pretensions with postmodern strategies when entrenched symbolic prerogatives such as God the Father, male ministerial authority/supremacy or the orthodoxy of dogma are at issue. Both forms of intervention can effect dramatic, if different, changes. Juxtaposing gender and genre opens possibilities for a fresh reading of sacred texts. Bringing this type of feminist theory into dialectical discourse with present scholarship on religion results in a powerful deconstruction of the homogeneous image of world religions represented by mainstream scholarship. Each essay lays bare fissures and gaps in the edifice of the different world religions. Texts, stripped of a meaning received through authoritative exegesis, reveal, in the process of re-reading, meanings that the official versions had not acknowledged.

The papers of this research network reflect a diversity of approaches using both gender and genre as analytic tools. As such, they illustrate the creativity that continues to animate the study of women in religion. Their various treatments of the question of gender illustrate how it resonates with the particular genre the writer uses or is studying, and provides ample evidence of the new pathways that are opening up for women in the study of religion. In contrast to the United States, where the clash of ethnic and cultural communities is more pronounced, and where the intellectual discourse reflects an activist stance, Canadian scholarly discourse tends to be more theoretical in a way that nevertheless affirms diversity. The essays in the volume fall naturally into two groups: the first section consists of papers that provide insights into how the concept of gender (male) is embedded in traditional texts, structures and symbols. They also highlight the nuances that can be discovered when a woman reads or investigates material from her own gendered perspective. The second section is more innovative in experimenting with either different forms of genre or critiquing traditional forms from an original and feminist perspective. Together, they exemplify the richness and complexity that enliven contemporary feminist scholarship.

Gendered Perspectives
The first five papers of this section — those of Schuller, Joseph, Dickey Young, Dumais and Goldenberg — use gender in diverse ways as a tool to illustrate the absence or silence of women in traditional forms of interpretation. In Schuller and Joseph, gender is a pivotal notion for dissecting aspects of the two normative Western religions — Christianity and Judaism. Schuller's survey of the different interpretations of Genesis 1-3 documents that the customary exegeses of this passage owe more to the extrapolation of socio-political interests than to a close reading of the text. Schuller depicts the changes wrought by feminist approaches but does not attempt to adjudicate amongst competing claims for the best way to decipher gender according to genre specifications. Instead, she simply indicates the profusion of forms available, and does not imply that this proliferation is without friction, but believes such richness can lead to more informed and constructive developments.

In contrast, Norma Joseph is more urgent in her demands. The basic premise of her essay is that for a woman to achieve recognition as a Jew, she should be subject to all the obligations and privileges that have been accorded to men. In Judaism, for Joseph, gender is both a tool for change

but also the basis of an appeal to the foundational impulse of full participation in the kingdom of God. She gives an impassioned affirmative response to her own question as to whether one can be both an orthodox
Jew and a feminist.

Goldenberg, an atheistic Jew, has a very different take. She develops
a gendered perspective on the psychology of religion by using James
Jones' book on contemporary psychoanalysis and religion as a starting
point. Goldenberg's discomfort, both with God-talk and the emphasis on
religion itself, is based on her critical observations that the presence pre-
siding over much of these reflections in psychology of religion is a male-
identified God.

While Schuller, Joseph and Goldenberg have questioned the monolithic male voice, both Dumais and Dickey Young discuss the developments that flourish when a woman regards religion in a positive way from
her own gendered perspective.

Monique Dumais explores the theme of women's experience as a
pivotal notion in all aspects of theological reflections. She surveys the
work of three Christian thinkers, Elisabeth Schüssler Fiorenza, Mary
Daly and Ellen Leonard, as they seek to incorporate women's experience
in their reformulation of human nature and its relationship with a divine
principle. Such a revisioning from the perspective of gender also implies
a reclamation of the genre of history (from which women have been
largely excluded), as well as a transformative engagement with structures
that have operated with a model of domination and division rather than
inclusion and pluralism.

In a more general fashion, Pamela Dickey Young surveys the developments in theology in the ten years since she started teaching feminist
theology in 1981. In the intervening years, the domain of feminist theology has both broadened and narrowed. On the one hand, Dickey Young
describes the new pluralism that has resulted from the voices of women,
different from those of middle-class, white, American females. These
new voices contest any normative understanding of "woman's experience." She alerts us that the construct of gender is not one that leads to a
unanimous consent of all women. Perhaps the subject of gender is leading to the emergence of feminist theologies, rather than one comprehensive field or genre. Dickey Young hesitates to predict the future of such
diversity—but she raises the crucial issue of possible fragmentation.

The issue may not be one of fragmentation, but rather an acknowl-
edgment of the multiple dimensions and claims that arise when questions
of class and race are added to the potent notion of gender. In-built hierarchies which entail domination and oppression are thus subjected to
scrutiny. The two papers of Spence and McDonough both raise, in different ways, the topic of the colonialization of spiritual values. The two essays examine the position of women within Native Canadian beliefs and
Islamic traditions from the vantage point of colonialism and the struggle

against it. The imposition of "alien" values and norms through domineering colonial powers led, in both cases, to a search for origin and identity, although with different results. In situations of oppression, the least advantaged people, usually women, are, more than others, exposed to loss of identity on the one hand and to coercion to maintain or regain traditional values on the other. Patriarchal values of the white society were imposed on the Native communities of Canada who were despised as "uncivilized" because their women held decision-making power in contrast to women in the colonial system. McDonough's nuanced presentation takes into account the ravages of colonization on a people's spirit, and of the need to recuperate from such a perceived loss to one's strength and esteem. Neo-patriarchy, as an aspect of neo-traditionalism, can seriously impede the various attempts of women to reformulate the medieval codes of law which are often promoted as an ideal. This is a sensitive issue, for Western women can no longer automatically assume superiority and expect women of other religions to comply. In most non-Western religions, women are trying to maintain a delicate balance between reform of their own traditions and a refusal to capitulate to Western values.

Western women need, then, to be particularly careful on two counts. One is to refrain from simplistic generalizations regarding their own status (which is all too precarious); the other is not to presume that their standards are of a universal nature by which the position of women in all religions can automatically be evaluated.

Genre Explorations
The essays in Part 2 reflect how the recognition of different genres enhances feminist critiques of religion. Gender and genre thus become a powerful combination. Genre studies allow for the examination of non-canonical material in ways that expose the encoded pervasiveness of the dominant male discourse. They also permit the employment of specific forms of critical and psychoanalytic theory, not without certain reservations, to uncover unconscious and hidden gender bias in religious texts.

Eva Neumaier-Dargyay investigates certain Buddhist texts attributed to the "fathers of the canon" but intended for lay patrons of the Buddhist traditions. Thus, Dargyay argues, a privileged male voice inscribed a misogynist tone in the texts whose professed purpose was to show the path to enlightenment. Qualities associated with women, even when viewed in a positive light, such as a bodhisattva's compassion, are still encoded in patriarchal structures that deny women access to the centrality of the tradition. Thus, she argues, despite the absence of a supreme God perceived as male, the Buddhist traditions exhibit a thinking deeply influenced by that of the dominant, i.e., male, gender.

Katherine Young focusses on a particular art form — film — and, within that form, a particular genre — Hindi popular romance — to assess the role of women in Hindu society today. She examines reviews of these films (another genre in itself) to assess the subtleties by which changes in the traditional female role are being evaluated. Even the sex of the film reviewers illustrates just how gender affects the reception of the genre and the loaded effect of such interpretations on a society in flux.

Still within the confines of genre, but in a different vein, Francine Michaud researches the wills of women of the thirteenth and fourteenth centuries that are housed in the archives of the city of Marseilles. Thus, she introduces gender, in the form of women, into a genre, i.e., wills, which usually has been seen as a territory of privileged men. This innovative approach allows her to shed light for the first time on the spiritual orientation of women of that period other than nuns or vowed women.

A Chinese novel is the subject of Fan Pen Chen's enquiry into patriarchal mores. Chen's feminist perspective overturns the genre's conventions that viewed women only as appendages (of either benign or malign import) in a male-centred saga. Her psychoanalytic reading illustrates that the seemingly vindictive or rebellious behaviour of the women is explicable to a woman reader who perceives the women involved utterly confined to degrading or subordinate situations. The female protagonist's "viciousness" finds a "natural" explanation if her life circumstances are acknowledged. Her reading challenges the male-monopolized structures of the society that used religion and literature to reinforce its exclusionary values.

Legge and Tomm introduce a new genre, wherein women express their own spiritual quests in language that acknowledges a holistic interconnectedness. Their language is markedly different from the male spiritual confessions, where the ego usually predominates, and reflects their own awareness of their embodied consciousness. While Legge celebrates the joys and struggles of a feminist ethics that reshapes the genre's legalistic code so as to understand relationship not simply as passive witness, but active engagement, Tomm explores the problematic area of identity—what does it mean today for women to have a *self*? Tomm proposes a new genre of a mutually interactive model between the two modes of essentialism and constructivism. She then proposes ways that this enriched dialogue can support discussions of the body, of language and of an embodied spiritual consciousness.

With reference to new genres created by women in religion, no one has been more imaginative in both word and form than Mary Daly. She has led many women on a "be-dazzling" voyage beyond the confines of patriarchal religion. Daly envisages an innate energy, particular to women, that she calls "pure lust." Marsha Hewitt draws attention to the similarity of these ideas to Marcuse's concept of "women" as a power that can heal the ailing human society. Hewitt's work is both an appreciation and a caution. She argues that Marcuse's eros and Daly's celebrations of poetic metamorphosis are insufficient to effect the radical reordering of the very structures of society and the injustices that are thereby perpetrated.

In conclusion, Morny Joy examines the conundrum of truth and its relation to women. She suggests a model that recognizes the varieties of gendered experience and of generic thematization that mark contemporary feminist thought. Similarly to Gerhart, Joy does not see that these approaches need to antithetical. Sensitive to context, different methods (and genres) can be employed depending on the circumstances. Such context-dependent awareness would seem to introduce a form of feminism that is not autocratic, dogmatic or unilateral in its pronouncements, but ready to be informed by and respond to the changing dimensions of the problems of gender in the world at large and religion in particular. Woman, the enigma, is the focal point in both Hewitt's paper and in Morny Joy's. Hewitt brings Marcuse and his feminine negativity into discourse with radical feminist thinkers, like Mary Daly, while Joy leads the reader from Nietzsche to Derrida in her exploration of whether one may speak of "woman" and/or "truth." She draws an arch from the multivalent positioning of postmodern thinking to hermeneutics, whose emancipatory potential she sees in its claim that all knowledge is situated within specific contexts.

Morny Joy
Eva K. Neumaier-Dargyay

II

SETTING THE THEME

Chapter 1

FRAMING DISCOURSE FOR THE FUTURE

Mary Gerhart

Introduction

This research network would seem to enjoy the best of circumstances. Canada is the nation of two major feminist languages, and according to the list of participants, the source of at least two feminisms. If there is an ideal place and time to work constructively beyond the stereotypes of Anglo-American and French feminism, we may expect it to be here and now. I have always been struck by the ability of feminist theology to work from as well as to go beyond traditional religious and cultural boundaries. It seems equally important that the boundaries within feminism be equally malleable. In this sense, the very fact of the existence of two paradigms — Anglo-American and French feminism — takes on importance. Together they provide a structural basis for enhancing rather than reducing the complexity of the issues. At the same time, the mutual concerns inscribed in them afford a recognition of the need to *interpret*, as well as to defend, advocate, assess and believe. The existence of two paradigms need not be divisive, even though it may be explosive when differences come to light. Indeed, with appropriate reflection, the differences in the two paradigms may be more productive than any uncritical agreement between them.

One of the anomalies of feminist and womanist theory is that, in spite of its celebration of diversity, there are relatively few occasions when we can draw with equal familiarity and expertise on two major areas of feminist theory. For Anglo-American feminists, Simone de Beauvoir, Julia Kristeva and Luce Irigaray often represent French feminism, while the work of Christine Delphy, Michele LeDoeuff and Annie Leclerc goes largely unmentioned.[1] Moreover, Anglo-American feminists continue to use the category, French *feminism*, in spite of the fact that the term is eschewed by many of the theorists to whom it is applied. French theorists, on the other hand, seem little affected by and at times even dismissive of the work of Anglo-American feminism.[2]

Let us state these generalizations at the outset. Anglo-American feminists tend to be best known as advocates of economic and political equality between women and men (in other words, they seek to erase the category "woman" insofar as it represents political and economic deprivation). French feminists tend to be characterized by their supporters as evocators of psychoanalytic categories for the exploration of sexual differences (in this sense, they seek to reinforce the category "woman").

And yet each has been charged with bringing about an effect opposite to their goal. By calling attention to the current status of women, Anglo-American feminists can be seen to reinforce the category "woman"! And by emphasizing the opacity of woman's experience, French feminists assimilate all who have similar experiences to the category "woman," regardless of gender — effectively blurring or deconstructing the boundaries of the category.

Since this research network includes participants from both French and Anglo-American feminisms, it offers the possibility of using the hermeneutical models of both selectively. Although some of the responses to these two models occasionally resemble conventional interdenominational disputes, it will be to our advantage to treat each model as a region of hermeneutical theory and to explore how they might reciprocally enrich each other as we plot a path forward for women and religion.

One of the most useful models for plotting a path forward can be found in the field of hermeneutical theory. Friedrich Schleiermacher and others made interpretation explicit as an aspect of knowing in the early nineteenth century. Hermeneutical theory made it possible to side-step the tradition of positivist thinking — a tradition which had certainty as its goal. By means of nineteenth-century hermeneutical theory, we can focus instead on the process of knowing, and we will not expect the results of inquiry to be certain. But how shall we characterize the results of inquiry? This is the question that Sandra Harding raised in her essay, "The Instability of the Analytical Categories of Feminist Theory."[3] Harding's daring response is to call the categories themselves "unstable." What argument can be made in support of this position? Assuming that there is a good reason to posit "instability" in the process of knowing, is instability best located at the level of categories employed? And if not there, where?

Hardy argues that there are currently two approaches to feminist theory. The first, called "standpoint or feminist successor science," has as its premise the substitution of either women or feminists for men as ideal knowers: the expectation is that "women [or feminists] are able to use political struggle and analysis to provide a less partial, less defensive, less perverse understanding of human social relations — including our relations with nature."[4] Standpoint feminism, then, critiques patriarchy by showing how "men's characteristic social experience . . . hides from them the politically imposed nature of the social relations they see as natural." The latter position does not indict individual males as sexist but rather recognizes that "dominant patterns in Western thought justify women's subjugation as necessary for the progress of culture, and men's partial and perverse views as uniquely and admirably human."[5] The second approach, called "postmodernist," relies on achievements of "feminist successor" scientists and also critiques them for being "still too firmly rooted in distinctively masculine modes of being in the world." The postmodern feminist suspects that successor science feminism still aspires to an epistemological structure of the "universalizing perspective of the master. That is, only to the extent that one person or group can dominate the whole, can 'reality' appear to be governed by one set of rules or be constituted by one privileged set of social relations."[6]

The postmodernist position does not escape criticism from Harding. Indeed, if anything, her criticism of postmodern feminism is harsher than her citations of the shortcomings of standpoint feminism. Postmodernist feminism appears "viciously utopian" and ironically "of a piece with masculine and bourgeois desire to justify one's activities by denying one's social, embodied location in history."[7] Perhaps most devastating is Harding's criticism of postmodernism's tendency to "support an inappropriate relativist stance":

> It is worth keeping in mind that the articulation of relativism as an intellectual position emerges historically only as an attempt to dissolve challenges to the legitimacy of purportedly universal beliefs and ways of life. It is an objective problem, or a solution to a problem, only from *the perspective of the dominating groups*. Reality may indeed appear to have many different structures from the perspectives of our different locations in social relations, but some of those appearances are ideologies in the strong sense of the term: they are not only false and "interested" beliefs but also ones that are used to structure social relations for the rest of us.[8]

Harding's explication of the feminist standpoint and the postmodern feminist approaches is especially helpful in the way that it places the two in a dialectical and mutually corrective relationship. The difficulty with Harding's position is that the title of the article, "the instability of feminist categories," invokes only the postmodern position—even though Harding intends it to apply to the situation of feminist theorizing in general. If postmodernism slights the "political struggles necessary to bring about change," and successor science "fails to challenge the modernist intimacies between knowledge and power or the legitimacy of assuming there can be a single, feminist story of reality," then, she argues, "we must resist the temptation to explain away the problem each addresses and to choose one to the exclusion of the other."[9] But it is only in postmodernism that the categories are unstable. Hardy is correct in her explication of the two positions and in her assessment that both are needed. But I think that her position might best be called one of "misplaced instability."

Nevertheless, the categories do pose a problem. From an epistemological perspective, they are the means by and through which we can conceive at all. In the following passage, Harding referred to two familiar categories as dichotomous:

> [D]ichotomies such as nature/culture are empirically false, but we cannot afford to dismiss them as irrelevant as long as they structure our lives and our consciousness. . . . Gender, like class, is not a voluntarily disposable individual

characteristic. . . . But the standpoint and postmodern tendencies within feminist theory place feminism in an uneasy and ambivalent relationship to patriarchal discourses and projects. Furthermore, these feminist appeals to truth and
objectivity trust that reason will play a role in the eventual triumph of feminism, that feminism correctly will be perceived as more than a power
politic – though it is that, too.[10]

I support Harding's attempt to call attention to the ambiguity in feminist
thought. But as the shift in rhetoric in the foregoing passage indicates,
her position is vulnerable to the criticism of a "misplaced instability." For
we do need categories in which to speak meaningfully – all the while
testing, pushing beyond, retracting, querying.

In Harding's proposal, where is the instability located? If "instability"
refers to the incompleteness or the changeableness of theory taken one
by one, or even feminist theory taken as a whole, then this feature is not
basically different from what we recognize to be the case with all theories. Have the theories themselves changed? Does "instability" point to
the expectation that as women (and men) and women's situations
change, new theories will be needed? It is not so much that formerly
"stable" theories are now best understood as "unstable"; it is rather that
the theories are both "stable" *and* "unstable." That is, the use of carefully
designed theories is always partial, pertaining to determinate or indeterminate data, and results – either by their effects or by their relations with
other theories – in both stabilizing and destabilizing the current situation.[11]

Taking Our Bearings from Recent Allies
"Women" and "religion" are concepts that seem to be self-evident. Yet
even casual conversation frequently shifts into argument when participants hold quite different understandings of either or both concepts. As
the overarching context for our research, then, I suggest that we join
those scholars who have called into question the two terms "women" and
"religion."

With respect to "woman," Denise Riley has raised the question of
"woman" both historically and philosophically in her book *"Am I That
Name?": Feminism and the Category of "Women."*[12] Early in the book she
observed that each person is constituted by multiple identities, many of
which are complementary: for example, I am a Caucasian woman born of
first-generation Americans with German and some French ancestry, a
professor of religious studies and theology, with interests in science and
mathematics and literature of several traditions and periods. Some of my
other identities are not always so compatible. Being a Midwesterner and
a New Yorker, a Roman Catholic and an American pro-choicer, raises
questions in different settings and with different degrees of intensity. According to Riley, we seldom invoke all our identities at once. Nor
do we necessarily carry every one of these identities into a public posi-

tion. For if we "go public," we must be willing not only to "take on" an identity but also, when necessary, to articulate our position over and against the perceived opposition to that position. In other words, there is a wide range of possibility—a range which is most visible when we voluntarily choose to move from reflective to political activity. We do not usually live our lives fully defined as any one of our identities. One of the necessary revisions of gender theory is to explore the development of interests over a lifetime in relation to plural identities. For example, Catherine Mowry LaCugna, for example, has proposed that one solution to the question of the ordination of women in the Roman Catholic tradition would be to regard ordination, for both women and men, as temporary: a person would be ordained for a specific communities for limited periods of time.[13]

But it is not enough to explore the concept of gender identity only in the abstract. Such exploration fails to address, for example, the continuing problem of violence against women. Who among us does not remember multiple examples—statistics on rape and battery, personal accounts of neighbours and friends, systemic denigration of the female? Taken within the context of religion, the concept of identity must take cognizance of the fact of violence. In his *Religion and Violence*, Robert McAfee Brown argued for a broadening of the understanding of "violence" and a reunderstanding of the term "religion" in relation to violence.[14] He charged that the popular understanding of violence included only overt personal violence. Brown broadened the spectrum to include overt institutional violence, covert personal violence and covert institutional violence. But Brown applied his analysis only to the issues of war, third world/first world relations and economic disparity.[15]

But violence based in gender hatred is not merely among that committed most frequently. Some have argued that the toleration of violence against women provides an implicit legitimation of other forms of violence. It is not necessary for us here to repeat the argument for this claim. But constructive efforts are needed to empower scholars in the discipline of religion to address the manifold issue of violence in relation to women. Beyond general thematizations of violence, we need reiterations of the relation between women and violence. If oppression of women is the basic paradigm which functions as a legitimation of other kinds of oppression, then we need more searching analysis of the role of gender wherever theological attention is brought to bear on the problem of identity. Besides Brown's analysis of religion and violence, which can be extended, four other resources can be invoked.

In order to raise public consciousness to the effects of violence based on gender, Judith Herman, the first resource, compares the effects of violence against women with the effects of wartime violence. In her book, *Trauma and Recovery*, Herman finds that the long-range effects in women on whom violence has been perpetrated resemble the effect of shock or injury on war veterans during military combat.[16] Herman is thus able to make visible the effects of long-term trauma which in women have been invisible in the public domain. Herman also assists in the religious thematization of violence against women when she creates an analogy between the victims of domestic violence with those in concentration camps during World War II, and death camps in Southeast Asia, Siberia, and South Africa. By showing that depression, loneliness, flashbacks, frayed memories, distorted feelings of guilt are not only similar but worse for those who suffer hidden, chronic violence in the home, Herman's book elevates the chances that violence against women will be less likely to be dismissed as pathetic or despicable. Although Herman's book comes primarily from a psychological and psychoanalytic background, it has ramifications that reach beyond psychology.

We can find similar shifts in the focus of some contemporary theologians. David Tracy, for example as a second resource, thinks that the "non-person" of the oppressed, as distinct from the "non-believer" who was the object of much traditional theology, is the more important reality to be faced in contemporary theology. In his book *Dialogue with the Other: The Interreligious Dialogue*, Tracy takes cognizance of the pluralism and ambiguity within as well as across religious traditions.[17] He goes back to William James' three well-known criteria for evaluating religious experience — immediate luminousness, philosophical reasonableness and moral helpfulness — and revises them for use in the new situation. For immediate luminousness, Tracy substitutes "suggestive possibility." This criterion allows the contemporary interpreter to acknowledge the ambiguity which characterizes the contemporary awareness of the complex role that any experience is likely to have in the life of an individual or community. For philosophical reasonableness, Tracy suggests "coherence with what we otherwise know or more likely believe to be the case," a criterion which allows us to assess life as a whole, including its margins as well as its commonalties. For moral helpfulness, Tracy introduces ethical-social-political-social criteria which are capable of reflecting both the complexity of the situation as well as the corrections, such as in the notion of "self." If one applies these revised criteria to questions involving explicit gender issues, the tension and ambiguities multiply — simply because of the strength of the stereotypes embedded in our political structures, in corporate advertising, and in our own self-consciousness.

Third, Rebecca Chopp's *The Power to Speak* draws upon French feminist semiotic theory and Christian theology, as she reflects on the theme of emancipatory transformation.[18] She concludes that "transformations occur in departures from and reformulations of ideas, theories, traditions, words, cultural forms, and economic practices. ..." For Chopp, the "discourses of Word and world will be more than a mere "no" to the prevailing social and symbolic structures, though they will offer a no to the "murderous effects" of those structures. Instead, "transformations occur in departures from and reformulations of ideas, theories, traditions, words, cultural forms, and economic practices." For Chopp, emancipatory transformation involves a change in the way we see: "Seeing differently feminism finds no totally new way of being and doing, as if a magic city from above could appear, but rather in the wandering and movement of a sojourn in the wilderness, feminism can discover and create new ways of dwelling."[19] Chopp eschews what she calls essentialist solutions to gender issues.

Recognition of the complexity of the contemporary situation, especially with respect to the issue of gender, can be found in recent studies of sacred texts as well. As a fourth resource, Mieke Bal acknowledges the complexity when she constructs a corresponding methodological complexity in her book, *Murder and Difference: Gender, Genre, and Scholarship on Sisera's Death*.[20] Indeed, she chooses as the biblical texts to be interpreted parts of Judges 5 and 4, which scholars agree represent two different treatments of Sisera's death. The basis of her choice is their appropriateness in accomplishing the goal of her study: to disclose how ideologies foster uniformity and the subordination of some groups to dominant groups. She understands hermeneutics to be preparation for critical practice. Since hermeneutics practised within disciplines is based on codes, "codes" can be viewed as "rule[s] of correlation institutionally tied to a group that projects its own interests upon it."[21] Bal applies four disciplinary codes and two transdisciplinary codes to the two accounts of Sisera's death; she analyzes the codes, on the one hand, in terms of their ability to differentiate meanings and, on the other hand, in terms of their inability to advance interpretation of the differences they uncover.

She credits the historical code, for example, with having developed two capabilities. First of all, this code can distinguish among the discrete sources which are identified in the two texts being studied. Second, by treating the texts as documents of a people, the historical code reconstructs the history of that people in terms of models. At the same time, this code suffers from a tendency to devalue the genre of poetry and to privilege binary oppositions, such as general/particular, individual/collective, and traditional/original.

Bal is less helpful in her assessment of the strength of the theological code. She credits it only with being able to distinguish enthusiasm and commitment as religious feelings which enable the Israelites to achieve an identity. This achievement in her eyes is severely curtailed by the way this code "joins an evolutionist perspective to a monotheistic commitment in a positive evaluation of war."[22]

The anthropological code, according to Bal, is capable of differentiating among cultural forms and practices, such as the division of labor and the ritual meaning of objects and actions and of accounting for the function of texts (oral and written) in a society. This code is not immune to the biases of premature closure, anachronism, ethnocentrism, and androcentrism, although it encourages a critical attitude toward them more than the historical and theological codes do.

The literary critical code distinguishes the compositional elements of a text, together with the sources of what we perceive as textually significant or beautiful. By distinguishing genres, this code can spot crucial differences of meaning otherwise likely to be overlooked. However, it has a weakness for dichotomizing categorization and for being unnecessarily polemical in relation to other disciplines.

Bal introduces two codes that are not confined to current disciplines. Both of these codes "float" among the previous codes. The thematic code is one of the most frequent codes to be invoked because in relation to disciplinary boundaries it is relatively underdetermined. It presupposes unity among the meanings of several texts and emphasizes the center of interest in each interpreter. However, the thematic code has serious weaknesses in that it masks anachronisms and destroys ambiguity.

The gender code, like the thematic code, is capable of distinguishing, rather than opposing or eliminating, texts which contain references to male and female. Bal thinks that this code is relatively free from the limitations of specific disciplines mentioned above so long as it is kept distinct from one's chosen "personal gender code" and the "gender code he or she assumes the other has adopted."[23] Bal uses the gender code to bring meanings constructed through the other codes into sharper focus.

Bal has shown that the multidisciplinary recognition of code can enable a more critical hermeneutic practice. She also shows that the application of some kind of gender code to puzzling or hitherto otherwise unremarkable passages can yield new significance. More than the foregoing authors, Bal celebrates interdisciplinarity in recent scholarship. Nevertheless, all codes (in different ways), call into question both terms: "Women" and "religion."

A Radical Question: How to Get Beyond the Essentialist Debate

The essentialist movement is a good example of a critical movement reading a moment of crisis. It was inevitable, perhaps, that the feminist movement would at some point be challenged from within on the issue of epistemological coherence. As feminism has matured—from a realization that gender bias was systemic to a realization that the bias could be overcome in critical discourse and political action—feminists have had to confront their successes. First came the confrontation with racial and class differences. The challenge was to recognize differences among and across women's situations. The solution was by and large an effort to be inclusive in the strategies for overcoming oppression of women whatever their situation. Such attempts produced several major interest groups within the movement, such as womanists, women of color, lesbians, and bisexual women. With the new emphasis on diversity came a resistance to, as well as a new need for, defining similarity: the similarity could no longer be based in naive assumptions. So many questions about these assumptions had been raised that feminism could no longer revert to its former libertarian terms. This impossibility of going back to a previous moment in the debate was especially apparent with respect to the empiricist premise that biology is destiny, a premise which perhaps more than any other had been thoroughly discredited.[24]

Indeed, the essentialist debate emerged at a time when the need to affirm differences was at its height. At the same time, the limited success of political and economic efforts to improve the situation of women made it apparent that feminists had to unite beyond their differences: "the bottom line," some said, was a sense that "woman" is not just an appropriate term but an indispensable focus for political action.

I have heard several versions of an anecdote which makes an analogous point with respect to the term "race." Françoise Meltzer tells it as follows. A group of guest editors, discussing parameters for soliciting articles for a special issue of *Critical Inquiry*, were debating whether or not the terms "race" and "gender" were useful anymore, given that the referents formerly attached to each term had effectively been called into question. Suddenly a black man said, "Look, when I try to flag a cab outside Grand Central Station on a rainy night and several empty cabs pass by, I *know* there's something real about race." Meltzer suggested that there are good reasons to employ the term "women" when we are engaging in political action, and there are just as good reasons to be critical of the term when we are engaging in philosophical discourse. Meltzer defuses the problem of essentialism by legitimating the already existing plurality of references.

In her book *Essentially Speaking: Feminism, Nature and Difference*, (1989), Diana Fuss proposes a daring philosophical retrieval of not only the term "essentialism" but also the position which it designated.[25] Fuss thinks that

> In and of itself, essentialism is neither good nor bad, progressive nor reactionary, beneficial not dangerous. The question we should be asking is not "is this text essentialist (and therefore 'bad')?" but rather, "if this text is essentialist, *what motivates its deployment?*" How does the sign "essence" circulate in various contemporary critical debates? Where, how, and why is it invoked? What are its political and textual effects?[26]

Fuss argues, on the one hand, that "there is no essence to essentialism, that (historically, philosophically, and politically) we can speak only of *essentialisms.*"[27] Her most important contribution, however, is to show that the opposition given to essentialism by the constructivists is itself "a more sophisticated form of essentialism"[28] and that essentialism "underwrites theories of constructionism."[29] Fuss' strategy is not merely a show of logic. Rejecting the poststructuralist formulation of the essentialist/constructionist opposition, she carefully analyzes several representations of the opposition: the disputes over "reading as women"; Monique Wittig (anti-essentialist) vs. Luce Irigaray (essentialist); the current Afro-American debate over "the deconstruction of 'race' as an essential, natural, empirical category" and the effects of this deconstruction in literary criticism; the gay and lesbian controversy over "the constructionist hypothesis of invented homosexuality" and the essentialist practice of rallying people politically according to their sexual preferences.[30] Fuss concludes that

> we need both to theorize essentialist spaces from which to speak and, simultaneously, to deconstruct these spaces to keep them from solidifying. Such a double gesture involves once again the responsibility to historicize, to examine each deployment of essence each appeal to experience, each claim to identity in the complicated contextual frame in which it is made.[31]

Her conclusion suggests an effective pedagogy for overcoming the stand-off between essentialism and constructionism.

Within the field of religion, the essentialist debate can be found in the reluctance of many scholars to assign any positive meaning to the term "religion" and in the tendency to substitute for "religion," terms like "faith," "path," "way," "belief," "commitment."[32] The controversy over essentialism may also enhance the uneasy relationship between theological studies and religious studies.[33]

Further Strategies for Overcoming the Essentialist/Constructionist Stand-off

Fuss has already alerted us to the need for pedagogical strategies to overcome the stalemate between essentialism and constructionism. In this section I will both propose two new strategies for breaking the stalemate as it exists within the field of women and religion. Why do we need to get beyond the debate? Epistemological "paralysis" results when opposing terms, such as essentialist and constructionist, become mere labels and, devoid of understanding, are used to castigate anyone who dares question or countenance the opposing position. Both strategies are strongly heuristic; that is, they are process-oriented and their validity becomes most apparent in their use.

The first strategy can be called "metaphoric process." Since this research network has as its central theme, the path *forward*, it would seem that among the most promising new directions for women in religion is an epistemology which emphasizes the creation of new meaning. Metaphor has traditionally been a key term for novelty or newness of meaning. For twenty-two centuries after Aristotle, metaphor suffered a demise into mere decoration. But with the work of I.A. Richards in the 1920s and Paul Ricoeur in the 1970s, metaphor has been revived as a vehicle of new meaning. Presuming familiarity with Ricoeur's theory of metaphor, which distinguishes between dead and living metaphors and which emphasizes the new meaning resulting from the tension between established mean-

ings, I will sketch the theory of metaphoric process which a physicist colleague, Allan Russell, and I have developed to understand the creation of
scientific and religious understanding.[34] Then, as an example of new understanding that can result from metaphoric process, I will describe an
application of the theory to the problem of the goddess in the Hebrew
Bible.

Our theory distinguishes between analogy and metaphor. Analogy, in
our theory, is at the center of the process by which we come to know the
unfamiliar by comparing it with that which is familiar. An analogy, in
other words, relates an unknown to a known: "u" is like "k." In the analogical process, new meaning is not significantly different from what we
know in the first place. In terms of form and general shape, analogy enables us to understand an unknown in terms of a known—as, for example, in Aquinas' use of the known concept "habit" to understand the unknown concept "grace." Today, of course, the concept "habit" no longer
has the same connotation that it had in the thirteenth century, and for
many readers does not provide an effective analogical understanding of
grace.[35]

Metaphor, on the other hand, is the forced equivalence of two
knowns. Analogy is generally found in response to the question, "What is
an 'x'?" whereas metaphor is likely to be manifested as a "Eureka" experience. Unlike analogy, in which an unknown is understood in terms of a
known, metaphor is founded on two knowns. In Shakespeare's Sonnet 73,
"bare ruin'd choirs" force "boughs" to be understood as "choir lofts." Because each of the terms is firmly rooted in its "field of meanings," the
move toward equivalence meets resistance. In metaphoric process, the
fields of meanings to which the concepts ordinarily belong are distorted,
thrown out of lexical and semantic shape, when two concepts, rigidly embedded in the different fields, are forced together by the assertion that
they are the same. The distortion of the fields of meanings creates relationships among old concepts and incites a potential for ontological
change in the sense that an individual's "world of meanings" has undergone a change.

In 1990, Russell and I collaborated further with Joseph Healey, a
biblical scholar, in an application of our theory of metaphor to the Hebrew testament in an article for *Semeia*, entitled "The Sublimation of the
Goddess in the Deitic Metaphor of Moses."[36] In this article we argue that
metaphoric process can be found in the Mosaic texts when Moses is portrayed as equating Yahweh (God of the Exodus) with El, the God of the
Fathers. In the metaphoric pronouncement Yahweh=El (for example, in
Exodus 3:6), Moses effectively creates a new meaning for the God of all
the tribes of Israel.

But with this advance toward monotheism in the metaphoric act, the
postmetaphoric field of meanings no longer includes a Goddess with
whom a god could procreate. On the level of myth it becomes necessary

for the deitic conjunction Yahweh=El to arrogate the function of fertility. By excluding the Goddess, and hence the possibility of procreative union, the canonical God Yahweh came to represent only an abstract sense of fertility. Nevertheless, the Goddess, spouse of El, although formally absent in the postmetaphoric field of meanings of Yahweh, very likely remained active and alive. Indeed, there are some amazing remnants of her being worshipped as Asherah in the community that constituted Israel, as, for example, in this passage in Jer. 44:15-19:

> From all the men who knew that their wives were burning incense to strange gods, from all the women who were present in the immense crowd, and from all the people who lived in Lower and Upper Egypt, Jeremiah received this answer: "We will not listen to what you tell us in the name of the Lord. Rather will we continue doing what we had proposed; we will burn incense to the queen of heaven and *pour out libations to her, as we and our fathers, our kings and our princes have done* in the cities of Judah and the streets of Jerusalem ... was it without our husbands' consent that we baked cakes in her image and poured out libations to her?" (emphasis mine)

Here the fathers — presumably, the same fathers whose God was El — are said to have participated in the worship of Asherah. In this passage we can hear echoes not only of El, the God of the Fathers, but also Asherah, the Goddess of the Fathers.

On the basis of the frequent references to Asherahs in the Hebrew Bible (which, according to Winter, are best interpreted as shrines[37]), it seems reasonable to think that although the Goddess was hidden for generations in the formal religion, her worship continued, probably as a part of the women's ritual celebration of first menstruation, sexual initiation, marriage, pregnancy, childbirth, menopause — observances having to do with plant and animal culture, and death.

What has metaphoric process to do with essentialism? From Aristotle to the present, metaphor has most often been associated with genius or creativity. According to Aristotle, for example, metaphor-makers appear to pluck metaphors out of nowhere. We understand metaphor as coming from the insistence that a given concept in one field of meanings means the same as a given concept in another field of meanings. Notwithstanding the fact that there are different kinds of essentialism, most assume some delimitation of conceptual boundaries and resistance to certain other kinds of difference. In metaphoric process, resistance to a novel identification of two meanings from disparate fields is *de rigueur*: New meaning results from the radical overcoming of resistance to other than established meanings. Some day the gender revolution is likely to have as far-reaching effects as the Copernican revolution — a metaphoric process that equated the sun, instead of the earth, as center of the universe. The theory of metaphoric process is one way of accounting for both the magnitude and the breadth of the conceptual changes that must attend the conjunction of woman and the sacred, as well as to map the resistance to cognitive change that exists at the time of the creation of any specific metaphor.

Other strategies for overcoming essentialism are suggested by recent developments in genre and gender theory. In my book, *Genre Choices, Gender Questions* (1992), I take advantage of the common root in both "gender" and "genre" to show that much more can be made of the plurality of "kinds."[38] Gender is far richer and more useful as a social-historical-political construct than as a biological index, referring, as it does, to human beings who are androgynous, bisexual, homosexual, heterosexual, and transsexual, as well as those who become eunuchs, celibates, transvestites, and berdache.[39] And although genre is most often thought of in relation to the work of authoring, it plays a constructive role in the work of reading as well.

Specifically, with respect to the problem of essentialism, I explore three ways of "belonging to a genre": the traditionalist, the ideological, and the deconstructionist. With respect to the understanding of genre, the traditionalist view emphasizes the tension between singularity and commonality, between the individual and the category. Traditionalists are concerned primarily with aggrandizing the uniqueness of the individual text and frequently use genre for prescriptive purposes. Traditionalists tend to consider genres only at the height of their powers: the rise or decline of genres are of only derivative interest.

The ideological view is that genres are always systematically biased in their approximations of reality. Ideological critics are concerned primarily with the tension between texts and social contexts. Whereas traditionalists think of genres as being bound to one locality, ideological critics see genres as also inhering in opposing social relations. These relations depend on one another and can be found to exist in several cultures. The genres which most interest ideological critics are those which have the power to explain social privilege or oppression of one group by another.

The deconstructive view is that genres always exceed their stated rhetorical purposes. As a special form of ideology critique, deconstructionism shifts the focus of genre from social structures to the *language* of ideas, structures, and knowledge. The avowed enemy of essentialisms of any kind, deconstructionism sees genre as both destroying the individual text and as being targeted itself by individual texts for destruction. In the deconstructionist view, written texts and their genres "control" readers in a particular culture; likewise, a person's gender is "controlled" by the texts of her culture.

These contrasting views of "belonging" to a genre challenge us to develop strategies for employing the category of genre constructively. What might they also do for our understanding of gender? In my book I describe Julia Kristeva's tripartite model (which she called heuristic/synthetic) for feminist self-understanding as explicated in her essay "Woman's Time." On one level, her model is historical. Kristeva observed that the women's[40] movement can be understood to have had three phases or generations. In the first phase, women claim an equal part of the traditional benefits of being a member of society: for example, the right to vote, to participate freely in public as recognized professionals, to receive equal pay for equal work, to decide for themselves whether to bear children or not. In the second phase, women exercise a hermeneutics of suspicion with respect to the public realm as represented primarily by males. Feminists of the second phase seek to replace androcentric values with gynocentric ones and to transform the perceived attributes of feminine from negative to positive. The third phase moves to the locus of "personal and sexual identity." In this phase, the struggle for gender and individual identity is carried out in the lives of individuals – a struggle which is at the center of the gender conflict. In my book I coordinate Kristeva's tripartite model with the three ways of "belonging" to a genre and show how her model requires that the third phase presuppose some necessary continuation of the first and second.[41] Here, the conjunction of genre and gender studies returns us to the radical hermeneutical question with which we began our inquiry: to what extent does the field of women and religion imply an ongoing critique and reconstruction of both "woman" and "religion"?

I would suggest that women and religion as an area of specialization must preserve these radical questions as central to its path forward. As readers, scholars in this field might well understand themselves as engaging in gender- and genre-testing – a process that presupposes more than one way of reading a text. The wager is that by engaging in this process, we will experience a growing confidence in asking constructive as well as critical gender questions and a new competence in making effective genre choices.

Such confidence and competence make possible a way of overcoming two antinomies which have been noticed in recent feminist theory. The first arises from a conflict between a socioloy-of-knowledge perspective and a moral perspective. On the one hand, the "social construction of reality" is often assumed to account for everything that occurs, but on the other hand, the hermeneutics of suspicion seems to assume that historical figures could and should have eliminated gender oppression wherever it occurred. The second antinomy is that addressed in this paper. As we have seen, this antinomy of essentialism vs. constructionism may be rooted in the conflict between a political perspective and a philosophical perspective. On the one hand, a general concept of "woman" is necessary, especially for political action; on the other hand, it is necessary to eschew definitions in order to go beyond the status quo.

Asking gender questions and making genre choices provides a strategy for appropriating the elements of what has been variously perceived as contradiction or instability. This strategy requires more of our imagination than does any routine task of criticism. Madame de Staël employed historical genre considerations, for example, when she reflected on what conversation as a genre had become after the Revolution—when women were excluded from political life.[42] But her being a mistress and master of that genre far exceeded her historical observations about it—however important those observations also were.

Gender questions and genre choices are central to the task of "naming" both women and religion[43]—for what is naming, but plotting the future?

Notes

1 But see the collection of feminist writings, such as those of Mary Eagleton, ed., *Feminist Literary Theory: A Reader* (London: Basil Blackwell, 1986), and Toril Moi, *French Feminist Thought: A Reader* (London: Basil Blackwell, 1987), which include theorists from both continents.

2 See Morny Joy, "Equality or Divinity—A False Dichotomy?" *Journal of Feminist Studies in Religion*, 6 (Spring 1990): 9-24, on Luce Irigaray's review of Elisabeth Schüssler Fiorenza's *In Memory of Her*.

3 Sandra Harding, "The Instability of the Analytical Categories of Feminist Theory," in Micheline Malson et al., eds., *Feminist Theory in Practice and Process* (Chicago: University of Chicago Press, 1989), p. x.

4 Ibid., p. 25.

5 Ibid.

6 Ibid., p. 26.

7 Ibid.

8 Ibid., p. 27.

9 Ibid.

10 Ibid., p. 23-24.

11 In *Metaphoric Process: The Creation of Scientific and Religious Understanding* (Fort Worth: Texas Christian University, 1984), Allan Russell, my co-author, and I distinguish between typical theories in religion and in science on the basis of the preponderance of determinate and indeterminate data they attempt to understand.

12 (Minneapolis: University of Minnesota Press, 1988).

13 Catherine Mowry LaCugna, "Catholic Women as Ministers and Theologians," in *America*, 167 (10 October 1992): 238-44.

14 2nd ed. (Philadelphia: Westminster Press, 1987).

15 Although he does not address the issue of violence based on gender, he includes it among what he calls "new issues" in the revised edition.

16 (New York: Basic, 1992).

17 (Grand Rapids: Eerdmans, 1990.)

18 *The Power to Speak: Feminism, Language, God* (New York: Crossroad, 1989).

19 Ibid., p. 127-28.

20 (Bloomington: Indiana University Press, 1988).

21 Ibid., p. 2.

22 Ibid., p. 39.

23 Ibid., p. 111.

24 The premise does still reign in many parts of the world. The claim pertains strictly to the context of the debate and the resistance it might provide against those who in any way would forcibly perpetuate the premise.

25 (New York: Routledge, 1989).

26 Ibid., p. xi.

27 Ibid., p. xii.

28 Ibid.

29 Ibid., p. 118.

30 Ibid., p. xiii.

31 Ibid., p. 118.

32 Tracy, *Dialogue with the Other*, p. 53.

33 See the survey on the current state of the field of religion by Ray Hart in *The Journal of the American Academy of Religion* (October 1991): 715-827.

34 See Mary Gerhart and Allan Melvin Russell, *Metaphoric Process: The Creation of Scientific and Religious Understanding* (1984), and more recently an article, "The Cognitive Effect of Metaphor," in *Listening*, 25 (1989): 114-26.

35 Today the concept has many negative connotations, as in "drug habit."

36 Mary Gerhart, Joseph Healey and Allan M. Russell, "The Sublimation of the Goddess in the Mosaic Metaphor of Moses," *Semeia*, 51 (1993): 114-26.

37 Urs Winter, *Frau Gottin: Exegetische und ikonographische Studien zum weiblichen Gottesbild im alten Israel und in dessen Umwelt* (Göttingen: Vandenhoeck und Ruprecht, 1983).

38 (Norman: University of Oklahoma Press, 1992).

39 Berdache are "third sex" (or male gender-reversed) sacred persons who act as shamans among some Indian tribes in this country and in Chile.

40 Julia Kristeva, "Women's Time," in Nanerl O. Keohane et al., eds., *Feminist Theory: A Critique of Ideology* (Chicago: University of Chicago Press, 1981), p. x.

41 As Denise Riley has observed, however, the model can also be read as having the effect of destroying the category of "woman" altogether (*"Am I That Name?"* p. 110-11).

42 Ibid., p. 44.

43 Catherine Clement, a French feminist, wrote: "Even if somewhere it is true that rhetoric and vocabulary are formed by centuries of male cultural domination, to renounce the exercise of thought, to give it to them, is *to perpetuate*, as always when it is a matter of 'not being part of the system.' 'Be a feminist and shout'; an unchanged variant of 'Be beautiful and keep your tongue' " (" 'Enslaved Enclave,' New French Feminisms," in Mary Eagleton, ed., *Feminist Literary Theory: A Reader* [London: Basil Blackwell, 1986], p. 235).

III

GENDERED PERSPECTIVES

Chapter 2

FEMINISM AND BIBLICAL HERMENEUTICS: GENESIS 1-3 AS A TEST CASE

Eileen Schuller

The account of the creation of the world and the creation of Adam and Eve, its first inhabitants, serves as the beginning of the biblical story. These first chapters of Genesis, so short in length and so long in impact, will also serve for us as the starting point for a more generalized discussion of the relationship between feminism and biblical interpretation in the study of women and religion today. Now, in 1992, the coming together of feminist thought and criticism with the study of the Bible has resulted in an area of study with distinctive and ever-increasing subdivisions and an immense bibliography, too vast to cover in any comprehensive way in a paper of this length. A number of surveys of the field and various attempts at systematization and evaluation have appeared at regular intervals over the last decade, and these do not need to be duplicated here.[1]

That I choose in this paper to begin with a specific biblical text is not incidental, but in itself draws attention to certain features of the current state of scholarship. Until very recently (and this will come up again in the course of the paper) most scholarship in this area came from women trained in "classical" biblical studies (that is, in the historical-critical methodology of studying specific texts) who were introduced to feminist thought only later in their careers and then in a largely self-taught and self-selected manner.[2] Furthermore, feminist studies have, for the most part, followed the traditional demarcation between Hebrew Scriptures/Old Testament and New Covenant/New Testament;[3] that is, few feminist scholars actually write on "the Bible," but rather continue working in the specific area of their training. This means that, although much of our reflection about Gen 1-3 is applicable to the study of the gospels, for instance, feminist scholarship in the New Testament has had in fact a somewhat different emphasis and development from that which focused on the Old Testament.

In attempting to categorize the changing mosaic of feminist biblical scholarship, it has become commonplace to use the image of "three generations" or "three waves."[4] In this paper, I will survey, rather briefly, certain key articles on Gen 1-3 written by feminist scholars of the "first generation" (the end of the nineteenth century) and "second generation" (ca. 1973-1983). I intend to treat at greater length the "the third generation," recognizing that it is, of course, much more difficult to "map" work currently in progress. My intent is less to argue for or against a specific interpretation of Gen 1-3 than to understand what these various readings are telling us about the complex interrelationship of feminism and biblical studies. Although there are obviously some limiting factors in concentrating on a single passage, most key issues both in terms of the methodology and of the problematics of feminist biblical studies find resonance in this passage.[5]

Gen 1-3 has been, of course, a pivotal text, not only theologically, but also culturally in the shaping of Western civilization. Although there are surprisingly few references to Gen 1-3 in the rest of the Hebrew biblical tradition, these chapters became the focus of considerable attention from about the second century B.C.E. onwards (e.g., Sirach 24:25), into the New Testament era (e.g., 2 Cor 11:3, 1 Tim 2:9-15, 1 Pet 3:1-7) and the church fathers. The history of interpretation has been well documented, and need not be repeated here.[6] With a few notable exceptions, the "dominant reading"[7] has found this passage negative to women. Throughout the centuries, Gen 1-3 has functioned as the divinely sanctioned explanation of women's fundamental inferiority, and therefore as a legitimization of women's subordination to men in both societal and ecclesiastical spheres.[8] Thus, any attempt at bringing together feminist consciousness and the Bible must in some way be tested in these chapters.

The First Generation
Between 1895 and 1898, Elizabeth Cady Stanton, an American feminist and suffragist, along with a small committee of other women published *The Woman's Bible*, a commentary on those segments of the Bible (about one-tenth of the total) which "directly refer to women and those also in which women are made prominent by exclusion."[9] Although attempting to use the most advanced historical-critical methods of the day, the impetus for this work was not the cause of disinterested scholarship, but rather Stanton's recognition of the power which the Bible exercised in both civic and ecclesiastical circles, a power which "does not exalt or dignify woman."[10]

Although certain texts which would now be considered essential to the feminist agenda are omitted (most notably Gal 3:28), Stanton implicitly recognized the central importance of Gen 1-3 by the length of her commentary on these chapters. From our vantage point, it is fascinating to note how many of the factors that shape the discussion and are spiritedly debatèd in our day were already articulated in 1895. For example, Stanton contrasts the version of creation in Gen 1 with that of Gen 2-3, praising the first which "dignifies woman as an important factor in the creation, equal in power and glory with man," while condemning the second, which "makes her a mere afterthought."[11] When pressed to account for the difference in the two accounts, Canton blames "some wily writer" who "seeing the perfect equality of man and woman in the first chapter, felt it important for the dignity and domination of man to effect woman's subordination in some way."[12] More bluntly, she claims that "the second story was manipulated by some Jew"[13] thus introducing the issue of "blaming the Jews for patriarchy" which continues as a motif in feminist scholarship until the present.[14] Finally, in a move which anticipates even some of the language of Phyllis Trible, Stanton recognizes in Gen 2 "the courage, the dignity, and the lofty ambition of the woman"[15] in contrast to the "dastardly" conduct of Adam; in Gen 3:16, she points out that "what has been called the curse"[16] is rather a prediction, and thus descriptive of the results of the fall rather than normative for all times.

In light of the struggle today for women working from a feminist perspective to be taken seriously, both by their colleagues in the discipline of biblical studies and by their colleagues in the feminist movement as a whole, it is fascinating to hear Stanton lament that women scholars trained in Hebrew and Greek refused to be involved in the project lest their "high reputation and scholarly attainments might be compromised by taking part in an enterprise that for a time may prove very unpopular.[17] The desire of many to keep the feminist movement separate from issues of Bible and church is reflected in the 1896 resolution of the National American Woman Suffrage Association to disassociate itself totally from the "so-called 'Woman's Bible," The debate about whether the Bible is ultimately redeemable for women was already taking shape; feminists like Sarah Grimké and Francis Willard[18] believed that, once women read the Bible in the original languages and interpreted it for themselves, they would find it a resource and source of spiritual strength; Elizabeth Cady Stanton and her colleagues, though finding some words of hope in Gen 1 and isolated passages elsewhere in the Bible, ultimately concluded that "they cannot twist out of the Old or New Testaments a message of justice, liberty or equality from God to the women of the nineteenth century!"[19]

The Second Generation

An essay in 1973 by Phyllis Trible of Union Theological Seminary on Genesis 2-3 marked a turning point in the study of the Bible from an explicitly feminist perspective. Certainly there were others in the years immediately prior who had begun to articulate questions about the Bible and women,[20] but Trible's article, which was published simultaneously in an academic and a seminary publication, reprinted in a popular feminist reader, and then substantially enlarged in 1978[21] became in some ways, the classic statement both of the question and of the solution.

Refusing to be placed in a position of being forced to choose between her feminist beliefs and her Christian faith, Trible set out "to reread (not to rewrite) the bible without the blinders"[22] worn by male exegetes throughout the centuries. She combined an explicit feminist hermeneutic (understood as "a critique of culture in light of misogyny[23] with the methodology of rhetorical criticism as developed and understood by her mentor, James Muilenburg,[24] that is, an intrinsic reading of the text with close attention to the literary structure of words and motifs. The results of her beautifully written analysis (especially in the long form of the essay) convinced her that "rather than legitimating the patriarchal culture from which it comes, the myth places that culture under judgment. And thus it functions to liberate, not to enslave." Thus, for Trible, the text of Gen 1-3, when freed from the constraints of centuries of androcentric interpretation, shows itself to be positive and life-giving for women.

Since Trible's essay is relatively well known, I will not try to reproduce her arguments in any detail; as with any literary analysis, the effect is cumulative. Suffice it to say that key points would include (1) the *inclusio* structure of the text itself which makes the entrance of woman "the culmination of the entire movement, in no way an afterthought"[25] (as opposed to the traditional reading which views woman as inferior because she was created last); (2) the interpretation of "Adam" as a sexually undifferentiated creature[26] until Gen 2:21-24, so that man and woman come into being simultaneously; (3) the claim that *ezer* "helper" is not a term of inferior rank (given that God is frequently described with the same term) and particularly not when joined with *kenegdo* (New Revised Standard Version "as his partner"), an expression of equality;[27] (4) careful analysis of the phrase "she shall be called woman" (Gen 2:23) to show that it is radically distinct from the naming formula used to express Adam's domination over the animals; (5) the argument that the serpent speaks to Eve, not because she is gullible and weak, but precisely because she is—to use Trible's oft-quoted phrase—"intelligent, sensitive and ingenious" in contrast to Adam who is "passive, brutish, and inept;"[28] (6) finally, understanding of the "curses" of Gen 3:115-19 as descriptive, not prescriptive, a perversion of the intent of creation, thus calling for repentance and a return to woman's original freedom and equality.

Trible's reading of Gen 2-3 must be taken in conjunction with her much briefer exposition of Gen 1:27 "male and female he created them," where she analyzes the operation of vehicle and tenor in the working of metaphor to show how sexual differentiation bespeaks not hierarchy but equality.[29] These two studies enjoyed unprecedented influence and "stunning success"[30] throughout the 1970s and early 1980s. Indeed, Trible's reading of Gen 1-3 was so widely adopted that for a time it looked like "among feminist theologians it ["depatriarchalizing"] would seem to have established a new orthodoxy."[31]

Yet the impact of this "epoch-making paper"[32] can only be fully understood when it is viewed as an expression of the agenda and goals of the much broader movement of "reformist" feminist scholars. In the

1970s it became standard to divide feminists into two groups:[33] the "reformists" who sought to combine an explicit feminist perspective with an explicit faith (usually Christian[34]) commitment; and the "rejectionists" who judged that the Bible was hopelessly patriarchal and corrupt, with no message of salvation for women. The rejectionists understandably wrote little about the Bible; it was the reformists who judged it possible and thus made the attempt to speak both to a broad-based liberal church constituency and to the world of the university.[35] Yet although Trible began her *Journal of the American Academy of Religion* article with a reference to Kate Millett and *Sexual Politics*, her real dialogue partner is the world of the church (and less directly the synagogue), not the university or the secular women's community. Even in the lengthier version of her essay, there are few references to current developments in the field of literary criticism per se, and no evidence of interaction with feminist literary critics who were beginning to write at the same time.

Today, it is easy to be highly critical of some of the unexamined presuppositions and ready optimism of "second generation reformists." Yet they did attempt, in their day, something radically new: within the church they articulated for the first time the problematics of the Bible for women, and in the academic milieu they stubbornly refused to abandon a text that they and many women experienced as central to their identity and a source of liberation.

The Third Generation
Though Trible's reading of Gen 1-3 enjoyed immense popularity for many years, it in no way provided the last word, and a number of recent articles have once again taken up this text. In these studies, we can see in microcosm some of the diversity and turmoil which mark feminist biblical hermeneutics in the 1980s and early 1990s.

For instance, in 1981 and 1989, Phyllis Bird returned for another look at Gen 1,[36] a text which both Stanton and Trible judged to be one of the Bible's most positive statements of the fundamental equality of women (in contrast to the more problematic Gen 2-3). Bird presented a detailed exegetical study of Gen 1:27b "male and female he created them" within the framework of Gen 1:26-28, and concluded that 1:27b is to be read with 1:28 as a specification of sexual differentiation which is a necessary prerequisite for the commandment to be fruitful and multiply. That is, in contrast to Trible, this is not a statement about male and female in the image of God or about equal dominion, but a much more limited statement by the Priestly tradition (P) about fertility, describing a biological pair, not social relationships. The implication for Bird is clear: "the incongruous portrait of P as an equal-rights theologian is removed and Genesis 1 can be read in harmony with the rest of the Priestly work"[37] – a work which is thoroughly androcentric in outlook. Thus, although Bird has used the well-established historical-critical methodology and approach, she comes to a quite different reading of the text, a reading that calls into question any assumption that even Gen 1 provides a simple and clear biblical statement of the equality of women.

Although Bird's essays illustrate continuity with the methodology of the second generation, many of the changes to be observed in feminist study of the Bible must be understood as part and parcel of more extensive and rapid changes in the entire field of biblical studies. We are seeing the collapse of the hegemony of the historical-critical approach,[38] and a two-pronged thrust into an approach to the Bible through the application of and in dialogue with current literary theory (structuralism, reader-response criticism, deconstructionism, etc.) and an approach through social scientific methodologies, especially those linked to a liberation hermeneutic.[39] Here I can only examine a representative sample of recent studies on Gen 1-3 and conclude with more questions than answers about future directions.

Literary Studies
In 1987, the feminist literary critic, semiotician and narratologist, Mieke Bal, published an important essay on Gen 1-3 as a chapter of her book *Lethal Love: Feminist Literary Reading of Biblical Love Stories*,[40] a study of five biblical women (Bathsheba, Delilah, Ruth, Tamar and Eve), "women who bring death." *Lethal Love* was the first of a trilogy on the Bible, the other two dealing specifically with the book of Judges and developing in a more theoretical manner the "codes" of reading, particularly the gender code.[41] In *Lethal Love*, Bal is concerned "not with what is really written, but with why what is written is thus read."[42] Understanding the "reception" of the text in a broad sense to include how it is "read" in popular commentaries, children's Bibles and art, Bal demonstrates that the dominant reading of biblical stories about women has been monolithically misogynist, a denial of the importance of women and a denigration of their worth.

What is distinctive to Bal is her determination to explain why readers, beginning with Paul, have falsely read Genesis in the way they have. Thus, she introduces the concept of "the retrospective fallacy": that is, readers have projected the accomplished characters Adam and Eve, who appear only at the very end of Gen 3 with the naming of the characters, onto the previous textual elements which lead to the production of the character. For Bal, "the concept of character is at once a cause of the sexist myth and a means to deconstruct it."[43] Thus, the core of Bal's essay carefully works out the steps in the narrative construction of the character Eve—from a sexually undifferentiated being, to a sexually differentiated being capable of awareness, speech and choice, to the finally fully formed character who is named Eve; only at the end of the story, does the "myth of Eve" begin.

The similarity of their work invites comparison between Trible and Bal,[44] and so doing we see in bold relief some of the ways in which feminist biblical studies is changing. It is certainly not an exaggeration to say that Bal is on the cutting edge of much that is happening in biblical studies today. As author of five books in six years, plus a continuous stream of articles,[45] her work was the subject of a major session at the 1990 annual meeting of the Society of Biblical Literature, and a lengthy review article acclaimed her latest book as "the most important book in biblical studies in a generation."[46] Yet her own training and intellectual home is not in biblical studies as a discipline, but in narratology, semiotics, structuralism, psychoanalysis and the critical philosophy of Habermas. She has turned to the Bible "for a time"[47] to test her theoretical persuasions against a body of literature which was, at first, almost totally unknown and radically foreign in language and culture. Thus, with Bal, the starting point for study of the Bible has shifted from the church and theological concerns to the broader arena of literary, and especially feminist literary, criticism. It is a new experience for the biblical scholar to have to hunt up literary journals and books published by Indiana University Press in order to read about Genesis! On the other hand, her allegiance to the technical vocabulary and theoretical background of her own disciplines, as well as the difficulty of her style and presentation[48] have meant that Bal has been ignored by much of more "mainstream" biblical studies; it is not by chance that the most of the standard biblical journals of the academy and the church have so far featured few substantial reviews of her books.[49]

But the issue goes beyond that of the self-isolating language of discourse of various disciplines. In describing her own relationship to both the Bible and feminism, Bal writes: "I do not claim the bible to be either a feminist resource or a sexist manifesto. That kind of assumption can be only an issue for those who attribute moral, religious or political authority to those texts, which is precisely the opposite of what I am interested in."[50] That is, many of the very questions which are at the core of Trible's interest and passion (and of vital concern for many of her readers) are simply non-questions to Bal. Underlying Trible's methodology was a quest for the "true" meaning of the biblical passage,[51] a meaning to be found in the text, the recovery of which is of salvific importance since this is a "sacred text." For Bal, criteria are expressed in the language of plausibility, adequacy and relevance,[52] not the language of truth; the Bible has been of importance in the cultural development of Western civilization, but there is no assumption of its normativity for belief or praxis. The dialogue between church and academy and the conviction that it is not only possible but also desirable to speak to both—features which marked the "reformists" of the second generation—are no longer a given.

Although I have singled out Mieke Bal, I do not mean to imply that she is the only scholar who has studied Genesis from a literary perspective. Indeed some of the most interesting reflections on Gen 1-3 have come from women who are writing solely as literary critics, and have no explicit ties with the world of feminist biblical scholarship.[53] Furthermore, in a most helpful and perceptive recent article,[54] Pamela Milne has examined how Gen 2-3 has fared when examined from a structuralist perspective. After surveying a variety of studies, she observes that structural analysis of these texts (in whatever divergent ways structural analysis has been applied) inevitably concludes that the fundamental structure of these texts establishes a binary opposition (e.g., "man" over against "woman and animal") which is hierarchical and oppressive to women; at the level of "deep structures" this cannot be altered or ameliorated by a rereading of surface details. At best, the logic of oppression upon which the text is built can be deconstructed,[55] though the power of the text to transmit its male mythology to the unsuspecting reader remains intact.

A final group of recent essays has applied the perspective of reader-response criticism to Gen 1-3. Drawing upon the speech-act theory of J.L. Austin, Susan Lanser explored the role of *context* in how linguistic communication is performed,[56] demonstrating (to give just one example) that the description of the tree, the prohibition of eating, the expectation of punishment all work together to create a context wherein Gen 3:14-19 must be read as God's verdict of male dominance even if the surface appearance allows other possibilities. Similarly, David Clines, as a practitioner of reader-response criticism as understood by Stanley Fish,[57] takes three key points of Trible's equalitarian reading (Eve as "helper," the naming of Eve, and the term *'adam*) and shows in each case how the reader is led to an androcentric reading.

Beyond an evaluation of the relative merits of individual points raised in each of these studies, what is most striking for our purposes is that the application of modern literary methods (structuralism, speech-act-theory, reader response criticism) has resulted in a text which is more, rather than less, problematic for women especially for women who take this text as a spiritual resource and guide. I wish to return to this point at the conclusion of my paper.

Social Scientific Studies

A recent book by Carol Meyers, *Rediscovering Eve*,[58] illustrates how some third generation scholars have turned to the social sciences for a methodology and theoretical framework for the study of the Bible. Even more so than with literary studies, much of the work is still exploratory, and here (in this movement away from the text per se, to a reconstruction of social reality via the texts) developments in New Testament scholarship (in particular the work of Elisabeth Schüssler Fiorenza) have followed a somewhat different path.

Although one section of *Rediscovering Eve* does treat Gen 1-3 specifically (see below), the "Eve" of this book is really "Everywoman" of Ancient Israel. Meyers argues that it is a fundamental methodological error to think that we can come to know the life of this ordinary woman from the biblical text which is male, urban, and elite; however, an interdisciplinary approach utilizing anthropology (particularly gender theory), comparative ethnology and "the new archaeology," offers the possibility of recovering much about the social world of women in the highland areas of Canaan in the premonarchic era (1120-1000 BCE). The centrality of the household as the economic unit, the demands of pioneer highland terracing agriculture, coupled with a significant population decline at the end of the Bronze Age, all produced conditions that made the involvement of women in food production and the bearing of many children essential for economic viability; this resulted in "a context for gender neutrality and interdependence and of concomitant female power."[59]

For Meyers, this socio-economic reality is the hermeneutic key for reading Gen 2-3, a text which "can be counted among the best, not the worst, statements about women."[60] Meyers emphasizes the mythical, etiological and wisdom character of Gen 3:14-19, especially Gen 3:16a which she translates as "I will greatly increase your toil and your pregnancies." That is, the text served to provide ideological divine sanction for the intense physical labor and multiple pregnancies which were demanded for subsistence in premonarchic Israel—and cannot be presumed to have prescriptive validity in radically different socio-economic contexts.

Although Meyers is pleased to discover so much that is positive in the position of early Israelite woman and in Gen 2-3 (as she has recovered it, shorn of all postbiblical interpretations), she does not discuss in any depth the broader implications of her approach. Clearly Meyers' world of discourse is the academy, and on one level her work finds its validity within the larger framework of the recovery of Women's History per se.[61] In a brief and ambivalent statement she acknowledges that: "effecting current social change is not central to our goals here, yet the search for origins has an important—though indirect—role to play."[62] That is, given the discovery of a "golden age" in ancient Israel (or, in New Testament, Schüssler Fiorenza's early Christian "discipleship of equals"), what relationship does this have to contemporary praxis? Is this reconstructed socio-historical reality somehow necessarily a model or a prototype for women today? In its own way, social scientific analysis raises again what Letty Russell has called the "Midas" issue of feminism—that is, whatever question feminists touch, either in terms of the text or in terms of social reality, the discussion ultimately turns into a question of authority.[63]

Final Remarks
As the above survey indicates, something has changed in third generation feminist scholarship, though it is perhaps too early to pinpoint and name

the critical moves as opposed to more idiosyncratic and short-lived explorations. In the early 1980s, the "cutting edge" task was defined as exploring "the tension between historical-critical scholarship and feminism."[64] In the early 1990s, historical-criticism is only one component (and indeed somewhat secondary), as the focus shifts to a complex variety of literary approaches (reader-response criticism, structuralism, narratology, deconstructionism) on the one hand, and social anthropology and historical imagination, on the other. The bifurcation of biblical studies as a whole into literary and social-sciences streams carries over to feminist scholarship; until the present there has been little constructive dialogue between scholars like Bal and Meyers, even when they study the same text.[65] It remains to be seen whether feminist scholarship will continue to submit to the agenda set by "the guild," or whether the more inclusive, non-dualistic feminist impulse can find expression in bringing these together. A recent essay by Phyllis Bird articulates the conviction that "literary art and social presuppositions are so interrelated in any literary work that adequate interpretation requires the employment of both literary criticism and social analysis."[66] Exploration of how in fact to bring the two together seems a promising direction for the future.

That contemporary literary theory and social scientific methodology has made an important contribution to feminist biblical scholarship is obvious. What is less clear is whether the flow is solely unidirectional, that is, is there some contribution that feminist biblical scholarship can make to other disciplines? I have found very little written that even asks the question; closest is a single reference in a footnote to an unpublished paper that suggests, in a more general way, that "biblical hermeneutics could provide to literary theory a valuable 'chastening perspective' about the relationship between reader and text."[67] Perhaps it is at this point that recent "womanist" writing will have much to contribute. It is only in the last few years that the voices of American black women have been heard at all within the academy.[68] We are now discovering a living and vital tradition coming from women who have experienced the oppression of the Bible in its starkest forms but who continue to read and derive life and strength from this same Bible. Exactly how these women read needs to be explored in depth. The phenomenon poses a challenge to much of contemporary literary theory which is at a loss to provide a theoretical framework to explain such an "odd" use of a text. The lived experience of these women raises new questions about the relationship of reader and text.[69]

That third generation scholars are in dialogue with broader feminist thought and theory is apparent from even a cursory examination of bibliographies and footnotes in the essays on Gen 1-3.[70] The establishment of the *Journal for the Feminist Study of Religion* in 1985 has served to bring at least some important biblical studies articles to the attention of feminists in other fields of religion. However, very few works on biblical studies appear in feminist journals per se.[71] French feminist theory is only very recently being drawn upon in any significant way; indeed, at times where it has been used, the result has been more misunderstanding than enlightenment.[72] For the most part, feminist biblical scholars continue to draw upon feminist theory and apply it secondarily, rather than attempting to be creators and innovators within the broader domain of feminist thought.

As indicated at various places throughout the paper, the language of "reformist" and "rejectionist" has served over many years to name fundamental divisions and orientations within feminist scholarship. At present, although these terms linger on, there is a growing sense that they no longer fit, and may in fact be contributing to the problem of clarifying emerging trends.[73] Not only is the terminology of rejectionist or "nonreformist" fundamentally negative, it is misleading in so far as it does not "adequately acknowledge the possibility of a starting point significantly outside the realm of reformist concern."[74]

But as much more feminist biblical studies takes as its starting point and partner in dialogue literary criticism, social sciences, or women's studies more broadly defined[75] the links which formerly existed between church and academy are rapidly disappearing. Even on the level of individuals there are few women willing or able to be part of both worlds. Though there are gains in such a change of direction, there are also losses.[76] Indeed as feminist biblical scholarship becomes ever more diverse both in methodology and in fundamental orientation in this third generation one of the basic challenges will be whether literary critics and social scientists, women whose home is the academy and those whose home is the church/synagogue, can share both the language and the will to continue to speak with one another in mutually enriching and understandable ways as we continue to study the same texts.

Notes

1 For example, Mary Ann Tolbert, "Defining the Problem: The Bible and Feminist Hermeneutics," *Semeia*, 28 (1983): 113-26; Carolyn Osiek, "The Feminist and the Bible: Hermeneutical Alternatives," in Adela Yarbro Collins, ed., *Feminist Perspectives on Biblical Scholarship* (Chico: Scholars Press, 1985), p. 93-106; Katherine Doob Sakenfeld, "Feminist Uses of Biblical Materials," in Letty M. Russell, ed., *Feminist Interpretation of the Bible* (Philadelphia: Westminster Press, 1985), p. 55-64; also "Feminist Biblical Interpretation," *Theology Today*, 46 (1989): 154-68; Phyllis Trible, "Five Loaves and Two Fishes: Feminist Hermeneutics and Biblical Theology," *Theological Studies*, 50 (1989): 279-95; Jo Ann Hackett, "Woman's Studies: and the Hebrew Bible," in R.E. Friedman and H.E.M. Williamson, eds., *The Future of Biblical Studies* (Atlanta: Scholars Press, 1987), p. 141-64.

2 This is illustrated in a recent collection of essays by women who all studied at Harvard University in the 1970s and 1980s and have since then incorporated a feminist perspective into their work, Peggy L. Day, ed., *Gender and Difference in Ancient Israel* (Minneapolis: Fortress Press, 1989).

3 The terminology to be used for the canon of literature considered as scripture by Christians and Jews is itself a matter of much discussion today in biblical studies; here I have followed the usage adopted by the New Revised Standard Version.

4 Sometimes surveys begin only with the present century, but most often there is an effort to honour the nineteenth-century feminists by inclusion in the schema — though the remembrance of their work is a result of, rather than a cause of, second generation feminism.

5 Because of the focus on Gen 1-3, what is not treated at length in this paper is the type of scholarship which is not based on a text but instead seeks to "place women in the social world of ancient Israel," e.g., Phyllis Bird, "Israelite Religion and the Faith of Israel's Daughters: Reflections on Gender and Religious Definition," in David Jobling, Peggy Day, and Gerald Sheppard, eds., *The Bible and the Politics of Exegesis* (Cleveland: Pilgrim Press, 1991), p. 97-108.

6 For example, J.A. Phillips, *Eve, The History of an Idea* (San Francisco: Harper & Row, 1984); Gregory Allen Robbing, ed., *Genesis 1-3, History of Exegesis: Intrigue in the Gardin* (Lewiston: Edwin Mellen Press, 1988); for the interpretation of Gen 1-3 in the apocrypha and pseudepigrapha, see Bernard P. Prusak, "Woman: Seductive Siren and Source of Sin?" in Rosemary Ruether, ed., *Religion and Sexism* (New York: Simon and Schuster, 1974), p. 89-116.

7 The terminology is from Mieke Bal, *Lethal Love: Feminist Readings of Biblical Love Stories* (Bloomington: Indiana University Press, 1987), p. 2.

8 For a classic statement of eleven key points in this misogynist interpretation, see Phyllis Trible, "A Love Story Gone Awry," in *God and the Rhetoric of Sexuality* (Philadelphia: Fortress, 1978), p. 73.

9 Preface, *The Woman's Bible*, 1 August 1995, p. 5; reprinted by the Coalition Task Force on Women and Religion, Seattle Washington, 1974, fourteenth printing 1989.

10 Ibid., p. 12.

11 Ibid., p. 26.

12 Ibid., p. 21.

13 Ibid., p. 119.

14 To give the title of a much-quoted article by Judith Plaskow, "Blaming the Jews for the Birth of Patriarchy," *Cross Currents*, 28 (1978): 306-309. This on-going issue was the topic of a 1990 doctoral thesis from Temple University by Katharina van Kellenbach, "Anti-Judaism in Christian-Rooted Feminist Writing and West-German Feminist Theologians."

15 Preface, *The Woman's Bible*, p. 24.

16 Ibid., p. 27.

17 Ibid., p. 9.

18 For these and other early feminists see Carolyn de Swarte Gifford, "American Women and the Bible: The Nature of Woman as a Hermeneutical Issue," in Collins, *Feminist Perspectives on Biblical Scholarship*, p. 11-33; Dorothy Bass, "Woman's Studies and Biblical Studies in Historical Perspective," *Journal for the Study of the Old Testament*, 22 (1982): 6-12; also the bibliographies cited therein.

19 Ibid., p. 214.

20 For instance, Krister Stendahl, *The Bible and the Role of Women* (Philadelphia: Fortress Press, 1966), or even L. Swidler who had already coined the catchy phrase "Jesus was a feminist," *Catholic World*, 212 (1971): 177. Trible acknowledges that certain of her arguments were already formulated, although as isolated points without a broader theoretical framework, by male exegetes such as W. Brueggemann ("Of the Same Flesh and Bone (Gen 2:23a)," *Catholic Biblical Quarterly*, 32 [1970]: 541-42) and Edwin Good, *Irony in the Old Testament* (Philadelphia: Westminster

Press, 1965), p. 84 n.6.

21 Phyllis Trible, "Depatriarchalizing in Biblical Interpretation," *Journal of the Ameri-can Academy of Religion*, 12 (1973): 39-42; "Eve and Adam: Genesis 2-3 Reread," *Andover Newton Quarterly*, 13 (1973): 251-58, reprinted in C. Christ and J. Plaskow, eds., *Womanspirit Rising: A Feminist Reader in Religion* (New York: Harper & Row, 1979), p. 74-83; "A Love Story Gone Awry," p. 72-143.

22 Trible, "Depatriarchalizing in Biblical Interpretation," p. 31.

23 Trible, "Clues in a Text," *God and the Rhetoric of Sexuality*, p. 7.

24 James Muilenburg, "Form Criticism and Beyond," *Journal of Biblical Literature*, 88 (1969): 1-18.

25 Trible, "A Love Story Gone Awry," p. 102.

26 Ibid., p. 141, n. 17 Trible abandons the terminology of androgyny which she had used earlier, in favor of understanding "the earth creature [as] either humanity or proto-humanity."

27 In her later work, Trible sees *ezer* as connotating superiority, with *kenegdo* temper-ing this to mutual equality ("Five Loaves and Two Fishes," p. 291).

28 Trible, "Depatriarchalizing," p. 40.

29 Trible, "Clues in a Text," p. 12-21.

30 To quote the verdict of Mary Ann Tolbert in "Defining the Problem," p. 122. In addition to her impact on the English-speaking world, Trible has been the English-speaking feminist biblical scholar who continues to be quoted in other countries, e.g., Inger Ljung, *Silence or Suppression: Attitudes Toward Women in the Old Testa-ment* (Stockholm: Almqvist & Wiksell, 1989).

31 Mary Nyquist, "Gynesis, Genesis, Exegesis and the Formation of Milton's Eve," in Marjorie Garber, ed., *Cannibals, Witches, and Divorce: Estranging the Renaissance* (Baltimore: Johns Hopkins University Press, 1987), p. 162.

32 David J. A. Clines,"What Does Eve Do to Help? and Other Readerly Questions to the Old Testament," *Journal for the Study of the Old Testament Supplement Series*, 94 (Sheffield: Sheffield Academic Press, 1990): 25-48.

33 The terms "reformist" and "revolutionary" were first used by Sheila Collins, *A Dif-ferent Heaven and Earth* (Valley Forge: Judson, 1976), p. 41, and popularized by Carolyn Christ, "The New Feminine Theology: A Review of the Literature," *Reli-gious Studies Review*, 3 (1977): 203-204. This terminology subsequently becomes standard, at least as general categories (see n. 2). Carolyn Osiek ("The Feminist and the Bible") uses "revisionist" with much the same meaning as "reformist." Some-times a third category of "loyalist" is added to include women who seek to bring to-gether an evangelical perspective with certain feminist insights.

34 Relatively few Jewish feminist scholars have written specifically on the Bible, usually treating it within the larger context of *halakah*. Interestingly, it was Trible's essay "Depatriarchalizing in Biblical Interpretation" which was included in one of the first Jewish feminist readers, Elizabeth Koltun, ed., *The Jewish Women: New Perspectives* (New York: Shocken, 1976), p. 217-40. For a critique of Trible from a Jewish per-spective, see Nancy Fuchs-Kreimer, "Feminism and Scripture Interpretation: A Contemporary Jewish Critique," *Journal of Ecumenical Studies*, 20 (1988): 539-41.

35 It is interesting to note how little difference there is in content or methodology be-tween books published by an academic press such as Scholars Press (e.g., *Feminist Perspectives on Biblical Scholarship*) and a religious press such as Westminster (e.g., *Feminist Interpretation of the Bible*). Similarly, from the articles themselves, it is of-ten virtually impossible to know whether the author is writing within the university or seminary context.

36 Phyllis Bird, "'Male and Female He Created Them': Gen 1:27b in the Context of the

the Priestly Account of Creation," *Harvard Theological Review*, 74 (1981): 129-59; "Genesis 1-11 as a Source for a Contemporary Theology of Sexuality," *Ex Auditu*, 5 (1989): 31-44. Bird's conclusions here are a radical reversal of her earlier optimism that "the P formulation implies an essential equality of the two sexes" ("Images of Women in the Old Testament," in *Religion and Sexism*, p. 41-88).

37 Ibid., p. 156.

38 For example, Robert Morgan and John Barton, *Biblical Interpretation* (New York: Oxford University Press, 1988).

39 For this division, see Norman K. Gottwald, *The Hebrew Bible: A Socio-Literary Introduction* (Philadelphia: Fortress, 1985), p. 20-34.

40 This essay had first appeared in French in 1985 in *Femmes Imaginaires: L'Ancien Testament au risque d'une narratologie critique* (Paris and Montreal: Hurtubise, 1985), and then first in English as "Sexuality, Sin and Sorrow: The Emergence of the Female Character (A Reading of Genesis 1-3)," *Poetics Today*, 6 (1985): 21-42; also reprinted in Susan Sulieman, ed., *The Female Body in Western Culture* (Cambridge: Harvard University Press, 1986), p. 317-38.

41 Mieke Bal, *Murder and Difference: Gender, Genre, and Scholarship on Sisera's Death* (Bloomington: Indiana University Press, 1988), and *Death and Dissymmetry: The Politics of Coherence in the Book of Judges* (Chicago: University of Chicago Press, 1988).

42 Bal, *Lethal Love* (Bloomington: Indiana University Press, 1987), p. 39.

43 Ibid., p. 319.

44 Although I will highlight the differences in approach of these two scholars, there are clearly similarities in their reading of Gen 1-3. Interestingly, in the 1986 version of her essay, Bal praises Trible and "her seminal study on the feminine in the Bible which marked an important step in feminist theology" ("Sexuality, Sin and Sorrow," p. 321). That phrase is omitted in the 1987 version! Bal had indicated that she would discuss the relationship between her reading and Trible's more explicitly in a forthcoming book.

45 Most recently, Mieke Bal, "The Point of Narratology," *Poetics Today*, 2 (1990): 727-50; "Murder and Difference: Uncanny Sites in an Uncanny World," *Journal of Literature and Theology*, 5 (1991): 11-20.

46 David Jobling, "Mieke Bal on Biblical Narrative," *Religious Studies Review*, 17 (1991): 1-10; the quotation is from p. 9.

47 Bal's own account of her journey to biblical studies is traced in "Murder and Difference: Uncanny Sites in an Uncanny World," p. 11-12.

48 See Jobling's critique, "Mieke Bal on Biblical Narrative," p. 7, on this point in his otherwise most laudatory review. On another occasion, in "Feminism and 'Mode of Production' in Ancient Israel," *The Bible and Politics of Exegesis*, p. 249, Jobling has drawn attention to Bal's lack of familiarity with basic current work in biblical history and archaeology.

49 A brief book notice did appear in *Zeitschrift für die Alttestamentliche Wissenschaft*, 99 (1987): 454-55, and *Vetus Testamentum*, 38 (1988): 380 (which chooses to point out that Bal "makes no secret of her atheistic feminist standpoint"). The inability to fit Bal into standard categories may account for the fact that reviews of her work have appeared more often in general periodicals (*Theology Today* [1989]: 348-50; *Journal of Religion* [1989]: 395-96; *Union Seminary Quarterly Review* [1991]: 333-41).

50 Bal, *Lethal Love*, p. 1.

51 For a critique of this neo-orthodox quality of Trible's approach, see Elisabeth Schüssler Fiorenza, *In Memory of Her: A Feminist Theology Reconstruction of Christian Origins* (New York: Crossroad, 1983), p. 19-20.

52 Bal, *Lethal Love*, p. 13.
53 For example, the essay of Mary Nyquist, "Gynesis, Genesis, Exegesis and Milton's Eve"; also Patricia Parker, "Coming Second, Woman's Place," *Literary Fat Ladies: Rhetoric, Gender, Property* (New York: Methuen, 1987), p. 178-233.
54 Pamela J. Milne, "The Patriarchal Stamp of Scripture: The Implications of Structuralist Analyses for Feminist Hermeneutics," *Journal of Feminist Studies in Religion* (1989): 17-34; also in a semi-popular version, "Eve and Adam: Is a Feminist Reading Possible?" *Bible Review* (1988): 11-21, 39.
55 This is the approach taken by David Jobling, "Myth and Its Limits in Genesis 2:4b-3:24," in *The Sense of Biblical Narrative: Structural Analysis in the Hebrew Bible* 2 (Sheffield: *Journal for the Study of the Old Testament*, 1986): 17-43; Milne gives a critique of the limitations of his attempt. Other scholars have recently looked to deconstructionist tactics to reveal literary strategies at work in the interests of patriarchal ideology, e.g., Esther Fuchs, "Structure and Patriarchal Functions in the Biblical Betrothal Type Scene," *Journal of Feminist Studies in Religion*, 3 (1987): 7-13; Danna Nolan Fewell, "Feminist Reading of the Hebrew Bible: Affirmation, Resistance and Transformation," *Journal for the Study of the Old Testament*, 39 (1987): 77-87.
56 Susan Lanser, "(Feminist) Criticism in the Garden: Inferring Genesis 2-3," in Hugh C. White, ed., *Speech Act Theory and Biblical Criticism* (Decatur, GA: Scholars Press, [1988] (=*Semeia*, 41 [1988]: 67-84).
57 Clines, "What Does Eve Do to Help?," p. 21-22.
58 Carol Meyers, *Rediscovering Eve: Ancient Israelite Women in Context* (New York: Oxford University Press, 1988); this work incorporates a series of earlier studies by Meyers.
59 Ibid., p. 187.
60 Carol Meyers, "Recovering Eve: Biblical Woman Without Postbiblical Dogma," in J.F. O'Barr, ed., *Women and a New Academy: Gender and Cultural Contexts* (Madison: University of Wisconsin Press, 1989).
61 In the Preface of her book, Meyers describes her intellectual journey from traditional biblical studies to women's studies; see also "Women and the Domestic Economy of Early Israel," in Barbara Lesko, ed., *Women's Earliest Records from Ancient Egypt and Western Asia* (Chico: Scholars Press, 1989), p. 265-81.
62 Meyers, *Rediscovering Eve*, p. 8.
63 For this particular formulation, see Letty Russell, *The Household of Freedom: Authority in Feminist Theology* (Philadelphia: Westminster, 1987), p. 12. The issue of the authority of historical reconstruction has been more extensively discussed in terms of the New Testament, particularly Schüssler Fiorenza's work; for a perceptive reflection in theological terms, see Mary Ann Tolbert, "Protestant Feminists and the Bible: On the Horns of a Dilemma," in Alice Bach, ed., *The Pleasure of Her Text: Feminist Readings of Biblical and Historical Texts* (Philadelphia: Trinity Press International, 1990), p. 12-14. Mieke Bal raises the same question from a non-theological, feminist perspective in her review of Meyers' book (*Journal of the American Academy of Religion*, 57 [1990]: 511-13).
64 The definition given by Adela Yarbro Collins in the Introduction to the Society of Biblical Literature Centennial Volume, *Feminist Perspectives on Biblical Scholarship*, p. 2.
65 For the recent, though brief, review of Meyers' book by Bal, see n. 54.
66 Phyllis Bird, "The Harlot as Heroine: Narrative Art and Social Presuppositions in Three Old Testament Texts," *Semeia*, 46 (1989): 119-39.

67 Taken from Lanser, "(Feminist) Criticism in the Garden," p. 82, n. 23. The reference is to "The Will to Power in Biblical Interpretation," a paper by Joseph Sitterson delivered at the Modern Language Association Convention, 1986.

68 Although "womanist theology" has been explored for some time, work on the Bible specifically is more recent: e.g., Renita Weems, *Just a Sister Away: A Womanist Version of Women's Relationships in the Bible* (San Diego: Lua Media, 1989) and "Reading Her Way through the Struggle: African American Women and Bible," in Cain Hope Felder, ed., *Stony the Road We Trod* (Minneapolis: Fortress, 1991), p. 57-80; Clarice Martin, "Womanist Interpretations of the New Testament: The Quest for Holistic and Inclusive Translation and Interpretation," *Journal of Feminist Studies in Religion*, 6 (1990): 41-61; Cheryl Townsend Gilkes, "Mother to the Motherless, Father to the Fatherless: Power, Gender and Community in an Afrocentric Biblical Tradition," *Semeia*, 47 (1989): 57-85.

69 In a sense the question is not so different than that posed by women who characterize themselves as "loyalists" and whom feminist biblical scholarship has largely ignored; for all sorts of reasons of cultural and religious background, it seems easier to deal with the more (apparently) esoteric "womanist" phenomena.

70 It is notable that a very small core of articles are quoted repeatedly. Two common works are: Elaine Showalter, "Introduction: The Feminist Critical Revolution," in *The New Feminist Criticism: Essays on Women, Literature and Theory* (New York: Pantheon, 1985); Michelle Zimbalist Rosaldo and Louise Lamphere, eds., *Women, Culture and Society* (Stanford: University of California Press, 1974).

71 Articles in a journal like *Signs* deal more with the history of women in the biblical period than with a biblical text (e.g., Ross Kraemer, "Monastic Jewish Women in Graeco-Roman Egypt," 14 [1989]: 342-70).

72 For example, Luce Irigaray's review of *In Memory of Her*, "Égales à qui?" *Critique*, 43 (1987): 420-37, and the response by Morny Joy, "Equality or Divinity: A False Dichotomy?" *Journal of Feminist Studies in Religion* (1990): 3-24. For a successful and provocative use of the categories of Julia Kristeva, see Carol Newsom, "Woman and the Discourse of Patriarchal Wisdom: A Study of Proverbs 1-9," in *Gender and Difference*, especially p. 156-57.

73 See the discussion of Judith Plaskow and Carol Christ, eds., in *Weaving the Visions: New Patterns in Feminist Spirituality* (San Francisco: Harper & Row, 1989), p. 6-7. Though their earlier volume *Womanspirit Rising* was very influential in establishing the terminology, the struggle now is to name the "real division between and within women . . . while we would no longer use the terms reformist and revolutionary."

74 Peggy L. Day, "Biblical Studies and Women's Studies," in Klaus K. Klostermaier and Larry W. Hurtado, eds., *Religious Studies: Issues, Prospects and Proposals* (Atlanta: Scholars Press, 1991), p. 207, n. 6.

75 Jo Ann Hackett, "Women's Studies and the Hebrew Bible," p. 141-64.

76 Within a very short period of time there are increasing indications that church and academy are operating with simplistic and outdated understandings of what the other is doing. For example, much theological discourse in the churches about Gen 1-3 is carried on as if Trible were the absolute and final word, blissfully unaware of and unresponsive to the challenges to her interpretation which we have examined. On the other hand, the options available for women who approach the Bible theologically are sometimes presented almost as a caricature, without any awareness of the more sophisticated hermeneutical approaches of scholars such as Elisabeth Schüssler Fiorenza, e.g., *Bread Not Stone: The Challenge of Feminist Biblical Interpretation* (Boston: Beacon, 1984), and Sandra Schneiders, *The Revelatory Text* (New York: Harper Collins, 1991).

Chapter 3

THE FEMINIST CHALLENGE TO JUDAISM: CRITIQUE AND TRANSFORMATION[1]

Norma Baumel Joseph

The cantor swayed back and forth, her lovely soprano voice leading us in prayer, as she rocked her baby to sleep. It was Rosh Hodesh, the new moon, and we were gathered in prayer and celebration. Women praying, babies mewing, children playing — quite natural for us though strange too! Women wrapped in prayer shawls look so Jewish, so different. Our personal goals vary, our group experience is one of innovation in the context of tradition. We are seeking a vehicle of deeper involvement, a public expression of commitment. There have been times of exquisite singing but also moments truly off-key. There have been times of rare religious celebration, of laughter and joy, of hesitation and doubt and questioning. Yet they have been anchored by our concern to be part of the Jewish experience. These new experiences in the context of ancient patterns form the base of a feminist Judaism.[2]

The feminist critique of Judaism is well under way. The resultant transformation is just beginning. For many Jewish feminists, the world of traditional religion is hopelessly patriarchal[3] and irredeemable. In *The Changing of the Gods,*[4] Naomi Goldenberg predicted that placing women at the centre, allowing the feminist critique to penetrate and transform the tradition, would so alter it as to render it no longer recognizable as Judaism. Agreeing with her, yet not caring about religion at all, many feminists walked away completely. Others, still in agreement with Naomi, but unwilling to relinquish their own spiritual needs, entered new and different religious communities. Feminist Jews[5] disagreed with her prediction and attempted to remain.[6] They had a vision of a Judaism that should and could include them: a feminist Judaism.

One thing is certain, Judaism and the Jewish community of the twenty-first century will not look like today's communities of Montreal, New York or Jerusalem. Whether due to historic, political, economic or other factors; whether due to internal process or external influence; all living cultures change. They are dynamic by definition — stasis is found only in anthropology museums. In the past, Judaism has experienced radical challenges and has been transformed thereby. For example, the Hasidic movement threatened the ideology and the political structure of the existing community of the late eighteenth and early nineteenth centuries. Not only do we recognize Hasidism today as Jewish, but for some, Hasidim (pl.) are the quintessential Jews. Likewise, feminist Judaism, with its vision of women at the centre, will not necessarily destroy Jewish continuity. A Judaism that is enriched and transformed by feminism is germinating and is recognizable as Judaism.

One of the ingredients necessary for cultural continuity is knowledge of and confidence in the vitality of the tradition. Continuity is about past tradition flowing within the power of communal life.[7] If people feel empowered by their tradition, then changes will be felt as occurring legitimately within it.[8] Feminist Jews contend that, just as Jewish schools for girls did not end Jewish life but enhanced it, neither do women's prayer and prayer groups, female scholars and female names of God necessarily signal the demise of a vibrant Judaism. Furthermore, they argue, if feminist Jews do not participate in the process of defining and determining the future of Judaism now, it will change without them—without any recognition of their needs, vision, ability and God-given creativity.

To Be a Jew

The central premise of contemporary feminist Judaism, the transformation key, is that women are Jews. So simply put, most would agree. But the concomitant results are quite revolutionary. Any obligation incumbent on a Jew should be incumbent on a female Jew. Any privilege should also extend to female Jews. Anything a Jew can and should do, a female Jew can and should do. It is interesting to note that though in some sectors of Judaism privileges have been extended to women, the concomitant obligations and responsibilities have not. Feminist theologians such as Judith Plaskow have cogently argued that women must participate in the process of defining the meaning of Judaism, Jewish, Jew.

In an early and influential essay, Cynthia Ozick wrote "The only place I am not a Jew is in my synagogue."[9] Recognition of this factor, of the alienation and restriction of women, is a necessary prologue, a first step in the generation of a feminist Judaism. Accepting the legitimacy of the grievance and the unacceptability of the inequity necessitates a conceptual shift. Firstly, it means that women can no longer be the "other." Too much of Jewish life has been defined with men at the representative, ritual and legal centre. In the Bible, references to the people Israel or the children of Israel is in male grammatical form and is frequently defined by commentaries as applicable to men only. According to the Talmud (TB *Shabbat* 62a) women are a separate juridical group. Many of the laws pertaining to them and their status presuppose an otherness and a subsequent marginality.[10]

Secondly, it means that women are not just progenitors of Jews. Female Jews are not simply mothers, daughters or sisters. They may be all of those, but their relationship to God, tradition and people is not circumscribed by those relational characteristics. Complementarity is not equality when one partner is the norm. Feminists claim that, since according to tradition, the covenant with God is central in Judaism, female Jews must be completely, directly and independently included in that covenant. The quest no longer pursues illusive concepts such as equality or complimentarity, but rather centrality.

For feminist Jews, being in the covenant means direct, indispensable, active, public participation in all aspects of community life. It means being recognized as responsible and competent, with the same moral and religious obligations. It means that women's moral agency and judgement is integral to the future shaping of Judaism. The message of Genesis 1 is that men and women were created equally in the image of God. Feminist Judaism embraces that recognition and responsibility. The consequences can be quite revolutionary.

What is at stake is not only adding women in, which has already taken place in many sectors. It is not *merely* giving women equal access or even equivalent positions, which also has occurred in certain spheres. It certainly is not confined to bemoaning the discrimination and deprivation. Placing women at the centre "risks" a perceptual and conceptual shift that challenges the very nature of and continuity of contemporary Judaism. The problems are manifold. How does change get legitimated? How does one accept innovation without destroying a meaningful past? How is it possible to create new ceremonies while keeping alive a cherished link to an extraordinary tradition? What happens to those who are content and do not want change? How is it possible to establish a sense of continuity for future planning? How is it possible to avoid that transitory and arbitrary feeling that anything goes? What will it take to substantiate the paradigm shift? And, the quintessential question, will it be good for all of us Jews?[11]

I believe that it is worth the risk. More importantly, along with feminist Jews such as Cynthia Ozick and Blu Greenberg, I am compelled by the conviction that "Torah" requires it. I trust in the tradition of my ancestors that was both strong enough to survive and flexible enough to adapt. I have confidence that ultimately it will be good for all the Jews.

Ritual as Access

Despite all the inherent difficulties and trepidations, feminists have understood the imperative of critique and transformation.[12] Theorists first argued that the target had to be ritual, others insisted that the primary target should be theological, historic or legal. Regardless of all the cogent arguments, the initial stages focused on the ritual arena, mainly because of the nature of Judaism and the ensuing needs of the larger community of women who understood the primacy of participation. In Judaism, rituals of both synagogue and home are the access to religious life. Women were always ritual actors and even, though seldom recognized, experts in the domestic sphere. Concerned with food and holiday preparation, women managed the creation of *sacred* space in their homes. But Judaism remained defined by male public activity. Contemporary life turned women's attention to this public expression and experience of religion. To be a Jew is to have ritual responsibilities—and the more the better. Women were exempt or excluded from crucial communal ritual.

As ritual defines and refines life, and as it is the mode of doing as well as being Jewish, feminists insisted that there was no substitute for participation. Standing passively on the sidelines risks disengagement, estrangement, alienation. Private performance was considered important but not sufficient.

Life cycle rituals were the obvious first targets of this grass roots movement. Birth rituals[13] and Bat Mitsvah ceremonies[14] have appeared in every phase and community of Jews. That is not to say that every Jew will celebrate a *Simḥat Ha-Bat* or *Britah* for a newborn female; but many will have access to some form of birth ritual that recognizes and *publicly celebrates* the fact of the child's existence as a new Jew. To be sure, traditional Judaism always recognized a new birth. The father would go to synagogue as soon as possible to name the child. No mother, no baby, no celebration. The new forms of celebratory ritual do not contravene tradition; they augment it to capture the moment of God-involved creativity and the attendant religious attention bestowed upon female Jews. Similarly, when a girl reached the age of twelve, she was traditionally considered a Bat Mitsvah, responsible to the commandments (TB *Bava Kamma* 15a). However, there was no public celebration or ritualization of that religious moment.

> *In 1956, my female classmates and I turned twelve. On our respective birthdays we each became a Bat Mitsvah, a juridical adult in terms of ritual according to Jewish law. We understood the new level of ritual performance expected of us; now we had to fast on Yom Kippur (the Day of Atonement). The world of Jewish ritual observance descended upon us completely and* quietly. *We lived through this potentially momentous change in our lives and status privately. The only public sign of change was our absence from the men's section, although most of us had long ago stopped sitting with Daddy. It was so quiet that I don't remember anyone ever saying Mazel Tov! Did anyone ever teach us about being "twelve and one day," about all those ritual responsibilities? How did we know?*

> *In the following year, at age thirteen, the boys in our class experienced the same legal ritual transformation in a radically opposite form. To use the word* same *in this context is* absurd. *Each boy was publicly tested and feted — proclaimed adult by the adult world — religiously and socially acknowledged as having entered the community of Jews. In every conceivable way their Bar Mitsvah differed from ours, while supposedly meaning the same thing.*

> *I was proud to be a Bat Mitsvah and even enjoyed being a woman in the women's section. But of that momentous change — I expected no recognition and got none!*[15]

Today, in an ever-increasing array of creative possibilities, Bat Mitsvah celebrations, focussing public recognition on female Jews, are found in most sectors of the Jewish community from secular to hasidic. Female Jewish children of age twelve can publicly proclaim "Today I am a Jew!" The form and context of that event differs — for some it is limited to an announcement in a newspaper, for others it is a private party, some have school-centred celebrations, for many it involves some form of synagogue performance and prominence—but the fact and effect of the public recognition remains the same. Women are acknowledged as necessary participants in the covenantal community. Each individual child has an opportunity to proclaim her attachment to the people, and the community publicly claims and welcomes her.[16]

There have been numerous other developments in the ritual arena of women's life celebrations.[17] Some have changed marriage ceremonies, a few have added rituals to mark significant moments in their professional lives,[18] while others have felt the need to celebrate the onset of menarche and menopause.[19] The transformation has begun. What will Judaism be like for these women who will have a memory of their public positive identification as Jews? What will their contributions be and where will they lead?

Most clearly, the present score-card indicates a great unleashing of creativity and vitality. Nothing has been destroyed via these ritual inclusions and some claim that, on the contrary, the tradition and the community have been revitalized.[20] Most significantly, it is still recognizably Judaism, and the impetus for change as well as the creative process has found its base amongst the community of women and not in the male-dominated hierarchical institutional framework.

Herstories and Celebrations

Jewish feminists have also addressed themselves to the historical, calendrical and liturgical cycles. At the very outset, women sought ways to incorporate their experiences and voices in holiday celebrations. In North America today, feminist *Seders*[21] are occurring in many different communities as women grapple with Passover festivities. *Ushpizin*[22] ceremonies, welcoming female ancestors on the holiday of Sukot, have been generated.[23] Not all holidays have been visited with a feminist revision, but one of the most intriguing developments has been the reclamation of *Rosh Hodesh* ceremonies. Beginning in the 70s, Jewish women seeking greater personal and communal religious expression found a lost women's holiday.[24] The new moon holiday, *Rosh Hodesh*, has been adopted and adapted, celebrated, studied and sanctified by a plethora of Jewish women's groups in the Western world. The growth of these groups, not all of whose members claim to be feminist, speaks to the pervasive need for positive communal religious experiences in which women are at the centre and can focus on their religious lives as Jews. Some of the groups are study groups, many are prayer groups.[25] Some meet on the new moon itself,[26] others meet monthly on the Sabbath or on a weekday night. Many of the prayer groups have organized into a network with their own newsletter.[27] Some of the activities are replicas of male prayer or study patterns, others focus on new rituals only. All are innovative. The *Rosh Hodesh* development confronts three separate areas of the feminist Jewish agenda: women's herstory, prayer and ritual. It challenges the theoretical basis of the feminist agenda by implicitly raising questions about separation/integration, reclamation/revisionism, body-reductionism/embodiment, and imitation/innovation.

> *On a Shabbaton we had nowhere to place our ritual participation. Well, after heated arguments with some of our male partners we thought, "maybe we would separate and try our own service." But—separate is not equal! I knew that. Would this new experience be a means to an end or a dead end? Was our effort to pray going to leave us invisible or revealed? I never expected the genuine result—long-term prayer with women is now an end in itself for many of us.*

> *I am still troubled by the thorny problem of separation versus integration: should we continue our distinctive services? Should we have separate women's studies departments or "mainstream"? How does this differ from the existence of separate Jewish studies departments?*

Rosh Hodesh

Since the Jewish ceremonial calendar is lunar, the new moon is remembered in prayers, but today there are no associated festivities. Yet women in the past were said to have celebrated this day. Rabbinic documents indicate that once a month Jewish women would take a holiday from their daily routine. Traditional reasons given for this focus on women included their special piety, their bodily monthly cycle, their historic righteousness, their special role in the redemption from Egypt or their refusal to participate in the golden calf episode. In late medieval times, the day's festivities and association with women fell into disuse. Some say the rabbis disliked the fact that women spent the day gambling! Some rabbis are still dissatisfied with the way women are celebrating the holiday today.[28] The historical implication is clear, women had a herstory that has been lost or denied. For some feminist Jews, the requisite reaction was to explore that herstory and restore women to Jewish history.[29] For many it coincided with attempts to gain equal access in contemporary congregations. For others the next obvious step was to reclaim female separate celebrations and restore prayer to women. Neither path is mutually exclusive. All reinforce each other.

The resultant growth of women's prayer groups is both fascinating and unsettling. Initially, separate women's prayer groups appeared to reflect the needs of Orthodox women. Those groups that are associated with the Women's Tefillah Network are all committed to *halakhah*—Jewish law. These women were the ones who appeared to be most restricted in their own synagogue service. The prayer group offered individual women an opportunity to lead the congregation in prayer, to have an *aliyah*—the honour of being called to the Torah—to carry the Torah, to speak, to sing; to do all the things men do. Interestingly, although Reform, Reconstructionist and Conservative congregations offer women major participatory roles, some women from these sectors and even *secular* women found the need to share prayer with women-only groups.

Restoring prayer to women involved many different facets and efforts from different elements in the feminist community. Women had to learn to pray. Many women who had prayed all their lives suddenly realized that they were missing basic knowledge and skills. Never having led services, they simply did not know how. The imposed passivity had left its mark. Religion requires action, involvement, knowledge. For some, the traditional prayers were unable to convey female religious devotion. Some created their own style of service. Some, like Marcia Falk,[30] used their poetic skills to write new non-gendered prayers. Others, like Chava Weissler,[31] explored the 'hidden from history' prayers — *tekhinnes* — of European women. Their work exposed and expressed women's private devotion and public participation. The prayer groups benefited from all these converging elements. The new and the old mixed in distinctive liturgical styles of the diverse groups.[32] The spread of these groups is slow, but their presence and influence is felt in many other environments.[33]

Women at the Western Wall

It was refreshing to be amongst women who cared so much about prayer, Israel, Judaism and community, and about each other's needs and sensibilities. There were many disagreements, but all were voiced with mutual respect. Some felt we should go without the Torah so as not to create an incident; others wanted us to pray with the Torah but in the hotel. Some suggested that we pray at a different section of the Wall, others wanted us to pray where there was no meḥitsa or else on the other side. The majority wanted to go to the Kotel — to reclaim that place, with a Torah — to reclaim our attachment to that sacred symbol. The law of Moses is ours and we are the people Israel.

After long discussions, we decided to go. We would dress respectfully, and those who wished to wear their Tallitot (prayer shawls, permitted according to Rabbenu Tam and Rambam) would.

The thorniest issue was how to deal with the press. We did not want them there, but we had been informed that they already knew of our plans. I cannot emphasize enough that our desire was to do this quietly, without fanfare, to pray and to celebrate a quiet religious moment together.

There was a great deal of discussion on what kind of a service we should conduct. For some of us, it was imperative that we do everything according to Halakhah, Jewish law. Let me clarify one crucial point at the outset. According to Jewish law, it is permissible for a woman to carry, kiss and read from the Torah scroll. In order to satisfy the needs of the group and to be as inclusive as possible, a lot of compromises had to be made. For some women, praying with a meḥitsa, partition, was against their principles, while for others some parts of the service violated their sense of prayer. Some of us gave up the opportunity to chant a favoured part of the service so others could participate. Many women had very specific ideas on how to proceed, varying from the confrontational to the invisible. Yet, by the time we went, we were united in a way seldom experienced.

7 a.m. came quickly. No other session could have got us up and out at that hour! We were tingling with expectation, and warmed by our sense of camaraderie. As our two buses left the hotel, we verified the plans and procedures. When we arrived, Dafna went to inform the security guards of our intentions. They were surprised but very supportive. We walked forward slowly and were amazed to find a wall of cameras facing us. Tension mounted as the reporters engulfed us. But we found our way quickly and quietly to the Kotel.

We were there . . . actually there. At the Kotel. With our Torah.

As we started praying, the local women reacted, some with distraction, some with curiosity, some with fascination. One women became very upset and berated us. She even hit our backs to try and stop us! Rayzel's voice led us in song. Deborah's command to "focus" kept us on track.

We concentrated on praying and eliminating distractions. We did not look at the photographers, we did not look at the men. We looked only at our prayer books. We tried to block them out and listen only to the voices of the different women as they led us in prayer . . . women's voices praying, nervous . . . even tentative . . . but potent, eloquent and legitimate.

As the Torah service started, the tension increased. At this moment, we were breaking with the past. Women had prayed here, but never before had they chanted the Torah portion. Three women were called forward, each to say the appropriate blessing and read her portion.

WOMEN HAD ALIYOT AT THE KOTEL. That sentence is so easy to type, so difficult to explore and express. As Rivka Haut was later to state, we felt we had reclaimed the Torah for women. Not out of anger, but out of love and commitment. In a moment of religious significance, we declared our part in the covenant of Israel. We are the people. It is our Torah. The Kotel is ours, too.

In 1988, at the First International Jewish Feminist Conference in Jerusalem, a group of over 80 women went to the Kotel (the Western Wall) on Thursday morning to pray. This was a natural extension of the women's daily prayers at the conference. Women from all sectors gathered together for the first time in history to take a Torah to the Kotel and conduct services there. Individual women had prayed there for as long as the Wall attracted Jewish worshippers, but this was the first time women tried to pray as a group with prayer shawls and Torah.

As a result of that moment in time, some Israeli women continued to go to the Wall to pray on *Rosh Hodesh*. They were increasingly attacked, verbally and physically. Finally they turned to the State's secular courts. Subsequently, the North Americans formed a separate group—ICWK (the International Committee for Women of the Kotel), hired their own lawyers and, in 1989, after being refused entry to the area, joined the suit. The case rests on Judaic and Israeli law—not always identical.

The case is still pending. It is a landmark case. It represents the first time in history that Jewish women's religious rights were argued in a court of law. The women involved represent thousands of Jewish women. Money was collected from almost every branch of the contemporary Jewish community. Of course, not everyone is involved, not everyone cares,[34] some disagree.[35] But those dedicated to the case, who see it as symptomatic of the feminist battle in the Jewish community, have learned some valuable lessons and had incomparable religious experiences.

Women's prayer groups and women at the Kotel focus attention on women as ritually and spiritually active. It brings their experience out into the public domain. It allows women to proclaim: I am a Jew and Judaism's sacred text and space are mine too! It is by no means the only possible expression or experience for feminist Jews. There are many other forums. Some include weekend retreats of which there are a growing number. The most famous and enduring is the B'not Esh yearly retreat.[36] Many volunteer women's organizations are experimenting with Jewish experiential weekends for women.[37] In all of these moments there is a growing sense of the power of women as they come together for religious expression and experience.[38]

As with the prayer groups, they raise possibilities and problems. Most stimulating and somewhat unexpected was the exhilaration of praying with women. And this is precisely one of the unsettling facets. What are feminists proclaiming by creating something for women only? What are they acceding to, who are they denying? Separate but equal was used to segregate and restrict women—how can it be justified for women? It is understandable that in the process of placing women at the centre, women will find greater support and harmony with other women. Feelings of pride and accomplishment of sharing and caring are prevalent in women-only groups. Does that necessitate a separatist agenda? Is it possible to remain distinctive, to hear women's voices, to celebrate women, in integrated environments? Is it possible to disconnect sometimes and unite at others?

On Including Women

There are three distinct modes available for female ritual expressions. Women can be integrated into a previously male sphere, they can construct parallel but separate modes, and they can create totally new practices. Elements of all three approaches have been woven into new ceremonies. By focusing on women as public religious figures, by naming women as Jews, all these disparate attempts are radical and transformative. Yet each pattern poses serious questions of concept and strategy.

If the option is to be integration, and women are accepted into all male spheres, is the result equality or sameness? Does it affirm women as Jews or mask their femaleness? Does it make them more male-like and therefore equal? Is it symptomatic of the valuation of everything male and the devaluation of the female? Is it a sharp cry to "let me be like you" or is it a more subtle demand to "let me in so that I can change you"? Is it the profound claim let me in because I belong?!

The greatest effort has taken place in moving towards the integrated mode. The Reform, Reconstructionist, Conservative (and even in some areas, Orthodox) movements have made attempts to be more inclusive.[39] Except for the Orthodox, they have all opened their rabbinic seminaries to women. Again, except for the Orthodox and some Conservative congregations, women can have the honour of an *aliyah*, be counted in the *minyan* – quorum – and participate in other ways in the service. Yet, in all these endeavors, there have been major setbacks and no conclusive transformation.

In 1846, the Reform movement declared men and women equal, but women were given no sphere of action to exercise that equality. Feminist Reform Jews argued that they were offered an equal share of a theory but no practice.[40] It was not until 1972 that the first female rabbi was ordained by the Reform seminary. Only now, in the 90s, is the Reform movement addressing the problem of an androcentric liturgy. The Reconstructionist movement opened its doors to women from its inception. However, though women were present, their femaleness was not allowed to penetrate the halls of academia. Curriculum changes are only slowly being made today. And still the Rabbinical Reconstructionist College does not welcome female appellations for God.[41]

The Conservative movement went through a series of paroxysms in its attempt at integration. They began with *aliyot* for women in the 50s, which was quietly passed but never universally accepted and rarely practised. The next stage in the 70s focussed on the inclusion of women in the prayer quorum, the *minyan*. Again, peculiar to the non-authoritarian structure of Jewish religious institutions, some congregations and their rabbis accepted the decision of the law committee, but many refused and went through a time of bitter controversy. The 80s brought the debate to the arena of women in the rabbinate, which was even more divisive. Today, the issue of women in the clergy, including women as cantors, appears to be causing a great rift in the movement and amongst the teachers in the Jewish Theological Seminary.

Yet, feminists claimed, none of these steps attacked the problem at its source. Declare all women Jews – equally obligated – and the rest falls into place. Why are only female rabbinic students in the Conservative seminary obligated to all rituals? Is it because they are more male-like, having entered a male career? If women in the movement do not have to pray with phylacteries, why is it incumbent on female rabbis? The preceding list of grievances is not a condemnation of the different attempts nor an assertion that integration does not work. Rather, it is an attempt to chart the feminist challenge and to clarify the problems.

No path is totally without risk or immediately successful. Integration, the inclusion of women in all spheres of the Jewish endeavour, is the basis of much of the transformation that has successfully taken place. However, no denomination has yet been fully transformed. As a result, there has been an increase in all types of experimental groups. In traditional and non-traditional egalitarian services, men and women together are attempting to forge a path of shared non-sexist religious rituals. Many are non-denominational, few have hired clergy. Some have been very successful and have been in existence for more than a decade. They form a small but important influence and offer a much-needed option. Thus, choices are available, possibilities do exist; but transformation is not yet fully in place. "Not yet" means — there is progress, there is hope, there is work.

As mentioned above, prayer or *Rosh Hodesh* groups suggest a different model. Women's separating from mixed congregations becomes both a political as well as an existential act. The choice to separate can arise from a sincere commitment to, enjoyment of, and celebration of women. Women's groups are free to develop a special sense of femaleness and female bonding. They can explore, express and elaborate on the specialness of being a female Jew.[42] However, conceptually and strategically, separate and equal is not an indisputable choice. If the feminist critique insists that woman be called "Jew," regardless of gender, are separate Jewish women's groups reverting to a gender-restricted view of the tradition? In a patriarchal world, perhaps it is necessary to isolate women so as to call attention to their special attributes and unique experiences. Is this the only way? Is it only one of the ways on a road to integration? Is it an end in itself? Feminists have lobbied against exclusionist policies, yet is this not gender-based exclusion? Ironically, some women-only groups are very selective and have not even allowed many women to join.[43] Others are so inclusive as to lose all definition and purpose.[44]

In an important essay on the methodological approach to the study of women and religion, Rita Gross noted the need for studies that focused on both exclusionary as well as inclusionary rituals.[45] Inclusion is not always available or easy. It is not even always desirable. Exclusion may not always be desirable, but it is one of the many strategies available to women in the throes of a search for self and group bonding. Yet, it is a strategy fraught with danger. Separation can lead to isolation, detachment, fragmentation and seclusion. Are separate women's prayer groups merely a disguise for the continuation of the age-old pattern of traditional segregation? Are they a dead end for women? Does their existence take the pressure off the Orthodox and malestream community to respond? Are new rituals for women performed in women-only environs a celebration, or a path to invisibility? When lesbian feminist Jews hold separate services, are they "allowing" the heterosexual world to ignore their religious needs and experiences or are they establishing a distinctive addition to Jewish practice?[46]

Creativity and Continuity

Within both integrated and separatist agendas, experimentation has created new modes of expression. Inclusive and feminist liturgies are slowly appearing. Marcia Falk has been writing new blessings that have no gender reference[47] and musicians such as Debbie Friedman have been writing songs that, amongst other things, recall biblical women.[48] New prayer books are now being published that begin to look at female representation. One of the most inspiring developments is in the field of *midrash*. *Midrash* is homiletic interpretation of scripture. Many legends have passed into the learning and lore of Judaism through *midrash*. Today, women are creating feminist *midrash*[49] that gives voice to women's experience and questions. Many of the tales present biblical women as strong and vibrant characters, others expose women's life experiences. Many raise difficult questions about the biblical treatment of women that frequently went unanswered.[50] Most allow contemporary women to "enter the story"[51] so that they can feel the strands of their lives connected to the tradition and collective memory of their people.

New rituals, new prayers, new stories, new patterns of leadership and interaction have invigorated the community. However, here too, theoretical and strategic concerns apply. Firstly, Naomi Goldenberg's challenge remains: how to accept the new without destroying the old? Any innovative move must respond to the challenge of continuity as well as the very real need for legitimacy and familiarity. Old rituals are known, have a history and are therefore comfortable.

> *My great-grandmother lit Sabbath candles in Europe, and when I repeat that act every Friday night, I somehow manage to connect with her. I use my mother's candlesticks, joining her to my action. When my daughter stands at my side, the chain of continuity is tangible. We know that thousands of women are doing the same thing at that very moment. The connection to a past, present and future, expands and authenticates our experience.*

The new must somehow be integrated with the old so that the experience of continuity is preserved. Perhaps, *Rosh Hodesh* groups, *midrash* and birth rituals all manage to maintain the feeling of continuity by clothing the feminist transformation in Jewish symbols and patterns.

A Case of Legal Inequity

Yet some of the old patterns must be totally eradicated or radically changed. For example, Jewish divorce law poses serious difficulties and is an obstacle to any sense of female equality.[52] The biblically determined procedure requires that the male be the divorcing agent. There is no power of the court to decree a divorce, nor may the woman give the *get* (divorce document). The woman must wait, sometimes eternally, for the man to agree voluntarily to divorce her. This has led to intolerable conditions of extortion and oppression. The Reform movement eliminated the whole procedure. Those in the traditional camp, unwilling to abandon the legal system, have worked on various solutions but as yet none have been implemented that are fully successful.[53] The problem rests in the very structure of the law as well as in the male rabbinic courts that apply the procedures. Women and men from many different affiliations have been struggling with different approaches. One important consequence is that women have reached across borders to help each other and work together.[54]

Many would like to believe that this is a minor problem of Jewish law. Those women and men who have been dealing with the devastating effects of this problem know full well the real dimensions. For many Jews, this situation speaks not only to the position of women in Judaism, but also challenges any claim the Judaic system has to justice and ethical principles. If this is the way law and rabbis can allow women to be treated, then. . . . The wave of fury is growing; who knows what it will engulf.

The result of this particular battle will be radical. Women must be able to find justice when the law is applied — most would agree. Women must be involved in finding and defining the solution — many would agree. Women must be actors/authors in the process of making and applying the law — only some would agree.[55]

Perhaps, one of the most exciting and contentious platforms is that which posits women within the Jewish legal system. Some women have begun that hard road toward scholarship in Jewish law.[56] What will Judaism be like when women are the decisors — the legal decision makers? The potential for change as well as for chaos is embedded in the system; the outcome is not yet in sight.

If one of the residual demands is greater involvement of women in the process and procedures of Jewish life, is the implication that women will do it better? Certainly, male-only councils have not attended to the needs of women. Furthermore, women, whose social upbringing and experience is different, will be able to make a distinctive contribution to Jewish law and life. So the argument grows for women's increased involvement in all levels of Jewish life. But is there an underlying reductionism? Is the claim that women do it better reducible to some form of "anatomy is destiny"? More concretely, are new rituals for women that focus on the female body also in danger of introducing a reductionist mode?[57]

The challenge is to celebrate and not reduce; to recognize and not romanticize; to consecrate and not ignore. Women are embodied, and it is necessary to celebrate and ritualize special moments in their physical/spiritual life cycle. Rosemary Reuther once wrote that "the significance of our movement will be lost if we merely seek valued masculine

AUGUSTANA UNIVERSITY COLLEGE
LIBRARY

traits at the expense of devalued feminine ones."[58] On the other hand, Rachel Adler warned that creating religious metaphors solely out of our biological experience will not be constructive.[59] Finding the balance between old and new, between individual and community, between a bodily or historical locus, between unity and diversity—those are the challenges of feminist Judaism.

On Speaking to God

Jewish feminist creativity is thus challenged and challenging. It is alive and well and Jewish. Despite all the questions and disputes, the feminist critique has developed into a nascent feminist Judaism. Though the initial efforts were focused on ritual and historical metaphors, some feminists recognized that discussions about the theology of Judaism required careful attention.[60] With the publication of Judith Plaskow's book *Standing Again at Sinai: Judaism From A Feminist Perspective*,[61] the classic mythic structure has also been placed on the agenda. She argues that women's experience can lead to a new understanding of Torah as sacred text, Israel as community, and most importantly, God as Creator/Redeemer. Again, the challenge is to find a Jewish, feminist and authentic way to call upon God[62] and recognize Her presence in our lives. Old metaphors were rediscovered[63]—God is our Mother—[64] female attributes were reclaimed, and God was found to have female names—*Shekhinah*.

There are various formulations of feminist Jewish thealogy[65] but the general deliberation has slowly begun to have an impact on the established community. The previously mentioned liturgical changes reflect a growing awareness of the theological critique and have resulted in some innovative terminology. Traditional Jewish monotheism need not be destroyed by pronoun changes.

> *I believe that it is salvific and transformative to conceive of God as Female. It shocks us out of the idolatry of seeing God as Male. God created humans in God's image; male and female God created them; God's image is male and female. In this search for relationship with God and for understanding, it is also necessary to recognize the need for a plurality of images. God is infinite, and our ability to comprehend is limited. God's infinity must allow a variety of possible "faces"; our finiteness requires a variety of access modes. God appears as Father, Mother, Feeder, Tailor, Matchmaker, Lover, King, Creator, Judge, Comforting Presence, Disappointed Parent, Warrior, Healer.*

> *No one image can contain the infinity of God: neither male nor female.*

> *The question of my relationship to God must include a whole series of concerns starting with how I talk to God—prayer—and how I speak about God—theology. The case might be made that the present Jewish feminist quest for identity will centre on God.*

> *Feminist theology has developed in the context of story, too. One of the earliest was Judith Plaskow's "Applesource".[66] It was theologically and humanly playful,*

speculative, worrisome, stimulating, challenging. I am reminded of a story that is so evocative, I still use it in the classroom. Elie Wiesel wrote a forceful story about a man who changes places with God. What an imagination! What theological audacity! But the ultimate challenge was Carol Christ's retelling of that midrash *in a feminist mode.*[67] *It described a woman's powerlessness and pain. It expressed a woman's anger at God for allowing "all this" to happen to me. And then, it brought forth a God who is female, who has not been known, who yearns, who suffers and is a companion in our suffering. No impersonal God; no ground of being; no dry systematic philosophic treatise could have expressed my feelings and made sense of my religious yearning as that story did. The difficulty in relating to God in the modern world is finding the fitting (kosher) story or metaphor and the appropriate mutual expectation. . . . God's presence in our lives is a becoming – a never-ending-story.*[68]

The significance of the theological discussions is the growing concern with a thoroughgoing articulation of feminist and Jewish interests. The unfolding of new hermeneutical paradigms that express women's religious experience and need can be both a source of the feminist transformation and a resource for Judaism as a whole.

Education: An Arena Transformed

The greatest resource and perhaps most successfully transformed arena of Jewish life is to be found in the world of education and scholarship. At the beginning of this century, in a very gradual and imperceptible way that, nonetheless, has had revolutionary results, Jewish women were given access to Jewish knowledge. Both in the religious and secular worlds, women entered the halls of learning and transformed them.

The study of Judaism and Jewish texts has not always been open to women. Debates concerning the propriety of teaching women emanate from early rabbinic literature. The Talmud states that women were considered exempt from the obligation to study Torah (TB *Berakhot* 20b, *Kiddushin* 34a). The prooftext is the biblical verse (Deut 11:19), "And you shall teach them to your children," the last word commonly translated as "your sons and not your daughters" (*Sifrei* Deut 46). In fact, the Mishnah in *Soṭah* 3:4 and the ensuing talmudic debate posits the question of whether women were even allowed to study.

This is not to say that women were not educated – some were even noted for their scholarship – but rather to highlight the problematic nature of women's education in Jewish history and law.[69] Throughout the medieval period most women were not taught in a formal or systematic manner. They were primarily expected to learn all that they needed at their proverbial *mother's lap.* As late as the nineteenth century one noted rabbi claimed that women were never taught from books.[70] Although new research indicates that there were some female scholars, the consistent expectation was that ordinary women would glean everything they needed from observation and informal parental guidance. The majority of women could not read Hebrew, prayed in Yiddish and were unable to study Judaic texts.

As Jews entered the modern world, this attitude became increasingly problematic. Women, like men, needed formal education in order to ensure the transmission of Judaism from generation to generation. Some rabbinic leaders approved this new development, but the transformation occurred because of the vision and perseverance of one woman, Sara Schenirer (1883-1938).[71] The resultant Beth Jacob movement was immensely successful, creating an environment in which the once forbidden, or at least debatable, education of Jewish females was now to be considered a *mitsvah*, a commandment, available to all girls, not just the exceptional ones.[72] This decision inaugurated a new era with wide-ranging repercussions. Jewish girls were to be publicly, professionally and communally educated in Jewish subjects. Modern Judaism is significantly different from previous eras in part because of its attitude towards, and unique development of, the education of its female children.[73]

Feminist Judaism grows out of and is nourished by the education of female Jews. Finally, women can say *we know of what we speak*. Finally, women can look to women scholars and leaders for information, knowledge, interpretation and explanation. Finally, women can contribute on an equal plane. The rapid and recent growth of schools created just for women to study Judaic texts is encouraging, even though many insist that they are not feminist.[74] Many streams, from many different sources, can combine to create a tidal wave. The waters of Torah — of women studying Torah — have washed over the Jewish world and refreshed it.

The focus on women in Judaism in the academic world, and the subsequent increase in research, have contributed enormously to the transformation.[75] There are a significant number of scholars, most of them female, who have concentrated on *filling in the gaps*.[76] As more biographies are written, the corpus of information on individual women's lives and the distinctive historical experience of women has necessarily come sharply into focus.[77] This spotlight, then, informed by feminist theory, creates a whole new approach with a suggestive set of new research questions and directions.[78] There are now exciting new studies in fields such as women and Bible, literature, history, immigration, resistance, Talmud, late antique Judaism, synagogue, Germany, America, labour movements, Yiddish literature, prayers, rabbinics, Jewish philosophy, Israel. Research has yielded impressive amounts of new information that have resulted in "a broad challenge of the paradigms and methods of research within the academy based on gender as a category of analysis."[79]

However, the question remains: How far has this wealth of knowledge penetrated both the academy and the community? In 1990, the journal *Modern Judaism* dedicated two volumes to "take stock of where the various fields that comprise modern Jewish studies presently stand."[80] Twenty-one experts wrote essays that were to give a picture of the best of modern Judaic scholarship and its future directions. One of those essays, by Susannah Heschel, does focus on women's studies. Another, by Shulamit Magnus on German Jewish history, integrates research by and about women into the total corpus of scholarly work in her field. Five of the remaining nineteen articles were written by women. Other than one by Gershon Hundert, the rest do not include current research on women. Furthermore, according to Susan Shapiro, although progress has been made, there is not yet a transformed, balanced curriculum. The different disciplines are at disparate stages.[81] This means there is more work to be done. And it is not only in matters of research topics and academic disciplines. Women who have been working in these fields have been marginalized. Hence, there are now two separate groups for them and separate journals for their publications. There is a Jewish woman's caucus at the Association for Jewish Studies and a similar group at the American Academy of Religion. *Lilith*, *Bridges* and *The Journal for Feminist Studies in Religion* all specialize in publishing work that is women-centred. Mainstream journals obviously print women's studies articles, but still there is a need for specialized publications. Although Paula Hyman's essay indicated that women's history is reshaping "traditional conceptions of Jewish history and culture,"[82] the doubt remains that it is not yet[83] a thoroughgoing process.

Moreover, the response of the Jewish world to these scholars and their respective scholarship has not reached total acceptance or even acknowledgement.[84] Examples of female scholarship, leadership and participation from the past are neither well known nor proclaimed as precedents for current developments. Thus, although the work of Weissler on women's prayers and Weissman on women's education present women's distinctive experiences and extrapolate the ensuing religious and revolutionary significance, few wish to apply the lessons. Nevertheless, as scholars continue to unearth herstory, the transformation process will continue and will gain that feeling of legitimacy and continuity. Links with women from the past stimulate and strengthen the process.

Feminist scholarship, women's greater educational opportunities and increased communal participation have also led to the fitting presence of women in the rabbinate.[85] The issue of women as rabbis appears to present the community with a radical change, yet one could argue that, not only is this a natural outgrowth of women's education, but that there have been historical precedents. Women speaking in public places is not new, though perhaps rare. Certainly, the biblical figures of Miriam and Deborah stand as clear prototypes. Women as teachers of the community are also not unheard of, from Hulda, Beruriah, Asnat Barzani, Miriam Shapira Luria and, today, Nehama Leibowitz. Perhaps the combination of function and place, that of giving a sermon from the pulpit, is remarkable. Yet, here again, one can name women such as Bat Halevi, Dulcie of Worms, Eidele, daughter of the rabbi of Belz, and most famous, Hannah

Rachel Werbermacher, the "Maid of Ludomir." All these names are precedents, links in a chain of Jewish endurance and vigour; links in a chain of women recognized and sought for their knowledge of Jewish law and lore. Thus, as research into the arena of herstory combines with women's contemporary communal activism, feminist Judaism will develop the necessary ambience of legitimacy and authenticity as it continues to confront the tradition.

Judaism of the twenty-first century will be different from the nineteenth, but it will be recognizably Jewish even with women at the centre. There will be an increment in female lay and professional leadership, and women's rituals will continue on their glorious path of creative expansion. Feminist *midrash* will yield a whole new set of stories and paradigms. Women will increase their participation in synagogue life, while they maintain a strong attachment to women-only groups and organizations. Academic research will continue its present growth pattern, and schools for women's study of Judaica will flourish. Liturgy changes will take longer to be accepted. Women as law makers and decisors will take the longest to reach a normative standard. There are many problems, pitfalls and obstacles. Questions of strategy and theory have not yet been resolved. Feminist Jews are frustrated, excited, disappointed, encouraged, disheartened, exhilarated, worried, confident.

As a scholar and teacher, I am clearly acting in congruence with Jewish religious norms. Yet, as female scholar I challenge those very norms, both by simply being female and by using a feminist critical approach. The ethical struggle deepens as I learn more, speak out more forcefully and as I become more attached to and more estranged from that very community. Can I not make a claim on that community that it sustain me? And to what degree must I respond to its claim that I sustain it? What right do I have to work to transform the Jewish world according to my vision? How can I not?

Notes

1 I would like to thank Morny Joy, Michael Oppenheim and Leslie Orr for their helpful comments on earlier drafts.
2 This paper presents two distinct perspectives. Its main purpose is to describe the current developments in the realm of feminism and Judaism. It is based on and develops out of sixteen years of academic research and scholarship. It is a feminist enquiry in so far as it tries to focus on the transformation of a religious tradition under the impact of the feminist challenge.

The second perspective is that of a partisan. In this voice, my own experiences are presented. Feminist writing has explored the autobiographical mode incorporated into the theoretical. The strength and potential of this method seems appropriate in this context. Italics and indentation will be used to indicate the shift from invested scholar to involved participant.

Operating in both modes, theoretical questions impinge on narrative and description. The feminist, Jew and scholar in me discerns inconsistencies and contradictions more frequently than solutions or theoretical integration.

3   The nature of patriarchy is not uniform. The diverse facets must be differentially ex-
    plored historically. See Carol Meyers, *Discovering Eve: Ancient Israelite Women in
    Context* (New York: Oxford University Press, 1988), for her chapter on the different
    form of Israelite patriarchy and its effects on women's place in the cult and culture
    of ancient Israel. Gerda Lerner's *The Creation of Patriarchy* (New York: Oxford
    University Press, 1986) adds significantly to the feminist inquiry into this area.

4   Naomi R. Goldenberg, *The Changing of the Gods: Feminism and the End of Tradi-
    tional Religions* (Boston: Beacon Press, 1979).

5   The difference between Jewish feminists and feminist Jews is not mere word play. It
    rests on which category is considered the noun and which the modifying adjective.
    While there are many feminists who are Jewish, only some are attempting to use
    feminist theory and methodology to transform (modify) Judaism. See: Shulamit
    Magnus, "Re-inventing Miriam's Well: Feminist Jewish Ceremonials," paper deliv-
    ered at *The Uses of Tradition*, The Henry N. Rapaport Conference, Jewish Theologi-
    cal Seminary, 1991; Judith Plaskow, *Standing Again at Sinai* (New York: Harper &
    Row, 1990); Ellen Umansky, "Females, Feminists, and Feminism: A Review of Re-
    cent Literature on Jewish Feminism and a Creation of a Feminist Judaism," *Femi-
    nist Studies*, 14 (Summer 1988): 349-65.

6   The number of books and articles published in the last decade attests to the growth
    of this phenomenon.

7   I am indebted to Michael Oppenheim for this insight.

8   I will come back to this topic later in the paper.

9   Cynthia Ozick, "Notes Toward Finding The Right Question," *Lilith*, 6 (Spring
    1979). Reprinted in Susannah Heschel, ed., *On Being A Jewish Feminist: A Reader*
    (New York: Schocken, 1983), p. 120-51.

10 See Rachel Biale, *Women and Jewish Law* (New York: Shocken Books, 1984) for an
    excellent initiation into the field.

11 The angst of this question is not easily expressed. One eloquent articulation of this
    conflict is found in Blu Greenberg's book *On Women and Judaism: A View from
    Tradition* (Philadelphia: Jewish Publication Society, 1981). See also her article on
    female cantors, "Women as Messenger of the Congregation: Musings of an Ortho-
    dox Jewish Feminist," *Women's Tefillah Network Newsletter* (July 1988). Blu main-
    tains that feminism has "had a powerful impact on Jewish life and community" and
    that this is a positive though slow transformative process ("Feminism Within Or-
    thodoxy: A Revolution of Small Signs," *Lilith*, 17 [Summer 1992]: 11-17).

12 Rebecca Alpert persuasively wrote: "We must use our Jewish womenspirit as a pow-
    erful force for transformation" ("Our Lives Are the Text: Exploring Jewish
    Women's Rituals," *Bridges* [Spring 1991]: 77).

13 Daniel Leifer and Myra Leifer, "On the Birth of a Daughter," in Elizabeth Koltun,
    ed., in *The Jewish Woman: New Perspectives* (New York: Schocken, 1976), p. 21-30;
    Toby Fishbein Reifman, ed., *Blessing the Birth of a Daughter: Jewish Naming
    Ceremonies for Girls* (Ezrat Nashim, 1976).

14 Richard Siegal et al., eds., *The Jewish Catalogue* (Philadelphia: Jewish Publication
    Society, 1973); Susan Weidman Schneider, *Jewish and Female* (New York: Simon &
    Schuster, 1984).

15 This recollection is excerpted from a longer version which is published in *Lifecycles:
    Jewish Women on Life Passages and Personal Milestones* edited by Rabbi Debra
    Orenstein (Woodstock, Vermont: Jewish Lights Publishing, 1994).

16 Rita Gross explores women's rituals as access to the sacred in "Menstruation and
    Childbirth As Ritual and Religious Expression Among Native Australians," in

Nancy Auer Falk and Rita Gross, eds., *Unspoken Worlds* (California: Wadsworth, 1989), p. 257-66.

17 Penina Adelman, *Miriam's Well: Rituals for Jewish Women Around the Year* (Fresh Meadows: Biblio Press, 1986).

18 *Lilith* magazine frequently lists new rituals for women, e.g., new ceremonies for: "Turning 12: Becoming a Woman," and at p. 60: "A Ceremony of Wisdom," 21(Fall 1988). Rabbi Elyse Goldstein went to the *mikveh* when she received her rabbinic ordination (Rabbi Elyse Goldstein, "Take Back The Waters," *Lilith*, 15 [Summer 1986]: 15-16).

19 *Lilith*, 1/2 (Winter 1976), 21 (Fall 1988), 22 (Fall 1989). Shulamit Magnus, "More Light on Menarche," *New Menorah*, second series (Winter 1985); Penina Adelman, *Miriam's Well*; Irene Fine, *Midlife: A Rite of Passage & The Wise Woman: A Celebration* (San Diego: Women's Institute for Continuing Jewish Education, 1988).

20 Magnus ("Re-inventing Miriam's Well") claims that at the same time these rituals for women are creating a path for feminist Judaism, they have resulted in a creative amalgam that is reshaping Judaism.

21 Esther Broner, *The Telling* (San Francisco: Harper & Row, 1993).

22 Refers to the traditional ritual of inviting male ancestors to the family meal in the *Sukah*.

23 Toronto, Fall 1992; Israel, Fall 1992.

24 Arlene Agus, "This Month is for You," in Koltun, ed., *The Jewish Woman*, p. 84-93. See also Adelman *Miriam's Well*.

25 For a description of the liturgy and practice of some of the groups, see Rivka Haut in Susan Grossman and Rivka Haut, eds., *Daughters of the King: Women and the Synagogue* (New York: Jewish Publication Society, 1992), p. 135-38.

26 Such as the one I founded with friends thirteen years ago in Montreal.

27 The Women's Tefillah Network was founded by Rivka Haut. The Newsletter is available from: Esther Farber, editor, WTN, 4625 Delafield Ave., Riverdale, NY 10471.

28 Ironically, women praying has aroused even greater ire than gambling. Many Orthodox rabbis have written against such groups. Rabbi Hershel Schachter, "Go Out in the Footsteps of the Sheep" (in Hebrew), *Beit Yitzhak*, 17 (1984): 118-34; Rabbi J. David Bleich, "Religious Experience?" *Sh'ma* (18 October 1985): 146-49; Moshe Meiselman, *Jewish Women in Jewish Law* (New York: Ktav, 1978), ch. 8-9. For a detailed list see Grossman and Haut, *Daughters of the King*, p. 152.

29 Elisabeth Schüssler Fiorenza (*In Memory of Her: A Feminist Theological Reconstruction of Christian Origins* [New York: Crossroad, 1983]), discusses the theoretical and methodological task of returning women to religion and religion to women. New scholarly works on Jewish women in history are appearing almost daily. For specific studies see the work of Bernadette Brooten and Chava Weissler. An excellent resource is Judith Baskin's *Jewish Women in History* (Detroit: Wayne State, 1991).

30 Marcia Falk, *The Book of Blessings: A Feminist Jewish Reconstruction of Prayer* (San Francisco: Harper & Row, 1992).

31 "The Traditional Piety of Ashkenazic Women," in Arthur Green, ed., *Jewish Spirituality: From the Sixteenth Century Revival to the Present* (New York: Crossroad, 1987), p. 245-75; "Women in Paradise," *Tikkun*, 2/2 (April 1987): 43-47 and 117-20.

32 Women's prayer has been associated with and strengthened by new developments in liturgical music, religious poetry and ritual garments.

33 A recent United Jewish Appeal conference in New York (June 1991) began with a women's prayer service. In Toronto, a joint feminist prayer service was held at the

Ontario Institute for Studies in Education conference, *Jewish Women's Voices: Past and Present*, 1993.

34 Very few Israeli feminists are involved. It took some time for the Israel Women's Network to get involved and by that time the court refused their entry. Prayer groups are mostly a North American phenomenon, though there are some European groups. Only recently have prominent Jewish feminists recognized this as an authentic feminist cause.

35 Judith Plaskow, "Up Against The Wall," *Tikkun*, 5/5 (July 1990): 25-26.

36 Martha Acklesberg, "Spirituality, Community and Politics: B'not Esh and Feminist Reconstruction of Judaism," *Journal of Feminist Studies in Religion*, 2 (Fall 1986): 109-20. There are a growing number of such groups, including the New England *Ahayot Or*. It would be interesting to collect the names of the dispersed groups and begin writing the herstory.

37 B'nai Brith Women Canada has had such weekends for the past four years.

38 Some female rabbis meet biannually and have formed a Woman's Rabbinic Network. Rabbi Elyse Goldstein, in a personal communication, has said that the renewal and spiritual high experienced on these retreats is unique and incredibly valuable.

39 Ann Lapidus Lerner, *Who Hast Not Made Me A Man* (New York: American Jewish Committee, 1977); Susan Weidman Schneider, *Jewish and Female* (New York: Simon and Schuster, 1984); Heschel, *On Being a Jewish Feminist* (1983).

40 Riv-Ellen Prell, "Dilemma of Women's Equality in the History of Reform Judaism," *Judaism* (Fall 1981): 418-26.

41 Arthur Green, dean of the Seminary, wrote that God "is a relatively genderless male deity" (*Sh'ma*, 16 [10 January 1986]: 35).

42 In Judaism the act of separating is required and sanctified. There is even a special ritual — *havdalah* — that marks the end of the Sabbath and the separating powers of God. Yet traditional Judaism also included the need to separate men from women, which led to a restriction of role and a loss of status.

43 Some are chosen on the basis of religious affiliation, others on sexual identity, while still others nominally allow all to attend but insist on certain standards or practices that prevent others from sharing.

44 Inclusion poses difficult and unforeseen traps. Is the included person allowed in as a different entity or despite their difference? Tolerance is not the same as respect or equality. Some Christian groups will accept me despite my Jewishness or because of it, but not with it. Some male establishments accept women despite their femaleness, or because of it, but not with it. The difference is subtle and not always applicable. Women should be hired for jobs without reference to their gender; but they should not be hired despite it.

45 Rita Gross, "Androcentrism and Androgyny in the Methodology of History of Religions," in Rita Gross, ed., *Beyond Androcentrism: New Essays on Women and Religion* (Montana: Scholars Press, 1977), p. 7-19.

46 Julie Greenberg, "Seeking a Feminist Judaism," in Melanie Kaye Kantrowitz and Irene Klepfisz, eds., *Tribe of Dinah* (Vermont: Sinister Wisdom Books, 1986). Also see discussion in Christie Balka and Andy Rose, eds., *Twice Blessed: On Being Lesbian, Gay and Jewish* (Boston: Beacon Press, 1989).

47 Marcia Falk, "Notes on Composing New Blessings: Toward a Feminist/Jewish Reconstruction of Prayer," *Journal of Feminist Studies in Religion*, 3 (Spring 1987): 39-53. Also see her translation of *Song of Songs* in *Love Lyrics from the Bible* (Sheffield, England: Almond Press, 1982). There are new and interesting prayer books on the market now. For example, *Kol HaNeshama* and *Sim Shalom*.

48 See Debbie Friedman, tapes and sheet music. She is only one amongst a growing number of lyricists and educators.
49 Judith Plaskow, "The Coming of Lilith," in Rosemary Ruether, ed., *Religion and Sexism: Images of Women in the Jewish and Christian Traditions* (New York: Simon and Schuster, 1974), p. 341-43. This *midrash* was originally titled "Applesource" and appears that way in Koltun, *The Jewish Woman*, p. 8; Jane Sprague Zones, ed., *Taking the Fruit: Modern Women's Tales of the Bible* (San Diego: Women's Institute for Continuing Jewish Education, 1989); Naomi Graetz, *Male and Female S/He Created Them* (privately published, copyright by Naomi Graetz, 1988); Seymour Mayne, "Down Here," *Viewpoints*, 17/1 (1989): 8.
50 See the stories about Dinah and the Introduction to Kaye et al., *The Tribe of Dinah*. Recent stories have been written about Miriam and Judith in *Bible Review* and *Biblical Archaeological Review*. Also, mention is made of the potential for stories about Jepthah's daughter in the documentary film *Half the Kingdom* (National Film Board, Canada).
51 Magnus, *More Light on Menarche*, p. 7.
52 Biale, *Women and Jewish Law*; Irwin Haut, *Divorce in Jewish Law and Life* (New York: Sepher-Hermon Press, 1983); Eliezer Berkovitz, *Jewish Women in Time and Torah* (New Jersey: Ktav, 1990); Norma Baumel Joseph, "Jewish Women and Divorce," *Viewpoints*, 12/8 (December 1984): 1-2.
53 Individuals and groups have been working diligently to come up with a solution that will fix the problem for all Jews. Many groups have pushed for civil legislative solutions. In Canada, an amendment to the federal divorce law was enacted in 1990. Following that, New York legislature made changes to its divorce code. Presently countries such as Israel, Italy and Australia are examining the Canadian Act as they grapple with solutions within their own civil codes. There are also recommendations for *halakhic* solutions. ICAR, the International Coalition for Agunah Rights, has been formed to press for just such a resolution (1175 York Avenue, New York 10021).
54 The Canadian Coalition of Women for the GET has been very successful both in Canada and on the international scene.
55 Many Jews would not like to see women in the role of legal decisor. Some feminists think that law is not a feminist mode. See Judith Plaskow, "Halakhah as a Feminist Issue," *The Melton Journal* (Fall 1987): 3-5; Biale, *Women and Jewish Law*, claims that women must become involved in the very process of giving birth to the law.
56 There are a growing number of female rabbis, but few are experts in Jewish law. There are also non-rabbi scholars, whose knowledge of the law and judgement is sought. It will take time for the decisions of this group to be acknowledged and become effective precedents.
57 Cynthia Ozick argues against the increase of women's rituals that focus on the body as a betrayal of feminist and Judaic premises. See "Bima: Torah as Matrix for Feminism," *Lilith*, 12-13(Winter-Spring 1985): 47-48.
58 "Motherearth and the Megamachine," in Carol Christ and Judith Plaskow, eds., *Womanspirit Rising: A Feminist Reader In Religion* (San Francisco: Harper & Row, 1979), p. 51.
59 "Full Participation in Jewish Life," *Face to Face*, 5 (Spring 1978): 17. See also her "I've Had Nothing Yet So I Can't Take More," in *Moment* (September 1983): 22-28. Her point was the need for feminist Jews to focus more attention on historical events – the major focus of Judaism – rather than just on rites of passage.
60 Judith Plaskow, "The Question is Theological," in Heschel, ed., *On Being a Jewish Feminist* (1983), p. 223-33.

61 (San Francisco: Harper & Row, 1989).

62 Many feminist Jews have staunchly maintained their faith in a monotheistic Judaism while denouncing a male monotheism. Different feminist groups, including some Jewish feminists, have proclaimed their faith in ancient goddess traditions. Authors such as Savina Teubal, *Sarah The Priestess: The First Matriarch of Genesis* (Athens, OH: Swallow Press, 1984), claim to have unearthed a goddess tradition within Judaism. Regrettably, some feminists have blamed the Jews for the death of the Goddess. The anti-semitism implied in these claims is discussed by Annette Daum and Judith Plaskow in Evelyn Torton Beck, ed., *Nice Jewish Girls: A Lesbian Anthology* (Boston: Beacon Press, 1989), p. 289-309. Tikva Frymer-Kensky's new book, *In The Wake of The Goddesses* (New York: Free Press, 1992), clarifies the historical and cultural pattern of goddess worship against which the biblical tradition operates. It is a welcomed scholarly analysis.

63 Phyllis Trible, "Depatriarchalizing in Biblical Interpretation," in Koltun, ed., *The Jewish Woman*, p. 217-40.

64 Dr. J.H. Hertz, ed., *The Pentateuch and Haftorahs* (London: Soncino Press, 1968), Isaiah 66:13. See comment by Hertz on sentence 13, p. 946.

65 Ellen Umansky, "Creating a Jewish Feminist Theology: Possibility and Problems," in Judith Plaskow and Carol Christ, eds., *Weaving The Visions* (New York: Harper & Row, 1989), p. 187-98.

66 Plaskow's *Midrash*, "The Coming of Lilith," originally entitled "Applesource," appeared in *Religion and Sexism* (see note 48), and has been reprinted in several places. See her analysis in Carol Christ and Judith Plaskow, eds., *Womanspirit Rising* (New York: Harper & Row, 1979), p. 198-209.

67 Carol Christ, "Women's Liberation and The Liberation of God: An Essay in Story and Metaphor," in Koltun, ed., *The Jewish Woman*, p. 12.

68 Parts of this section come from a letter I wrote to a friend for publication in a book on philosophy. Michael Oppenheim, *Mutual Upholdings: Fashioning Jewish Philosophy Through Letters* (New York: Peter Lang, 1992), p. 168-71.

69 Biale, *Women and Jewish Law*, p. 29-41; Saul Berman, "The Status of Women in Halakhic Judaism," in Koltun, ed. (1976), p. 119-24; Arthur Silver, "May Women Be Taught Bible, Mishnah and Talmud," *Tradition*, 17 (Summer 1978): 74-85.

70 For an overview, see Deborah Weissman, "Education of Jewish Women," in *Encyclopaedia Judaica, Year Book* (Jerusalem: Keter, 1986-87), p. 29-36.

71 Deborah Weissman, "Bais Yaakov: A Historical Model for Jewish Feminists," in Koltun, ed., *The Jewish Woman*, p. 139-48.

72 Weissman, "Education of Jewish Women," p. 34.

73 The specific conception and pattern of some of these changes are explored in an article by myself for a special edition on Jewish Women in North America, "Jewish Education for Women: Rabi Moshe Feinstein's Map of America," in *American Jewish History*, special editor Pamela Nadell, forthcoming 1995.

74 Vanessa Ochs, *Words on Fire: One Woman's Journey Into The Sacred* (New York: Harcourt Brace Jovanovich, 1990).

75 For a review of the field see, Susannah Heschel, "Women's Studies," *Modern Judaism*, 10 (1990): 243-58; Susan E. Shapiro, "Voice from the Margins: Women and Jewish Studies," *Association for Jewish Studies Newsletter*, 4 (Spring 1990): 1-2, 4.

76 Vanessa Ochs, "Jewish Feminist Scholarship Comes of Age," *Lilith*, 15/1 (Winter 1990): 8-12.

77 There are many biographies to be consulted, e.g., Glueckl of Hamelin, Lily Montagu, Maimie Pinzee, Dona Gracia Mendes, Golda Meir, Manya Shochet, Rachel Varnhagen.

78 Paula Hyman, "Gender and Jewish History," *Tikkun*, 3/1 (1988): 35-38.
79 Heschel, "Women's Studies," p. 243.
80 Steven Katz, "Editor's Introduction," *Modern Judaism*, 10/3 (October 1990): v. The second volume is vol. 11/1 (February 1991).
81 Shapiro, "Voice from the Margins," p. 2, 4.
82 Hyman, "Gender and Jewish History," p. 35.
83 Not yet means there is hope, there is work, there is progress.
84 Ruth Wisse, consistently critical of Jewish feminism, recently referred to the number of papers on women at the annual Association of Jewish Studies conference as "comical" (The *Jerusalem Report* [January 1992]: 40). For various responses, see *Midstream* Symposium, "Does Judaism Need Feminism?" (April 1986).
85 Simon Greenberg, ed., *The Ordination of Women Rabbis* (New York: Jewish Theological Seminary, 1980), p. 127-85.

Chapter 4

FEMINIST THEOLOGY: FROM PAST TO FUTURE

Pamela Dickey Young

When I taught my first course in feminist theology in 1981 I had a file box containing a virtually complete record of the then-available published resources in feminist theology. Today, testimony to changing times, such a collection would fill several diskettes and would probably even then not claim to be exhaustive.

One can gain an overview of feminist theology in a variety of ways. Anne Carr's *Transforming Grace: Christian Tradition and Women's Experience* and Ursula King's *Women and Spirituality: Voices of Protest and Promise* both contain chapters that summarize what has happened in feminist theology. The older *Womanspirit Rising*, edited by Carol Christ and Judith Plaskow, and the more recent *Feminist Theology: A Reader*, edited by Ann Loades, provide surveys of feminist theology by offering a selection of representative readings. I myself tried to furnish something of a survey of feminist theological method in *Feminist Theology/Christian Theology*.[1]

Rather than repeat what has already been said in summary, I want here to reflect on a major change in the way in which the term "feminist theology" has been used over the past thirty years. When the term "feminist theology" has been used, to what has it referred? I think that such an exercise will tell us much about where feminist theology has been and where it is going. I then wish to outline some questions and issues that I think are crucial for feminist theology today.

Contemporary feminist theology is usually seen to begin with Valerie Saiving's 1960 article "The Human Situation: A Feminine View."[2] In this ground-breaking essay, Saiving raises the question of experience that becomes central to feminist theology (although the actual term "feminist theology" is not used until later). She opines that women do not experience the world in the same way men do and thus that traditional theological definitions (in this case, of sin and salvation) do not apply to women in the same way as they do to men.

Although the subtitle of *Womanspirit Rising* is "A Feminist Reader in Religion," and although one of its editors, Carol Christ, coined the term *thealogy* to replace the masculine form *theology*, still in the early years of feminist critique, "feminist theology" was a term applied to all feminist criticism of religion. In their introduction to *Womanspirit Rising*, Christ and Plaskow used headings such as "Creative Tensions in Feminist Theology," where "feminist theology" includes all the religious options represented in *Womanspirit Rising.*

Thus, "feminist theology" was usually used as a catch-all term, including feminist biblical criticism, feminist history of Christianity, etc., but also including what Christ and Plaskow call the "revolutionary" option, the option of feminists who "believe that the essential core of the traditions is so irreformably sexist that it is pointless to tinker with them in the hope of change."[3] Thus, in the early period of feminist writing on religion (roughly until the early 1980s), it was all "feminist theology." It is also the case that in this early writing the major focus was usually criticism of existing tradition rather than the formulation of constructive alternatives.

This blanket use of the term "feminist theology" gives us a number of insights. First, it illuminates/betrays the origin of feminist criticism of religion in those who either were or had been Christian (or possibly Jewish, although "theology" is not a term traditionally used in Judaism). Early feminist criticism of religion was almost entirely directed at Christianity and Judaism. Second, it also pinpoints the beginnings of feminist criticism of religion in a time just before religious studies came prominently into its own as something distinct from theological studies. Third, the use of the term "theology" points to a pervasive Western influence in the earliest feminist critiques. The women writing this "feminist theology" were Western women whose religious mindset was, broadly speaking, "theological."

A basic feminist consensus arises as "feminist theology" develops. Feminists recognize that, traditionally, theology has been done by, for, and about men. In traditional theology, women are usually ignored or caricatured, not described at all or falsely described. Such false naming of women has fostered social, political, and religious structures that systemically and systematically subordinate women. Feminist theology focuses on women's experience. It tries to name the experiences of women and to ask how these experiences might make an impact on theological thought if they are taken seriously. Noting that often the world has been cast into dualisms by traditional religions, dualisms of spirit or mind over body, God over humanity, male over female, humanity over nature, and so forth, feminist theology seeks a holism that appreciates difference but does not use it to create hierarchical relationships of "power over." Feminist theology will accept nothing as theologically adequate which does not promote the full humanity of women.

As "feminist theology" developed (as more and more was published), it became clear that more than "theology" was being written. Feminist critique of Christianity and Judaism was broadened to include critique of other major world religious traditions. Feminist construction of non-traditional alternative religious patterns moved beyond Christian, Jewish or even theistic patterns. Feminist history, feminist hermeneutics (biblical and otherwise), feminist literary criticism, critical theory—all these could not so easily be encompassed by the term "theology."

Today, the term "feminist theology" would not commonly be used to refer to all feminist study of religion or spirituality, but would, rather, usually be used "to relate to feminist writings closely connected with or at least arising out of Christian theological concerns."[4] Indeed, I use the term here to focus not on feminist biblical hermeneutics or feminist church history (for which there are also burgeoning specialized literatures) but to focus on the more strictly theological pursuits usually encompassed by the terms "systematic theology" and, to a certain extent, "theological ethics." Encompassed within this definition would be the work of such feminists as Rosemary Radford Ruether, for example, in her book *Sexism and God-talk,* or Anne Carr's *Transforming Grace* or Letty Russell's *Human Liberation in a Feminist Perspective* or *Household of Freedom*.[5] All these books seek to raise feminist questions and to explore if and how those questions might be answered by articulating new and different understandings of the Christian tradition. Such works as these draw on the insights and questions of feminist biblical scholarship and history as they look to the Christian texts and tradition and ask if the patriarchy there is inevitable or reformable. They raise questions about what authority is and what holds authority in the lives of feminist Christians. (Indeed, Letty Russell aptly notes that "whatever feminist theologians take up transforms itself into an authority problem."[6]) They also seek to draw centrally on women's experience and propose how the experiences of women are to be included in theological work today.

The works by Ruether, Russell and Carr to which I refer by way of example treat the traditional questions of systematic theology. With new eyes they look at doctrinal questions and propose new patterns of thinking and new ways of talking, whole new constructive theologies. How shall we talk about God, about salvation, about Jesus Christ, about the church? Hosts of articles by a wide variety of feminist theologians treat individual doctrinal questions from a feminist point of view. Central to this treatment is the recognition that thought and activity are intimately related and thus, that what we say theologically and how we act in the church and in the world are connected. Feminist constructive work is crucial to the ongoing enterprise of Christian theology as well as to changed social structures in the world. For example, Ruether proposes that we begin to write and think not of God, but of God/ess.

> If God/ess is not the creator and validator of the existing hierarchical order, but rather the one who liberates us from it, who opens up a new community of equals, then language about God/ess drawn from kingship and hierarchical power must lose its privileged place. Images of God/ess must include female roles and experience. Images of God/ess must be drawn from the activities of peasants and working people, people at the bottom of society. Most of all, images of God/ess must be transformative, pointing us back to our authentic potential and forward to new redeemed possibilities. God/ess-language cannot

validate roles of men or women in stereotypic ways that justify male dominance and female subordination.[7]

There are also feminist theologies that consider whether one can be Christian and feminist at the same time, but decide, ultimately, that this is impossible. Both Mary Daly in *Beyond God the Father* and Daphne Hampson in *Theology and Feminism* deal with traditional doctrinal questions as well as the activity implied or endorsed by various doctrinal positions.[8] But in the end they do so, not to reformulate Christian theology, but to pronounce it impossible from a feminist point of view. Daphne Hampson argues that Christianity is neither true nor moral.

The question of the truth of the Christian picture of the world has increasingly come to be raised during the last two hundred years. In our age this has become an urgent question for many people and many others have left Christianity behind them. The further questions which feminism raises — to an extent to which, I would contend, this has not been raised before — is that of whether it is moral. It is possible to say that Christian beliefs are "symbolically true." But if one does not believe them to be symbolically "true" but false to one's belief in human equality, there is no point in having made this sideways move. It is precisely at the level of symbolism that, feminists are saying, the Christian story has harmed women. Thus many a feminist no longer has any use for Christianity.[9]

Although the scope of the term "feminist theology" has narrowed in some ways, it has broadened in others. Feminist theology today is taking a variety of forms and coming from new sources. Women of colour, lesbian women, women from outside North America are beginning to add their voices, their experience, to reflection on traditional theological topics.[10] Such contributions broaden the range of experience that must be accounted for in theological thinking. Such voices make us aware that there is no one thing called "women's experience" which can be easily named and pinpointed and used in formulating Christian theology. For example, Jacquelyn Grant, a womanist theologian, makes the point that black women's experience of Jesus as liberator has been different from white women's experience of Jesus' maleness as oppressive. "To locate the Christ in Black people is a radical and necessary step, but an understanding of Black women's reality challenges us to go further. Christ among the least must also mean Christ in the community of Black women."[11] Luz Beatriz Arellano, from Nicaragua, says:

Out of their participation in the suffering of our people while also battling through their own struggle, women discover a new image of Jesus — a Jesus who is brother and sister, in solidarity on the journey toward liberation, the people's journey and their own journey; a Jesus who is a *compañero* [colleague, fellow revolutionary] in building the new society.

Jesus' face is present in all the men and women who endure weariness and give their life for others. Jesus is identified as God, man and women, standing in firm solidarity with the struggle.[12]

In addition to feminist theologies growing out of the traditional doctrinal model, there is a whole genre of narrative theology emerging from women, where theology and personal journey are intertwined, where autobiography is theology. Anyone familiar with the history of Christian theology will recognize that this is not a new theological pattern. Many of the Christian theological classics, Augustine's *Confessions*, for instance, or Bonhoeffer's *Letters and Papers From Prison* take the form of personal narrative. The difference here is that the speakers are women. The narrative form is more accessible, both for teller and hearer, to a wider variety of women from a wider variety of backgrounds, than is the traditional academic form of theology. Women without formal theological education or detailed knowledge of the history of the Christian tradition can communicate their faith, and thus, their theological understandings. Letty Russell and several others have edited a book entitled *Inheriting Our Mothers' Gardens* which contains the narrative theological reflections of women from Africa, Central America, the Caribbean and Asia, women of colour, women from non-dominant groups.[13] Kwok Pui-lan, for example, tells her own story about being a Christian woman in a society that is not dominantly Christian, Hong Kong.[14] Marta Benavides speaks of her childhood in El Salvador, and then says:

Our solidarity [that of the people of El Salvador] is a reflection of a God who is with us as *Compañero*. The passages of the Bible, such as those in Isaiah about the new earth, tell us that God's plan is for each and every one of us to live in justice and freedom. When God's new creation is fulfilled, we will have the real garden in which everyone can dwell as companions in peace.[15]

The narrative pattern of theology also extends to fictional forms. Often feminist fiction portrays a spiritual journey and gives insight into theological themes and questions. Many feminist theologians are looking to fiction as an entrée into experience that is not their own.[16]

Because feminist criticism recognizes that thought and activity are intimately related, it is impossible to draw a hard and fast line between feminist work in what has traditionally been called systematic theology and feminist work in theological ethics.[17] Feminists begin with the contexts in which women find themselves and the issues that arise in those contexts. They both reflect on and implement strategies for social change. Feminist theologians are asking a variety of questions about the interrelationship of Christian teaching and activity with regard, for example, to poverty, violence against women, the sexual abuse of women and children, and environmental issues. Creative theological work on doctrines such as the atonement begins with consideration of child abuse.[18] Environmental concerns give rise to new views of God.[19]

As is clear from the topics mentioned above, feminist theologies are seeking to broaden the traditional topics of theological concern. For instance, marriage has long been a topic for theological reflection. But in her book *Fierce Tenderness*, Mary Hunt asks why friendship has never been central to theological concern. She devotes her book to theological reflection on friendship. "I suggest that when women (and other previously excluded people) enter theological debates, the issues under consideration will shift. For example, women experience friendships as a plural experience including other human beings, ourselves, and the divine. The personal/communal split is meaningless. Multiple friendships are a simultaneous, not a competing, experience."[20]

In addition to the narrative form mentioned above, feminist theologians are seeking a variety of forms of theological expression. One such alternative is explored by Rebecca Chopp in *The Power to Speak: Feminism, Language, God*. Influenced by post-modern hermeneutic theories, Chopp "seeks to examine and construct feminist theology as discourses of emancipatory transformation that proclaim the Word to and for the world."[21] Chopp's interest is in a linguistic model where proclamation is a central act of feminist theology. She seeks to develop feminist theology as a new and liberating discourse.

Both the greatest strength and the greatest challenge in feminist theology today is its diversity. Feminist theologians agree that one must begin with experience and context. Thus, there is a pressing need to foster the new theological voices that are just beginning to be heard, voices from a variety of global locations, voices of women of colour, voices of lesbians, voices of poor women. And yet, when experience and context are taken seriously, we come up against the fact that there are an endless number of experiences and contexts. Early on in feminist theology, as in feminist thought generally, there was an assumption made that "woman" was one category and that one could define what "women's experience" was. But as new women's voices enter the dialogue, the variety and diversity of voices shows us how difficult it is to make statements for "women." Here, the strength of this diversity is in the richness and depth it adds to our thinking.

But the challenge of this diversity is the challenge of fragmentation. How can feminists privilege diversity without fragmenting into "communities" of one? The feminist movement arose as women began to recognize shared oppression. Feminism gains its strength from acknowledgement of shared social and political goals. Collectivity is an important value in feminist theology. Feminist theologians need to keep looking for what they share with one another at the same time as they do not gloss over the differences of experience and context or of theoretical or practical commitments or outlook.

While women are subordinated in different ways, they may have some similar constraints on their moral agency under particular historical conditions—for example, women, despite their differences, are more vulnerable to violence. Hence, we must resist both a simple acceptance and a rejection of the differences among women. Instead, we will aim to empower each woman to specify the particularities of her own life, to learn the causes of her sufferings and to name the sources of her hope.[22]

The gains of feminism are great but fragile; in church, in university, in society. Too much fragmentation could easily allow a return to the previous status quo. But feminists also have to be serious with themselves about who exactly has and has not benefited by current gains. White, middle-class, North American feminist theologians need to be clear about how their own privilege has affected their theological thinking.

The fragmentation of the once all-encompassing term "feminist theology" into a variety of feminist studies of religion is also a strength and a challenge for feminist theology today. Again, the abundance of available material presents the problem that one can no longer be conversant with all of it (unlike my file box days). The danger this presents to feminist theology is the danger of being marginalized. It would not be conducive to the health of feminist criticism if feminist scholars who sought to remain within or to study traditions such as Christianity or Judaism found themselves separated from other feminist scholars of religion who took that to be impossible. In traditional scholarship, the tendency has always been to exploit theoretical difference for academic gain. Feminist study is multidisciplinary. There is much in terms of theory that needs to be shared by feminists across traditional disciplinary lines. Feminists, including feminist theologians, need to find creative ways to value and discuss difference without marginalizing those whose conclusions differ from one's own.

One very large issue on the agenda of feminist theology (not less than on the agenda of other feminist scholars) is the question about the nature of making claims to "truth." Feminists have rightly been wary of claims that are said to hold true for all cases, when they see a multiplicity of cases simply ignored as not worth considering. And yet, many feminists have also seen a problem with claiming that all points of view are equally valid, for this would allow the claims of oppressors equal status with the claims of the oppressed. In feminist theology, there is the additional issue of the status of the tradition in which one finds oneself, and how one will evaluate its claims to truth or validity.

Some feminist theologians have been content with the option of a complete and total relativism. Sheila Davaney suggests that "a feminist theology that carries through the insights of historical consciousness more consistently will move away from the appeal to ontological grounds for its validity and will eschew referential models of knowledge."[23] This is often combined with a call for the pragmatic choice of feminism.

Feminist visions would be understood as thoroughly human constructions sharing the same *ontological* status as male perspectives. The validity of these

competing "regimes of truth" would be judged not according to which was
"closer to reality" but upon the pragmatic grounds of what kind of existence
these visions permitted or inhibited.[24]

Yet other feminists are wary of the implications of such thoroughgoing
relativism.[25] Marjorie Hewitt Suchocki, for example, argues against relativism and for "a shift of judgment from ideological ground to ethical
ground, along with an open recognition of the conditioned nature of the
norm of justice we bring and a commitment to critical exploration of the
norm in the very dialogue wherein it is brought to bear."[26] Still other
feminists (myself included), while recognizing difficulties in attaining
agreement about the nature of "truth," are not willing to abandon entirely the possibility of making truth claims.[27]

A major and ongoing question within Christian feminist theology today is the question of how to bring together past and present. Christian
theology is connected to a history that is patriarchal; it is connected to the
biblical documents. Is the Christian past normative for feminist theology?
How can one do Christian theology beginning from women's experience?
How does one conceive of the biblical documents and how does one use
them in feminist theology? In general, there is agreement that feminist
theology must grapple with the biblical texts and must take women's experience seriously. But how to characterize the fact that the authority of
both varies from feminist theology to feminist theology. In my book
Feminist Theology/Christian Theology, I explore some of the ways in which
feminists have answered these questions, and I offer my own constructive
proposals for theological method.[28]

One issue that I myself think will become crucial to feminist theology
as it interacts with a growing feminist literature on other religious traditions is the question of Christian feminism relating to other religious
feminisms. There is a need for interreligious dialogue among women, in
particular among feminists — dialogue that assumes religious commitment, and yet seeks to understand the commitments of another.[29] Here, I
think feminists have much to offer, as shared commitments to the cause
of women provide an excellent basis for beginning discussion. Religious
pluralism also points to the need for serious theological thought about
the implications of the present pluralistic world for a Christian feminist
theology. Must a Christian point of view be imperialistic? Can Christian
theology make room for understanding other faith commitments? How
do commitment to Christianity and commitment to feminism relate to
one another in a world where other feminists have other religious commitments? Thus far, feminist theologians have written very little on these
questions, and yet I think these are questions that need to be addressed
by feminists.[30]

Most feminist theology to date has taken the Christian religious symbols, such as God, Jesus Christ or the church, at face value. Thus, it has
looked at the overt maleness or femaleness of the symbols in relation to

the status and roles of women and men and asked whether such maleness or femaleness can be altered or supplemented. Feminist theology needs to begin to grapple seriously with questions about the depth meaning of symbols and texts. For example, does changing the way we talk about God from male to female or to gender-neutral terms bring about the changes feminists desire, both in how we think of the symbol and how it functions to influence social structures? Here feminist theologians need to be in dialogue with feminist hermeneutics and with feminist philosophical and anthropological studies of symbol formation.[31]

Feminist theology espouses the idea of a church of equals that is not found embodied in any institutional church. It is a constant struggle and a constant issue for feminist theologians who call themselves Christians to know how to relate to existing Christian communities. Some feminists have chosen the option of "women church"—egalitarian and women-positive communities that exist outside or alongside traditional institutional structures.[32] A continuing issue for feminist theologians is finding new ways of being church and relating to the institutional church.

In North America today, we have now what amounts to two generations of feminist theological scholarship. The first generation of scholars are all self-trained feminists; they taught themselves to be feminist theologians; they invented feminist theology as they went along. But now there is an emerging group of feminist scholars who themselves had feminist teachers and mentors. It remains to be seen just how this will influence theological work. Clearly, one of the outcomes is in sheer volume of work on feminist theology, and in particular large numbers of doctoral theses on feminist topics. Not so many years ago women were advised not to write dissertations on feminist topics so as not to "typecast" themselves as *only* interested in feminism.

It is difficult to summarize what is happening in Canadian feminist theology today in part because so much of what is happening is in small group discussions and in feminist liturgical celebrations.[33] In the Canadian academy, most of the women who are theologians are also feminists, most of them first-generation feminists, and many of these women have done some of their publishing in the area of feminist theology. Many more teach courses on feminist theology or include feminist theology in the courses they teach. Many of the feminist doctoral students I meet seem to be coming at feminist theology through feminist ethics.

The themes that arise in feminist theology generally arise in Canadian feminist theology. An additional richness in the Canadian context is the work being done by Francophone feminist theologians who tend to draw more readily on European feminist thought than their English-speaking counterparts. Canadian feminists are seeking to name a Canadian context for feminist theology that differentiates it from its American counterpart.[34] In one attempt to articulate it, Ellen Leonard describes: "three transitions which are shaping the Canadian context: from survival in the wilderness to the survival of the world; from colonial status to global responsibility; from maintaining French and English culture to the acceptance and affirmation of pluralism."[35]

It is difficult to predict where feminist theology will be twenty years hence. The past thirty years of feminist theology has charted new waters. A large agenda has already been set. Much has been accomplished, but much more awaits serious feminist reflection and action. Transformation of church and society according to feminist aims has barely begun. New questions and issues will arise. New generations of feminist scholars and thinkers will undoubtedly continue to foster lively and critical feminist theologies.

Notes

1   Anne E. Carr, *Transforming Grace: Christian Tradition and Women's Experience* (San Francisco: Harper & Row, 1988), see especially p. 95-113; Ursula King, *Women and Spirituality: Voices of Protest and Promise* (Basingstoke and London: Macmillan, 1989), see especially p. 160-205; Carol Christ and Judith Plaskow, eds., *Womanspirit Rising: A Feminist Reader in Religion* (San Francisco: Harper & Row, 1979); Ann Loades, ed., *Feminist Theology: A Reader* (London: SPCK, 1990); Pamela Dickey Young, *Feminist Theology/Christian Theology* (Minneapolis: Fortress, 1990). For an extensive bibliography of material up to 1988, see Shelley Davis Finson, ed., *Women and Religion: A Bibliographical Guide to Christian Feminist Liberation Theology* (Toronto: University of Toronto Press, 1991).

2   Valerie Saiving, "The Human Situation: A Feminine View," *The Journal of Religion*, 40 (April 1960): 100-12, most easily accessible in Christ and Plaskow, eds., *Womanspirit Rising*, p. 25-42.

3   Christ and Plaskow, eds., *Womanspirit Rising*, p. 10.

4   King, *Women and Spirituality*, p. 161.

5   Rosemary Radford Ruether, *Sexism and God-Talk: Toward a Feminist Theology* (Boston: Beacon, 1983); Anne Carr, *Transforming Grace*; Letty Russell, *Human Liberation in a Feminist Perspective: A Theology* (Philadelphia: Westminster, 1974); Letty Russell, *Household of Freedom: Authority in Feminist Theology* (Philadelphia: Westminster, 1987).

6   Ibid., p. 12.

7   Ruether, *Sexism and God-Talk*, p. 69.

8   Mary Daly, *Beyond God the Father* (Boston: Beacon, 1973); Daphne Hampson, *Theology and Feminism* (Oxford: Basil Blackwell, 1990).

9   Ibid., p. 45.

10 See, for example, Jacquelyn Grant, *White Women's Christ and Black Women's Jesus: Feminist Christology and Womanist Response* (Atlanta: Scholars Press, 1989); Carter Heyward, *Touching Our Strength: The Erotic as Power and the Love of God* (San Francisco: Harper & Row, 1989); Chung Hyun Kyung, *Struggle to the Sun Again: Introducing Asian Women's Theology* (Maryknoll, NY: Orbis, 1990); Virginia Fabella and Mercy Amba Oduyoye, eds., *With Passion and Compassion: Third World Women Doing Theology* (Maryknoll, NY: Orbis, 1988).

11 Grant, *White Women's Christ and Black Women's Jesus*, p. 217.

12 Luz Beatriz Arellano, "Women's Experience of God in Emerging Spirituality," in Fabella and Oduyoye, eds., *With Passion and Compassion: Third World Women Doing Theology*, p. 137.

13 Letty M. Russell et al., eds., *Inheriting Our Mothers' Gardens: Feminist Theology in Third World Perspective* (Philadelphia: Westminster, 1988).

14 Kwok Pui-lan, "Mothers and Daughters, Writers and Fighters," in ibid., p. 21-34.

15 Marta Benavides, "My Mother's Garden is a New Creation," in ibid., 137.

16 See Marilyn J. Legge, "Colourful Differences: 'Otherness' and Image of God for Canadian Feminist Theologies," *Studies in Religion/Sciences Religieuses*, 21/1 (1992): 67-80.

17 The literature of feminist theological ethics is a growing one and I only treat here what impinges most directly on theological concerns more narrowly defined.

18 See Joanne Carlson Brown and Carol R. Bohn, eds., *Christianity, Patriarchy and Abuse: A Feminist Critique* (New York: Pilgrim Press, 1989); Rita Nakashima Brock, *Journeys By Heart: A Christology of Erotic Power* (New York: Crossroad, 1988).

19 Sallie McFague, *Models of God: Theology for an Ecological, Nuclear Age* (Philadelphia: Fortress, 1987).

20 Mary E. Hunt, *Fierce Tenderness: A Feminist Theology of Friendship* (New York: Crossroad, 1991), p. 10.

21 Rebecca S. Chopp, *The Power to Speak: Feminism, Language, God* (New York: Crossroad, 1989), p. 3.

22 Legge, "Colourful Differences," p. 74-75.

23 Sheila Greeve Davaney, "Problems with Feminist Theory: Historicity and the Search for Sure Foundations," in Paula M. Cooey et al., eds., *Embodied Love: Sensuality and Relationship as Feminist Values* (San Francisco: Harper & Row, 1987), p. 93.

24 Ibid.

25 See the cogent criticism of Davaney offered by Carol P. Christ, "Embodied Thinking: Reflections on Feminist Theological Method," *Journal of Feminist Studies in Religion*, 5/1 (Spring 1989): 7-15. See also Rebecca Chopp, "Feminism's Theological Pragmatics: A Social Naturalism of Women's Experience," *Journal of Religion*, 67 (1987): 239-56. Chopp combines pragmatism as a criterion of judgment with what she calls "social naturalism."

26 Marjorie Hewitt Suchocki, "In Search of Justice: Religious Pluralism from a Feminist Perspective," in John Hick and Paul F. Knitter, eds., *The Myth of Christian Uniqueness: Toward a Pluralistic Theology of Religions* (Maryknoll, NY: Orbis, 1987), p. 150.

27 In my current work on feminism and religious pluralism, I argue that feminists should not abandon metaphysical arguments.

28 Young, *Feminist Theology/Christian Theology*; see also Elisabeth Schüssler Fiorenza, *Bread Not Stone: The Challenge of Feminist Biblical Interpretation* (Boston: Beacon, 1984); Carr, *Transforming Grace*; Ruether, *Sexism and God-Talk*; Russell, *Household of Freedom*.

29 Maura O'Neill, *Women Speaking, Women Listening: Women in Interreligious Dialogue* (Maryknoll, NY: Orbis, 1990). See also the series of videos of a World Council of Churches interfaith dialogue among women made by Studio D of the National Film Board of Canada, and distributed under the title *Faithful Women*.

30 See Rosemary Radford Ruether, "Feminism and Jewish-Christian Dialogue: Particularism and Universalism in the Search for Religious Truth," and Marjorie Hewitt Suchocki, "In Search of Justice: Religious Pluralism from a Feminist Perspective," in Hick and Knitter, eds., *The Myth of Christian Uniqueness*, p. 137-48, 149-61.

31 See, for example, in Caroline Walker Bynum, "Introduction: The Complexity of Symbols," in Caroline Walker Bynum et al., eds., *Gender and Religion: On the Complexity of Symbols* (Boston: Beacon, 1986), p. 1-20.

32 See, for example, Rosemary Radford Ruether, *Women Church* (San Francisco: Harper & Row, 1985), and Elisabeth Schüssler Fiorenza, "Women Church: The Hermeneutical Center of Feminist Biblical Interpretation," in *Bread Not Stone*, p. 1-22. At the Canadian Theological Society meetings in June 1992, a panel consisting of Ellen Leonard, Doris Dyke, Rebecca McKenna and Lillian Perigoe presented "Glimpses of Women Church in Canada."

33 For an attempt to gather the names and interests of Canadians involved in feminist theology, see *Canadian Network Resources for Feminist Theology and Spirituality*, compiled by the Ecumenical Decade Coordinating Group in Toronto. (A new edition was compiled in 1992.) For a look at what was happening in Canada, but particularly in the United Church of Canada up to about 1988, see Ruth Evans, "'Behold I Am Doing a New Thing': Canadian Feminist Theology and the Social Gospel," in Harold Wells and Roger Hutchinson, eds., *A Long and Faithful March: Towards the Christian Revolution 1930s/1980s* (Toronto: United Church Publishing House, 1989), p. 153-65.

34 See Ellen Leonard, "Experience as a Source for Theology: A Canadian and Feminist Perspective," *Studies in Religion/Sciences Religieuses*, 19/2 (1990): 143-62, and Monique Dumais, "Les femmes théologiennes dans l'Église," *Studies in Religion/Sciences Religieuses*, 8/2 (1979): 191-96.

35 Leonard, "Experience as a Source for Theology," p. 149.

Chapter 5

LE CONCEPT "EXPÉRIENCES DES FEMMES" DANS L'AVÈNEMENT D'UNE THÉOLOGIE FÉMINISTE*

Monique Dumais

La théologie féministe recourt dès son avènement au concept "expériences des femmes" pour bien démarquer sa spécificité. Peut-on avoir une théologie féministe sans se référer aux "expériences des femmes"? En 1974, Sheila A. Collins présente "l'expérience comme le creuset d'où les théologies surgissent."[1] Elle reconnaît que l'utilisation des "expériences des femmes" n'est pas facile pour les femmes et les place dans une situation de conflit avec l'autorité constituée, reconnue, gardienne de ce qui est vrai. Elle distingue alors deux sortes de théologiennes féministes: des réformistes et des révolutionnaires. Les premières conservent intacte la tradition chrétienne tout en la libérant des distorsions culturelles touchant l'infériorisation des femmes.[2] Les secondes font partie d'une "minorité cognitive" selon l'expression de Peter Berger;[3] elles voient la société d'une façon différente et cherchent à expérimenter de nouvelles voies.

Il n'en demeure pas moins que les théologies féministes, qu'elles soient réformistes ou révolutionnaires, trouvent leurs sources dans les "expériences de vie des femmes" et la réflexion sur ces expériences qui proviennent du mouvement de libération des femmes.[4] Carol P. Christ le confirmait en 1977 dans sa revue de la littérature se rapportant à la théologie féministe: "L'expérience doit devenir une nouvelle norme pour la théologie."[5] En effet, la plupart des théologiennes féministes ont organisé leurs réflexions en tenant compte des expériences des femmes.

Je me propose donc dans cette communication de mettre en évidence trois types d'utilisation du concept "expérience des femmes": d'abord la nouvelle herméneutique biblique proposée par Elisabeth Schüssler Fiorenza, ensuite l'utilisation radicale et exclusive faite par Mary Daly, enfin l'intégration de ces expériences dans le contexte canadien accomplie par Ellen Leonard. Pour chaque auteure, je tenterai de travailler selon les lieux suivants: le lieu d'émergence, le lieu de valorisation, le lieu d'engagement. Ce travail de repérage selon ces lieux reçoit son sens d'une préoccupation éthique cherchant à montrer l'impact dans une praxis, des recherches théologiques féministes. Celles-ci ne sont pas pure gratuité, elles visent à développer une autre appréhension du monde afin de favoriser une nouvelle relation avec le divin et une entière participation des femmes dans les institutions religieuses.

Elisabeth Schüssler Fiorenza: une nouvelle herméneutique biblique
Dans sa classification des divers courants du mouvement religieux des femmes, Elisabeth J. Lacelle en distingue trois: para- ou post-chrétien, chrétien post-chrétien et chrétien réformiste-transformateur.[6] C'est dans ce dernier courant qu'elle assigne un rôle significatif à Elisabeth Schüssler Fiorenza, exégète féministe. Celle-ci est surtout connue pour son livre *In Memory of Her*;[7] elle a également écrit *Bread Not Stone*[8] et plusieurs autres contributions dans des ouvrages collectifs.

Lieu d'émergence
Dans quel contexte surgit le concept "expériences des femmes"? Sous quel angle est-il abordé? Quels traitements méthodologiques reçoit-il? Telles sont les questions qui m'apparaissent pouvoir circonscrire le lieu d'émergence du concept étudié.

A la recherche d'une définition des "expériences des femmes" dans l'oeuvre d'Elisabeth Schüssler Fiorenza, j'ai trouvé ce passage dans *En mémoire d'elle* qui contient des éléments révélateurs:

> Tandis que les femmes en tant que groupe partagent une expérience commune et que les femmes sont engagées dans la lutte pour la libération des femmes, la perception et l'interprétation individuelles de l'expérience de l'oppression qu'elles subissent ainsi que la formulation concrète des valeurs et des buts de leur libération varient considérablement selon les femmes.[9]

Expérience commune partagée par des femmes, expérience d'oppression subie, lutte pour la libération des femmes, voilà trois éléments qui forment la trame de la recherche poursuivie par Elisabeth Schüssler Fiorenza, trois éléments qui organisent sa quête réflexive, qui lui donnent l'ardeur nécessaire pour accomplir sa tâche herméneutique et reconstructive des textes de la tradition chrétienne, surtout ceux de l'Église primitive.

Dans *Bread not Stone*, publié en 1984, Elisabeth Schüssler Fiorenza est encore plus explicite en affirmant qu'"elle prend comme critère herméneutique l'autorité de l'expérience des femmes qui luttent pour la libération,"[10] et qu'elle se sert de ce critère pour discerner dans la Bible ce qui a servi à l'oppression des femmes ou ce qui a contribué à leur libération. Elle insiste sur le fait que la Bible est "un prototype historique" qui doit être perçu comme un héritage, "comme du pain plutôt qu'une pierre" qui "apporte à l'église des femmes le sens d'une histoire en marche aussi bien qu'une identité chrétienne."[11] A cet effet, elle développe une quadruple herméneutique critique féministe: l'herméneutique du soupçon, l'herméneutique de la proclamation, l'herméneutique du souvenir et l'herméneutique de l'actualisation créatrice.[12]

L'herméneutique du soupçon "prend comme point de départ l'hypothèse que tous les textes bibliques et leurs interprétations sont androcentriques et remplissent des fonctions patriarcales."[13] Dans ce travail de détection, Elisabeth Schüssler Fiorenza souligne que "les textes de la Bible, qu'ils soient neutres par rapport au féminisme ou qu'ils soient même positifs à cet égard, peuvent contribuer à renforcer les structures patriarcales quand ils sont proclamés ou enseignés en vue d'assurer un comportement patriarcal et d'inculquer des valeurs d'oppression."[14] En conséquence, une herméneutique féministe de la proclamation veille à ce que le lectionnaire, les célébrations liturgiques, la catéchèse ne gardent pas-les textes qui sont identifiés comme sexistes ou patriarcaux. L'herméneutique du souvenir apporte un contrepoids à l'herméneutique féministe de la proclamation en permettant d'aller au-delà des textes androcentriques, en mettant en évidence et en valeur l'histoire des femmes dans la religion biblique.[15] Enfin, l'herméneutique d'actualisation créatrice travaille à présenter les histoires bibliques selon une perspective féministe, "à reformuler les visions et les commandements bibliques selon une perspective des disciples égaux, de créer des amplifications narratives des restes (remnants) féministes qui ont survécu dans les textes pa-triarcaux."[16] Il s'agit d'un processus de re-vision créatrice qui utilise tous les moyens disponibles à l'imagination artistique: créativité littéraire, mu-sique, danse.

Ces quatre formes d'herméneutique nous indiquent clairement l'investissement important d'Elisabeth Schüssler Fiorenza dans son travail d'exégèse critico-historique de la Bible. Elle se donne "un nouveau magistère", celui de l'Église des femmes.[17] Ainsi, tout est scruté, en fonction de la libération des femmes pour combattre une oppression qui a pesé sur elles.

> Une interprétation théologique féministe de la Bible qui a pour canon la libération des structures sexistes d'institutions et de valeurs intégrées oppri-mantes doit, dorénavant, maintenir que seulement les traditions non sexistes et les traditions non androcentriques de la Bible et les traditions non oppri-mantes de l'interprétation biblique ont une autorité théologique de révélation si la Bible ne continue pas d'être un outil d'oppression pour les femmes.[18]

Lieu de valorisation

Le concept "expériences des femmes" est utilisé par Elisabeth Schüssler Fiorenza pour mettre en valeur deux dimensions importantes: l'égalité et la solidarité. Elles sont poursuivies constamment et se déploient dans toute l'argumentation de la spécialiste en exégèse néotestamentaire.

L'étude "Word, Spirit and Power: Women in Early Christian Communities"[19] a préparé de façon évidente le terrain pour *In Memory of Her*. La reconstruction de l'histoire de l'Église primitive montrait à Elisabeth Schüssler Fiorenza la possibilité d'une vue alternative aux structures ecclésiales animées par un pouvoir mâle qui ont traversé les siècles, il s'agit d'"un mouvement égalitaire, contre-culturel, à plusieurs dimensions." [20] Ce mouvement ne définissait pas les rôles de ses membres en fonction du sexe, mais selon leur engagement de foi dans la communauté chrétienne. Une évidence s'est imposée: "Les femmes, dans ce mouvement égalitaire, n'étaient pas des figures marginales mais ont exercé un leadership responsable."[21] *In Memory of Her* s'attache à démontrer la dimension égalitaire en s'appuyant sur de nombreuses références bibliques et historiques.

> L'ampleur de la souffrance des femmes dans le patriarcat religieux doit être remémorée et explorée structurellement afin de libérer le pouvoir émancipateur de la communauté chrétienne qui, théologiquement, est enraciné, non pas dans le dimorphisme sexuel et spirituel, ni dans la domination ecclésiale patriarcale, mais dans une vision égalitaire et dans des relations sociales altruistes qui ne peuvent pas être ramenées au "genre" masculin ou féminin.[22]

Ainsi, elle a constaté que le leadership des femmes faisait partie du mouvement chrétien primitif: "en tant que mouvement contestataire à l'intérieur de la Palestine, de la Syrie, de la Grèce, de l'Asie Mineure et de Rome, il a mis en question et s'est opposé à l'éthos patriarcal dominant par la praxis de l'égalité des disciples."[23]

Cette praxis de disciples égaux a donné lieu à une "solidarité à partir du bas."[24] Elisabeth Schüssler Fiorenza a rassemblé toutes ses énergies pour faire valoir "l'héritage des femmes", tel qu'elle l'annonce dans son introduction. Le titre même de son ouvrage, *In Memory of Her*, signale sa détermination à mettre en évidence tout ce qui a été tu, fait silence, tenu invisible au sujet des femmes. L'Évangile de Marc quand il relate "l'onction de Béthanie" ne mentionne même pas le nom de cette femme qui reçoit Jésus d'une manière si généreuse, en lui versant "un parfum de nard, pur et très coûteux (Marc 14, 3); on lui doit toutefois d'avoir retenu ces paroles de Jésus: "En vérité, je vous le déclare, partout où sera proclamé l'Évangile dans le monde entier, on racontera aussi, en souvenir d'elle, ce qu'elle a fait" (Marc 14, 9). On se rappelle l'histoire de Pierre, celle de Judas, ne faut-il pas s'étonner du fait qu' "On se rappelle le nom du traître mais on a oublié le nom de cette disciple fidèle, parce que c'était une femme."[25] Elisabeth Schüssler Fiorenza s'oppose à une position féministe qui ne tiendrait pas compte des racines bibliques, et il lui importe de rattacher l'expérience religieuse des femmes contemporaines à celle de nombreuses générations de femmes qui nous ont précédées dans notre histoire chrétienne. Une herméneutique critique féministe doit nous permettre de retrouver nos soeurs ancêtres qui ont été "à la fois victimes et sujets participant à la culture patriarcale,"[26] de saisir comment elles ont pu contribuer à l'avènement de l'Église chrétienne. Le projet scientifique vise à émanciper la communauté chrétienne de ses structures patriarcales et de son attitude androcentrique pour que l'Évangile soit vraiment salvifique, perçu comme une base de libération pour les femmes aussi bien que pour les hommes. Le passé remémoré dans ses étapes de souffrance et de libération est une force subversive qui entraîne un changement, qui débouche sur un avenir. "Une telle 'mémoire subversive' ne garde pas seulement vivants les espoirs et les souffrances des femmes chrétiennes du passé, mais elle permet aussi que se développe une solidarité universelle entre toutes les femmes du passé, du présent et du futur, unies par la même vision d'avenir."[27]

Lieu d'engagement
L'exploration des "expériences des femmes" n'est pas purement spéculative, elle ouvre des avenues pour des formes d'engagement. Dans *Bread Not Stone*, Elisabeth Schüssler Fiorenza suggère une "praxis d'émancipation";[28] elle assigne comme but au mouvement féministe dans le domaine religieux, une auto-affirmation des femmes, l'exercice du pouvoir, et la li-bération de l'aliénation, de la marginalisation et de l'exploitation supportées par le patriarcat.[29] Dans *In Memory of Her*, elle dégage trois grandes possibilités d'engagement: la ré-écriture, une spiritualité propre et de manière plus culminante, le leadership des femmes exprimé dans l'*ecclèsia* des femmes. "La tentative de "réécrire" les femmes jusque dans les débuts de l'histoire chrétienne ne devrait pas seulement rendre aux femmes leur histoire des débuts du christianisme, mais aussi permettre une perception plus riche et plus précise de ces débuts."[30]

Le volumineux ouvrage *In Memory of Her* manifeste l'engagement d'Elisabeth Schüssler Fiorenza à rendre les femmes à l'histoire, à leur redonner leur sens dans une tradition chrétienne qui s'est efforcée de les évincer. La tâche est hardie de montrer comme la postérité de l'Église primitive a tenté de faire disparaître l'égalité hommes-femmes présente dans le premier siècle de l'ère chrétienne. L'étude du passage de l'Épître aux Galates (3, 28) et des différentes modifications pauliniennes, des codes de morale domestique dans l'Épître aux Colossiens (3, 18-4, 1), dans la première Épître de Pierre (2, 11-3, 12) fait voir les différents méandres où passe la rivière de l'égalité tantôt affirmée, tantôt déniée. Peu importe, il faut aller de l'avant et signaler la présence d'un courant égalitaire dans les débuts de l'Église, en faisant l'inventaire de tous les lieux où les femmes ont connu des possibilités d'affirmation et d'action.

Un deuxième aspect de l'engagement, c'est celui du développement d'une spiritualité féministe. Celle-ci exprime non seulement les expériences de libération des femmes, mais aussi les luttes et les souffrances vécues par nos soeurs ancêtres dans la religion patriarcale. Elle constitue un lieu qui doit devenir une tradition où les femmes se retrouvent et célèbrent les merveilles de Dieu. Cette spiritualité s'élabore sur une base critique où les expériences des femmes sont scrutées, dévoilées, identifiées dans les injustices qui les accablent.

> Comment pouvons-nous désigner le pain eucharistique et dire "ceci est mon corps" tant que les corps des femmes sont battus, violés, stérilisés, mutilés, prostitués et utilisés à des fins mâles?... L'ekklèsia des femmes doit donc rétablir le corps des femmes comme l'image et le corps du Christ. Elle doit dénoncer toute violence contre les femmes comme sacrilège et soutenir le pouvoir moral des femmes et leur capacité à prendre des décisions pour tout ce qui touche à leur vie spirituelle qui embrasse le corps et l'âme, le coeur et les entrailles.[31]

L'"*ekklèsia* des femmes," c'est l'expression choisie par Elisabeth Schüssler Fiorenza pour indiquer le point ultime de son désir concernant les femmes dans la religion chrétienne. L'image et la vision du peuple de Dieu, de celui que représentent les femmes dans leur quête de libération de toutes formes d'oppression contribuent à susciter une *ekklèsia* des femmes. Ainsi, le mouvement féministe ne serait plus en marge de l'Église, mais serait "l'incarnation, la concrétisation constitutive de la vision d'une Église qui vit en solidarité avec les opprimés et les démunis dont la majorité sont des femmes et des enfants qui dépendent des femmes."[32] Cet engagement dans l'*ekklesia* des femmes ouvre toutes les possibilités de célébrer toutes les forces de libération qui sont à l'oeuvre.

> Alors seulement nous serons capables de dire de manière adéquate ce que nos soeurs ancêtres ont fait "en mémoire d'elle." En rompant le pain et en buvant à la coupe, nous ne proclamons pas seulement la Passion et la Résurrection du Christ, mais nous célébrons aussi celles des femmes de la religion biblique.[33]

C'est également dans cette ekklèsia des femmes que pourra s'affirmer et se confirmer un leadership des femmes, celui qui aurait pu émerger à partir de Marie-Madeleine. Elisabeth Schüssler Fiorenza a constaté dans ses recherches que "les gnostiques et d'autres groupes se fondent sur ces traditions (celles des évangiles canoniques) pour considérer les femmes disciples comme des autorités apostoliques aptes à recevoir la révélation et un enseignement secret."[34]

Le christianisme patristique a par la suite minimisé l'importance des femmes disciples et de leur chef, Marie-Madeleine, en mettant de l'avant des hommes apôtres, Pierre, Paul, les Douze. Il n'en reste pas moins que Marie-Madeleine est présentée dans les quatre évangiles canoniques comme le premier témoin du Christ ressuscité. Luc signale bien que les onze apôtres ne sont pas capables d'accueillir les paroles des femmes leur racontant une apparition de Jésus et concluent que c'est du radotage et ne les croient pas (Luc 24, 11). La pente de non-réception du témoignage des femmes est ardue à remonter, mais une herméneutique critique féministe permet de trouver des éléments de reconstruction de la première communauté chrétienne plus positifs envers les femmes.

Les recherches d'Elisabeth Schüssler Fiorenza contribuent éminemment à nous donner une nouvelle herméneutique des écrits bibliques où les expériences des femmes sont restaurées dans leur dynamisme. Ces expériences sont perçues avec tout le poids d'oppression transmis par les structures patriarcales et la force de libération surgie d'une prise de conscience de l'histoire des femmes. Des valeurs d'égalité hommes-femmes et de solidarité entre les femmes apparaissent dans le mouvement des disciples de Jésus. Elles trouvent une confirmation praxéologique dans une ré-écriture de l'histoire des femmes, dans le développement d'une spiritualité féministe et dans l'émergence d'une *ekklèsia* des femmes.

Mary Daly, une utilisation exclusive

Mary Daly utilise les expériences des femmes d'une manière autre qu'Elisabeth Schüssler Fiorenza. Je qualifie cette manière: "une utilisation exclusive", car Mary Daly entend donner aux expériences des femmes un sens nouveau hors des moules patriarcaux. Formée d'abord en théologie, puis en philosophie,[35] elle préfère se rattacher à la philosophie;[36] les titres de ses livres le manifestent clairement: *Beyond God the Father: Toward a Philosophy of Women's Liberation*,[37] *Gyn/Ecology. The Metaethics of Radical Feminism*,[38] *Pure Lust: An Elemental Feminist Philosophy*.[39] De plus, elle considère avoir dépassé l'étape réformiste de son premier ouvrage: *The Church and the Second Sex*, pour lequel elle fait en 1975 une introduction très critique; elle situe désormais son entreprise dans le courant d'un "féminisme radical."[40]

Lieu d'émergence

Ne pourrait-on pas dire avec une certaine note d'humour que Mary Daly a réussi une fervente dénonciation du système patriarcal. Elle présente sa méthode comme "une méthode gynocentrique", qui "n'exige pas seulement le meurtre des méthodes misogynes (un exorcisme intellectuel et affectif), mais aussi une extase."[41] Elle commet donc "le crime de méthodicide" annoncé dans *Beyond God the Father*, confirmé dans *Gyn/Ecology* qui est "une forme de déicide," puisque la méthode a le statut de dieu, elle peut par conséquent parler dans *Pure Lust* "d'une tradition de méthodicide."[42]

La méthode de Mary Daly consiste à sortir du patriarcat pour pouvoir donner un sens intensément positif à tout ce qui a trait aux expériences des femmes, en somme déployer une "gynocentricité." Ainsi, le patriarcat est dénoncé sous toutes ses formes nécrophores:

1) comme une période de danger extrême: "This book is being published in the 1980s — a period of extreme danger for women and for our sister the earth and her other creatures, all of whom are targeted by the maniacal fathers, sons and holy ghosts for extinction by nuclear holocaust, or, failing, that, by contamination, by escalated ordinary violence, by man-made hunger and disease that proliferate in a climate of deception and mind-rot. Within the general context of this decade's horrors, women face in our daily lives forces whose intent is to mangle, strangle, tame, and turn us against our own purposes."[43]

2) comme un système de mort: "The Most Unholy Trinity of Rape, Genocide, and War is a logical expression of phallocentric power."[44]

3) Le titre d'un de ses livres, *Pure Lust*, explique Mary Daly, se réfère en premier lieu à: "the deadly dis-passion that prevails in patriarchy—the life-hating lechery that rapes and kills the objects of its obsession/aggression. Indeed, the usual meaning of lust within the Lecherous State of patriarchy is well known. It means "sexual desire, especially of a violent self-indulgent character: LECHERY, LASCIVIOUSNESS."[45]

4) comme un État engendrant et perpétuant le sadisme, un "sadostate": "She may experience and be informed about atrocities against women, and yet she is unable to feel sustained rage against the perpetrators of the atrocities, and incapable of acting against the men who are the originators, rulers and controlling legitimators of the sadostate."[46]

Le patriarcat poursuit l'effacement et la destruction des femmes de plusieurs façons. Dans *Beyond God the Father*, Mary Daly a montré comment "dans un monde sexiste, le système de symboles et les appareils conceptuels ont été des créations mâles. Celles-ci ne reflètent pas l'expérience des femmes, mais fonctionnent plutôt pour falsifier leur propre image et leurs expériences."[47] Dans *Gyn/Ecology*, elle étudie de façon extensive cinq rites spécifiques qui ont massacré et qui massacrent le corps des femmes: le suttee en Inde, le bandement des pieds en Chine, les mutilations génitales en Afrique, la destruction par le feu des sorcières en Europe, les interventions gynécologiques sur le continent nord-américain.[48]

Dans *Pure Lust*, Mary Daly fait voir comment le patriarcat entraîne la destruction des sensations premières: "en nous privant d'un rapport avec les sons, les significations, les rythmes, les liens cosmiques, désignés comme 'cet alphabet archaïque.'"[49] et aussi: "en détériorant nos capacités sensorielles dans des espaces de travail au décor uniformisé, aux fenêtres scellées, dans un environnement sonore homogénéisé, sous éclairage constant."[50]

Plus encore, le système patriarcal s'attaque au corps des femmes, en lui faisant subir "des atrocités gynocides," telles que le viol, les coups, l'inceste subi par les filles.[51] Cette sortie contre le patriarcat s'oriente vers l'exaltation des éléments primordiaux: le feu, l'air, la terre, l'eau qui permettent à nos sens d'être mis en communication d'une façon naturelle et sauvage.[52] Ainsi, les femmes peuvent retrouver leurs racines et faire partie de leur race dont il sera question plus loin. Il s'agit de se livrer à un véritable travail d'exorcisme de tout ce qui nous a été imposé à travers Eve[53] et de savoir donner un sens positif aux mots, en les situant dans leur contexte étymologique. Ainsi, le mot "lust" peut se charger de sa connotation reliée au mot latin *lascivus*, signifiant "licencieux, folâtre," pour se rattacher à sa luxuriante croissance de la terre ou des plantes.

Premièrement donc, *pure lust* définit l'exultation, l'espoir, l'hilarité, l'accord/ l'harmonie cosmiques de ces femmes qui choisissent de s'échapper, de suivre les voies du coeur et de bondir hors de leur condition de servage: en nous liant et nous alliant avec les Éléments, en nous branchant avec l'aura des animaux et des plantes, en nous mettant en communion planétaire avec les étoiles les plus éloignées.[54]

Cette méthode gynocentrique se définit dans *Gyn/Ecology*: "spinning in a time/space,"[55] qui pousse au vertige de la création.[56]

Spinning is creating an environment of increasing innocence. Innocence does not consist in simply "not harming." This is the fallacy of ideologies on nonviolence. Powerful innocence is seeking and naming the deep mysteries of interconnectedness.... It must be nothing less than successive acts of transcendence and Gyn/Ecological creation.[57]

Lieu de valorisation

L'utilisation du concept "expériences des femmes" par Mary Daly donne lieu à une valorisation qui est signifiée en totalité dans sa proposition du mot "Be-ing." En scindant en deux le mot anglais "Being," elle veut le libérer de son sens abstrait d'"être" et "lui rendre sa dynamique originelle à savoir celle de l'être en devenir, étante et non celle d'être là, passivement."[58] Elle emploie aussi le mot "Metabeing" dans *Pure Lust*: "The word Metabeing is used here to Name Realms of active participation, in the Powers of Be-ing."[59] Cette valorisation des "expériences des femmes" dans le Be-ing cherche premièrement et ultimement à donner une intégrité aux femmes. La référence au mot anglais "Re-member" sous sa forme scindée en deux permet de saisir le sens de ces retrouvailles ontologiques.

Thousands of women struggle to re-member ourselves and our history, to sustain and intensify a biophilic consciousness. Having once known the intense joy of woman-identified bonding and creation, we refuse to turn back. For those who survive in the only real sense, that is, with metapatriarchal consciousness alive and growing, our struggle and quest concern Elemental participation in Be-ing. Our passion is for that which is most intimate and most ultimate, for depth and transcendence, for recalling original wholeness.[60]

Ainsi l'époque du démembrement (dismemberment) subi par les femmes sous le système patriarcal est dépassée. Il fallait toutefois aux femmes avoir "le courage existentiel de se confronter à l'expérience du néant (nothingness)" pour se défaire des définitions, modèles patriarcaux et parvenir à une situation de participation plus entière dans la réalisation d'elles-mêmes.[61]

Les femmes font donc partie de ce mouvement, de la Race des femmes. Là encore, Mary Daly joue sur les différents sens d'un mot anglais, celui de "race," donnés par le dictionnaire Merriam-Webster. Elle acquiesce au sens premier de "race": "l'action de se précipiter en

avant, courir," comme rendant bien compte du mouvement des femmes.
Un autre sens de "race": "fort ou rapide courant d'eau qui coule dans un
lit étroit" indique que l'Etante élémentale doit couler dans des lits étroits
en raison de ses options fort rétrécies. Une troisième définition de "race"
comme "mer forte ou hachée, celle qui fait naître la rencontre de deux
marées," s'applique à la Race des femmes souvent entraînée dans "des
marées, des houles et des rythmes qui sont élémentaux et effets de ren-
contres cosmiques."[62]

L'effet de gynergie est en pleine action; il s'agit de "retrouver
l'énergie qui nous a été ravie par une politique sexuelle,"[63] de mettre en
évidence la puissance (potency) des femmes—"a potency that needs to
be actualized."[64]

> Be-Witching is the actual leaping/hopping/flying that is Metamorphosis, and
> that is encouraged by the context of Be-Friending. It is the series of movements
> that constitute that shift of degree which can transform the confining path of
> the circle. Be-Witching, then, is the succession of transformative moments/
> movements of be-ing that are Metamorphic, macromutational. It is the crea-
> tion of Fairy Space.[65]

Lieu d'engagement

Depuis *The Church and the Second Sex*, paru en 1968, Mary Daly a par-
couru toute une trajectoire d'investissements par rapport aux
expériences des femmes. Alors qu'elle parlait de "confrontation, de dialogue, de collaboration entre les personnes des deux sexes" (p. 178)[66] d'
"une meilleure compréhension entre hommes et femmes,"[67] elle fait
dans ses livres subséquents "un saut qualitatif au-delà de la religion
patriarcale."[68] Cependant, Mary Daly se défend bien de confier aux
femmes une "mission," celle de sauver le monde d'un désastre
écologique. "I am affirming that those women who have the courage to
break the silence within our Selves are finding/creating/spiraling a new
Spring. This Spring within and among us makes be-ing possible, and
makes the process of integrity possible."[69]

La proposition gynocentrique délivrée avec intensité par Mary Daly
peut être considérée sous plusieurs angles praxéologiques, et j'en
souligne quelques-uns. Tout d'abord, Mary Daly nous invite à nous inve-
stir dans une réalité autre: "Spinning new time/space," c'est le troisième
passage de *Gyn/Ecology*. Elle plaide particulièrement pour un "enspirit-
ing":

> Enspiriting is breathing, be-ing. The Self enspirits the Self and others by en-
> couraging, by expanding her own courage, hope, determination, vigor. To en-
> spirit is to be an expressive active verb, an Active Voice uttering the Self ut-
> terly, in a movement/Journey that spirals outward, inward. In this Active
> Voicing, the Self Spooks the spookers. She affirms the becoming Self who is
> always Other. She dis-covers and creates the Otherworld.[70]

Ce passage à un monde autre entraîne un nouveau rapport avec les mots: les femmes emploient de nouveaux mots et travaillent à transformer et rappeler (transforming/recalling) des sens des mots anciens. Elles doivent se donner le pouvoir de nommer, un pouvoir qui leur a été ravi.[71] Mary Daly ne craint pas d'affirmer que son entreprise est "Un-Theology" ou "Un-Philosophy" et que "*Gyn/Ecology* is the Un-field/Ourfield/Outfield of Journeyers."[72] Le "courage de nommer"[73] prend toute son ampleur quand elle veut désormais parler de "Dieu" non pas comme un nom mais comme un verbe. Elle veut communiquer un pouvoir actif aux mots, les délivrer d'un carcan de passivité. Ainsi, Dieu est un verbe, "le plus actif et dynamique de tous,"[74] le Verbe des Verbes."[75] C'est dans la transcendance de ce Verbe que les femmes entendent participer, vivre, agir et avoir leur être.

L'avènement d'une "conscience biophylique"[76] est l'intention majeure de Mary Daly. Le lien avec le cosmos, avec les éléments fondamentaux tels le vent, le feu, la terre, l'eau, constitue la trame régénératrice de tout le nouveau tissage/spirage, la réalisation de l'alliance cosmique annoncée dans *Beyond God the Father*.[77] Cette conscience biophylique se développe entre les femmes qui forment une sororité. Dans sa nouvelle introduction féministe post-chrétienne à *The Church and the Second Sex*, Mary Daly affirme: "This is becoming a credible dream, because a community of sisterhood was coming into being, into be-ing."[78] Dans *Beyond God the Father*, elle consacre deux chapitres à mettre en évidence les liens de la liberté qui sont en train d'advenir entre les femmes. Dans le chapitre 5: "The Bonds of Freedom: Sisterhood as Antichurch" elle fait voir la menace que constitue la sororité vis-à-vis une Église constituée sur un modèle hiérarchique et forte d'une autorité dominatrice. Dans le chapitre 6: "Sisterhood as Cosmic Covenant"[79] elle se lance dans la perspective d'une sororité qui résulte d'un profond accord des femmes avec elles-mêmes et parmi elles-mêmes et qui progresse harmonieusement avec un environnement qui est au-delà, en-dessous et tout autour d'un non-environnement constitué par les brisures et les barrières du patriarcat.

L'utilisation du concept "expériences des femmes" par Mary Daly est marquée par une sortie fulgurante du territoire patriarcal. Aucun compromis ne peut être fait avec un modèle, des perceptions, des définitions qui ont dominé et contribuent à détruire le potentiel des femmes plutôt qu'à l'accomplir. C'est pourquoi Mary Daly dénonce hardiment le patriarcat comme un système de mort qui représente un danger constant pour les femmes. Elle tente de déployer la gynergie, afin que les femmes puissent atteindre leur intégrité et devenir "Be-ing." Cette quête explosive la conduit à un engagement pour une réalité autre, nouvellement nommée, dans l'avènement d'une conscience biophylique où les femmes développent des liens de sororité.

Ellen Leonard, une intégration dans le contexte canadien

Un texte tout récent d'Ellen Leonard fournit une intéressante application sur les possibilités de l'intégration de l'expérience des femmes dans le contexte canadien.[80]

Lieu d'émergence

Ellen Leonard constate que "l'expérience a toujours été utilisée en théologie, mais que sa fonction n'a pas toujours été reconnue."[81] Cependant, un profond changement s'est manifesté dans l'utilisation de l'expérience comme source de la théologie; elle a entraîné "la correction de préjugés (bias). Désormais les expériences ignorées auparavant deviennent un lieu de référence (source) pour la réflexion théologique."[82] Une nouvelle épistémologie est donc en cause. L'expérience présente devient un lieu important pour la théologie; elle apporte des corrections vis-à-vis des expériences passées qui ne doivent pas toutefois être reléguées aux oubliettes. Ellen Leonard apporte deux formes de théologies contemporaines "correctives": 1) contextuelles — pour montrer qu'une théologie est soumise à son propre contexte culturel; 2) féministes — pour dépasser des théologies androcentriques.[83]

Lieu de valorisation

Ellen Leonard combine donc deux séries d'expériences, celles des femmes et celles cultivées dans le contexte canadien. Elle considère les expériences des femmes selon quatre catégories: les expériences d'oppression sous leurs multiples formes incluant les expériences de harcèlement sexuel et de violence, les expériences d'être une fille, une soeur, une mère, les expériences d'avoir un corps de femme, avec ses propres rythmes tels que les menstruations, la ménopause, les expériences de conscientisation croissante de sororité avec les femmes de partout.[84] Du côté canadien sont signalées trois transitions importantes: de la survivance dans la nature sauvage à la survivance du monde; du statut colonial à une responsabilité globale; du maintien des cultures francophone et anglophone à l'acceptation et l'affirmation du pluralisme.[85]

Ainsi, Ellen Leonard a établi en trois points un parallèle entre les deux types d'expériences, où se trouvent valorisées les expériences des femmes dans un contexte canadien. Premièrement, alors que le Canada a effectué le passage d'une survie dans la nature sauvage à une préoccupation pour la survie du monde, des féministes réfléchissent sur la transition d'une identification des femmes à la nature à une préoccupation des femmes pour l'écologie. Deuxièmement, comme le Canada est sorti du statut de pays colonisé pour s'engager dans une responsabilité pour la planète, ainsi les femmes s'affranchissent d'une position de personnes dominées pour parvenir à celle d'une actualisation de leurs capacités. Enfin, comme le Canada tente de se situer au-delà du maintien de deux cultures distinctes en reconnaissant un pluralisme culturel, le mouvement des femmes libère les femmes de leur rôle spécial pour accueillir les nombreuses voix différentes des femmes.[86] Ces changements dans la condition des femmes montrent comme les féministes rejettent une structure hiérarchique et une pensée dualiste qui dévalue le corps et la nature, comment elles cherchent une façon de vivre en convivialité avec la nature, en communion avec leurs soeurs et les êtres humains.

Lieu d'engagement

Cette intégration des expériences des femmes dans un contexte canadien oblige à repenser la théologie, particulièrement l'image de Dieu et à revoir l'anthropologie, la christologie et l'ecclésiologie.[87] Ellen Leonard se réfère à la critique de Mary Daly au sujet de l'image de Dieu comme un être humain mâle et de couleur blanche; à la perception étonnante d'Alice Walker, une femme noire dans The Color Purple; à l'invitation d'Elizabeth Johnson à présenter les multiples images de Dieu à partir de la riche diversité de l'expérience humaine; aux modèles de Dieu comme une mère, une amoureuse et une amie du monde développés par Sallie McFague. Un élargissement de la compréhension en anthropologie, en christologie et en ecclésiologie permet d'aller au-delà d'un système de domination d'un sexe par l'autre, de reconnaître la sagesse et le courage de nos soeurs dans la foi, de voir le Christ comme un symbole d'affirmation (empowerment) de chacun et de chacune, de la mutualité et de la diversité des frères et des soeurs dans l'Église. A la place du symbole de la pyramide dans l'Église, il faudrait voir, comme le suggère Letty Russell, "l'image de l'arc-en-ciel comme le paradigme de la diversité et de l'inclusivité dans l'Église."[88]

Ellen Leonard conclut de façon significative son étude:

> Dans mon expérience de femme canadienne, je reconnais la présence de Dieu qui m'appelle à être responsable pour ce monde, à travailler pour l'affirmation de tous les peuples, particulièrement des femmes, et à entendre les voix de mes soeurs et de mes frères dans ma communauté locale et dans la plus grande communauté du monde.[89]

Conclusion

Sheila Greeve Davaney a remis en question en 1987 une utilisation du concept "expérience des femmes" dans une analyse de textes de trois théologiennes féministes américaines, Elisabeth Schüssler Fiorenza, Rosemary Radford Ruether et Mary Daly.[90] Elle fait à leur égard deux critiques majeures: 1) elles se livrent à une "fausse universalisation"[91] d'un type d'expériences de femmes qui est le propre d'un groupe particulier, celui des blanches, ignorant la diversité et la multiplicité des expériences des femmes de différentes classes, couleurs, races; 2) elles s'appuient subrepticement sur un fondement ontologique: pour Schüssler

Fiorenza et Ruether, c'est une réalité divine – Dieu/Déesse qui participe aux luttes de libération et de prise de pouvoir; pour Mary Daly, c'est l'essence innée des femmes.[92] En somme, Sheila Greeve Davaney réclame de faire appel à "des normes pragmatiques plutôt qu'à des fondements ontologiques,"[93] et de se référer à "des expériences concrètes et particulières."[94]

Carol P. Christ a réagi[95] à l'argumentation de Sheila Greeve Davaney en admettant qu'il puisse y avoir une ambiguïté dans une oeuvre mais en ne reconnaissant pas les accusations présentées contre les trois théologiennes féministes. Elle réexamine particulièrement le livre *In Memory of Her* d'Elisabeth Schüssler Fiorenza; elle montre que celle-ci ne fait pas une affirmation universelle et objective de Dieu, mais qu'elle se réfère à sa propre expérience et affirmation. Carol B. Christ propose plutôt une attitude d'engagement puisqu' "elle croit que le féminisme a le potentiel pour améliorer le monde";[96] elle ne prétend pas à une neutralité intellectuelle qui est de toute façon seulement un embarras, mais plutôt de reconnaître et d'affirmer les conditions du temps et de l'espace, qui limitent nos perspectives aussi bien qu'elles leur donnent un pouvoir distinctif de perspective.[97]

La présente étude a permis de faire voir que les théologiennes féministes trouvent donc par l'utilisation du concept "expériences des femmes" des possibilités multiples d'intégrer le vécu des femmes dans la science théologique. Elles manifestent de façon variée leur tempérament de chercheuse et diverses voies de réflexion. Elisabeth Schüssler Fiorenza, Mary Daly et Ellen Leonard apportent une contribution remarquable à la participation des femmes dans un savoir qui a été réservé pendant près de deux millénaires à des clercs mâles. Le discernement des lieux d'émergence, de valorisation et d'engagement du concept "expériences des femmes" chez chacune de ces trois chercheuses – et il y en a d'autres qui sont à l'étude – signale des perspectives intéressantes sur les plans herméneutique et éthique.

Notes

1 Sheila A. Collins, *A Different Heaven and Earth* (Valley Forge, PA: Judson Press, 1974).

2 Ibid., p. 41.

3 Peter L. Berger, *A Rumor of Angels. Modern Society and the Rediscovery of the Supernatural* (New York: Doubleday, 1969).

4 Collins, *A Different Heaven*, p. 43.

5 Carol P. Christ, "The New Feminist Theology: A Review of the Literature," *Religious Studies Review*, 3/4 (October 1977): 204.

6 Elisabeth J. Lacelle, "Le mouvement des femmes dans les Églises nord-américaines," *Études*, 363/5 (novembre 1985): 543.

7 Elisabeth Schüssler Fiorenza, *In Memory of Her: A Feminist Reconstruction of Christian Origins* (New York: Crossroad, 1983); traduit en français par Marcelline Brun: *En mémoire d'elle.* (Paris: Cerf, 1986), Cogitatio Fidei, p. 136. Je me référerai à la traduction française.

8 Elisabeth Schüssler Fiorenza, *Bread Not Stone: The Challenge of Feminist Biblical Interpretation* (Boston: Beacon Press, 1984).

9 Schüssler Fiorenza, *En mémoire d'elle*, p. 32.

10 Schüssler Fiorenza, *Bread Not Stone*, p. 8.

11 Ibid., p. xvii.

12 Ibid., p. 15.

13 Ibid.

14 Ibid., p. 18.

15 Ibid., p. 19.

16 Ibid., p. 21.

17 Pamela Dickey Young, *Feminist Theology/Christian Theology: In Search of Method* (Minneapolis: Fortress Press, 1990), p. 26.

18 Schüssler Fiorenza, "Toward a Feminist Biblical Hermeneutics: Biblical Interpretation and Liberation Theology," in L. Dale and Brian Mahan, eds., *The Challenge of Liberation Theology: A First World Response* (New York: Orbis Maryknoll, 1984), p. 108.

19 Schüssler Fiorenza, "Word, Spirit and Power: Women in Early Christian Communities," in Eleanor McLaughlin and Rosemary Ruether, eds., *Female Leadership in the Jewish and Christian Traditions* (New York: Simon and Schuster, 1979), p. 29-70.

20 Schüssler Fiorenza, *En mémoire d'elle*, p. 31.

21 Ibid.

22 Ibid., p. 150.

23 Ibid., p. 214.

24 Ibid., p. 230.

25 Ibid., p. 11.

26 Ibid., p. 69.

27 Ibid., p. 72.

28 Schüssler Fiorenza, *Bread Not Stone*, p. xvii.

29 Ibid., p. xv.

30 Schüssler Fiorenza, *En mémoire d'elle*, p. 15.

31 Ibid., p. 477.

32 Ibid., p. 468.

33 Ibid., p. 478.

34 Ibid., p. 422.

35 Mary Daly, *The Church and the Second Sex.* (New York: Harper & Row, 1975), p. 7.

36 Mary Daly, *Beyond God the Father: Toward a Philosophy of Women's Liberation* (Boston: Beacon Press, 1973), p. 6. New edition with an original Reintroduction by the author in 1985.

37 Ibid.

38 Mary Daly, *Gyn/Ecology: The Metaethics of Radical Feminism* (Boston: Beacon Press, 1978).

39 Mary Daly, *Pure Lust: Elemental Feminist Philosophy* (Boston: Beacon Press, 1984).

40 Daly, *Gyn/Ecology*, p. 1, cf. Mary Daly, *Notes pour une ontologie du féminisme radical*, traduit par Michèle Causse (Montréal: L'intégrale, 1982, hereafter *Notes*). Voir aussi Elisabeth J. Lacelle, "Le mouvement des femmes," p. 544-45.

41 Daly, *Gyn/Ecology*, p. 23.

42 Daly, *Pure Lust*, p. 30.

43 Ibid., préface, p. ix. Traduit dans *Notes*, p. 5.

44 Daly, *Beyond God the Father,* p. 122.

45 Ibid., p. 2.

46 Ibid., p. 60.

47 Ibid., p. 7.
48 Daly, *Gyn/Ecology*, p. 111.
49 Daly, *Pure Lust*, p. 10.
50 Ibid., p. 63-64.
51 Daly, *Beyond God the Father*, p. xiv, 118.
52 Daly, *Pure Lust*, p. 11.
53 Daly, "Exorcising Evil from Eve: The Fall into Freedom," chap. 1 in *Beyond God the Father*, p. 44-68.
54 Daly, *Notes*, p. 10.
55 Daly, *Gyn/Ecology*, p. 4, 23.
56 Ibid., p. 414-17.
57 Ibid., p. 413-14.
58 Explication de Michèle Causse dans *Notes*, p. 26.
59 Daly, *Pure Lust*, p. 26.
60 Ibid., p. ix.
61 Daly, *Beyond God the Father*, p. 23-24.
62 Daly, *Notes*, 7; *Pure Lust*, p. 259.
63 Daly, *Beyond God the Father*, p. 124.
64 Daly, *Pure Lust*, p. 373.
65 Ibid., p. 388.
66 Daly, *The Church and the Second Sex*, p. 178. Références à la traduction française.
67 Ibid., p. 200.
68 Cf. Édition de 1975, *The Church and the Second Sex (with a New Feminist Postchristian Introduction by the Author)*, p. 50; "The Qualitative Leap Beyond Patriarchal Religion," *Quest*, 1/4 (Spring 1975): 20-40.
69 Daly, *Gyn/Ecology*, p. 21.
70 Ibid., p. 340.
71 Daly, *Beyond God the Father*, p. 8.
72 Daly, *Gyn/Ecology*, p. xiii.
73 Daly, *Beyond God the Father*, p. 28.
74 Ibid., p. 33.
75 Ibid., p. 34.
76 Voir "biophilia" dans Mary Daly, *Websters' First New Intergalactic Wickedary* (Boston: Beacon Press, 1987), p. 67. See also *Notes*, p. 5.
77 Ibid., p. 155-78.
78 Daly, *The Church and the Second Sex*, p. 14.
79 Daly, *Beyond God the Father*, p. 155-78.
80 Ellen Leonard, "Experience as a Source for Theology: A Canadian and Feminist Perspective," *Studies in Religion/Sciences religieuses*, 19/2 (1990): 143-62.
81 Ibid., p. 143.
82 Ibid., p. 146.
83 Ibid., p. 148.
84 Ibid., p. 147.
85 Ibid., p. 149.
86 Ibid.
87 Ibid., p. 155.
88 Letty Russell, "Women and Ministry: Problem or Possibility," in Judith Weidman, ed., *Christian Feminism: Visions of a New Humanity* (San Francisco: Harper & Row, 1984), p. 75-92. Cited in Leonard, "Experience as a Source for Theology," p. 161.
89 Leonard, "Experience as a Source for Theology," p. 162.

90 Sheila Greeve Davaney, "The Limits of the Appeal to Women's Experience," Clarissa W. Atkinson et al., eds., *Shaping New Vision Gender and Values in American Culture*, The Harvard Women's Studies in Religion Series (Ann Arbor and London: UMI Research Press, 1987), p. 32-49.

91 Ibid., p. 32, 48.

92 Ibid., p. 42.

93 Ibid., p. 47.

94 Ibid., p. 48.

95 Carol P. Christ, "Embodied Thinking: Reflections of Feminist Theological Method," *Journal of Feminist Studies in Religion*, 5/1 (Spring 1989): 7-15.

96 Ibid., p. 14.

97 Ibid., p. 15.

Chapter 6

PSYCHOANALYSIS AND RELIGION: A FEMINIST ATHEIST'S PERSPECTIVE ON RECENT WORK*

Naomi R. Goldenberg

My work in the psychology of religion is influenced by two evolving bodies of theory—psychoanalysis and feminism. Although I am a secularist, many scholars working in the field of psychology of religion hold to portions of a religious view the world. My colleague, James Jones, is such a scholar. In this essay, I will use Jones' recent work as a foil to develop a psychoanalytic, feminist perspective on the psychology of religion.

In his book, *Contemporary Psychoanalysis and Religion: Transference and Transcendence* (New Haven: Yale University Press, 1991), Jones looks at religious ideas through object relations theory, a branch of Freudian psychoanalytic thought that stresses the importance of past and present relationships in the construction of human experience.[1] Since Jones' work appeared soon after the publication of *Returning Words to Flesh: Feminism, Psychoanalysis and the Resurrection of the Body*,[2] my book on a similar theme, I feel that a comparison of our perspectives will give the reader a good idea of my specific points of difference within a central discussion in the field. For me, as will become clear in the pages that follow, atheism and feminism are the cornerstones on which an effective approach to the psychology of religion must be built.

As we all know, Freud had very definite ideas about where psychoanalysis and religion ought to stand in relation to one another. Throughout his work, he states that his science of psychoanalysis must be opposed to religion. In the *New Introductory Lectures*, he writes with characteristic directness that "of the three powers (art, philosophy and religion) which may dispute the basic position of science, religion alone is to be taken seriously as an enemy."[3] For scholars of the psychology of religion, Freud's attitude toward religion is a key problem in the field. Whatever we do with Freud's antipathy to religion, whether we agree with it, disagree with it, modify it or analyze it, we feel compelled to react to it. Thus, the description of psychoanalysis and religion as eternal antagonists has framed a central and (just as eternal) agenda for the construction of theory.

One of the things that interests me about this issue is a paradox I see involving the place of deity in Freud's work. Although Freud never wavered in his atheism, and although he certainly never made a place for God in psychoanalysis, in the last chapter of *The Future of an Illusion*, which, by any standard, ranks as one of his major treatises opposing the maintenance of religion, Freud proposes a god for psychoanalysis. According to Freud, "our God," that is, the god of scientists and psychoanalysts, is Logos, who, he says, operates "within human limits-so far as external reality, 'Ananke,' allows. . . ."[4]

I, who, like Freud, consider myself to be a "godless Jew," find this statement very interesting. Are we to understand Freud's mention of a god for psychoanalysis to be wholly rhetorical? Or could we consider it in another way, as, perhaps, a somewhat playful suggestion that there are some types of gods that may be compatible with psychoanalysis — that there are some gods that even godless Jews might maintain?

In the course of thinking about Jones' book and contrasting it with my own work, I began to understand that our differing opinions about the proper relation between psychoanalysis and religion could stem from the fact that we are actually concerned with two different kinds of gods — one that, like Logos, already has a place in the traditional, Freudian atheistic structure of psychoanalysis, and one which does not. A goal of Jones' work, I think, is to make a home for a god, who, in Freud's edifice, is left homeless. Before I can elaborate further on the idea that Jones and I approach the psychology of religion differently because we differ in ways that might be termed "theological," I want to present and comment upon what I understand Jones' ideas to be about the place of religion in relation to psychoanalysis. As you will see, even though we are headed in different directions, we do share opinions that enable us to carry on an interfaith dialogue before we part company to attend to separate types of shrines.

Jones' first principle, as I see it, is this: Because of the application of newer, object relations models of human development, psychoanalysis, both in theory-building and in therapy, should reopen the discussion of religion and religious belief. I agree with this whole-heartedly. Freud's assertion of atheism has caused too many analysts to avoid the subject of religion both in their theorizing and in their clinical work. Unlike Freud, who actively engaged the subject of religion in several major works, his followers tend to shrink from the topic. The result may be that a good number of analysts actually need religionists to give them food for thought — to furnish them with ideas that could be helpful in their clinical work. Two years ago, a group of analytic candidates told me this when I was invited to speak at one of their institute's classes in Montreal. I was surprised that several of them who had been seeing patients for a number of years said that they were often perplexed when religion entered an analysis. Perhaps it took a roomful of candidates to admit to a measure of confusion about this topic in therapy, but I suspect the uncertainty might be fairly common among practising analysts. For this reason, I expect that a book like Jones', which approaches the topic with grounding in both psychoanalysis and religion, will find an audience among analysts.

One thing we might learn from discussion of the subject is that a form of "plea-bargaining" often occurs in relation to religion. I take the term "plea-bargaining" from the British analyst Dennis Duncan, who, in a talk before the Psychoanalytic Society of Eastern Ontario,[5] suggested it as a description of what often happens in analysis. According to Duncan, analysts and patients frequently strike an unspoken bargain analogous to the sort used in legal systems to allow a trial to proceed. Analyst and patient agree that something of importance will not be discussed for the time being. In an extensive analysis, the sensitive topic will be investigated eventually. But, in some less thorough treatments, it may never be broached. Even so, a good deal of analytic work might be accomplished.

In a discussion of Jones' book with a reading group in Ottawa, one analyst told me of a patient he had had who was studying to be a priest. After a few years, the therapy ended to the mutual satisfaction of both with the patient's vocation remaining undisturbed. From this vignette and from the remarks of the Montreal candidates, I have begun to think that the picture of the contemporary Freudian analyst who tramples on every patient's religious connection is a false one. Much Freudian-type analysis probably proceeds without extensive interrogation of a patient's religious affiliation or sentiments. Religion may well be a domain for plea-bargaining in many an analysis – it could be a subject that a good number of analyst/patient pairs agree not to touch. There is much to learn about this. It is my hope that *Contemporary Psychoanalysis and Religion* will contribute to some discussion about the ways in which analysts do handle religious material in their clinical work.

The most developed and convincing point in the book is that, like art and literature, religious activity and experience should be considered a field for the expression of "object relations," that is, for the type of psychological linkages an individual makes both intrapsychically and with the world. Religion, Jones argues, is a legitimate domain in which to observe the "vicissitudes of interaction"[6] that a person has with "objects." These objects are formed by the interactions of both an external social and material reality and an internal dynamic composed of memory, "phantasy"[7] and emotional attachment. Jones is right when he emphasizes that the external and internal "objects" discussed in object relations theory refer to processes of interaction rather than to static entities.

The case studies in Jones' book show how patients' involvement with religious objects, that is, with religious images, ideas and social groups changes as their therapy has wider effect in their lives. In general, for each of the four patients discussed – Harold, Sylvia, Barbara and Martin – "God" or "the universe" changes from being a harsh, judgmental, cold, angry force to being more loving, accessible, forgiving and complex. For example, at the conclusion of Harold's therapy, he abandons his attachment to a God of wrath. "I know how destructive it is to live under that kind of punishing regime," he says. "I am a parent and I would never,

ever treat my children that way. I've learned my lesson and what it's done to me. I could never do that to them. If I know better than that, surely God does. God is surely even a better parent than I am."[8]

One way in which Harold expresses this new understanding of God is by teaching a class about business ethics in his church. This activity shows Harold's increasing capacity to take responsibility for his own life instead of blindly following a set of rules.

A similar change takes place for Sylvia. Her progress in therapy allows her to interact with her idea of God in ways that are freer and more flexible. As her life becomes fuller, her understanding of God becomes broader. At the conclusion of her treatment, she switches churches and professes her new understanding of God. "God is no longer a judge," she says. "I used to prefer judgmental religion; now I feel it does harm, it's not good. I see God as more forgiving. I see parts of Scripture about God's love that I never saw before."[9]

Harold, Sylvia, and the two other patients, modify their patterns of object relations through their therapeutic relationship with Jones. The therapy enables Harold and Sylvia to have more satisfying ties with both the external work of their churches and with the internal world of their God. These religious changes should be seen as reflections of changes in therapeutic transference. For these patients, the change from a judgmental, unforgiving God to a more flexible, loving one bodes well for the future. I would argue that Harold and Sylvia need not give up such ideas of God to achieve psychological health. Since their religious involvements carry much life history and thus much meaning for them, I would not want to deprive them of the opportunity to live out and deepen the sense of identity that religion carries for them.

Likewise, if Harold and Sylvia were artists, I would expect good therapy to help them maintain a satisfying connection to their art. I would not expect successful therapy to require an abandonment of art as an activity for the expression of fantasy[10] or as an avenue offering social ties to the world. Instead, I would hope that successful therapy would enable the art of Harold and Sylvia to be freer, to express a broader range and greater depth of feeling, and to afford them more pleasure and fulfilment.

Thus far, Jones and I see eye to eye about the relationship of religion to psychoanalysis. We both take Winnicott's direction in considering "religious feeling" as part of a "whole cultural field" that includes such phenomena as "play" and "artistic creativity and appreciation."[11] I agree that an object relations orientation in the psychology of religion "would investigate the way in which individuals' religious beliefs, experiences, and practices reflect the dynamics active in their construing of experience and in the deep structure of their internalized relationships."[12]

Despite our shared opinion that religion is a legitimate domain for the investigation of a person's object relations, Jones and I disagree on a matter of substance. I believe that psychoanalysis should treat religion as

a complex cultural phenomenon like art, work, friendship, family and political ideology. Jones, on the other hand, gives it special treatment. This
privileging of religion, or rather, of what he calls "the sacred" is complicated. Often he refers to "the sacred" as if it were a person with whom
everyday relations were possible. The following two instances in *Contemporary Psychoanalysis and Religion* stand out: "In the transference, the patient's basic patterns of relating and making sense of experience are
acted out and modified. It is hoped that this change will reverberate outside the consulting room to affect the patient's relations with friends,
lovers, children, coworkers, and the sacred."[13]

And, later he writes: "Presumably this newfound capacity [for growth
and development] might be reflected in a new relationship to the cosmic
or the sacred as well as to friends, lovers, colleagues, and clients."[14]

This looks like a mere sleight-of-hand. I am tempted to say "now,
wait a minute—I can't agree on those commas. To me, 'the sacred' does
not belong in the same series as friends, lovers and co-workers." I consider 'the sacred' to be a mystification of the depth of human psychological feeling about social and physical experience. To my way of thinking,
relations with friends, family, lovers, co-workers and the varied textures
of the material world are what makes life worth living. 'The sacred' is a
term which actually interferes with our understanding of the profundity
of our ties to people and to the world. But let's return to my understanding of the unique place that Jones gives religion in human experience.

As I understand it, Jones' privileging of religion over other cultural
formations is a way of reserving a certain measure of non-human mystery
for what he terms "the sacred." His work points toward a psychoanalysis
of religion in which "there would be nothing childish about acknowledging connection to a self-sustaining universal matrix."[15] To justify this nod
to religion, Jones uses object relations theory to make an analogy to religious mystery. "If selves necessarily stand in relation," he concludes, "it is
not necessarily irrational to ask if this complex of selves in relation does
not itself stand in relation."[16]

I admit that such statements are modestly phrased and seem to open
up avenues of important inquiry. Nevertheless, this Jewish atheist is suspicious. I feel thought shutting down as theistic awe enters the prose. In
relation to what does Jones want our complex of selves to stand? Although he says he is not trying to prove the existence of God,[17] he does
want to begin the psychological investigation of religious phenomena
with what he calls "the human experience of the sacred."[18] By making
this his starting point, by assuming an irreducible thing called "the sacred" in human experience, he seems to be closing off inquiry into the
very things I want to use psychoanalytic theory to investigate. Many people in the field of the psychology of religion fear the reductive powers of
psychoanalysis when it is used to approach religious phenomena. In contrast, I am more concerned about protecting psychoanalysis from being

reduced by spirituality. I don't want psychoanalysis to treat "the sacred" as a taboo subject that is fenced off from inquiry by reverence and the attribution of mystery. Jones and I both want to use object relations to find out more about religious thought and experience. However, while he believes that we can learn more by according "the sacred" more reverence, I feel that such an attitude would cause us to learn less.

I suggest that atheism is an important cornerstone of the psychoanalytic epistemology developed by Freud. Freud thought that he was following the scientific method and the way of reason. Belief in God would have placed limits on Freud's curiosity — would have hampered him in probing the complexities of the human mind. Because Freud was always looking for the human factors behind behaviour, feeling and thought, the psychoanalysis he initiated could enlarge our sense of who we are beyond the awareness of consciousness without positing a larger, non-human matrix for experience. His godlessness enabled him to expand our concept of what it means to be human.

Jones says that the image that some of his patients have of God is too much of a caricature. "They have a very clear idea of who and of what God is, even though they don't believe in him and I must observe in passing that their images are often of a God I wouldn't believe in either."[19]

I find myself thinking similar things about Jones' image of Freud. If Freudian theory really were as inflexible as he presents it, I wouldn't find it worth reading. Descriptions of Freud's work as "atomistic,"[20] and as an example of "rigid dualism"[21] with a "single-minded focus"[22] driven "by linear causality"[23] do not ring true. At one point in his text, Jones praises what I consider to be a particularly jargon-laden, awkward bit of the psychoanalyst Hans Loewald's prose.[24] By way of introducing this passage, Jones says that these are "words Freud could never have said."[25] Yes, I thought, Freud wrote too well. And Freud's body of work, which was awarded the Goethe Prize for Literature in 1930, develops a rich, nuanced spectrum of theory that has had the power to initiate much varied psychoanalytic research.

Object relations theory itself has its source in Freud's work.[26] Portions of *Three Essays on a Theory of Sexuality*, written in 1905, suggest that the sexual instinct is first directed toward the mother, who is the first object. It is in this early work that Freud makes the statement that later became a foundation of object relations theory: "the finding of an object is in fact a refinding of it."[27] This direction in Freud's thought eventually pushed followers like Melanie Klein to investigate early childhood with psychoanalytic methods. Object relations theory is in fact a continuation of Freudian theory. While Jones tends to emphasize the ways in which object relations theory departs from Freud, I see it as an extension of Freudian principles. It results from pushing the Freudian search for answers about human behaviour back in time to infancy and early child-hood.

Freud's atheistic approach toward human psychology has epistemo-logical value, as does his ambivalence toward Judaism[28] and his tendency to deflate humanity's "greatly valued higher activities."[29] These are quali-ties that Jones criticizes, along with William Meissner and Hans Loewald, two writers in the field of the psychology of religion who favour a theo-logical world view.[30] In contrast, I place a high value on Freud's ex-pressions of ambivalence and irreverence. The ability to tolerate am-bivalence and ambiguity is a hallmark of psychological health, according to many object relations theorists. That Freud both valued and criticized elements of Jewish tradition broadens the range of his thought.[31]

Furthermore, I think Jones' and Loewald's sensitivity to Freud's view of sublimation is misplaced. What is so very wrong with the idea that "there is some element of sham or pretense in our greatly valued higher activities?"[32] Why should we want to see art, politics and religion as above such things as lust, aggression and anality? Good psychoanalysts, like good comedians, should be reminding us of the less-than-noble wishes behind our noble ideals. To my mind, the cultivation of such a taste for irony and scepticism acts to curb human grandiosity and makes it harder for patriotism, chauvinism and missionary zeal to get out of hand.

I see Freud's irreverence as part of his insistence that psychoanalysis be maintained as a secular inquiry that should treat nothing as sacred, nothing as taboo. Because analysis is reductive, that is, because it is al-ways leading us back to see the interplay of our history with our present time, it is always involved in questioning the apparent facts of conscious-ness. By seeing psychoanalysis as "reductive," I do not mean that I con-sider it to be literalizing — that is, I do not see psychoanalysis as restricting meaning to a single explanation. Instead, I understand "reductive" in the sense of its Latin root, *reducere*, to lead back. Analysis deepens our un-derstanding of the present by leading us back to the textures of past ex-perience. I consider active, secular psychoanalytic interrogation of reli-gious phenomena more promising than a modified analytic approach — one that, as Jones says, would start by considering the sacred as one of "the psyche's most fundamental experiences."[33]

We already have a psychology with the starting point that Jones pro-poses. I am referring to Jungian theory which attributes human psycho-logical characteristics to the dance of non-human archetypes. In the Jun-gian system, the psychologist's task is to lead patients to see the so-called timeless "archetypal" reality behind their personal psychological experi-ences. Jung conceived of the contents of archetypes as unseen, irrepre-sentable, and ultimately unknowable forces that transcended the world.[34] His idea that our thoughts and behaviour are largely influenced by entities outside of our bodies and our physical environment is a gross departure from the major premises of psychoanalysis laid down by Freud.[35]

In my essay, "Looking at Jung Looking at Himself: A Psychoanalytic Rereading of *Memories, Dreams, Reflections*,"[36] I try to show how Jung used his theory of archetypes and quasi-mystical forces to shield himself from looking at the influence of his family on his own psychology. I fear that if we construct a psychoanalysis of religion based on object relations as one which stops short of analysing what are termed "sacred experiences," we will duplicate some of the obfuscation in Jungian technique. And, I think, we will fail to take note of important characteristics of religious thought.

In order to illustrate the value that a secular, psychoanalytically inspired approach to religious ideas can have, I'd like to discuss some of the assumptions standing behind Jones' construction of "the sacred." If we do not regard "the sacred" as something other than a fundamental datum of human experience, we may uncover some of the psychological and cultural contingencies that compose the various versions that people have of it.

First, I want to comment on the similarity of the four case studies that Jones presents. As I noted earlier, for each patient, God changes from a judgmental, severe, cold force to one that is loving, forgiving and encouraging. After their therapy, Harold, Sylvia, Barbara, and even Martin (who remains an atheist), find God or the universe to be more complex and accepting. This change parallels Freud's account of what happens to the super-ego in analysis. The personal development of Jones' patients also fits other analytic formulations — (e.g. D. W. Winnicott's "true self" and Melanie Klein's capacity for "reparation")[37] — that describe the deepening of a personality that can occur in a successful analysis. I prefer these analytic descriptions to religious ones because I think they encourage more investigation of particular history and experience.

Furthermore, I wonder about contingencies related to gender in the type of "sacred" that we find in *Contemporary Psychoanalysis and Religion*. I realize that I am on shaky ground here because Jones never quite declares what he believes the sacred to be. However, he does select the ideas of certain theologians to quote on the subject, and I find these ripe for feminist, psychoanalytic inquiry. For example, Jones presents Paul Tillich's understanding of God in the following manner:

> For Tillich, we must begin with God, for God is the beginning of everything. The power of existing makes everything else possible. God alone was, as the Torah says, "in the beginning." The known world remains absolutely dependent on God to keep it from utter nothingness. That is the meaning of the term God. To experience God, then, is to move from the experience of ontological shock — the dread that comes when we confront the precariousness of life — to the realization of the power of being itself, the experience of the source that sustains existence in the face of nothingness and provides the basis for the courage to live in the face of life's inevitable uncertainty.[38]

When I read this paragraph I hear themes resonant with a young child's perception of a powerful, and perhaps, terrifying mother. After all, it is a child's mother who is first charged with the task of providing the child with the courage "to live in the face of life's inevitable uncertainty" when life itself is most vulnerable. It is a mother who "is the beginning of everything," and who is usually responsible for keeping "the known world" from "utter nothingness" and for mitigating "dread" at the "precariousness of life."

I think that a psychoanalytic perspective on such theological statements might connect them up with fears, fantasies and memories in a manner that reveals gender within ideas of "God." Because Jones' book juxtaposes theology with object relations theory, it makes questions about deity and gender especially apparent. In fact, all of the theologians from whose work Jones quotes in *Contemporary Psychoanalysis and Religion* seem to me to be proposing a maternal power as their god. Schleiermacher's God as the "whence of our feeling of absolute dependence"; H. R. Niebuhr's "God as the single power behind all the powers that impinge on us"; Tillich's "God as the ground of our being"; and Buber's epigram that "all lines of relation meet in the Eternal You" are, to my mind, adult formulations of childhood perceptions concerning a primary caretaker. This line of thought does not reduce theology for me. On the contrary, it makes theology more interesting.

It is interesting to note how central the problem existence itself is in the work of male theologians. Why is it that women theologians do not find the fact of existence such a worry? Whenever the concept of "being" enters the work of a thinker like Mary Daly, it is understood as referring to possibilities of experience linked to social practice. In contrast, male theologians (e.g., Tillich) are interested in discussing ontological anxiety—a condition beyond the influence of a person's history and position in the social world. Jones' discussion of Tillich[39] made me wonder if, in addition to Tillich's two categories of "ontological" and "neurotic anxiety," we should be contemplating a third one of "masculine anxiety."

Certain types of male theology and psychology may traditionally have coped with such masculine anxiety by constructing various models of a grandiose self. Jones' discussion of Kierkegaard's stages of consciousness suggests this possibility:

> Kierkegaard saw human consciousness passing through three stages. First was the aesthetic, the search for pleasure that drives for repetition as we seek to re-experience pleasure. But repetition leads to boredom, for even the most intense pleasures turn stale after a while. At first the aesthete deals with the staleness of one pleasure by going on to another, and then another. But if he is at all self-reflective, eventually the experience of boredom will call the whole search for pleasure into question.
>
> The person then moves on to the ethical stage where he seeks meaning in life through committing himself to something outside of himself. At first he

gives himself wholeheartedly to his new ideal, but eventually he falls short of its demands, and so the ethical leads inevitably to a realization of human finitude and failure, if not to guilt and despair. And so the ethical, rather than bringing meaning to life, results in a new level of pain. The person is still inwardly divided, for he is looking to something outside of the self to give meaning to life. At this point, the person can give up the search (a process Kierkegaard calls "resignation") and, thrown back on himself by the failure of the ethical stage, find the divine within.[40]

I see these stages as an apt reflection of a particular type of experience that is largely possible only for white men of the middle and upper classes. These are the people whose position in the world enables them to dabble in pleasures without entanglement. Because such detachment can be a lifestyle, "commitment" to other people can be seen as an option, as something one can try for a while until one gives up on others and withdraws into oneself. Jones uses these stages to present us with a theological version of what some object relations theorists call "the search for the transforming object." However, I read the material as a description of a male quest for transformation—one that ends up in idealizing a grandiose individual self. Such a formulation may also be present in the work of Jung in which a huge, individuated, four-part self is proposed as the goal of life.[41]

The work of feminist theorists who posit a more permeable, relational idea of a self offers a refreshing alternative to the overblown, independent one emphasized in male thought. Writers such as Carol Gilligan, Catherine Keller, Anne Klein and several eco-feminist theorists[42] depict human selves in ways that are more in harmony with object relations theory than those described by the male theologians whom Jones cites in his book. True, it is important to acknowledge that Martin Buber thought about "the sacred" or "God" in a "thou-ish" way. But it is more important to read contemporary feminist theorists who are in even greater harmony with object relations theory.

There are many feminist theorists who are saying much the same thing as the object relations analysts. Human beings, say these theorists, are constructed in large part by their social, political, economic and linguistic circumstances.[43] Thus, as feminist philosopher Naomi Scheman phrases it, "questions of meaning and interpretation [in psychology and philosophy] cannot be answered in abstraction from a social setting."[44] This stress on the social context of experience actually extends the perspective of object relations theory which sometimes concentrates too narrowly on the social world as seen from a baby's perspective. To psychoanalysts, mother is the social context of baby, while to feminist theorists, mother and baby are both embedded in a bigger world. Object relations emphasizes the infant's immediate human environment, while feminist theory tries to understand the larger social conditions which make each particular human environment what it is.

The Goddess movement, like object relations theory in particular and feminist theory in general, is concerned with expanding awareness of the conditions which make lives what they are. Starhawk, a well-known witch and feminist priestess, describes the Goddess as existing in the complex connections of the entire universe:

> Each individual self is linked by ties of blood and affection to the coven, which in turn is part of the larger human community, the culture and society in which it is found, and that culture is part of the biological/geological community of Planet Earth and the cosmos beyond, the dance of being which we call Goddess.[45]

In addition to encouraging an empathic relation to the world, another quality that Jones attributes to religion is the capacity to promote "re-immersion in the primary process."[46] He cites Loewald and Winnicott as writers "who agree that one of the tasks of religion is the cultivation of this richness of consciousness."[47] This objective is also one that I find carried much further in feminist thought. The use of literature, poetry and art as a basis for doing philosophy and theology has been a practice of feminist thought for at least two decades. I therefore strongly suggest that a psychoanalysis of religion founded on object relations theory make extensive use of women's writing.[48]

I see Jones' "sacred" and that of the theologians on whom he relies as suffused with a longing for an idealized maternal presence — that is, for a nurturing, totally accepting caretaker and environment. Yet, in certain parts of *Contemporary Psychoanalysis and Religion*, I feel that this maternal sacred is clothed in a particular style of male drag. Toward the end of his book, in his discussion of Nietzsche's observation that men must have gods, Jones mentions the drive of *homo religiosus* to latch "onto one object or another without regard to whether the object can bear the full weight and range of the experience of the holy or fulfill all social and psychological functions of the sacred."[49] To me, to ask "the sacred" to be well-rounded, dependable and responsible is to conjure up an image of God-the-hero, God-the-father, or God-the-benign bureaucrat. Like so many images of male authority, this kind of God is supposed to be able to handle whatever may come. I find it a culturally specific portrait of a senex god — a portrait of an old man who is in charge.

If we see "the sacred" only in senex terms — that is as an old man who is eternally serious and authoritative, we will be excluding from our theories a myriad of gods, goddesses, nymphs, satyrs and spirits who have animated human imagination for millenia. Dionysius, Aphrodite, Persephone and Priapus were manifestations of the "sacred" to the Greeks and none of them tried to live up to the mission of the sacred that Jones' text seems to be recommending. In addition to the Greek pantheon, consider the Trickster figures and animal spirits of Native American religions. None of these manifestations of the sacred conforms to the portrait of an all-encompassing sacred that can "fulfill all . . . social and psychological functions."

With this rather contentious observation about Jones' idea of the sacred, let us return to our initial concern. I do believe that the varieties of gods and spirits I have just invoked have some place in psychoanalysis as Freud conceived it. Images of powerful, specific desires such as those personified in the figures of Aphrodite and Dionysius are present in psychoanalysis. Metaphors for human thought processes like Logos are there as well. Furthermore, analytic reflection is thoroughly immersed in homage to the power of embodied, historic parental images whose forces are like gods creating the human world.

Although psychoanalysis can offer some accommodation to these kinds of powers, it cannot make a place for a deity that transcends the human material and psychological environment. I think it is this kind of God that Jones would like to see welcomed into psychoanalysis, or at least not shut out entirely. Psychoanalysis already accepts my kinds of deities – that is, the limited ones that give names to currents within human psyches. For this reason, I see no cause to reject the relationship between psychoanalysis and religion that Freud proposed.

I am convinced that feminist thought in religion and psychoanalysis, particularly as exemplified by object relations theory, is pushing the psychology of religion in the same direction. Both systems of theory are concerned with articulating the interconnection of human beings with each other and with all the things which make up the body of the world. This mutual interest in the social and physical context of human experience makes feminist religious thought and object relations theory natural allies and should provide important subject matter for scholars in the psychology of religion for many years to come.

Notes

*Portions of an earlier version of this essay have previously appeared in the *Journal of Pastoral Psychology*.

1 Object relations theory is a highly influential offshoot of earler Freudian theory developed in Britain out of the work of analysts such as Melanie Klein, W.R.D. Fairbairn, D.W. Winnicott and Michael Balint. This body of theory is often contrasted to the classical approach to psychoanalysis, which is frequently termed "instinct theory" or "drive theory." For a comprehensive bibliography and a good introduction to object relations theory, see Jay R. Greenberg and Stephen A. Mitchell, *Object Relations in Psychoanalytic Theory* (Boston: Harvard University Press, 1983).

2 Naomi Goldenberg, *Returning Words to Flesh* (Boston: Beacon, 1990).

3 Sigmund Freud, *The Standard Edition of the Complete Psychological Works of Sigmund Freud*, 24 vols., ed. James Strachey (London: Hogarth Press, 1953-1974), 22: 160. All quotations are from the edition reprinted in 1973. Hereafter, "SE" will be used to refer to *The Standard Edition*.

4 Freud, SE, 21: 53.

5 Dr. Duncan's lecture, "Plea-bargaining in Psychoanalysis," was presented to the Psychoanalytic Society of Eastern Ontario in Ottawa on March 31, 1991.

6 James W. Jones, *Contemporary Psychoanalysis and Religion: Transference and Transcendence* (New Haven: Yale University Press, 1991), p. 6.

7 In the work of Melanie Klein and her followers, the work phantasy is used to refer to the mental representation of instinct. In contrast, "fantasy" is the more general term describing a wide range of wishful conscious or unconscious psychic activity.

8 Jones, *Contemporary Psychoanalysis and Religion*, p. 103.

9 Ibid., p. 72.

10 See above n. 7.

11 Jones, *Contemporary Psychoanalysis and Religion*,p. 60.

12 Ibid., p. 63.

13 Ibid., p. 84.

14 Ibid., p. 94.

15 Ibid., p. 135.

16 Ibid.

17 Ibid., p. 113.

18 Ibid.

19 Ibid., p. 44.

20 Ibid., p. 22.

21 Ibid., p. 42.

22 Ibid.

23 Ibid., p. 32.

24 The passage that Jones finds so impressive is quoted from Hans Loewald's *Psychoanalysis and the History of the Individual* (New Haven: Yale University Press, 1978), p. 61. As quoted in Jones, *Contemporary Psychoanalysis and Religion*, p. 53-54, Loewald writes: "The range and richness of human life is directly proportional to the mutual responsiveness between these various mental phases and levels. . . . While [rational thought] is a later development, it limits and impoverishes . . . the perspective, understanding, and range of human action, feeling, and thought unless it is brought back into coordination and communication with those modes of experience that remain their living source, and perhaps their ultimate destination. It is not a foregone conclusion that man's objectifying mentation is or should be an ultimate end rather than a component and intermediate phase." I consider such prose inferior to Freud's work both in style and tone.

25 Jones, *Contemporary Psychoanalysis and Religion*, p. 53.

26 See Greenberg and Mitchell.

27 Freud, SE, 7: 222.

28 Jones, *Contemporary Psychoanalysis and Religion*, p. 36.

29 Ibid., p. 51.

30 Jones agrees with Meissner in *Psychoanalysis and Religious Experience* (New Haven: Yale University Press, 1984), p. 56 that Freud's criticism of religion is to be considered a neurotic symptom. As quoted in Jones, *Contemporary Psychoanalysis and Religion*, p. 36, Meissner writes: "As we have seen, Freud's interweaving of these complex [religious] themes rides on a powerful undercurrent that stems from unresolved infantile conflicts. Deep in the recesses of his mind. Freud seems to have resolved that his truculent spirit would never yield to the demands of religion for submission and resignation. . . . Freud was never able to free himself from these deep-seated entanglements and their associated conflicts, and ultimately what he taught us about religion, religious experience, and faith must be taken in the context of these unconscious conflicts." And, on p. 51 Jones quotes Loewald in *Psychoanalysis and the History of the Individual*, p. 75, as writing that Freud's "view of sublimation always

smacks of reduction. It also implies there is some element of sham or pretense in our greatly valued higher activities."

31 The work that best demonstrates Freud's complex analysis of Judaism is *Moses and Monotheism*, SE, 23: 3-207. In this book Freud criticizes Jewish tradition for its obsessiveness yet, at the same time, praises it for encouraging an "advance in intellectuality." (p. 111-15). Another interesting example of Freud's appreciation for his Jewish heritage is his 1926 "Address to the Society of B'nai B'rith," SE, 20: 273-74. Freud writes: "there was a perception that it was to my Jewish nature alone that I owed two characteristics that had become indispensable to me in the difficult course of my life. Because I was a Jew I found myself free from many prejudices which restricted others in the use of their intellect; and as a Jew I was prepared to join the Opposition and to do without agreement with the 'compact majority.'" (Freud is referring to Ibsens' *Enemy of the People*).

32 Jones, *Contemporary Psychoanalysis and Religion*, p. 51, and n. 30 above.

33 Ibid., p. 116.

34 Jung's theory of archetypes is discussed frequently in his writings. For an early formulation of the concept see C. G. Jung, *The Collected Works of C. G. Jung*, 20 vols., ed. William G. McGuire et al., transl. R. F. C. Hull, Bollingen Series, (Princeton: Princeton University Press, 1954-79), 9(1): 78-79. For Jung's last formulation of the theory see Jung, *The Collected Works*, 8: 215. For a more extensive critique of archetypal theory, please see my articles "A Feminist Critique of Jung," *Signs*, 2/2 (Winter 1976): 443-49; "Feminism and Jungian Theory," *Anima*, 3/2 (Spring 1977): 14-176; *Changing of the Gods: Feminism and the End of Traditional Religions* (Boston: Beacon Press, 1979), p. 54-64; and "Archetypal Theory and the Separation of Mind and Body: Reason Enough to Turn to Freud?" in *Returning Words to Flesh* (Boston: Beacon Press), p. 71-95. My earlier essay on the evolution of the concept of archetype in Jungian theory is "Archetypal Theory after Jung," in *Spring 1975* (Zurich: Spring Publications) p. 199-220.

35 See Freud, SE, 14: 60-62.

36 See Goldenberg, *Returning Words to Flesh*, p. 116-45.

37 See D. W. Winnicott, *The Maturational Process and the Facilitating Environment* (London: Hogarth Press and the Institute of Psychoanalysis, 1979), passim; Melanie Klein, *Love, Guilt and Reparation and Other Works 1921-1945* (New York: Delacorte Press, 1975), passim.

38 Jones, *Contemporary Psychoanalysis and Religion*, p. 127.

39 Ibid., p. 126.

40 Ibid., p. 123-24. See also Sören Kierkegaard, *Fear and Trembling* and *Sickness unto Death*, transl. W. Lowrie (Princeton: Princeton University Press, 1941).

41 Jung discusses the self and the goal of individuation in many of his writings. See, for example. C. G. Jung, *The Collected Works*, 11: 468-69.

42 See Carol Gilligan, *In a Different Voice* (Cambridge: Harvard University Press, 1982); Catherine Keller, *From a Broken Web* (Boston: Beacon Press, 1986); Anne Klein, "Finding a Self: Buddhist and Feminist Perspectives," in Clarissa Atkinson, Constance Buchanan and Margaret Miles, eds., *Shaping New Vision: Gender and Values in American Culture* (Ann Arbor, Mich.: UMI Research Press, 1987), p. 191-218; Carol Christ and Judith Plaskow, eds., *Weaving the Visions: New Patterns in Feminist Spirituality* (New York: Harper & Row, 1989).

43 See essays in Sandra Harding and Merrill B. Hintikka, eds., *Discovering Reality: Feminist Perspectives on Epistemology, Metaphysics, Methodology, and Philosophy of Science* (Dordrecht: D. Reidel, 1983).

44 Naomi Scheman, "Individualism and the Objects of Psychology," in Harding and Hintikka, eds., *Discovering Reality*, p. 225-44.
45 Starhawk, "Ethics and Justice in Goddess Religion," in Charlene Spretnak, ed., *The Politics of Women's Spirituality: Essays on the Rise of Spiritual Power within the Feminist Movement* (New York: Doubleday, 1982), p. 418.
46 Jones, *Contemporary Psychoanalysis and Religion*, p. 133.
47 Ibid., p. 134.
48 A classic on this theme is Carol P. Christ's *Diving Deep and Surfacing: Women Writers on Spiritual Quest*, 2nd. ed. (Boston: Beacon Press, 1986).
49 Jones, *Contemporary Psychoanalysis and Religion*, p. 123.

Chapter 7

ABORIGINAL WOMEN AND RELIGION

ANU KAN SAN TOK AHE MANI WIN
(Translation from Sioux:
"Bald Eagle Woman Who Leads")

Doreen Spence

I would like to begin this paper by giving my thanks and deepest gratitude to the Native elders who have taught me the traditional ways and spiritual values that have shaped my life. They have been my source of strength and inspiration throughout the years ... their knowledge and guidance have been invaluable.

I am presenting here a written statement of what is essentially for Aboriginal people an oral tradition. This is in contrast to the tradition of European peoples, which is a written one. All teachings for Aboriginal women are passed on through legends and stories. My grandmother, great-grandmother, and women elders moulded me into the person I am today. My great-grandmother, especially my Kookum, was my teacher. These teachings are part of sacred lore, and cannot be communicated to anyone who has not undergone the training. Therefore my statements are more of an evocative nature, so as not to disclose this sacred ritual knowledge.

Values are passed along through sharing these oral traditions and stories. For instance, when you use the drum, the circle is a sacred symbol, and the music represents the heartbeat of Mother Earth. Stories are told from the time of beginnings as well as ones that are associated with specific ceremonies.

All things are created as unique entities of the Creator. For example, the eagle is a sacred bird. It is said to be the highest flying bird—closest to the Creator. The eagle teaches us to view everything from above. To receive an eagle feather is regarded as a high honour, and must be respected as such. In traditional healing circles, there is the passing of an eagle feather, which gives strength and courage to talk. All things have a meaning, and each must be respected for their sacred space.

Look at a tree, it has life, it has a spirit. A plant, also, has life and a spirit. Mother Earth is a living being. She has her own blood—the streams and the rivers. She has her own bones—the rocks and mountains. She has her own nerves—the energy lines and magnetic fields. She has her own regulatory cycles—such as water returning to the lands.

The Creator has given us two ears to hear the message clearly and concisely, two eyes to view the world, and one mouth to give our message — the message that comes straight from the heart. It must always be sacred, clear, and truthful.

Take the rock — the rock teaches us strength. On my own rock, I have a turtle painted. The turtle teaches me to take time out and go within — to pull in and revamp on a daily basis. This is particularly imperative when things get rough — a turtle withdraws and pulls its head and feet in. I have learned from the turtle when it is necessary for me to turn within and examine my feelings, and take time out to gain a new perspective.

I take time out every day to thank the Creator for the life that has been given to me. It was said by my great-grandmother that our people thanked the Creator at least four times a day for their blessings — morning, noon, evening, and last thing at night.

Everything is of the earth. Whenever we take from the earth, we must give something in return. Often this is accomplished through giving thanks in a specific sacred manner by giving tobacco to Mother Earth to thank her for what we removed.

Sweetgrass is used for purification. The braids of grass represent body, mind, and spirit. The use of sweetgrass is an essential component of Aboriginal spiritual ceremonies. Other herbs, such as sage, are also used in the same manner.

We must learn that everything that goes around comes around. We are not a web of life, but merely a thread of it. Everything an Indian does is done in a circle. The circle has no beginning and no end, and is representative of friendship and unity. Life has four stages — childhood, youth, adulthood, and back to childhood.

The four elements — water, air, fire, and earth — are very important in Native spirituality. All are part of the same physical world. All must be respected for their gift of life. Similarly, the four directions — East, South, West, and North — are very important to Native spirituality. Each direction represents certain strengths and characteristics.

The Sacred Hoop teaches us that human beings have four aspects to their nature — physical, mental, spiritual, and emotional. Each of these areas must be developed equally in a healthy, well-balanced person through the use of will power.

There are also four symbolic races — Red, Yellow, Black, and White. All are part of the same human family. All are brothers and sisters living on the same Mother Earth.

Our minds are reflected in the work we do in educating people about Native traditional values through projects such as bridging the gap. Our bodies are reflected in the action we take to preserve and heal others as well as the earth through activism, such as church and environmental groups. Our emotions are reflected in the manner in which we interact with others, and in the way we take care of the needs of both others and ourselves. The spirit is reflected in the healing circle where we learn to heal our spirits that we might continue to work in a strong and hope-filled manner.

All of these teachings are very much alive and are being handed down to our children and our grandchildren. Ours is not a religion, but I view it more as a way of life, in which we interact with each other and with every living creature, plant, rock, mineral, bird, and tree in a respectful and loving manner.

The Historical Dimension

The role of women has been central to the handing down of these teachings. In traditional society, Native women have been honoured as the Centre of the Circle of Life. In Canadian society today, however, Native women hold the dubious honour of occupying the lowest position of socio-economic status of all the diverse groups that make up the mosaic of Canadian culture groups. Statistically, we are the least educated, least employed and lowest paid in the realm of the material hierarchy. We watch as our babies die at a rate three times higher than any others. We pray for the safety of our teenagers who kill themselves six times more often than those of other cultural groups. We watch our sons taken off to jail—65% of them will be there before they turn twenty years of age. We know that there is up to a 90% chance that our children, if they survive at all, will not succeed in the white man's school system. Our daughters are seven to nine times more likely to be sexually abused than they are to graduate from high school. We know that our husbands have a small chance of living past their thirty-fifth birthday if they are lucky.

Although we represent only 2% of the general population, we are more likely to be the victims of domestic abuse—20-40% of women in Calgary's emergency and second-stage shelters are Native—but have the least chance of escaping the vicious cycle. "Poverty increases violence; unavailability of employment or education results in poverty, thereby perpetuating the cycle of violence."[1]

One could say that Native women, through their treatment by the rough hands of society, are in the same condition as our Mother Earth, who is excessively violated by the hands of our greedy industrialists. Many parallels can be drawn between the women who were once viewed by society as the bringers of all human life and the degradation of Mother Earth who was the provider of all things. The degradation began when Native women, who once controlled and lived according to the Creator's Law, fell under the control of the White Man's Law.[2]

In traditional culture, Native communities live in harmony with their world. "The people," as nearly every indigenous group label themselves as its literal meaning, have equal respect for their sisters and brothers, mothers and fathers in the plant, animal, earth, rock, and sky world. Women, children, and men, too, share equal places in the system of life.

Young, old, male, and female play their roles to the cycle of time, each contributing their full measure throughout the circle of existence. Creation myths often express the underlying values of a particular culture, where many Native beliefs show their understanding of women's roles by stating that the woman was created first (Puabo) or that women and men were created simultaneously (Iroquois, Mohawk, and Ojibwa). Native woman is of the earth. She nurtures, nourishes, and heals in the same way the Earth does. Her reproductive power is sacred and she has great natural healing powers that derive from her spiritual connection with the earth.[3] In contrast, European (Jewish and Christian) belief holds that Adam was the prototype, while Eve was almost an afterthought, created from his "spare rib."

Traditional Native women were direct leaders in the home and in caring for the family. Social status is ascribed at birth. Women have been the central force strengthening families, clans, bands, and nations. Networks centred on kinship through the mother/women were the primary determinants in deciding where to live after marriage. Their advice and decisions were often sought for spiritual, economical, and political aspects of their tribal life.[4]

To be forced to live a life today that is totally in contrast to this and out of one's own control is a source of constant stress, and leads to weakness and demoralization of individuals and entire communities. We, as Native women, have been forced into coerced dependence upon paternalistic policies of the federal government. The power of women has thus been eroded, but not entirely. Traditionally, women have the status to put men in positions of executive power and remove them if they were not acceptable. The men will ask for their wisdom. The power of traditional women was never more obvious to the astonished eyes of the world as it was in the events that unfolded at Oka in the summer of 1990. We saw the Clan mother, with a few choice words, command the AK-47-toting Mohawk soldier to turn on his heels and back off from the invading army. Traditional women are integral members of their societies. Their power is derived directly from the family system. The Iroquois Confederacy, to which the Mohawks are a member, is both matriarchal and matrilineal.

Clan mothers are chosen for their wisdom and ability and play a leading, although most often indirect, role of government. Again, look at Oka—it was women, such as Ellen Gabriel, who kept the international world informed of negotiations, strategies, and conditions of the Mohawk position vis-à-vis governments. Clan mothers negotiated with the armed Quebec Sûreté and the Canadian Army. Mohawk women calmed the terrifying situation on many occasions—giving time for cooler heads to prevail. Mohawk women, through the long nerve-wracking summer, were the upholders and enforcers of the Law of Harmony.[5]

How then have the colonizer's laws—white man's laws, as they are also known in Indian Country—viewed Native women? They attributed superiority to the man because he walked ahead of the woman.

> You would see a man walking ahead with his bow and arrow, women walking behind with small children, hauling the *travois*. It looked like she's doing all the hard work. But there is a reason why that man walked ahead. It was to protect his wife and family and clear the way for them. As much as the traditional man would honor Mother Earth for her gifts, so would he honor womanhood.[6]

Colonizer laws placed the Native women in the same position of inferiority as their own women, which was a grievous mistake. The complexities of the modern political processes have, as a result, thrown Native women from a leadership role into one of subordination in contemporary society. This has not only created a stereotyped image of the Indian woman as the exploited concubine of the whiteman, but initiated policies which contribute to manifestations of social ill-health, alcohol and drug abuse, high suicide rate, and family breakdown. "The stress of dependence upon federal policies leads to uncertainty, physical illness and disease."[7] The traditional mode where Native women entered into customary marriages which were monogamous, freely entered by both parties, and long-lasting, has been shattered. Instead derogatory language and condescension became obvious.

Governor Simpson, a federal bureaucrat, was quoted as saying that "He was appalled . . . at the degree of control native and métis women had over their white husbands."[8] Simpson's journal also called these men "Sapient councils of their Squaws" and stated these men should "guard against indiscretions which these 'frail brown ones' are so apt to indulge in." Not surprisingly, Simpson labelled Native woman as "Copper-Gold Mate", "My Article" or "My Japan help-mate."[9]

Obviously, Simpson "introduced a strong emphasis on Social Class and a distinct note of racial prejudice," which would become the "Hall-mark of White Anglo-Saxon relationships" of the nineteenth century.[10] This view was based on the old double standard of what was appropriate sexual behaviour for male and female, as well as its Victorian corollary, which ascribed to women a purely sexual identity and three possible roles in life: virgin, mother, or whore.

Interestingly enough, Governor Simpson set out to fragment the Native women's unique position as leader of their tribes. "It must be understood that to affect this change, we have no petticoat politicians," he was quoted as saying.[11]

Thus, the discrimination began by legal process. "I want to get rid of the Indian problem," Deputy Superintendent of Indian Affairs, Duncan Campbell Scott, told the House of Commons in the early 1920s. "Our object is to continue until there is not a single Indian in Canada that has not been absorbed into the body politic, and there is no Indian question and no Indian department."[12]

In 1897 a Quebec civil servant wrote that "Before a quarter of a century is gone, perhaps the savages will be no more than just a memory. . . . Is it wise to sacrifice, for needs that are more fictional than real of this race that is leaving, the interests of the majority of the State?"[13] These arguments were repeated, virtually verbatim, by a judgement of the Quebec court of appeal in 1974 in the case against the Quebec government's hydro-electric project by the James Bay Cree.

Unfortunately, history has concerned itself exclusively with the lives and opinions of such famous men which have perpetuated the bleak views of Native women. This historical impact has bastardized our Native women and communities. We were thrown into a relationship with the Crown, through the *Indian Act*.[14] The *Indian Act* essentially was an excellent means of control. It is obvious that once we were herded onto reservations, the Indian agents and federal bureaucrats were more than able to exercise the ability to monitor every movement. We could not leave the reserves to visit other clans, bands, or reservations. In essence, if you had families or extended families on other reserves, you were denied the freedom to visit them. It is not surprising that it was not until the 1960s that our people were allowed to vote and the term "person" no longer meant an individual other than an Indian.

The obvious process of genocide continued from Governor Simpson's initial interventions. It desensitized us to our culture. This was reinforced through the Residential School process. It utilized Section 114 (2A) of the *Indian Act* which states: "The Minister may, in accordance with this act, establish, operate and maintain schools for Indian children. The Minister may require an Indian who has attained the age of six years to attend school."[15]

The tales of sexual, physical, mental, and emotional abuse that Native children faced for two decades are only now surfacing as legal issues in Canada. These children were taken from their families at a very young age — off to Indian Residential Schools — miles away from home, only to see their parents briefly each summer if they were lucky. Many weren't that lucky. Many, many children died in these "prisons," as our parents called them.

Here they were taught that everything "Indian" was evil. They were not to identify with anything Native. They were not even to use their given names. As such, they were victims in the long process of colonization which works the same way everywhere — its policies geared toward displacement and elimination of indigenous culture — genocide. The residential school, wherever it appeared, has always been a part of that policy. "As adults many consciously did not teach their children a Native language so that they might avoid the punishments incurred through its use at school," says an interviewee in *Resistance and Renewal*.[16] This was reiterated by my grandmother.

This process of paternalistic colonization has had the greatest impact on Native women. Not only did they lose their traditions, culture, and identity, they lost the traditional honour and stature for which they were acknowledged. They also lost the "bonding" ability of mothering and parenting skills. After all, if you can't identify with who you really are, you do suffer major social and emotional problems.

It is not surprising, then, that Native women face such horrendous socio-economic problems today. Family breakdown, social disintegration and assimilation policies have had the impact of increasing gaps in the support services for Native women. There are no present designated residences such as shelters, healing circles, social service facilities (outside of jail) specifically for Native women. One thing we know for sure is that the central force of control and manipulation has placed us in a position of submissiveness. This compounds the oppression of a mainly white male system because it denies Native women many basic freedoms and rights. The present problems of non-consultation of Aboriginals on issues concerning all our policies of governing is in direct conflict with the Canadian Charter of Rights and Freedoms.

It was not unexpected to see the Oka situation hit the national and international news when it provided evidence of respect towards women still remaining. Yet the demeaning treatment of Native women by society at large persists. As a result, it is fitting that Max Yalden of the Canadian Human Rights Commission called for the *Indian Act* and the Department of Indian affairs to be dumped, deeming them "paternalistic and colonial relics of the past Ottawa should replace with constitutional and legislative action, recognizing the unique status of Natives and treat them as equals."[17]

We must open our minds, emotions, and spirits, for we have been imprisoned in tight little worlds of man-made creations. As part of this diminution, Native women have been traumatized beyond comprehension. To illustrate this, I would like to share a personal evaluation. "It's one thing to be a woman in this Society, it's another thing to be a minority, but God help you should you be a Native woman. It's a double whammy."

As our elders have said, it is through education that change will come. We must come back to the sacred circle of life and educate people of all nations as to the spiritual value of Aboriginal peoples and the positive value that brings to *all* life. There is currently an upsurge in Native people returning to the traditional teaching and values. There is a need for healing in our global community. The elders say that there will be a time of coming together, a time of healing. As keepers of the earth, we will take our rightful place in leading our brothers and sisters from all nations to peace and harmony. And the vital role of women in this process will be restored.

Notes

1 Statement of Bob Hawkesworth NDP, MLA for Calgary Mountainview, Meeting with Native Women and Outreach Workers, 22 August 1990, Calgary, Alberta.
2 Mililanni Trasil, recorder, "Summary of the Gathering—day 1," *Fire Weed: A Feminist Quarterly*, 22, "Native Women" (Winter 1986): 28-30.
3 Osennotion and Skonaganlikird, "Our World," *Canadian Woman Studies/Les Cahiers de la femme*, 10 (Summer/Fall 1989) :8
4 As told to Jane Silman, *Enough is Enough: Aboriginal Women Speak Out* (Toronto: The Women's Press, 1987), p. 226.
5 During the Oka Crisis, September-October 1990. National and International Television.
6 Richard Wagamese, "Ancient Law of Harmony," *Calgary Herald*, 1 October 1990.
7 Bob Hawkesworth NDP, MLA for Calgary Mountainview, Meeting with Native Women and Outreach workers, 22 August 1990, Calgary, Alberta.
8 Kathleen Jamieson, *Indian Women and the Law in Canada: Citizens Minus* (Ottawa: Advisory Council on the Status of Women/Indian Rights for Indian Women, 1978), p. 8.
9 Ibid., p. 9.
10 Ibid.
11 Ibid.
12 George Erasmus, "Twenty Years of Disappointed Hopes," in Boyce Richardson, ed., *Drumbeat* (Toronto: Summerhill Press, 1989), p. 11.
13 Ibid.
14 Osennotion and Skonaganlikird, "Our World," p. 12.
15 *Indian Act*, R.S.C. 1956, c. 40, s. 28.
16 Celia Haig-Brown, *Resistance and Renewal: Surviving the Indian Residential School* (Vancouver: Tillacum Library, 1988), p. 110.
17 *Canadian Human Rights Act*, R.S.C. 1976-77, s. 63 (2).

Chapter 8

THE IMPACT OF SOCIAL CHANGE
ON MUSLIM WOMEN

Sheila McDonough

The most salient characteristic of most Muslim women's lives at present is that their cultures are caught up in rapid social change. There are estimated to be over a billion Muslims in the world currently living in many countries, from Indonesia through South Asia to the Arab world and Africa. Any generalization about the status of Muslim women cannot easily be applied to so many diverse cultural situations. To be a Muslim woman today might have different implications for social roles and self-understanding, depending on whether the person is still, as most Muslim women are, part of a village agrarian hierarchical culture or a city dweller. It would also be relevant to ask many questions about the context: what city, country, class, and education. The attitudes of the husband would also be significant. All these issues would have bearing on what kind of life experiences the particular woman might have had.

Since the beginnings of cross-cultural feminist studies in the late seventies, most authors of general books on Muslim women have been well aware of the difficulties of handling so much diversity and have tried to deal with it by including chapters about different Muslim cultural situations.[1] To make any statement that might apply to all, or even to a majority of Muslim women is as difficult as making any statement that would apply to all Christian women. These two religious cultures have in common the diversity of national, educational, and social backgrounds of their many adherents. This is the first issue we should acknowledge in approaching this subject.

Secondly, we should recognize that many Muslim societies have been subjected to colonization at the hands of European nations, and currently to economic domination by outsiders, and that this experience of humiliating subjugation by foreigners is a crucial factor in shaping much contemporary Muslim discussion about the need to recover distinctive identity. This issue is important as background in considering matters relating to the self-understanding of contemporary Muslim people. Many Muslims, male and female, think of feminism as a characteristic of what they perceive as the morally decadent foreign culture that has been their oppressor for the last two hundred years.

The transition from the hierarchically ordered structures of the medieval Islamic civilizations[2] to the new structures of industrialized societies has been particularly abrupt and painful in many parts of the Muslim world because the changes have been imposed, often harshly, from outside. The British exiled the last Mughal emperor of India and seized control of the country for themselves after the failed revolt of 1857. Almost every part of the Muslim world has suffered similar exploitation, often made worse because the foreigners have been contemptuous of Islamic values and traditions. The violence done to a community's sense of self by imposed transition of this kind is one of the main reasons for the intensity of the quest for identity characteristic of many recent Muslim thinkers.

The impact of domination by outsiders has varied in different Muslim contexts, depending on which foreign nation has been in charge, on whether the control has been political, as well as economic, and how alienating the experience of colonization has been. The author of a recent study on the persistence of patriarchy in Algeria has argued, I think persuasively, that patriarchy has been more persistent in Algeria than in the neighbouring regimes of Tunisia and Morocco because the French domination of Algeria was more extensive and severe.[3] One important issue we must consider in looking at Muslim women's lives is the increase of neo-patriarchy in a number of Muslim countries. It is true that the issue is more significant in some Muslim nations, as opposed to others, but it is also true that the tendency seems to be increasing throughout the Muslim world at present.

From this perspective, we should consider neo-patriarchy as an aspect of neo-traditionalism. I will use the latter term rather than fundamentalism to refer in a general way to the new revival movements among Muslims: the "neo" helps indicate that this is a new phenomenon, and not a simple reversion to medieval patterns of life and thought. Neo-patriarchy is a reactive movement to social change which seeks to embrace some new elements, such as technology, and the end of medieval kingship, while rejecting others, such as the separation of religion and politics, and the full participation of women in public life.[4] Movements of this type are active throughout the Muslim world, particularly in cities and among students. The neo-traditionalists usually claim that they represent a more authentic form of Islamic identity than do the other groups and leaders competing for the allegiance and support of Muslim populations.

Since the disappearance of kingship and foreign dominance in the years following World War II, parliaments in most Muslim countries have been struggling to determine the personal and family laws that would be appropriate for their people. Each country has worked out its own legal code, and no one model has been acceptable for other Muslim countries. This diversity is in itself a new development, because a greater uniformity had characterized the medieval codes. In the first instance, the Prophet Muhammad, during the last ten years of his life, had been the political, economic, military, and judicial head of the new community that had been established following the dictates of the new revelation, the Qur'an.

This experience of living according to revelation has shaped Muslim expectations as to the nature of an ideal social order.

After the death of the Prophet Muhammad, his followers attempted with varying degrees of success to live according to the norms established by the first community of believers. In the ninth century, about two hundred years after the death of the Prophet, some members of the community succeeded in working out and writing down a structure of religious law, the Shariah, which has since served to indicate a normative ideal primarily for ritual practice and personal law. Sunni Muslims have generally accepted four schools of Islamic law, and Shia Muslims have their own. Thus, the Shariah represents a normative ideal, but in actual practice scholars have agreed to accept differences of opinion on certain issues. In medieval Islam, the Shariah functioned in society as an effective source of personal and ritual law, although the rulers also enacted various other forms of legislation separate from the Shariah. The Shariah was never the exclusive source of the community's law, but it always served to indicate an ideal. It was generally believed that by the tenth century the major content of the Shariah has been worked out by the scholars.

Since most issues affecting women come under the heading of personal, as opposed to commercial, criminal, or military law, these issues, in the medieval period, were normally dealt with according to the Shariah. In the modern period, the issue becomes more complex, because the nation state is playing a new role in shaping laws of all kind. Fundamental to the Shariah question is the issue of the role of the Ulema, scholar-jurists, in a modern state. Since the medieval kings have disappeared, the role of the Ulema as advisors to kings no longer exists. Thus, in a modern state, the question arises: how are the Ulema to relate to an elected body of legislators? Since the Ulema are the traditional experts on personal law, and hence on the role of women, the status of the Ulema in society affects the making of laws relating to women. In the case of Iran, the Ulema have taken control of the state since the revolution of 1979. In the instance of Turkey, the Ulema were excluded from law-making authority by the Turkish revolution of the 1920s which opted to use the Swiss legal code. Most other nations have preferred some third possibility in which the Ulema are consulted, but do not have final authority.

Another question is whether the training institution of the Ulema, the *madrasa*, should remain unchanged, and indeed whether women might aspire to be members of that class. Some nations, notably Egypt, have modernized the curriculum and standards of training for the Ulema, particularly in the respected university of al-Azhar, which has been a centre of religious scholarship since the tenth century. In most Muslim countries, however, the nature of religious education has not changed much, and that means that the *madrasa*-educated Ulema often find themselves at odds with the graduates of modern universities, who usually dominate the government. They are even more at odds with many female university graduates. New forms of political organization involve new structures of making and imposing laws, and new types of universities, and these new developments undercut the traditional positions and prestige of the Ulema. When there is an increase in neo-patriarchy, as in Algeria, it usually follows that the Ulema are being granted more responsibility for personal law. The situation is complicated further by the actual neo-traditionalist organizations, which usually support the Ulema to some extent, but are not merely adjuncts to these religious scholar-jurists.

The major neo-traditionalist organizations, such as the Jamaat Islami of South Asia and the Muslim Brotherhood of the Arab world, have emerged in the context of new industrialized cities like Delhi and Cairo. The leadership of these groups has usually come from laymen rather than from the Ulema; the organizations have become powerful in part because they have provided services to the poor in the cities. They have strong, well-organized groups, which serve their members with many forms of needed service such as youth groups, men's and women's groups, help with jobs, education, health, funerals, and other needs characteristic of rural immigrants to big cities. These groups have members from many different backgrounds, and their effective organizational patterns make them a powerful social force.

The example of women's dress indicates certain characteristics of the thought and practices of these new organizations. They explicitly claim to be recovering the original heritage, but they are adapting their understanding of that heritage as they move away from more medieval patterns of existence to survival in the new industrialized world. For example, in some traditional societies, women were veiled in a way that covered face and hands as well as bodies. These newer groups stress covering the body and the hair, but leaving hands and face uncovered. In the latter case, a woman can move easily through difficulties posed by modern life, such as traffic jams, whereas completely veiled women were more totally restricted to staying home. The dress which leaves the face free serves to signal to men that the woman should not be bothered as she moves about, and it leaves her free to pursue her activities.

Two of the factors encouraging the improvement in women's situation everywhere in the world are education and the vote. In the Muslim world, as elsewhere, much remains to be done in these areas, but for our purposes here, let us recognize that these neo-traditionalist groups have not usually opposed either women's education or suffrage. Some of them prefer to insist on the separation of the sexes so they want female education done separately all the way through graduate education.

The man whose teachings are the most widely read of all the neo-traditionalist writers is Mawlana Mawdudi of India and Pakistan.[5] His books have been translated into many languages and have been extremely influential in every part of the Muslim world. He emphasizes that

Muslims will recover their cultural power through moral firmness and strength. His writings portray Western society as corrupt, exploitative, and coldly inhumane, with no family values, mutual support, or caring manifest in the lives of its citizens. His writings are particularly vivid in their portrayal of these evils, but the perception that Western societies are morally inferior to Muslim societies is very widespread in the Muslim world. The neo-traditionalists exploit this negative stereotyping of the morally decadent West, but almost all Muslims share this feeling to some degree.

The neo-traditionalists consciously and unconsciously exploit the fear and fantasies about the rampant and unrestrained sexuality which many Muslims imagine characterizes Western societies. The fervour to have neo-traditionalists control the industrializing Muslim nations is at least partially related to determination to retain control over sexual mores so that the imagined dissolution of family life and values many not take place. In Mawdudi's writings on birth control, he argues explicitly that sexuality should be understood as designed for purposes of procreation, but that unrestrained sexuality must be combatted.[6] Although medieval Muslim religious thought did not develop a notion of natural law and even stressed an opposite idea, namely a philosophy which saw no link between space-time instants other than the creative power of God, neo-traditionalist thinkers like Mawdudi emphasize natural law.

The natural for women, in Mawdudi's thought, is to be fertile and devoted to the well-being of husband and children. The unnatural for a Muslim woman would be to practise birth control so that she would reject her natural maternal impulses and give way to an immoral quest for sexual gratification. In Mawdudi's imagination, if the woman goes in for unrestrained sexual abandonment, she will lose her nurturing capacities and become self-centred and wicked. This fear of the uncaring, sexually depraved female is one of the major themes stimulating Muslim fears of social change. None of the Muslim neo-traditionalists is opposed to technology, or to the transformation of the material conditions of living. But there is a great fear of the loss of family solidarity and caring relationships.

The practical results of such attitudes can be recognized in legislative changes. As we noted earlier, the political scientist Peter Knauss has discerned an increase in neo-patriarchal attitudes expressed through legislation in Algeria. Knauss argues that the severe attempts to control women are exemplified in the legal codes of 1984 which are harsher than the laws of 1981. The legal issues, which have been problems for all newly emerging Muslim societies, include polygamy, legal age for matrimony, divorce by verbal repudiation, equal access to divorce, maintenance for divorced women, control by the husband over the wife's freedom of movement, and the right of the woman to choose her husband. In the 1984 code, as implemented by neo-traditionalists in Algeria, the matri-

monial guardian of the girl is required to be present at the marriage and
can prevent the marriage, and polygamy is permitted. The right of the
woman to work outside the house depends on the permission of the husband, to whom the wife must be obedient, and divorce is the exclusive
right of the husband, except in certain limited cases.[7] The determination
to control seems to be hardening.

Neo-patriarchy can be understood, at least in part, as an effort to
combat the possible disintegration of the known social order. We can
gain some insight into the feelings of anomie and despair in some Muslim
societies from the writings of Muslim novelists. An Arab oil engineer,
Abdel Rahman Munif, has written a powerful novel about the destruction of an ancient way of life in one small village. In the novel, *Cities of
Salt*, oil is discovered near the village. As a result, much money flows into
the pockets of local officials, but the people are uprooted and confused.
They have to leave the homes where their people have lived for generations, and the men have to work at construction jobs for the Western engineers who arrive to exploit the oil. Some of the people are driven mad
by this experience, some become corrupt and exploitative, and others retreat into depressed states of alienation. The novel conveys a vivid sense
of the total confusion of the people who cannot understand what has
happened to them.[8]

In *Cities of Salt*, one illuminating scene occurs when the men, who
have left their village to work in a harbour unloading goods for the
American oil engineers, see a boat full of American women in bikinis.
The impact of this exposure to the nakedness of women has a profoundly
disturbing effect on the Arab men. Some become haunted and obsessed,
even maddened by the impact of a form of sexuality they have no way to
relate to. The Muslim men are horrified by a society in which men care-
lessly flaunt their women for all to see and frightened by their inability to
restrain their reactions. Muslim men and women can easily conclude
from such experiences that Western women who would so display themselves could have no honour, self-respect, or virtue. They also conclude
that the men have no respect for the women. The villagers perceive the
moral world of the engineers as a world of wealth, power, and depravity.

The fact that the author is himself an oil engineer means that he
knows that the perceptions that the two groups, the villagers and the engineers, have of each other are not entirely correct in either case. The
novel is powerful precisely because it suggests the impersonality of the
forces at work. The people find their world disintegrating for no reasons
they can understand, and those doing the destruction have almost no idea
of the fruits of their actions in terms of the local people. The absence of
communication between the groups is one of the main reasons for the
tragedy.

We can also gain insight into these societies from the work of anthropologists. Although the people of the *Cities of Salt* novel are imagi-

nary, they do, nevertheless, reflect a culture which the author knows did exist in the world he knew. One excellent anthropological study of a similar Muslim society, one in which the medieval life-styles have scarcely changed, is *Behind the Veil in Arabia*, a study of the people of Oman, in the southern part of the Arabian peninsula. The author's research offers valuable insights into gender roles, and into the self-understanding of men and women within this traditional culture. It is a culture in which the women have been very heavily veiled, much more so than in most Muslim societies. The men and women have led highly segregated lives.[9]

The people of this society perceive themselves as part of a harmonious social order, in which roles and values are well integrated in the personalities of the people. Because of the segregation, neither the males nor the females have much knowledge or understanding of how persons in the other group see themselves. However, members of each gender have strongly internalized codes relating to proper and respectful behaviour. Living according to these codes is understood to promote harmony and balance in social existence. Since the ruler is very conservative, this society presents one of the most segregated forms of Muslim life that has existed. Within that context, however, the understanding is that males and females have complementary natures and roles. The men are expected to be the political, religious, and family authorities, and to deal with all aspects of public life. The women have the major responsibility for the home and child-rearing: they have no economic responsibilities.[10] The author characterizes what she perceives of the self-understanding and values of the men as follows:

> Even among their peers and equals, they seem reticent and reserved, striving towards a performance of gracefulness and style that honours the integrity of others and offers offense toward no one, women included. To praise women would be incompatible with their sense of modesty, to derogate them would be inconsistent with their sense of pride.[11]

Wikan comments that both males and females value respectful and modest behaviour towards persons of the other sex; each person feels part of a meaningful whole. Within their different realms, males and females both feel the need to internalize standards of honour. Wikan observes that anthropologists have often stressed the importance of honour for men, but that they have usually failed to understand that the females also value their personal honour. The women of Oman, in talking with Wikan, maintained that external controls, such as the veil, could not prevent prostitution and adultery if individual men and women had bad characters. The self-respect of the women came from their internal standards of morality and self-regard and the respect of their friends. She describes how the women understand their duties and rights: "As the women see it, a woman is entitled to consideration and respect, a view to which their experience testifies."[12] She notes that the women have a strong sense of modesty and that they have faith in the inherent justice of their system.

It seems to me that much of the tragedy of the contemporary Muslim world, as suggested by the *Cities of Salt* derives from situations in which social change has not been occurring as a result of leadership from within the community making self-conscious choices that could build on the internal strengths of the people. I can see a link between the imaginary people of the novel and the actual people described in the anthropological study of Oman. The Arab author of the novel imagined his people disintegrated and driven mad by too rapid and insensitive social change. It is the nature of the change, its speed and dehumanizing character, rather than anything intrinsic to the people, that makes for disintegration. It seems to me that the people of Oman represent something of what Muslim culture was like in many parts of the world before the impact of the impersonal and debilitating forces of modernity. One is left with the question as to whether social change could possibly come about in some less stressful and alienating fashion.

This is not to say that a woman who tried to move out of the restrictions of a society like that of Oman would have an easy time. Her difficulties would arise from her attempt to become a new kind of being, a type incomprehensible to both the males and the females, because she would be moving beyond established boundaries. In describing the conflicts resulting from women taking on new roles, some writers have used the phrase "the unveiled voice" to indicate how startling it is in such a society to hear speech of a kind that has never been heard before.

An example of such a person is Amatalrauf al-Sharki, born in 1958 in North Yemen. It was radio that initiated the changes in Amatalrauf's life. She started giving children's broadcasts on the local radio when she was twelve, and her voice was so good she was moved to news programmes. Her mother supported her, although the family believed she did this work while totally veiled. Her father supported her after another male relative tried to have her work stopped. The family's situation was insecure, because if a female relative were perceived by their social world as immodest, the whole family would suffer a loss of honour. They supported her ambition, but they knew she was taking risks. She writes of her feelings as she got older: "Inside me I didn't like that veil any more. I felt it was a big lie. . . . At the same time, I was not completely convinced that I should not wear the veil. That was around 1973 when I still thought that women were supposed to wear the veil and that was the way it was."[13]

She made friends with other working women, acted, still veiled, in some plays, taught in a literacy school, and developed a family affairs programme on the radio which became very successful. She and her mother, both still veiled, took part in a parade in 1972 to celebrate the Day of Revolution in Yemen. She wore a military uniform under her veil. Later she went to university in Egypt. When she returned to Yemen, she refused the veil and went on television unveiled. This was too much for her family, who felt themselves disgraced. She returned to Egypt.

This story seems to encapsulate the social reality of the processes that have been at work among Muslim women for over a hundred years. Muslim families are often very close, and the concern the parents felt for this strong-minded daughter is typical of the emotional distress occasioned by non-conforming children. It is significant to note the confusion felt by both parents and children as their different values create conflict. Most educated Muslim women today have mothers who were illiterate, and secluded, so the tensions involved in role changes across generations are severe.

Not all Muslim peoples have been completely overwhelmed by the impact of modernity. Some individual Muslim women have managed to move competently from their older cultural patterns into a new way of living. In an autobiography entitled *From Purdah to Parliament*, Shaista Ikramullah describes the enclosed world of her childhood in which modesty was inculcated in young girls at an early age. She also indicates, however, the strength of character of her mother and of many other women who wore veils outside the home. She shows the interest and complexity of their lives as they interacted with their friends in their enclosed female world and struggled to raise their children well.[14]

Shaista Ikramullah became interested in the struggle for India's independence as she matured in the thirties and began political life by making speeches to secluded women. This led her mother to restrict her further, on the grounds that this was improper behaviour in a young girl. After her marriage, however, her husband sympathized with her views and encouraged her political activism. So she went on to become a member of parliament, and subsequently one of Pakistan's representatives at the United Nations. In this fairly straightforward account, not untypical of many Muslim women's lives, one can recognize a reasonable transition from the mother's world to a new world of responsibilities and political activism for the daughter. But the worlds are still linked, by affection and respect. The strong character of the daughter is not unrelated to the strong and morally upright character of the mother. This point is similar to issues discussed by the anthropologist Wikan when she observed that anthropologists have often noted the cultural importance of male honour but have not acknowledged a comparable significance for women's dignity and self respect.[15] The veiling of women has been one aspect of the Islamic tradition, but the tradition has also stressed the moral autonomy of women as persons responsible to God, their Creator and their final Judge.

We will next consider the writings of several important Muslim women authors who perceive themselves as self-consciously advocating changes in the roles and status of Muslim women. One of the most controversial of these writers is Nawal El Saadawi. An Egyptian doctor and director of Public Health, she lost her position because of her writings, and was subsequently briefly imprisoned in 1981. Her books have particular importance because of her open discussion of incest, rape, and physical abuse within the family. She also deals with conditions in women's jails, and the experiences of prostitutes in Muslim cities like Cairo.[16] These issues are only beginning to be part of public discourse as a result of the work of women like El Saadawi. There is now a network of women seeking to raise consciousness on such matters. A newsletter published in France provides information about women under Muslim law.[17] The work of Nawal El Saadawi has opened the process of discussion of the abuses and suffering of women.

One of the best known Muslim feminist writers is the professor of sociology, Fatima Mernissi, whose book, *Beyond the Veil*, first published in 1975, has been reissued with a new introduction in 1987. Mernissi acknowledges that fundamentalism has grown in importance in the decade since she first wrote, but she is nevertheless optimistic about the future of Muslim societies. Her optimism comes partly from observation of the many changes taking place in actual life in Morocco such as attendance at beaches and television plays with amusing family conflict situations. She thinks that political rhetoric and real life are often far apart in contemporary Muslim societies. She acknowledges that the fundamentalist young males, often products of the same modern educational system as the unveiled females who oppose them, seek to affirm their cultural and masculine identities by advocating increased control over women.[18]

Mernissi says we should realize that women within the traditional societies were not entirely unaware that they were sometimes vulnerable to victimization by men. A veiled woman in a traditional society was often a person with a strong sense of honour and self-respect. Mernissi refers to the insights of her eighty-year-old aunt whose brothers had refused to give her her legitimate share of the inheritance. Mernissi's Aunt Hachouma thinks that men often cheat women if they can. She listens to her transistor radio and hears about events in the outside world. She interprets the Iranian revolution, and the fundamentalist activism of the young Arab males as further instances of men attempting to cheat and dominate women.[19] Mernissi argues that many Muslim women need to see political and economic realities as clearly as her old aunt does, and to learn how to take appropriate action.

Mernissi has published another volume entitled *Islam and Women* in which she ventures into the intellectual realms that had previously been restricted to male scholars. She discusses the formative period of the life of the Prophet Muhammad, the articulating of the Hadith collections, and the establishing of the orthodox codes of Islamic law. She considers in detail the contexts in which Qur'anic passages relating to women were revealed, and she also analyzes the sources of the Hadith stories that have most commonly been used to legitimate the subordination of women. She uses the classical methodologies for her work, but she also says there ought to be a greater attempt at synthesis. She recognizes that the classical legal scholars sought to limit their subjectivity and that they did so by including many diverse points of view. Her approach is to honour the great and sustained intellectual effort that has been involved over the centuries in articulating the Muslim science of jurisprudence, but she wishes to reopen certain issues, and to move the discussions further along.[20]

She understands the Prophet Muhammad to have been a person whose charm and gentleness of manner endeared him to all his followers, male and female alike, and to have been a man very sensitive to matters of justice. She understands prophecy to be the effective communication of a vision of a potentially better future; she thinks that persons who respond to the prophetic vision are transformed in their expectations and that they should be enabled to devise better and more humane political and economic structures. She says that the first Muslim women converted by the prophetic vision of the Qur'an experienced a liberating release from the situation in which they had been the property of males, with few rights of their own. Mernissi sees Surah 33:35 of the Qur'an as a powerful affirmation of the rights of women believers to be judged before God in the same way as the men are judged.

She also thinks, however, that the social context in which the Qur'an was revealed led to a restriction of the equality that the new revelation was bringing to women. Since the men gained much of their wealth through war and seizing booty, and since women were excluded from war, wealth tended to be in the control of men. Under these circumstances, the Qur'an affirmed the right of men to govern the women, since the men were in control of the sources of wealth. In a similar manner, she analyzes the original contexts of issues such as the veiling of women and the rights of husbands to punish wives, and suggests in every case a re-examination of the issues, based on discussions between men and women believers as to how they understand their faith. Her opinion is that the Muslim leaders after Muhammad, and in particular the Caliph Umar, were generally much less sensitive to issues of women's rights than the Prophet had been. She therefore maintains that greater knowledge among Muslim women of the roots of their tradition will lead them to understand the Prophet Muhammad much better as a person who had been filled with a vision of a better future. Her expectation is that a prophetic understanding for today would involve hope and readiness to work for greater social and economic justice.[21]

I would again note the significance of *madrasa* education with respect to these issues. It is a form of education which requires familiarity with the many texts of medieval law and with the reasoning of those early schools of law. It does not, however, encourage rethinking of the applications of the legal principles. Modernist Muslims have maintained that the

Qur'anic revelation taught basic principles such as justice and the equality of all Muslims, and that Muslims were expected to work out the specific applications of these principles differently in different historical contexts. Conservative Muslims usually argue that the revelation gave a final
system which is ahistorical and which can and should be applied in the
same way universally. Members of the Ulema class have been fairly consistent in many Muslim countries in advocating a strict adherence to the
classical Shariah because the uniform system of education they have received has encouraged them to think in this way. As long as the classical
form of religious education does not change, the Ulema are likely to continue to have the same convictions and attitudes. Mernissi's work, however, challenges the Ulema on their own grounds, and demands reopen-
ing of discussion of theological and legal issues relating to women.

In general, in most Muslim countries, the matter of opening mem-
bership in the Ulema class to women has not seriously been raised, as yet.
The traditional members would naturally oppose it, because it would be
an innovation. Also, more conservative Muslims have maintained that
menstruating women must not enter Mosques, and this would militate
against any significant role for women as religious leaders. It is possible
for women to become judges in the religious law courts, and, in a few rare
cases, this has occurred. Mernissi herself has been working with some
classically trained Moroccan jurists. There is little doubt that her work
will have a significant impact in the long run, but how long that process
may take is incalculable.

It is not impossible for women to achieve recognition for scholarship
on religious matters, although there are as yet few who have achieved this
goal. One example is Bint al-Shati of Egypt. She is a professor of Arabic
language and literature at an Egyptian university and has written more
than sixty books. She has written extensively about Muslim women's lives
during the lifetime of the Prophet and the first four Caliphs. She envisages these women as exemplary models for later believers. She sees them
as notable for their piety and modesty, but also for their courage in re-
nouncing traditional securities by opting to follow a new religion. She
considers herself conservative, but she conceives of the exemplary Muslim women as strong persons and she affirms the equality of all persons
before God.[22]

We also find women supportive of the neo-traditionalist movements.
One such woman writer is the Egyptian Zaynab al-Ghazali who was imprisoned along with male members of the Muslim Brotherhood in 1966.
She was released in 1971. Like her male counterparts, she believes that a
properly constituted Islamic system of government will bring justice to
everyone. She conceives of a one-party government headed by pious
Muslims. The logic of this argument is that democracy is man-made,
whereas the Islamic system is designed by God. She is like other vision

aries of this kind in imagining a transformed world in which present-day abuses will cease to exist.[23]

The neo-patriarchal attitudes of many of the young educated males, and their woman supporters, leads them to work together with the Ulema to create obstacles to changes in family law. Since the medieval monarchs have gone from most Muslim countries, the Ulema seek ways of exercising their influence within the context of the new models of political life. The young neo-patriarchal males see the Ulema as the upholders of traditional morality, which supports male dominance. As the Algerian case indicates, the more severe colonization has been, the more pressure seems to exist to recover threatened identity by reviving medieval hierarchical norms of family life. No one is suggesting reviving medieval forms of political life, or slavery, so only certain elements of the past are retained, and others are abandoned. The choice of which elements to retain is selective, and seems to focus on controlling women so that the hierarchical family does not change, even though the hierarchical political and economic orders have been transformed.

The Iranian case is the most extreme example of repressive family legislation. In Ayatollah Khomeini's writings, he has maintained that male superiority is manifest, and that "a woman who has entered into a permanent marriage is not allowed to leave the house without her husband's permission. She must submit herself to any pleasure he desires. . . . If a woman does not obey her husband . . . she is then sinful and is not entitled to food, clothes, housing or intercourse."[24]

From this perspective, women are defined as mothers and educators of children; their social existence is characterized exclusively by motherhood. Khomeini believes that a good nation will develop if the mothers are good. Conversely, since he envisages Western society as decadent and destructive of morality, the feminist movement is seen as a form of social disease, leading ultimately to the total decay of a culture.

The legal implications following from such a perspective stress punishment for females who deviate from the state's designation of their correct roles. In present-day Iran, women and men can be arrested for walking on the street if they are not married, or family members. The *hudood* punishments are the punishments based directly on the Qur'an. Most modern Muslim nations have qualified or modified them, but Iran applies them literally. This includes lashes and stoning for women and men convicted by the evidence of four male or equivalent witnesses. Women convicted of lesbian activity can also be flogged unless they repent before the judge.[25] The other Muslim nations that apply these punishments are Saudi Arabia and the Sudan.

The legal situation for Muslim women is volatile because the political situation in many Muslim nations is unstable: politicians sometimes compete with each other by promising to further Islamicize the country and to impose more restrictions on women. As we noted, this has occurred recently in Algeria, where the 1984 code is more restrictive than the 1981 one. In Pakistan, a Marriage Reform Code was passed in 1961 which restricted polygamy, raised the age of marriage, and established the need for registry of marriage and divorce. The neo-traditionalists have continued to object to these reformed marriage laws. The present government, in the summer 1991, said it would establish Shariah law, but in a manner that would not change the country's customs. This satisfies no one because it does not concede the control over women that the Ulema want, and neither does it guarantee more reforms in the interest of women. It is an awkward political juggling act trying to balance incompatible views.[26]

The Egyptian parliament has had numerous debates in recent years as to whether further restrictions on women should be imposed. The Muslims of India are also in turmoil over these questions. Although India is explicitly a secular state, with a population of eight hundred million, its one hundred million Muslim citizens are still governed by their own traditional code of personal law. The government has not yet dared to impose changes in Muslim personal law, lest further communal violence break out. In a controversial court case, an elderly Muslim woman, Shah Bano, after years of separation from her husband, was divorced. He, a lawyer, would not pay to support her, since Muslim law does not require that he do so. An Indian judge awarded her some support, but a public outcry broke out, because the judge had made comments about the Qur'an and Muslim law, and a higher court reversed the decision.[27] For many Indian Muslims, this decision is perceived as a victory against the efforts of the majority Hindu population to swallow up Islam. Ironically, it is the fundamentalist Hindu party, the BJP, that wants to bring Islamic personal law into line with reformed Hindu law, so that all citizens of India are subject to the same law. The more liberal Congress Hindus have favoured not interfering with the minority community.

Turkey has had the Swiss code since the early twenties, when the revolution led by Ataturk rejected the political and religious structures of the Ottoman empire. Religious life was separated from state control and became personal. This system has lasted over seventy years now, and the Turkish population continues to be over ninety per cent Muslim. A reform of this kind, which excludes the Ulema from legislative authority, and which changes personal law codes, is not necessarily unacceptable to a Muslim population. In modern Turkey, the problems of unemployment mean that women still do not participate as fully in economic life as men do.[28] Tunisia has also had a more liberal legal code since 1957.[29] The women's movements in most Muslim countries are aware that changing the laws is one important goal but that legal changes, without equivalent economic development and an increase in numbers of jobs available, will not solve all the problems of women.

The volatility of the legal issues is a symptom of the social and economic instability of the various nations. Bangladesh has a Muslim woman prime minister and a Muslim woman leader of the opposition. Although it is one of the poorest nations, subject to terrible natural disasters, the present government is opting to spend money on education rather than on the military, and this may have positive results. Other Muslim nations are spending huge amounts on arms, and this makes rational development more difficult. The issues of legal discrimination against women are linked with the wider matters of economic development and militarization of third world countries, and these are matters in which the Muslim nations tend to be caught up in the wider patterns of late-twentieth-century life.

The novelists of the Muslim world have been writing, directly and indirectly, about gender issues for over a hundred years. Recent North African literature tends to stress alienation and depersonalization.[30] Some of the writers imply the imminence of a destructuring of society in which males may lose their authoritative roles. Some writers suggest that the males hover on the brink of the loss of their traditional masculinity, must endure a demystification of sexuality, and are threatened by an implicit demand for a new form of being. One critic writes:

> Analysis of the novels reveals the use of a common narrative structure: the female character condemns personal and social failure, demystifies history and originates the liberation of man through the power of fantasy. She is therefore represented as a paradigm of the revolutionary ideal which must remain alive if man wants to be free.[31]

This kind of vision of a leap into a new form of being is by no means easy, given the chaotic economic and political realities in these countries. But it is not beyond imagination, either, as these writers indicate. The Muslim tradition contains strong elements of revolutionary idealism, linked with the images of Abraham, Moses, and Muhammad — images of exodus, *hijra*, going forth to create unimagined new forms of life and hope. One Muslim writer dreams about the future as follows: "Nous fonderons la science de l'amour. Les hommes sont reduits à aimer ou à se demettre. Et si cela s'appelle utopie, et si cela s'appelle mensonge, et si cela s'appelle délire, dites-moi ou est l'arme qui anéantira cette race de fous."[32] Writers of this kind are engaged in constructing imaginary worlds in which patriarchy may be transcended. But how long it may take to realize such dreams is another question.

Given the volatility of the political, social, and legal structures of the various Muslim nations, prediction would be unwise. The strength of the neo-traditionalist movements in the eighties was not foreseen, and what the nineties may bring forth remains to be seen. The Gulf War is relatively recent and its effects cannot yet be fully understood, although it is not hard to understand why that event may add to the alienation of many Muslims from Europe and America. If that happens, the forces of neo-patriarchy are likely to continue to be powerful, at least in the short run.

Notes

1 Some examples are: Elizabeth Warnock Fernea, ed., *Women and the Family in the Middle East* (Austin: University of Texas Press, 1985); Margot Badran and Miriam Cooke, eds., *Opening the Gates: A Century of Arab Feminist Writing* (Bloomington: Indiana University Press, 1990); Jane Smith, ed., *Women in Contemporary Muslim Societies* (Lewisburg: Bucknell University Press, 1980); and Lois Beck and Nikki Keddie, eds., *Women in the Muslim World* (Cambridge: Harvard University Press, 1978).

2 For insight into the structures of Muslim life in the Middle Ages, see Gustave von Grunebaum, *Medieval Islam: A Study in Cultural Orientation* (Chicago: University of Chicago Press, 1953).

3 Peter R. Knauss, *The Persistence of Patriarchy Class, Gender and Ideology in Twentieth Century Algeria* (New York: Praeger, 1987).

4 Several sources dealing with neo-traditionalist movements are Kalim Bahadur, *The Jama'at-Islami of Pakistan* (Lahore: Progressive Books, 1978); John J. Donohue and John L. Esposito, eds., *Islam in Transition: Muslim Perspectives* (New York: Oxford University Press, 1982); and R. Hrair Dekmejian, *Islam in Revolution: Fundamentalism in the Arab World* (Syracuse: Syracuse University Press, 1988).

5 Khurshid Ahmed and Zafar Ishaq Ansari, *Islamic Perspectives: Studies in Honour of Sayyid Abul A'la Mawdudi* (London: Islamic Foundation, 1979).

6 Khurshid Ahmed, *Birth Control: Its Social, Political, Economic, Moral and Religious Aspects*, trans. Abul A'la Mawdudi (Lahore: Islamic Publications, 1987).

7 John L. Esposito, *Women in Muslim Family Law* (Syracuse: Syracuse University Press, 1982). See also Norman Anderson, *Law Reform in the Muslim World* (London: Athlone Press, 1976).

8 Abdelrahman Munif, *Cities of Salt* (New York: Random House, 1987).

9 Unni Wikan, *Behind the Veil in Arabia: Women in Oman* (Chicago: University of Chicago Press, 1982). Another example is Elizabeth Warnock Fernea, *A Street in Marrakech: A Personal Encounter with the Lives of Moroccan Women* (New York: Anchor Books, 1980).

10 Wikan, *Behind the Veil*, p. 56.

11 Ibid., p. 60.

12 Ibid., p. 62.

13 Badran and Cooke, eds., *Opening the Gates*, p. 378-85.

14 Shaista Ikramullah, *From Purdah to Parliament* (London: Cresset Press, 1965).

15 Wikan, *Behind the Veil*, p. 71-73.

16 Nawal El Saadawi, *The Hidden Face of Eve* (Boston: Beacon Press, 1980).

17 Women living under Muslim laws, International solidarity network, Boîte Postale 23, 34790 Grabels, France. "Women living under Muslim laws is a network of women whose lives are shaped, conditioned or governed by laws, both written and unwritten, drawn from interpretations of the Koran tied up with local traditions. Generally speaking, men and the State use these against women, and they have done so under various political regimes." Dossier 5/6, 1.

18 Fatima Mernissi, *Beyond the Veil: Male-Female Dynamics in Modern Muslim Society*, rev. ed. (Bloomington: Indiana University Press, 1987).

19 Ibid., p. xiii.

20 Fatima Mernissi, *Islam and Women: An Historical and Theological Enquiry*, trans. Mary Jo Lakeland (London: Basil Blackwell, 1991).

21 Ibid., p. 61-64.

22 Ibid.

23 I. J. Boullata, *Trends and Issues in Contemporary Arab Thought* (Albany: SUNY, 1990), p. 124-27.

24 Freda Husain, ed., *Muslim Women* (New York: St. Martin's Press, 1984), p. 48-52.

25 Nayereh Tohidi, "Gender and Islamic Fundamentalism: Feminist Politics in Iran," in Chandra Talpade Mohanty et al., eds., *Third World Women and the Politics of Feminism* (Bloomington: Indiana University Press, 1991), p. 251-67. See also Guity Nashat, ed., *Women and Revolution in Iran* (Boulder, Colorado: Westview Press, 1983), p. 195-216.

26 For a good discussion of the women's movement in Pakistan, see Khawer Mumtaz and Farida Shaheed, eds., *Women of Pakistan* (London: Zed Books, 1987). For the most recent developments, see Arif Husain, "Form over Substance" *The Herald*, Karachi (June 1991): 43-48.

27 Shahida Lateef, *Muslim Women in India: Political and Private Realities* (New Delhi: Kali for Women, 1990), p. 192-201.

28 Janet Browning, *Ataturk's Legacy to the Women of Turkey* (Centre for Middle Eastern and Islamic Studies, University of Durham, England, 1985).

29 Norma Salem, "Islam and the Status of Women in Tunisia," in Husain, ed., *Muslim Women*, p. 141-68.

30 Anne-Marie Nisbet, "The Literary Treatment of Women in the Maghrebian Novel in French," in Husain, ed., *Muslim Women*, p. 100-10.

31 Ibid., p. 103.

32 Ibid., p. 109.

IV

GENRE EXPLORATIONS

Chapter 9

BUDDHIST THOUGHT FROM A
FEMINIST PERSPECTIVE

Eva K. Neumaier-Dargyay

Introduction

Typically, the West has focussed its exploration of the Buddhist tradition mainly on its elaborate philosophical and soteriological theory. Western scholars of Buddhism saw Buddhist thinkers, like Buddhaghosa, Nāgārjuna, or Tsong-kha-pa Blo-bzang grags-pa, as authentic representatives of their individual traditions, be it Sinhalese Theravāda, Indian Madhyamaka, or Tibetan Mahāyāna, and adopted them as their mentors and as superbly qualified for elucidating what Buddhist thought truly is. These Buddhist thinkers became, then, the fathers of the canon for a Western inquiry into the nature of Buddhist thought. That is, the canon as defined by Eastern patriarchy has defined the canon for an academic inquiry done by Western patriarchy. The fact that in this process of inquiry the Buddhist woman and the feminist concern remained shrouded in total invisibility was of no concern to the patriarchs of scholarship.

In their enterprise to unravel the true thought of Buddhism, modern scholars of the Western world mainly focussed on the scholastic and highly technical texts of Buddhism. Consequently, not only did the Buddhist woman remain hidden, but the Buddhist laity did as well. In cases where the laity's belief could not be further ignored, its religious practices were frequently discredited as "pre-buddhist," or "magic," or "folk religion." The scholastic, philosophical texts of Buddhism were written by monks to be studied by their peers. They were not intended for the lay or woman reader or student. As monks had vowed a celibate life, it is not surprising that woman did not figure prominently in these texts. With the absence of any anthropomorphic icon of the divine, male or female, no need arose to engage in a discussion of the "gender" of the ultimate – be it called *tathāgatagarbha*, *śūnyatā*, or whatever. Thus, Buddhism was largely seen as an "egalitarian" religion, a system where gender had no function. True, one is inclined to admit that, within such a homogeneous environment, where author and reader belong to the same gender and to the same privileged group, gender is not a contentious issue – in fact, no issue at all. Categories like gender and race arise only from difference, or *différance*. As long as the two are not pitted against each other, the fissure that divides them remains unrecognized.

But the authors of the great canon[1] of Buddhist thought also wrote simpler texts, like epistles and tractates, designed for the lay reader, who in many cases was a well-educated male aristocrat. We may surmise, however, that in some cases literate women of the privileged classes also read these texts. If we consider these texts, we get a wealth of information regarding how the authors of the canon wanted the Buddhist layman to consider woman and how he should treat issues of love, marriage, etc. For the purpose of our own inquiry here, I want not only to use texts of the canon, but also texts intended for the Buddhist laity which were nevertheless authored by the fathers of the canon.

In this contribution, I want to explore, from a feminist vantage point, certain key concepts of Buddhist thought that have been identified and defined by the male mainstream traditions of Buddhism. The questions that directed my inquiry were: what is Buddhism's vision of its woman followers? What gender speaks? What does the text say if the reader is of feminine gender? Does Buddhism have a potential for engaging in a feminist discourse? Can Buddhism speak to a woman of feminist proclivities? Does Buddhism address all of humanity in its thinking, or just one half of it, i.e., the men? Is the thinking of Buddhism conducive to the thinking of women? I shall also ask what kind of impact feminism has on the Buddhism of our own time, in Asia as well as in the West.

Certain key concepts of Buddhism are subject to this inquiry: (1) The assumption that suffering permeates all of life, and that it is most vividly experienced within those phases of life that are the traditional domain of women: birth, sickness, ageing, and death. Connected with the suffering of birth is the image of woman in a more general sense. (2) Compassion, mainly in its Mahāyānistic interpretation, is seen as a masculine virtue of the bodhisattva; thus "compassion" will be used as a vehicle for the exploration of gender stereotyping. (3) The problematic of "Self" and No-Self will be investigated in the light of recent psychoanalytical studies showing that in general women have a much weaker sense of self than men do, or none at all. Thus, one has to ask, is the question of Self relevant to woman? (4) Finally, the Buddhist vision of the "aim," the realization of the mystical transformation, is explored against the background of the woman's question. It will be argued that the theory of the asexuality of the consummate state is in contrast to the social and cultural reality of the lived tradition.

In this inquiry, the diversity and plurality of the Buddhist tradition ought to be fully recognized. The Buddhist texts make claims ranging from there being only one method for the achievement of liberating insight to there being 84,000 different methods. I will use texts considered representative by their own mainstream traditions as sources for this exploration. But space does not permit me to explore each individual tradition and its own diversification.

Woman: Locus and Cause of Suffering

The fundamental claim as formulated in the statement of the fourfold noble truth, the premise of all Buddhist traditions, is that suffering manifests itself in an examplary fashion in the birthing process, as well as in sickness, ageing, and death. Buddhaghosa (5th century CE) became the authoritative interpreter of the Theravāda tradition. He composed commentaries on almost all the major works of the Pamli *tripiṭaka*. Without exaggeration, we may hear in him the official voice of the Theravāda tradition. In his fundamental work, *Visuddhimagga* (Path of Purification or Path of Purity), he has the following to say about the gestation of the human fetus and about birthing:

> [W]hen this being is born in the mother's womb, he is not born inside a blue or red or white lotus, etc. but on the contrary, like a worm in rotting fish, rotting dough, cess-pool, etc., he is born in the belly in a position that is below the receptacle for undigested food (stomach), above the receptacle for digested food (rectum), between the belly lining and the backbone, which is very cramped, quite dark, pervaded by very fetid draughts redolent of various smells of ordure, and exceptionally loathesome. And on being reborn there, for ten months he undergoes excessive suffering, being cooked like a pudding in a bag by the heat produced in the mother's womb, and steamed like a dumpling of dough, with no bending, stretching, and so on. So this, firstly, is the suffering rooted in the descent into the womb.... The pain that arises in him when the mother gives birth, through his being turned upside-down by the *kamma* produced wind's [forces] and flung into the most fearful passage from the womb, like an infernal chasm, and lugged out through the extremely narrow mouth of the womb, like an elephant through a keyhole, like a denizen of hell being pounded to pulp by colliding rocks – this is the suffering rooted in parturition.[2]

In this passage, the mother's womb is pictured as a pit of filth, and the fetus pitied for being confined to this narrow space. I shall leave the exploration of this passage for the time when we have considered all the pertinent passages because the tenor, as we shall see, is quite repetitive.

In Buddhist thought, birth is not a mere physical event brought about through biological forces, but the result of actions of desire that were carried out in a previous life. The desire to exist is the main force driving the mind of the dead person into re-embodiment, and sexual desire as well as the desire for progeny drives the parents to sexual intercourse, which results in conception. Thus, the discussion of birthing is intricately linked with that of desire. Because the Buddhist discourse of desire knows only a heterosexual scenario, and because the author is invariably male, the object of desire is the female body.[3] As monks, the Buddhist fathers of the canon had a specific vision of the female body as the place of attachment leading to the most painful experience – birth.

Unquestionably, Nāgārjuna (second half of the 2nd century CE) is the foremost voice of early Mahamyamna. He authored two pieces intended for lay readers; these are the *Suhṛllekha* (A Letter to a Friend) and the *Ratnāvalī*.[4] Both works offer spiritual counsel and advice to one of the kings of the Śātavāhana dynasty of Andhra; some evidence points at King Vasiṣṭhīputra Pulumāyi.[5] The letter received broad publicity among the Buddhist community of India, as witnessed by the Chinese pilgrim I-tsing.[6] Bu-ston, monk-scholar of Tibet, and editor-in-chief of the first edition of the *tripiṭaka* in Tibetan, considers the letter to be a guideline for a lay person's spiritual life.

In this letter, Nāgārjuna, explores the different categories of unsalutary acts (v. 12-16), renunciation of sensual passion (v. 21-26), three evil types of women (v. 36), the good woman (v. 37), and the correct view of the body (v. 49-50). Among the unsalutary acts, Nāgārjuna predictably lists *dod chags*, usually translated as "attachment" with the tacit assumption that sexual attachment is meant (*Suhṛllekha*, v. 12).[7] Regardless whether they be centuries old or contemporary, these commentaries see the object of attachment not as a human being who permits us to encounter our own self in this interaction dominated by *eros*. The "object" is devalued for its compound nature (*zag bcas*). As the text speaks with a male voice to a male reader, the "object" of carnal desire (this phrase comes from the commentaries) is generally thought to be "woman" as the generic non-male. Woman here is seen as a thing, pretending to give pleasure while "in reality," i.e., in the life experience of celibate males, she gives only pain. She ought to cause pain because of her very own nature which, like the nature of every other object, is subject to change. This leads to a sense of disappointment and dissatisfaction on the side of the subject, i.e., the speaking male. Thus, the pain is a result both of the object's (i.e., woman's) nature, and therefore beyond control, and of the false expectation of the subject engaged in desire. This scenario constructs the erotic as an activity anchored in the male subject targetted at the passive feminine object. The female body does not deliver what the masculine desire expects. Therefore, the text argues, desire must be wrong, as it causes pain. The narrative does not leave room for desire and the erotic being an intersubjective activity where two individuals engage in an intimate and intricate interplay of desiring and acknowledging each other in their similarity and otherness. The masculine voice of the text does not provide a space where the object could reveal herself as a subject, and by doing so, the masculine subject deprives itself of an erotic encounter. The erotic is discounted as "attachment" or "carnal lust." The underlying assumption is that human desire strives for permanence in all our experiences of a pleasant and pleasurable nature. Is pleasure not nurtured by the sensation of *différance*,[8] by the constant shift of agency from self to other, by the constant change in the place of pleasure? Is not the assumption of an eternal pleasure an impossibility in itself? Is not the nature of pleasure given in its subtlety and fragility? How could something of eternal duration be gratifying and pleasurable? Would such an experience not spell final boredom?

The commentary by Mi-pham states that the king should see desire and the other unsalutary attitudes as his enemies.[9] If one should annihilate desire, it implies that the object of desire, i.e., woman, is equally unworthy. In this discourse, she cannot be acknowledged as other; she can only be exterminated. This leaves the masculine subject in a solitude so that, I am tempted to say, he is like a king without subjects—which makes him a no-king. The Buddhist discourse does not provide space for recognizing the "object" as other, and consequently deprives the agent of its mirror, which results in the dissolution of the agent: *anātman*, the Buddhist concept of negating self and identity.

In v. 36, Nāgārjuna warns his royal friend of three types of women who are not suitable as royal spouses. Their common characteristics are that they lack the social skills required of a queen: they will be allies of the king's enemies, or they attempt to influence the king, or they diminish his fortune. In the next verse, the author describes what kinds of spouses the king should seek. The suitability of these types of women is described in terms of social relationships. A wife ideally suitable for the king should be "kind like a sister"; "dear like a female friend"; one who cares for the king like a mother; or one who is subservient like a maid. Roles typifying the female gender are used by the text to specify the kind of wives suitable for his royal friend. Desirable female qualities, like kindness, affection, care and nurturance, and subservience, seem to be taken from an almost universal catalogue of womanly qualities as desired by men.

Geshe Rabten (1920-86), one of the most erudite Tibetan Buddhist monks who made it their task to teach Westerners (mainly men) in Buddhist thought, was deeply steeped in the tradition of Tsong-kha-pa. Geshe Rabten devoted a whole section of his book *The Essential Nectar* to the discussion of suffering and how one should meditate upon it. He ties the meditation of suffering together not only with the idea of hells and the fate of animals, but also with that of the hungry ghosts and shows that suffering is not restricted to the human species. In his introductory passage, he says: "Every suffering one experiences is the result of the ripening of a negative karmic imprint carried on one's mind. The worlds we find ourselves in are not separate from us but arise from our own mental imprints."[10] He sees the suffering experienced during birth mainly in terms of the suffering of the baby, not of the mother. He assumes that the fetus feels confined "in such a narrow, dark, wet space as the womb" which must feel "unpleasant."[11] At birth, he says, the mother may have access to pain-killers, but not so the baby.

At first glance, these texts seem to be unrelated to the gender issue; they seem to apply universally to both men and women, to humans as well as to all other living creatures. But do they really? These descriptions of suffering put woman in an uneasy position regarding the entire discourse about suffering. It is her body that is seen and described as a filthy and unpleasant place and that restrains the motility of the fetus. An adult monk's voice is speaking; his body sensation is displacing the fetus's sensation. Could the womb not be shelter and haven to the fetus, and the outside world with its cold and drafty air a threat or pain? To the monk, the womb is a prison that traps his fantasies and his desires. To him, it is a place that does not provide him with freedom of movement, the liberty to move in and out. To the monk, it is a forbidden and forbidding place, a place of awe and dread. How could a fetus be happy there, asks he who has no right to be there? The common male *angst* of the woman's procreative abilities is aggrandized in the monk's mind.[12] Between the lines, the text seems to say that woman is responsible for the space being so unpleasant for the imaginary fetus carried by the monk in his heart so pregnant with desire. The author of the text, the celibate monk, has every reason to consider this place unpleasant because it is to him a territory that is off-limits. So what is inaccessible to him becomes devalued in universal terms. The whole idea misses the fact that the womb is a place of great *jouissance*.[13]

Yet another apparent privileging of the masculine voice in these commentaries is the fact that the mother's pain of labour is discounted by the monk because she may have access to drugs. Her pregnancy of nine months does not warrant a sympathetic word. Her embodied experience is objectified, is made into a thing, when the monk says that her womb is dark and wet. Dark and wet — an almost classical definition of the *yin*. Is it mere coincidence, or a cross-cultural male objectification of the woman's body?

What does the text say to the reader who is a woman, a woman who identifies with the feminine gender role? Does her womb also become to her "filthy, dark, and wet"? What is the message a woman gets from these passages? Is it not that something is intrinsically wrong with her body, that she ought to be ashamed of her body if even the "compassionate teachers" see it as such? The text drives a wedge between the woman and her embodied experience. The monastic text has snatched away her body, with the result that then the woman's mind will be all the easier to be tamed and subjugated. No balance is provided for the female reader. No text, to my knowledge, speaks of the penis as a filthy, too narrow, too lonely place, a place, from which the semen, i.e., the "bone" of the child to begotten, is thrown out, ejaculated, evicted. No text of patriarchy narrates the experience of the semen shed, wasted, squandered, dropped from this place as too inadequate to hold the precious essence of life — although the texts praise the retention of the semen as the most desirable achievement. The Buddha never sheds a drop of semen. Why does the patriarchal text present only the female body in this negative light?

If we relate the Buddhist idea about suffering as being primarily located in the afflicted person's mind and as being a result of one's own actions, then the battered woman, the rape victim, has inflicted this suffering on herself. It is her mind that is tainted and abusive, and though the perpetrator's mind is equally distorted, there is a marked difference. This is that he is subject only to the suffering coming from his own state of mind, while the woman is subject to a trauma not of her present choosing. By psychologizing acts of violence and crime, Buddhism provides a frame of rhetoric that lends itself so readily to being used for pupuses perhaps not intended by the Buddhist thinkers. This may explain why Buddhism, until very recent times, did not aspire to improve the social and cultural conditions leading to suffering.

Compassion: The Bodhisattva's Prime Virtue

The Buddhist term *karuṇā* is usually translated as compassion. The Buddhist texts, like Kamalaśāla's *Bhāvanākrama*, distinguish between "ordinary" and "great" *karuṇā*. The ordinary *karuṇā* can be acquired and cultivated by ordinary people (*pṛtagjana*) who have embarked on the Mahāyāna path, while the cultivation of *mahākaruṇā* is the prerogative of the great bodhisattvas only. What is the difference? These texts distinguish between human beings for whom the realization of liberating insight is still at a great distance, and who, for this reason, are called "ordinary," and the great bodhisattvas who are at the verge of such realization. The first group is capable of "ordinary compassion" only, while the second group is capable of practising a "great," i.e., limitless compassion.

The Sanskrit word *karuṇā* is derived from the root *kṛ* which has the basic connotation of to do, to act, to bring forth. Consequently, *karuṇā* has the more narrow meaning of "appropriate action." When the Tibetans adopted Buddhism around the 8th century CE, they chose to translate the term as *snying rje*, which can literally be translated as "kindheartedness," thus shifting the meaning from the appropriateness of action to an emotional attitude.

Buddhaghosa discusses *karuṇā* in the context of the four celestial mental states (benevolence, compassion, empathy, and equanimity). These are four mental attitudes that are engendered through certain meditative deliberations. For Buddhaghosa, compassion manifests itself in the common response to the sight of a decrepit person, i.e., someone who begs for food while sitting in front of an asylum, his body covered with sores and infested with parasites. At such a pitiful sight, the monk ought to generate an attitude expressed in words such as "may this person find relief immediately." The next step in this contemplation is to pity a person who is not in an actual state of misery but whose character is such that it provokes the monk's pity; the wrongdoer is compared to a criminal who is about to be captured. That is to say, the focus shifts from a real observation to an imagined and possible scenario, from reality to fiction. Eventually, the monk will view everybody with compassion because all living creatures are in a state marked by the absence of liberating insight. The texts portray the monk as a person radiating compassion like the sun illuminates the universe with its light and warmth. He is the only still point in the endless quivering of pain.

The texts do not ask for taking action to alleviate the pain of the afflicted; rather, the texts are instrumental in creating a grandiose self. The monk defines the other according to what he sees as their deficiencies, and because they do not have what he has (i.e., the right insight), he pities them. He gets the feeling and satisfaction of having the right mental attitude, and the right, i.e., spiritually correct, insight, while all others are inferior to him. He can react with a feeling of being magnanimous. This kind of compassion is not the nurturance ascribed to woman but a method to develop and to display a noble and genteel character.

In Mahāyāna, the emphasis is changed. The plight of the other is now pictured in vivid colours; the compassionate response knows of no boundaries, no exception. The narrative, in its attempt to illustrate the limitlessness of this compassion, goes overboard. What is to the bodhisattva the ultimate compassion turns into ultimate cruelty for those affected by his actions (in most cases, his wife and his children). In other Mahāyāna texts, particularly in those devoted to the cult of Avalokiteśvara, compassion becomes a mode of interaction, a flow of communication between the particularities of the universe. It is seen as the primary potency that enables a universe of interdependence. In this context, the Buddhist term "compassion" comes close to what Audre Lorde calls "the erotic." She understands this term as "the nurturer or nursemaid of all our deepest knowledge."[14] To exhibit acts of compassion, particularly acts of universal compassion (*mahākaruṇā*) asks for a heroic disposition (one of the "perfections," *pāramitā*, a bodhisattva has to develop). Thus, compassion becomes the domain of the masculine gender.

The bodhisattva pledges to "assume the burden," i.e., the obligation to show all living creatures the path toward liberating insight. This is done with the following words: "Alone I assume the burden of causing all sentient beings to have happiness and the causes of happiness. Alone I assume the burden of causing all sentient beings to be free from suffering and its causes. Being a child of all these beings, if I do not try to make them happy, I will be shameless."[15] These are standard phrases found throughout the Mahāyāna literature. The male narrator, here Khensur Lekden quoting Tsong-kha-pa, puts himself in the position of a child, and as such, he wants to "repay" the kindness he had received from his mother. As the assumption is that each individual creature, human as well as not human, has been re-embodied innumerable times, it stands to reason that he had — at least in theory — once been the child of these innumerable creatures. With this rationale, the bodhisattvas feel responsible for all living creatures, and "assume the burden," as stated above. The monk transfers his moral agency to the role ascribed to the son: gratitude toward his mother. In other texts like sGam-po-pa's *Jewel Ornament*, the target of compassion, i.e., the figure of the mother, is described as being in a state of disability, as a blind old woman, teetering along the edge of an abyss. Who would not rush to help her, to rescue her?

In the Avalokiteśvara myth, as recorded, for instance, in the *Mani bka' 'bum*, Avalokiteśvara, the fledgling bodhisattva, resolves to practise universal compassion.[16] He "took on the burden" of making the path to liberating insight available to all sentient creatures. After eons of such arduous striving, he became fatigued and claimed "there is no hope that I will ever be able to help all living creatures to realize their aim." At that moment, his head burst into a thousand pieces. Amitābha, the Buddha and mentor of Avalokiteśvara, helps to put the pieces together, but, alas, they can be assembled only into a pyramid of eleven heads. But Avalokiteśvara's commitment to compassion is now unwavering. From now on, the bodhisattva is known as "Lord of Universal Compassion."

In the following, I want to examine these statements about compassion and to investigate the term as to whether it shows any genderedness. Ann Klein came to the conclusion that the Mahāyāna practice of compassion and relationality fostered the person's autonomy but permitted the maintainance of connectedness at the same time.[17] Reading the Buddhist texts exposes a male voice that sections itself off from the other, i.e., the figure of the mother, by picturing her disabilities. Compassion is not evoked for a strong, autonomous person, but for a blind old woman, a woman who cannot see. What is it that she cannot see? The truth, we may opine. Her ignorance warrants the knowing monk's compassion. His self becomes aggrandized through her lack of insight, lack of autonomy. (She cannot walk safely along the edge of the abyss.) Is this compassion built on relatedness, on connectedness? Is it not that this compassion is a means to aggrandize the monastic self, tormented by the abandonment syndrome?

Why, I want to ask the Buddhist texts, is there no talk of the love the healthy mother feels for her child? If the monk and bodhisattva had been the child of all creatures, then, one has to argue on the basis of this logic, he has been mother to all creatures once, too. Such an image, where motherhood is correlated with the figure of the bodhisattva, would empower woman. It would affirm woman's cultural role as nurturer and caregiver. But the bodhisattva figure is modelled upon the baby boy's experience. The vision of compassion, as rendered in most texts, is reflecting a dissymmetry of power and autonomy. The receiver of compassion is depicted as a needy person who lacks autonomy, while the giver of compassion is the hero.

The Avalokiteśvara myth invites a Freudian analysis. By violating the vow taken in the presence of Amitābha, the Father, Avalokiteśvara, fulfilling the role of the son, faces the fear of castration, symbolized through the "explosion" of his head. The castration is in a way "healed" when the son is willing to renew his commitment to observe the pledge. The submission of the son to the will of the Father results in a self that derives its sense of identity from seeing others, i.e., M/Other, in a situation of want. The son is rewarded for the pain of castration and its ensuing sensation of loss and deprivation through an opportunity to develop a grandiose self.

What happens if these texts are appropriated by a female voice? Can she see her mother, blind and fragile, stumbling along the edge of the abyss? Does the female reader construct a similar grandiose self? We don't know, because no records are left to us. If we follow modern feminist and psychoanalytic thinking, then we may read this scenario in a new light as providing an opportunity for woman-woman bonding. The daughter will recognize her own fate in her mother's suffering.[18] The Buddhist concept of compassion holds a potential for enriching a feminist search for spirituality, but the inscriptions of patriarchy have first to be deconstructed and finally erased from the texts before they can become inspiring to women.

No-Self for Women without a Sense of Self

> For there is ill but none to feel it;
> For there is action but no doer;
> And there is peace, but no one to enjoy it;
> A way there is, but no one goes it.[19]

These words of Buddhaghosa match closely those some contemporary women may use in describing their perception of selfhood and identity. First, I shall contrast the Buddhist sayings with statements made in modern feminist works; second, I shall attempt to highlight the differences apparent in the statements derived from two very different contexts, and third, I shall try to mark off areas of possible similarity.

In *Women's Ways of Knowing*, part of a chapter on received knowledge has the title "conceiving the selfless self"; it is not a discussion of Buddhism. Women, this study tells us, tend to define their personhood in terms of how the outside world ranks and classifies them: as a university graduate, as a senior clerk, or as a mother, for example. The authors, Field Belenky et al., speak of the "selflessness" and "voicelessness" of these women.[20] They see themselves not in terms of a Self but only in their use to others. That is, those others tell Woman (as a culturally constructed gender) who she is: no doer, none to feel emotion.

Jean Baker Miller found that women's sense of self is constituted through their experience of being related and connected with other people.[21] The locale of a woman's self is outside of herself. Gilligan perhaps cites the most telling statement given by a divorced, middle-aged woman who lived in a sophisticated university community: "As a woman, I feel I never understood that I was a person, that I could make decisions and I had a right to make decisions. I always felt that belonged to my father or my husband in some way, or church, which was always represented by a male clergyman."[22] Jessica Benjamin reasons that individuation (i.e, the development of a sense of centre of experience) happens in reaction to the experience of boundaries given in the "other" or the outside world.[23] One is inclined to say that with the psychologizing of the outside world, taken to its extreme in the Mind-Only School of thought (*cittamātra*), Buddhist thought had to lose its sense of self too. Mark C. Taylor states that, within Christian thinking, "self is a 'theological concept.'"[24] Thus, with the rejection of God as a valid concept to explain existence, its counterpart, or mirror, i.e., the self, had to be abolished too. Kristeva expands this discourse to realms considered with disgust which she terms the abject: vomit, excrement, decomposing bodies – they demarcate the boundary zones where self and other get into touch with one another, and define each other in this process.[25] In her article *Stabat Mater* she suggests that the maternal self, embodied as Virgin Mary in the Christian context, "knows no masculine body save that of her dead son, and her only pathos is her shedding tears over a corpse."[26] Is it then too far-fetched to suggest that Buddhism, by deconstructing God or the divine as source of the *"imago"* that the human existence is, had to accept the dissolution of the self as its corollary, and then tried to bar further erosion of the sense of being by emphasizing contemplation of ugliness, i.e., of the Kristevian abject? From its early days on, Buddhism cultivated meditation on ugliness: decaying corpses or excrements, blood and pus, all characteristics of the womb as described in Buddhist texts. Was such meditation a means to maintain some notion of selfhood while officially denouncing a reified concept of self (*ātman*)? By confronting the abject in its repulsiveness, the Buddhist practitioner is enabled to establish in an uncanny way a new sense of self (which in Buddhist terminology is called the *ahaṃkāra*) regardless of its abnegation in Buddhist theory. But this self, regained in such vicarious and bizarre ways, is a masculine self as the maternal, represented in the womb, is part of the abject which constitutes the self's boundaries.

What do Buddhist texts mean to say when they reject the concept of *ātman*, which is mostly translated as "self"?[27] Most textbooks of Buddhism seem to promulgate the idea that the Buddhists denied the self – and marvel about this strange project. As Pérez-Remón has shown in his comprehensive examination of the earliest Buddhist texts (*nikāya*), this was not necessarily the teaching contained in them. What these texts rejected was, according to Pérez-Remón, the identification of the self with the *skandhas*, the five groupings of tangible existence. Modern thought locates the self exactly in the domain of lived and embodied experience, that is, in Buddhist terminology, within the realm of the *skandhas*. Later commentators, like Buddhaghosa, took a more limited stance as they denied the existence of self in general. Despite such a theoretical stance, the lived reality had Buddhists think about a possible and acceptable formulation of a "centre of experience." Steven Collins formulates this need in the following way:

> [T]he Buddhist attitude to selfhood, to personality and continuity, is that impersonal mental and material elements are arranged together in a temporarily unified configuration. What unifies and prolongs this configuration is desire; it is in desire for the enjoyment of these constituents of personality, and for their continuance, that there arises for the unenlightened man "the conceit 'I am'" (asmimāna), a "conceit" which is not so much asserted propositionally as performed automatically by "the utterance 'I'" (ahaṃkāra).[28]

The "conceit" of which Collins speaks is the conflation of a metaphysical self, as accepted in some of the nikāya texts, with the self arising from the lived experience (skandha).

From the perspective of post-modern critical discourse, the metaphysical self has vanished precisely because of its intangibility; consequently, only the sense of selfhood stemming from lived experience remains. Men, in control and even creators of the Word of the Father, may still be inclined to relate their lived experience to a metaphysical reality. Feminist psychoanalytic theory argues that woman has no access to this realm of the symbolic; but psychological studies, like those by Field Belenky et al., also demonstrate that woman does not even find a sense of selfhood in her lived experience. I am asking the Buddhist texts which kind of "conceit" consisting in the conflation of a metaphysical self (denied to woman) with the sense of a centre of lived experience (unavailable to women) should be removed by woman? How can she remove what she has never acquired?

If post-nikāya Buddhist thought wants to alert us to the fact that lived experience provides a dynamic rather than static centre of continuance and selfhood which instills a sense of individuality, then woman, in her existential reliance on intersubjective connectedness, should have a better chance at understanding the nature of "no/self." But the Buddhist tradition never took up this thought. The Buddhist discourse of self and no-self is a discourse of the masculine voice only. Men, in their culturally privileged position, tend to identify the experientially constituted sense of self with a claim for a metaphysical self, but both avenues are denied to woman. However, even if this insight, i.e., that woman by her very nature is more in tune with the idea of no-self than man, had never been articulated in the Buddhist texts, could it be that it became vicariously acknowledged when the Buddhist system chose to symbolize the Perfection of Wisdom (prajñāpāramitā) in female form? An examination of these feminine hypostatizations is now appropriate.

The Symbolic Construction of the Metaphysical

In Buddhism, the metaphysical finds symbolic respresentation in anthropomorphic deities of masculine and feminine properties, and in non-anthropomorphic symbols, like a circle, the wheel, the tree. For present purposes, the only anthropomorphic symbolization of interest is the conceptualization of Goddess. Later, non-anthropomorphic symbolizations of a "feminine" nature will be examined.

In the modern discourse of the Goddess, a diversity of opinions is brought together in a *montage*, but there is a widespread sense that "Goddess" is a metaphor describing experiences of the feminine as a formative and sustaining power. The diversity comes forth in the symbols and symbolic structures evoked to express the Goddess, and in the ideas regarding the possibility of the Goddess' independent existence "out there." In contrast to the phallologocentric father god who resides in his transcendence, the Goddess *is* immanent. God the father is positioned in heaven, in a world-negating intangibility; the Goddess is seen as animating this world, the earth, the interaction and connectedness among women. She is immanent, tangible, open to human experience. In terms of the structure of language, "god" can be understood as an abstract noun, and "goddess" as a verb.

Carol Christ gave three prominent positions as to the quest of who or what the Goddess is: (1) a divine personification to be invoked in prayer and ritual; (2) a symbol of change as manifest in the life cycle (birth, death, rebirth) of living creatures, and in the rhythm of societies and cultures, and in the cycle of the seasons; and (3) an affirmation of the legitimacy and beauty of female power. Some women would see the Goddess as an independent entity "out there," while others see in the term a powerful metaphor and symbol narrating a new experience of gynocentric spirituality.

The metaphoric and symbolic understanding of the Goddess fuses sometimes with psychoanalytic discourse. The symbol of the Goddess takes on a personal meaning narrated within each woman's life in a different way. Theologically this heralded a new understanding of the ultimate, so different from the phallologic "I am who I am"[29] that marks the monotheistic/monolithic religions determining most modern Western thinking.

Buddhist thought generated various ideas, all of them more or less related to the concept found in the Goddess.[30] One may describe these ideas as various attempts to articulate the ultimate through symbols. This symbolized ultimate is established in a vital relationship with the human individual. The deity as an image becomes incarnate in the practitioner's mind who, in turn, will gradually develop the skill to absorb the deity's self. A spiritual metamorphosis begins to take place as the deity's self displaces the human self of the practitioner. The human individual turns into the deity. The deity mirrors the potential (the "holy") human being and lends her consummation to the practitioner's fragile psyche. There are many deities known in Buddhism, particularly in the Mahāyāna and Vajrayāna traditions; some are of a feminine appearance and character, others are of a masculine appearance and character. They can also appear "in union" which usually means that the masculine figure dominates the scene through size, the turn of his face toward the devotee, etc. Only one feminine deity in Buddhism occupies a position central enough (and does so in all Mahāyāna traditions) to be brought into discourse with the Goddess, and this is Tārā. Kuan Yin, who is sometimes celebrated as a feminine hypostasis of the buddhamind, became a feminine figure only in later periods of Chinese and Japanese Buddhism, while in earlier times, and in countries other than the two mentioned, Kuan Yin (better known by the Sanskrit name, Avalokiteśvara) remained of masculine gender.

Before we enter a discussion of Tārā, we should reflect for a moment upon the nature of these Buddhist deities, masculine or feminine. Most of the deities known to the Mahāyāna tradition cannot be traced outside of it; they seem to appear suddenly in the texts as manifestations of the "Buddha-as-Communal-Joy" (*sambhogakāya*). Consequently, they participate to a certain degree in the same numinous nature that is ascribed to the Buddha residing in nirvana. The tradition tells us that as manifestations of the Buddha's existence in communal joy they are also encompassed in Buddha-as-Reality (*dharmakāya*). The rationale is that Buddha-as-Reality has no means by which to engage in appropriate (i.e., empathetic or compassionate, or, as I like to say, "erotic") activity, and for this reason Buddha-as-Communal-Joy emerges. In this manifest form, although invisible to the naked eye of the non-awakened person, the Buddha's teaching is made accessible by acquiring the deities as a species of vicarious agents. In other words, the Buddhist deities are symbols of Buddha's salutary activity; their existence is confined to the symbolic exchange between the buddhamind, the practitioner, and the realm where this spiritual encounter occurs. The Buddhist deities have a different kind of reality than the Hindu deities. On the one hand, the Buddhist deities are considered as constructs of the psyche, products of the practitioner's inner yearning for consummation and enlightenment. On the other hand, they are "instruments" for Buddha's erotic interaction with the world. But, as it happens with the constructs of the psyche, particularly when fuelled by great desire, they gain a seeming life "of their own." Psychology speaks of "projections" that then become the target of transference. That is to say, the human psyche empowers its own constructs to such a degree that they appear as quasi-"real." They become a quasi-object, and gain the ability to act vicariously. This allows the psyche to transfer its repressed internalized objects onto these constructs in their seemingly "objectified" nature. For this reason, the symbolic speaks about the repressed internalized objects that otherwise remained hidden. The vicarious and adopted "objectified" nature of the Buddhist deities is sometimes borrowed from the repertoire of culturally defined and readily available symbols, such as the gods and goddesses of popular Hinduism and of tribal religions. None of the deities represents the fullness of buddhanature: this remains the property of Buddha-as-Reality (*dharma-kāya*).

In our declared intent to facilitate a discourse between the concept of Goddess and the Buddhist concept of deity and the ultimate, two avenues can be discerned: (1) to compare the Goddess with Tārā, as the most prominent goddess of the Mahāyāna pantheon, and (2) to compare the Goddess with Buddhist concepts of the ultimate, which necessarily lacks obvious gender definition, but which, as I intend to show, does not lack a subtly gendered nature.

Based on an examination of the legends associated with the Buddhist deities, Snellgrove assures us that the Buddhist goddesses, like Tārā, are hypostases of male bodhisattvas, like Avalokiteśvara.[31] That is, they are located in the realm of the symbolic. Nevertheless, Snellgrove believes he can observe that, when they enter a union with a male deity, they are not more than "handmaidens."[32] Yet when Tārā is visualized as a solitary deity, she becomes a powerful symbol of ego transformation: the deity's self displaces the human one of the practitioner who then adopts the deity's characteristics and properties. Tsong-kha-pa points this out in the following way: "In all these practices, one should increasingly gain the ability to cut off one's ordinary ego through the vivid appearance of the deity, and the ego of the deity: and for that reason it is not enough just to concentrate on forming the deity's body, but one must also concentrate upon making firm his (*sic*) ego."[33] That is to say that a feminine symbolic ego structure displaces the human, and potentially male, ego. Although affirming the symbolic nature of deities, some Buddhist masters also felt the deity to be physically present. One of them is dGe-legs rgya-mtsho (1641-1712), a not very well known but nevertheless influential Buddhist master and expert of the Graduated Path tradition (*lam rim*). He is recorded in his biography as saying that the flourishing of the buddha-teaching depends not only on the long life of scholars, such as the high-ranking lamas, but also on the continued existence of such famous statues as those in the Jo-khang that only seem to be statues but which are, in reality, Avalokiteśvara and Śākyamuni themselves.[34]

This concept of deity matches in a way that of the Goddess as an independently existent entity that can be evoked through rituals, prayers, and meditations. The question now arises as to how feminine is the character of Tārā? Nāgārjuna describes the Goddess in such way that a certain binary opposition gives structure to the visualization: the right hand is indicative of the conventional truth, the left hand of the absolute truth; her right foot stretched out is the abandonment of all defects of Māra, her left foot drawn back is the understanding of all good qualities.[35] These binary oppositions seem to be in accord with the modern understanding of how the two halves of the brain work, but no element typical of feminine gender can be distinguished. The text of the ritual evocation describes Tārā to some degree through aspects of domination and presence ("having eyes that flash like lightening") but the other describes her as embodying nurturance and protection (gift-bestowing ... mother, mother of all, protecting the entire world from ... terror, ... mother saving from all poverty).[36] She is said to have emerged from Buddha's face like Pallas Athena sprung from Zeus' forehead. In her culturally defined gender role, Tārā is also associated with terror and nightmarish visions from which she saves her devotees.[37] Psychoanalysis has elaborated on this theme of mother, the protector from the horror of abandonement, but also the source of depression and of deprivation, if the feeling of abandonment begins to dominate the psyche.

Tārā is not the primordial feminine potency that today's feminists desire, but she is certainly a powerful image expressing the culturally defined feminine gender role and placing it high in the symbolic structure of religion. Within the fold of the Buddhist belief, Tārā may hold the potential for inspiring and empowering women practitioners. If we use Kristeva's thinking as a frame of reference, then Tārā is phallic to the extent that she is placed in the order of the symbolic. But she is more than just the symbolic; she is also the "other," what Kristeva calls the "maternal." In the text's metaphorical language, the symbolic aspect of Tārā is expressed as "conventional truth" (em-bodied in her right leg, and right arm), and her "maternal" aspect as "ultimate truth" (her left leg and arm). Tārā oscillates between the representational realm of the symbolic where she can be described, where she articulates compassion on behalf of the Father (Avalokiteśvara), and a space where neither truth nor falsity reigns, where linear time collapses into the now. Kristeva says:

> A constant alternation between time and its "truth," identity and its loss, history and the timeless, signless, extra-phenomenal things that produce it. An impossible dialectic: a permament alternation: never the one without the other. It is not certain that anyone here and now is capable of it. An analyst conscious of history and politics? A politician tuned into the unconscious? A woman perhaps....[38]

Does this imply that Tārā could be perceived as more than the symbolic ... ?

Apart from perceiving the goddesses as bodhisattvas, feminine depictions of the ultimate figure prominently in Buddhism. It needs to be emphasized, however, that Buddhist texts are very firm in their rejection of any reified vision of the ultimate; they displaced the Hindu concept of an all-encompassing substance (*brahman* or otherwise) with the concept of emptiness (*śūnyatā*). While Hinduism, particularly in its Śaivaite tradition, uses phallic images, such as the *lingam*, the symbolized form of the penis, to render the absolute, Buddhism chose vacuity. Its prime symbolic representation is an empty circle. Any definition is in itself a futile attempt destined to destroy a view of reality that is fluid, open, ambiguous, and transparent. Emptiness in its philosophical descriptions, which are more descriptions of what it is not, rather than what it is, resonate with attributes usually associated with the feminine gender. They are expressions used for describing the ambiguity of the womb, its lack of boundaries, its hiddenness, yet source of all life. In tantric Buddhism, emptiness is symbolized as the womb. The *Hevajra Tantra* begins: "Om, homage to the noble Hevajra! Thus I have heard. At one time the Exalted One in the totality of his corporeal, vocalizing, and mental being, resided in the womb of the most honoured Adamantine Feminine."[39] The *Guhyasamāja Tantra*, commonly considered to be oldest Buddhist tantra (approximately 2nd century CE), refers to this symbolic vagina, which I prefer to call womb, as "the unspeakable mandala" from which everything arises.[40] This womb precedes, in an ontological sense, the existence of the Buddha. It is the matrix from which all Buddhas originate.

The Atiyoga tradition, as once cultivated in eighth-century Tibet, goes even one step further. It proclaims that unless one understands the buddhanature as feminine in its very being, no enlightening insight is possible. This particular tradition, which ceased to flourish in the ninth century, called the ultimate in its feminine symbolic nature Samantabhdrā, She Who Is All Good. A few references to the original texts may suffice to substantiate my claim: The *rDo la gser zhun* states that if the nature of All Good as a female (Samantabhdrā) is not grasped, the bliss of truth cannot be appreciated.[41] Another Atiyoga text, the Instruction on The Chain of [Doctrinal] Views (*Man ngag lta ba'i phreng ba*) ascribed to Padmasambhava, represents the five great elements as five "mothers" of "own being." It further says that the totality of what exists as compound and non-compound phenomena (this includes nirvana) is the feminine creative force (*chos bya ba mo*), i.e., "All Good" that is "own being" which exists from the primordial.[42] Thus, within the context of the Atiyoga literature, it is accurate to render the ultimate as of feminine gender. Later, however, when this tradition was incorporated into mainstream Tibetan Buddhism, Samantabhadrā became another consort added to a masculine hypostasis, Samantabhadrā. Patriarchy had taken over a spiritual tradition that had the potential to speak to women.

Another incongruity informs the Buddhist view of woman and Goddess. On the one hand, Buddhists adopted the view of the patriarchal cultures of their societies that woman is of inferior spiritual and intellectual capacities but, on the other hand, wisdom was always encapsulated in a feminine figure. One may argue that this was nothing but a figure of speech. To some degree, this may be so, but one may also consider the fact that in tantric Buddhism the practitioner takes a vow never to deride *any woman* because woman per se is wisdom. To make the situation even more confusing, some Buddhist texts are firm in stating that the state of buddhahood cannot be realized with a female body. Consequently, a woman who has reached such a sublime state of spirituality that she can enter nirvana has to exchange her female body for a male one. The question of how that would affect a woman, how she would feel with such an alien body, is never asked. In summary, the Buddhism of the Atiyoga and similar strands seems to harbour a potential to stimulate the spiritual quest of modern women. The ancient tradition with its lucidity, its "tested" quality may inform our modern searching for expressing the feminine in suitable terms. But one also has to acknowledge an overt trend in Buddhism of deriding the feminine.

Overall, the understanding of Buddhist feminine deities, like Tārā, remains ambiguous. She seems to be entrenched in the symbolic realm, phallic daughter of the Father Avalokiteśvara. At the same time, she carries in her vacuity, in her metaphorical womb, the unarticulated, unspeakable wisdom, which is beyond the grasp of object and subject, which is beyond the limitations of self and other. She is the matrix from which the buddhamind arises. In Kristeva's thinking, such is called the "maternal." It needs to be noted, however, that "maternal" is a loaded term for Kristeva, for it can signify "abject" as well as *jouissance*. Thus, Tārā is not only the phallic daughter of Avalokiteśvara, she is also the unspeakable truth of the primordial rendered in the metaphor of the darkness of vacuity. In this latter aspect, she is the wisdom expressed in the Atiyoga texts, which so vehemently reject any form of systematic meditation or of visualization, a wisdom that has no words, no symbols to reify itself.

The Challenge of Gender Sensitivity: The Transformation of Contemporary Buddhism

Members of the Western Buddhist communities are reported as saying that "the single most revolutionary aspect of Buddhist practice in the United States is that women are participating in it."[43] Certainly the fact that modern women of the Western world entered Buddhist communities as practitioners challenged the cultural determinism of Buddhism which until recently was an exclusively Asian religion. Western practitioners of Buddhism brought their own intellectual discourse to the Buddhist traditions. The interest in woman and her position within Buddhism arose as a consequence of developments in the Western world of the late twentieth century. For this reason, most publications dealing with the role of women in the Buddhist traditions, or exploring feminine traits within Buddhist thought, were written mainly by Westerners for Westerners.[44] Only during the last years of the 1980s did Asian women articulate their own interest in this topic.[45] The changes brought about constitute the organization of the communities, including the monastic ones: a rethinking of the role of the teacher; an attempt to recover the history of women in Buddhism; a challenge to the traditional role assigned to the nuns in Buddhism; and a desire to bring back full ordination for nuns.

In Asia, the roles women could play within the Buddhist traditions were predominantly defined by the individual cultural and social context rather than by any doctrinal viewpoint held by the religion. Thus, when Buddhist traditions began to take shape in the Western world, its own social and cultural context provided the parameters for the roles available to women in a Western form of Buddhism. The opportunities for women entering the Buddhist arena in a more visible form were further enhanced by the fact that, unlike in Asia, Buddhism in the West was not formally linked to the political institutions. Whereas in Asia the courtly culture could perceive of woman only as queen, as close relative of the ruler, and as concubine or courtesan, Western democracies did not impose such restrictions on the social organization of the Buddhist communities, nor did they invest the order with similar privileges and power. The kinds of restrictions and oppression imposed on Buddhist women in Asia are well illustrated in the account by Jiyu Kennet, the woman roshi guiding Shasta Abbey, a Zen monastery in California: "When I was in Japan, as a woman you could officially become a priest, but you didn't do it in public . . . because that would mean that the emperor would have to recognize that a woman existed. So you paid him four times the price that a man did, to get the certificate, and you did it in private."[46] In the West, women who joined the religious centres as practitioners lived, worked, and meditated there side by side with men. As serious lay practitioners, they frequently took vows of celibacy for a certain period of time while living in the religious centres. The term "monk" was redefined in this context by being applied to men and women who were serious about their religious practice. At Shasta Abbey, a concerted effort is made to fuse Japanese Zen tradition with American culture. Upon her visit to Shasta Abbey in 1981, Sandy Boucher felt that men and women had equal access to education and that women and men held positions of prestige and influence. Its roshi is an Englishwoman trained in Japan, and later more women received the title "roshi." All practitioners, men and women alike, are called "monks" and are addressed as "reverend."[47]

The Buddhist communities in the West provide a gender profile distinctly different from that prevalent among traditional Asian communities because the Western Buddhist women brought with them a perception of gender equality, or, at least, one of less severe oppression of women. Thus, it was the conceptual and societal changes marking the emancipation of women in the West that led to changes within the Buddhist communities of the West. The lack of a court culture into which the Buddhist order had been traditionally incorporated enhanced the possibilities for redrafting the social organization of the communities.

After a while, the changes happening in the communities of lay people affected the nuns' order. Karma Lekshe Tsomo, an American who became a Buddhist nun and who is living in Asia, rightly says:

> If ever there has been a silent minority among Buddhist practitioners, it is the nuns. Many people do not realize they exist. Even in traditionally Buddhist countries, nuns seem more or less invisible. . . . Now, emboldened by feminist thought, both Asian and Western sisters gradually are beginning to see themselves in a new light.[48]

The invisibility of the Buddhist nuns in the past is an astounding fact and one that raises serious questions about gender construction within the traditional Buddhist communities. The patriarchal societies of Asia gave women a recognized and acknowledged space only when they confined themselves to the roles of mothers and subservient wives. This recognition, however, was not available to celibate nuns. Consequently, there was no public recognition whatsoever of their existence or of the contribution they made to Buddhist belief and its practice. Even in countries like Tibet, where patriarchal structures were less restrictive and strident, nuns had no participation in the public representation and enactment of culture. This does not preclude that individual nuns were highly appreciated as advisor, spiritual guide, or counsel.

A turning point in the history of the nuns' order was the first conference of Buddhist nuns held in early 1987 in Bodhgaya, India. The most important issue on the agenda was the exploration of possibilities to bring back full ordination for women. (The *bhikṣunī sangha*, the order of fully ordained women renunciates ceased to exist in India long before Buddhism began to decline there. Only in countries following the Chinese Buddhist traditions does full ordination for nuns exist, but this practise does not receive recognition from other Buddhist traditions.) The discussion of such a possibility drew sharp criticism from some monks accusing the nuns of heading toward a schism – the worst possible offence in Buddhist ethics, comparable only to the slaying of an *arhant* or the shedding of the blood of a Buddha.

The main issue in reinstating a *bhikṣunī sangha* is that in most recensions of the *vinaya*, the body of monastic rules, it is said that for the ordination of *bhikṣunīs* ten fully ordained monks (*bhikṣu*) and ten fully ordained nuns (*bhikṣunī*) must be present. Thus, once the order of fully ordained nuns had disappeared, no new ordinations of nuns could happen. (In the Chinese *vinaya* tradition, the rules are more flexible and less defined.) The situation is further aggravated by the fact that different *vinaya* traditions are considered to be incompatible; in general, followers of one *vinaya* tradition cannot practise, i.e., live together, with members of another one. Furthermore, the different *vinaya* traditions resulted in different robes, etc. Thus, the discussion about reinstatement of the *bhikṣunī sangha* focusses on these technical aspects. However, this should not prevent us from recognizing the fact that the entire discussion is charged with emotions.[49] The nuns are faced with the task of getting enough support for the reinstatement of full ordination for women from influential monks without alienating the more conservative monks, and of working out the details so that the result permits the nuns to live in peace and harmony together. The opposition is strongest among the monks of those countries where they are integrated into the political structure, such as Thailand or Sri Lanka.

A concommitant issue is the education of nuns and their access to specialized Buddhist studies. Although the Buddhist scholars had produced a vast amount of literature, almost none of these works can be ascribed with certainty to nuns. Education, learning, and its practice in public debates were, and still are, the terrain of the monks. As women, nuns were confined to a low level of learning, if they had access to it at all. Frequently, they were as illiterate as their lay sisters — and despised for this reason by those who barred them from education. The Central Institute of Tibetan Higher Learning, a Buddhist university located in Sarnath, north of Benares, is theoretically open to women and nuns. In 1987, when I spent part of my sabbatical at this institution, there were about 800 boys enrolled, many of them novices, but only two nuns and two lay girls. The core subjects were taught by men, preferably monks, while optional subjects, like English, were taught by a woman teacher. There were no extracurricular activities for girls; they watched the boys playing soccer from the edge of the field. The girls could not be in residence as there were no dormitories for them; nor were there separate washrooms available. So they had to find accommodation in the town of Sarnath and walk for about twenty minutes to school, regardless of the intense heat during much of the year.

The opportunities for religious education for nuns varies greatly from country to country. In Taiwan, Buddhist women's colleges are popular and employ nuns as teachers who, as role models, encourage the female students to pursue a religious career. In Thailand, Sri Lanka, and Tibet, the opportunities for education are slim. In these countries, the education of a nun depends on adequate opportunities, i.e., access to a qualified female teacher and individual effort. Thus, the learning has a strictly private and individual character. It does not lead to a public status. Karma Lekshe Tsomo, herself a Buddhist nun, sums the situation up as follows:

> Unless structured systems of religious education are implemented soon, Buddhist women in these countries will remain disadvantaged for several generations hence. Though they may well progress spiritually despite learning handicaps, they will not be able to take their rightful places in the religious hierarchy as teachers, administrators, role models, and perpetuators of the *dharma*. Lacking a solid educational foundation themselves, they will have no footing from which to make a lasting contribution in the spread of Buddhist culture just at the very time when women's participation could have such a far-reaching and profound impact.[50]

Many Buddhist women in traditional Asian cultures seem to be convinced that, as women, they lack the intellectual and spiritual skills necessary for a vigorous pursuit of enlightenment. As nuns, they confine themselves to the chanting of prayers, to being subservient to the monks, and to the hope of a rebirth with a male body. Prayers like the one for a rebirth in Sukhamvati, the meditational realm of Buddha Amitābha, express these hopes articulately. When nuns seek a more thorough education, they have to confront the situation that the most qualified and learned teachers are invariably monks — and that for them the interaction with women is highly regulated and severely restricted.

In traditional Buddhism, the figure of the teacher was molded upon the teacher *par excellence*, i.e., Buddha Śākyamuni. Consequently, any female teacher would have been subsumed under the figure of the male teacher. The few known women teachers of the past remained exceptions amidst a sea of male teachers. As men, the teachers in traditional Buddhist settings enjoyed the privileges of high-ranking men who figured prominently in the public. One of these privileges was to have access to women outside of marriage. When Buddhist teachers came to the West, they continued to practise these habits. Some of the Zen priests had secret affairs with their female disciples. The scandal rocked the entire Zen community in the United States. The late Chogyam Trungpa, spiritual leader of Vajradhatu and Naropa Institute, indulged in alcohol and sex with his female disciples.[51] Some of the women felt betrayed, while others relished serving the master. Vicky Fitch, a disciple of Chogyam Trungpa, said: "I was Rinpoche's servant. I emptied his chamberpots, tied his shoes, cleaned his toilets, and did all that kind of work. . . . I've seen Rinpoche in outrageous postures, and yet every time I've seen that it's made sense to me, actually being there."[52] In some cases, the male teachers were seen as using the devotion offered to them by their female followers to veil their sexual advances. Some women conceded to the propositions more out of religious commitment and a feeling of obligation than out of their own desire. Some Buddhist women yearned for a female Buddhist teacher in the hope that such events would not repeat themselves there.

Nonetheless, in contemporary Buddhism, particularly in North America, female teachers are often well-educated women who use their authority with savvy. Such women have brought the figure of the Buddhist teacher back to a human level by declining the elevation to a godlike position as guru.[53] Women have become catalysts in transforming Buddhism from an ancient Asian religion into a contemporary religion which adjusts itself to all kinds of cultural contexts. It is all the more surprising that not much had been done in terms of a critical and analytical examination of the genderedness of Buddhist thought and doctrine. The kind of critique of Christianity exercised by such scholars as Rosemary Radford Reuther or Elisabeth Schüssler Fiorenza has still to come in the field of Buddhist studies.[54]

Recapitulation

The examination of the first statement of the fourfold noble truth of Buddhism revealed an uneasy association of woman with the source of human/male suffering. Compassion as the fundamental attitude of the bodhisattva relies on defining the object of compassion as Other, and it is in a state of disability and without autonomy. The idea that every living creature was once one's own parent also leads to the conclusion that oneself had been mother/parent to all other living creatures once. This would provide an affirmation of woman's cultural role as main nurturer and caregiver. But this opportunity is not appreciated by the Buddhist tradition. However, the core concept of Buddhist thought, i.e., that the nature of the cosmos can be described only as vacuity, emptiness, and that it transcends the realm of language and conceptual thinking, or the Word of the Father, to use a Kristevan phrase, harbours great potential for stimulating a feminist search for spirituality. In contrast to this, the Buddhist concept of No-Self is more critical, if investigated from a feminist perspective, since the general experience of women is that they do not have a sense of self. The anthropomorphic symbolization of "final meanings" — such as the Goddess Tārā, occupies an ambivalent place. On the one hand, Tārā is the Father's (here Avalokiteśvara) daughter; on the other hand, she symbolizes the maternal void (in a Kristevan sense), the unspeakable, the matrix from which all arises.

Contemporary Buddhism, particularly in North America, undergoes dramatic changes because of the influx of educated Western women who import their understanding of the position of women into the Buddhist traditions. Changes are mainly manifest in the areas of the organization of the monastic communities, in the female teacher, in promoting a better education for nuns, and in striving for the reintroduction of full ordination for nuns. But so far, little attempt has been made to examine Buddhist thought as to its gender proclivity.

I hope that this brief survey will show that bringing Buddhist and feminist thought into discourse is a fruitful enterprise, one that may diversify our search for understanding the human condition and the genderedness of symbolic systems.

Notes

1 When I use the term "canon" here, I understand it as it figures in modern critical discourse and not as a synonym for the scriptures of Buddhism (tripiṭaka).

2 Buddhaghosa, The Path of Purification (Visuddhimagga), trans. Bhikkhu Ñyānamoli (1956) (Berkeley: Shambhala, 1976), vol. 2, p. 569 f.

3 This issue was discussed by Roger Corless, Duke University, in his presentation "Beyond Acceptance: The Possibility of a Gay Male Spirituality in the Mainstream Religions" at the Annual Meeting of the American Academy of Religion at San Francisco in 1992.

4 Sieglinde Dietz, Die Buddhistische Briefliteratur Indiens (Inaugural diss., Universität Bonn, 1980), Vol. 1, p. 33 f.

5 Dietz, Indiens, p. 38.

6 J. Takakusu, trans., Record of the Buddhist Religion as Practised in India and the Malay Archipelago (A.D. 671-695) by I-tsing (Oxford: Clarendon Press, 1896), p. 162.

7 Leslie Kawamura, trans., Golden Zephyr — Instructions from a Spiritual Friend, Nagarjuna and Mipham (Emeryville, CA: Dharma Publishing, 1975), p. 16; Lozang Jamspal, Ngawang Samten Chophel, and P. Della Santina, Nāgārjuna's Letter to

King Gautamimputra (Delhi: Motilal Banarsidass, 1978), p. 8 f.; Georges Driessens, trans., *La lettre à un ami du supérieur Nāgārjuna: Une explication du Vénérable Geshé Ngawang Khyenrab d'après des commentaires tibétains* (Les Jacourets: Editions Dharma, 1981), p. 50.

8 I use here the term in its dual meaning of difference and deferral. The sensation of pleasure is different from its surrounding sensations, and it is grounded in a promise that its fulfillment will come in the future (J. Kristeva, *Revolution in Poetic Language*, trans. Leon S. Roudiez (New York: Columbia University Press, 1984), p. 255 n. 68).

9 Kawamura, *Golden Zephyr*, p. 17.

10 Geshe Rabten, *The Essential Nectar: Meditations on the Buddhist Path*, ed. Martin Willson (London: Wisdom Publications, 1984), p. 92.

11 Ibid., p. 122.

12 To most men, the womb is so awesome that they had to create the myth of the *vagina dentata*, about the dark cave where men loose their virility, where the power of the female "eats" away the male potency. Although this mytheme did not enter into the Buddhist literature, we may speculate that it nevertheless shaped and formed the monks' mind.

13 The intersection of Kristevan thinking and Buddhist theory is a fruitful field but too daunting to be dealt with here. A few remarks, however, may be helpful here. Kristeva understands *jouissance* as the only means to avoid being either master or slave of meaning, by mastery of it as well as passage through it (Leon S. Roudiez, ed., *Desire in Language* [New York: Columbia University Press, 1980], p. x). *Jouissance* is delight in difference, in the not-self-ness of self (Jean Graybeal "Joying in the Truth of Self-Division," in David Crownfield, ed., *Body/Text in Julia Kristeva: Religion, Women, and Psychoanalysis* (Albany, NY: State University of New York Press, 1992), p. 132 f. In tantric texts of Buddhism, the womb (*bhaga*, i.e., delight) is the place where the difference and otherness of (masculine) compassion and of (feminine) liberating insight is articulated and symbolically expressed through the metaphor of sexual union. Later, I shall return to the tantric strand within Buddhism.

14 Audre Lorde, *Sister Outsider* (Freedom, CA: The Crossing Press, 1984), p. 56. I have argued at other places (Plenary Session of the Annual Meeting of the American Oriental Society 1989 in Atlanta) that the two terms in their specific interpretations, as referred to here, have similarities and do overlap.

15 Jeffrey Hopkins, trans., *Compassion in Tibetan Buddhism* (London: Rider, 1980), p. 46.

16 E.K. Dargyay, "Srong-btsan Sgam-po of Tibet: Bodhisattva and King," in Phyllis Granoff and Koichi Shinohara, eds., *Monks and Magicians: Religious Biographies in Asia* (Oakville, ON.: Mosaic Press, 1988), p. 106 ff.

17 Anne C. Klein, "Gain or Drain? Buddhist Feminist Views on Compassion," *Wind Buddhist Cultural Forum*, Women and Buddhism, 6/1-3 (Spring 1986, Toronto: Zen Lotus Society): 105-16.

18 Nancy Chodorow, "Family Structure and Feminine Personality," in Michelle Zimbalist Rosaldo and Louise Lamphere, eds., *Woman, Culture, and Society* (Stanford, CA: Stanford University Press, 1974), p. 47.

19 Pe Maung Tin, *The Path of Purity* (London, 1971), p. 609, quoted from Joaquín Pérez-Remón, *Self and No-Self in Early Buddhism* (The Hague: Mouton, 1980), p. 11.

20 Mary Field Belenky et al., eds., *Women's Ways of Knowing: The Development of Self, Voice, and Mind* (New York: Basic Books, 1986), p. 51.

21 Jean Baker Miller, *Toward a New Psychology of Women* (Boston: Beacon Press, 1986), p. 83.
22 Carol Gilligan, *In a Different Voice: Psychological Theory and Women's Development* (Cambridge, MA.: Harvard University Press, 1982), p. 67.
23 Jessica Benjamin, *The Bonds of Love: Psychoanalysis, Feminism, and the Problem of Domination* (New York: Pantheon Books, 1988), p. 36 ff.
24 Mark C. Taylor, *Erring—a Postmodern A/theology* (Chicago and London: The University of Chicago Press, 1984), p. 35.
25 Julia Kristeva, *Powers of Horror: An Essay on Abjection*, trans. Leon S. Roudiez (New York: Columbia University Press, 1982).
26 Toril Moi, ed., *The Kristeva Reader* (New York: Columbia University Press, 1986), p. 175.
27 Joaquín Pérez-Remón, "Self and Non-Self in Early Buddhism," *Religion and Reason*, 22 (The Hague: Mouton, 1980): 7 ff.
28 Steven Collins, *Selfless Persons: Imagery and Thought in Theravāda Buddhism* (Cambridge: Cambridge University Press, 1982), p. 263.
29 The Hebrew phrase became incorporated in Western thought in the translation given here, although the original may equally well be translated as "I will be who I will be" thus indicating a greater fluidity of thinking than the "standard" translation does.
30 An aspect which warrants a whole paragraph is Kristeva's elaboration on truth as the unspeakable unconscious, the feminine, which, when embodied in a symbol becomes a phallus-substitute. See Julia Kristeva, *About Chinese Women* (1974) (New York: Marion Boyars, 1986), p. 37.
31 David Snellgrove, *Indo-Tibetan Buddhism* (Boston: Shambhala, 1987), Vol. 1, p. 151.
32 Ibid., p. 150.
33 Tsong-kha-pa, *sNgags rim chen po*, in *Collected Works* Dza, 56a, quoted from Stephen Beyer, *The Cult of Tārā: Magic and Ritual in Tibet* (Berkeley: University of California Press, 1973), p. 77.
34 Manuscript of 122 fols. (vol. ka: fol. 1-100; vol. kha: fol. 1-22) with title folio missing, composed by Phur-ru lcog Ngag-dbang byams-pa (1682-1762), photographic reproduction of the original manuscript in the possession of the *blon po* of Karcha (Zanskar, Ladakh), p. 126, line 4-5.
35 Beyer, *The Cult of Tara*, p. 80.
36 Ibid., p. 200.
37 Ibid., p. 229 f.
38 Moi, ed., *Kristeva Reader*, p. 38.
39 D.L. Snellgrove, ed., *The Hevajra Tantra*, London Oriental Series, 6 (London: Oxford University Press, 1959), Vol. 1, 2.
40 Benoytosh Bhattacharya, ed., *Guhyasamāja Tantra or Tathāgataguhyaka* (Baroda: Oriental Institute, 1967), p. 159, line 9.
41 NGB, Vol. 1, p. 499: *kun tu bzang mo'i spyod pas ma zin dge ba'i chos ni gang yang rung*. For a further discussion of a feminist reading of certain Buddhist texts and ideas see the publications by Anne Klein.
42 The short tractate is preserved in a number of collections, among them: 'Chi-med Rig-'dzin bla-ma, ed., *Selected Writings of Padmasambhava* (Leh: n.p., 1974), p. 1-18; Kong-sprul Blo-gros mtha'-yas, ed., *gDams ngag mdzod* (Delhi: n.p., 1971), Vol. 1, p. 16-26; cf. Ulrich Loseries, *Guru Padmasambhavas Instruktion 'Die Kette der Anschauungen'* (Friedrich-Wilhelm Universität, Bonn: n.p., 1989).
43 Rick Fields, *How the Swans Came to the Lake: A Narrative History of Buddhism in America* (Boulder: Shambhala, 1981), p. 363.

44 As, for instance, Karma Lekshe Tsomo, ed., *Sakyadhītā: Daughters of the Buddha* (Ithaca, NY: Snow Lion, 1988); Rita M. Gross, *Buddhism after Patriarchy: A Feminist History, Analysis, and Reconstruction of Buddhism* (Albany, NY: State University of New York Press, 1993); Jose I. Cabezon, ed., *Buddhism, Sexuality, and Gender* (Ithaca, NY: State University of New York Press, 1992).

45 This sequence of events is acknowledged by Karma Lekshe Tsomo in *Sakyadhītā, Daughters of the Buddha* (Ithaca, NY: Snow Lion, 1988), p. 18.

46 Sandy Boucher, *Turning the Wheel* (San Francisco: Harper & Row, 1988), p. 137.

47 Ibid., p. 133 f.

48 Ibid., p. 18.

49 See Karma Lekshe Tsomo, ed., *Sakyadhītā*, p. 252 f. where a traditional Tibetan monk puts forward his rigid view on this subject matter.

50 Ibid., p. 164.

51 Boucher, *Turning the Wheel*, p. 210-56.

52 Ibid., p. 242.

53 Ibid., p. 154.

54 Anne Klein made some attempts at a theoretical critique of Buddhist doctrine in some of her articles, and recently Rita M. Gross has also done so with her book *Buddhism after Patriarchy*.

Chapter 10

UPHOLDING NORMS OF HINDU WOMANHOOD: AN ANALYSIS BASED ON REVIEWS OF HINDI CINEMA

Katherine K. Young

The familial relationship between the sexes has always been a preoccupation of cinema everywhere; it can be seen as the key to the core of a culture, an index to the inner state of its being, and to the position of woman in society as a whole. It is, in other words, at the heart of the conflict between tradition and modernity. In the Islamic countries, the question of the position of woman has become the focal point of the attitude to modernization and its apparent concomitant, westernization. In a similar way in India, different religious groups are in varying degrees shaken by the basic changes brought about by modern industrialized society and perceive the position that women threaten to assume in it as an important symbol of a new social order (Chidananda Das Gupta, *The Painted Face*[1]).

The status of women in film has often been considered an indication of their status in society. In *Backlash*, for instance, Susan Faludi attempts to substantiate her thesis that there was a growing reaction to the women's movement in the 1980s by examining the subservient position of women in the films of that decade.[2] It is true, of course, that producers of popular Hollywood films often create them with an eye on the market and societal trends. Every minute of a commercial film costs an enormous amount of money; accordingly, no scene is superfluous.[3] If a backlash is occurring in society and portrayal of it is of great interest to film viewers, then producers will be interested in scripts reflecting or criticizing the backlash. A similar argument could be made for the two hundred Hindi ("Bollywood") films produced in Bombay, India, and watched by over fifteen million people daily. They, too, cost large amounts of money by Indian standards and may reflect the changing position of women in society or at least offer explorations of current horizons in the psychic make-up and gender roles of the country.

Hindi films have, in fact, long been recognized for their contribution to a pan-Indian popular culture. Plots, images and symbols—often drawn from traditional myths, epics, folk theatre or classical art—are generally fixed and known to the audience. Some elements, however, change. Aspects of urban life and Westernized values are incorporated and introduced in turn to provincial towns—thereby influencing "Indian ideas of the good life and the ideology of social, family, and love relationships."[4]

At the same time, regional forms of song and dance, after being transmuted in film through stereophonic sound and technicolour, are reintroduced to the local culture. "Even the traditional iconography of statues and pictures for religious worship is paying homage to film representations of gods and goddesses."[5]

As an initial point of departure for understanding the portrayal of women in Hindi films, I shall draw on specific film reviews and general discussions of the genre by (1) Indian feminists who write for *Manushi*, India's premier magazine dedicated to women's issues; (2) Sudhir Kakar, a psychoanalyst who has commented on gender in Hindi films; and (3) Chidananda Das Gupta, a film critic who has examined Hindi films in the context of larger societal trends. Of central concern is whether the reviewers think that traditonal norms of womanhood (*strīdharma*), which were once legitimated by Hindu values, are endorsed in the films or whether the reforms of Hinduism during the past century to improve the position of women are taking root. The perspectives of the reviewers will also be assessed with reference to changes taking place in Indian society. If there is consensus by the reviewers, this may reflect patterns occurring in the films. Although beyond the scope of the present discussion, the patterns detected in the reviews could be compared to an analysis based on formal properties — such as *mise-en-scène*, dialogue, colour, music, dramatis personae, space and time — to determine whether the reviewers have done justice to the films themselves.[6]

Traditional Roles of Womanhood: An Overview

To provide a background, I will present a brief description of the gender role of the conservative Hindu woman that emerged in the classical period of Hinduism. Because this role had influenced the lives of most upper-caste women during the medieval period — an especially difficult time in Indian history for Hindus, thanks to the domination first by the Muslims and then by the Western imperialists — it inspired the Hindu reform movement and then the women's movement of the nineteenth and early twentieth centuries. Although this role had been defined by and for the brahmin caste, it came to influence other communities as well. This occurred as a result of the process of sanskritization (imitation by the lower castes of brahmanical norms for upward mobility) and the universalization of these norms in the nineteenth century by the British who made them the basis of law.[7] It is important, therefore, to explore this role, being careful to understand it in its historical and sociological context and not as the only image of women in the Hindu tradition.[8]

This conservative role for women emerged during a period of internal crisis (6th century BCE — 4th century CE) which saw heterodox challenges to Hinduism in the wake of foreign invasions; massive economic changes resulting in an agricultural and urban economy, and population explosion. Again, after a liberal interlude during the Gupta dynasty (ca.

3rd-6th century CE) and spread of the bhakti traditions (especially 6th-9th century CE), it came to the foreground during the time of Muslim and British domination of the subcontinent, culminating in Tulsīdās' portrayal of Sītā as the ideal dependent wife in his eighteenth-century retelling of the epic *Rāmāyaṇa*.[9] The term *"pativrata"* best sums up this conservative role. *"Pativrata"* literally means a vow (*vrata*) for the husband (*pati*), either by a maiden to obtain a husband, or by a wife to ensure his health and longevity. It connotes chastity and loyalty to him (and by extension to the family) in thought, word and deed. Marriage and motherhood were, accordingly, the *sine qua non* of a traditional woman's life. Marriage was arranged by the families (rather than by the individuals concerned) on economic and status considerations; this involved the gift of a daughter accompanied by dowry and observance of strict rules regarding a candidate's suitability.[10] Females were married young in order to protect their virginity, a prerequisite for marriage. One corollary of this domestic orientation for the brahmin upper-caste woman was that she did not receive formal education. (Traditionally, this involved the study of sacred texts and the different branches of knowledge needed to interpret them.) Another was that she did not undertake work in the public realm and, in some communities, formal seclusion in the domestic sphere.

Thus, the conservative (upper-caste) woman's life was defined pre-eminently by her marriage and the ideal of *pativrata*. She was the protected; her husband the protector. According to the traditional lawgiver Manu, a woman should be dependent in youth on her father, during marriage on her husband, and in old age on her son.[11] Moreover, she was to be the servant; her husband was the master.[12] If her husband died before her, she was not allowed to remarry.[13] On the contrary, she was to endure inauspicious widowhood—it was believed she had caused her husband's death because of her lack of proper care—with an ascetic-like regimen that minimized her needs and controlled her desires. Or she could choose to perform *sati*, self-immolation on the funeral pyre of her husband, which was extremely rare but considered pre-eminently auspicious. *Sati* demonstrated a Hindu woman's loyalty to the husband (since she followed him in death), her enormous self-control (since her fortitude was akin to the yogic discipline of ascetics) and her benevolence to others (since the event generated merit for all.)[14]

This *pativrata* image certainly was influential in certain periods of Indian history, especially the medieval period. There are, however, some caveats. First, it is important to remember that it was only an ideal projected in texts written by men. And it did not make women completely subservient to men, as often claimed in today's popular press or anti-Hindu literature. Women also embodied power (*abalā*[15]) or generated it through the practice of vows—a form of asceticism adjusted to the domestic orientation of ordinary women but capable of generating power that could transform the behaviour of others, including deviant husbands, to ensure a just and moral world. Women, accordingly, represented culture; men, untamed nature (though in other contexts, the reverse occurred).[16] A woman, too, could exercise enormous power as a mother (since the mother-son relationship was particularly strong in India). She also attained power if she became the senior woman of the extended family, for this gave her authority over a number of women—younger sisters-in-law, daughters, daughters-in-law and nieces in the large extended family. Such a position allowed her to exercise managerial skills and political strategies to ensure the family's proper functioning and well-being. Senior women received respect as "elders" by the younger generation.

Second, it must be remembered that although some orthodox brahmanical communities viewed women as destined only for rebirth (though men could pursue salvation), others, either overtly or covertly, promoted salvation for married women. The overt approach saw women's practice of *vratas* (fasting for the welfare of others), *japa* (chanting the name of the deity) or *bhajans* (singing the deity's praise) as the means to the supreme goal. The covert approach paid lip-service to the importance of devotion to the husband as every woman's goal but allowed this concept to swing to devotion to God (another meaning of the word *pati*) and the goal of heaven or salvation.[17]

Third, it must be remembered that the lower-caste woman always had considerable independence, in part because of her labour in the public sphere, which provided economic power, and in part because she could romantically define her relationships and decision for marriage. In the traditional Hindu lawbooks, which enumerated the marital practices of all castes and regions, romance leading to marriage (called *Gandharva*) was acknowledged.[18] It was improper, however, for upper-caste women to entertain even the thought of romance, thanks to the high value placed on female chastity. An exception to this was a woman's relationship with a deity such as Lord Krishna or Lord Shiva as the Beloved (a romantic relationship safely limited to the spiritual realm). Besides the spiritual outlet, romance for the upper-caste woman could be vicariously experienced only through drama and poetry.[19] In contrast, the lower-caste woman was free to divorce and remarry and could have relationships, even marriage, with an upper-caste man.

Finally, it must be remembered that there were women who either ignored or defied the norms: tribal women who enjoyed a relatively egalitarian ethos; women of traditional matrilineal clans; *vesyas* (prostitutes); *gaṇikas* (courtesans known for their literary and artistic expertise[20]); *devadāsīs* (independent women in Tamil Nadu who gave donations to a temple—probably in return for honour and status—and in recent centuries became temple dancers known as the wives of a god);[21] and the *bhakta* saints (often upper-caste women who left their marriage—or avoided marriage altogether—for a spiritual quest).[22]

One of the most important traditional images of the independent woman was the *vīrāṅganā*. Although not well known to those outside the culture, the archetype of the warrior woman (*vīrāṅganā*) has had a long history in India.

> the *vīrāṅganā* [is] the woman who manifests the qualities of *vīryam* or heroism. . . . She is a valiant fighter who distinguishes herself by prowess in warfare, an activity normally reserved for men. She demonstrates her martial skills and courage by direct participation in combat, at the risk of her life; in fact, sometimes she dies in battle or takes her own life on the battlefield to avoid ignominious defeat. She is a leader of women and men, acting as head of state during peace and general in time of war. She adopts male attire, as well as the symbols of male status and authority, especially the sword, and she rides a horse. The *vīrāṅganā* is dedicated to virtue, wisdom, and the defence of her people. Above all, she is a fighter and a victor in the struggle with the forces of evil.[23]

The *vīrāṅganā* was the human counterpart of the warrior goddess. The most famous of such goddesses is Durgā, who rides into battle on her lion with weapons in her many hands to fight the demon Mahīṣa. Another is Kālī who defeats her enemies, drinks the blood of her victims and wears strings of their skulls as garlands.[24] The *vīrāṅganā* is the heroine of both folk theatre (*nautaṅkī*) and, in a milder version, real history (the warrior women Razia Sultana, Kurma Devi, Rani Durgavati, Chand Bibi, Tarabai, Ahalyabai Holkar and Lakshmibai[25]). Such independent roles for Hindu women were never actively encouraged by the Hindu tradition; once a woman had assumed such a role, however, it was acknowledged and often honored.[26]

The *pativrata* ideal (not to mention the culturally acknowledged exceptions such as the prostitutes, courtesans and temple dancers) was strongly attacked in the nineteenth century by the colonial powers and Christian missionaries, as they created a uniform civil law.[27] At the same time, the British Raj promoted ideals of education, work and voting rights for women (though the latter, ironically, had not yet gained acceptance in Britain itself!). The Hindu reform movement, initially led by brahmin men, addressed problems such as child marriage; lack of education; inheritance; and remarriage, as well as *sati* and widowhood. The reformers wanted to stop Western criticism of Hinduism, which had been blamed for the difficult situation of women.

Hindu women themselves quickly took up the challenge of reform. Their active participation in the fight for independence under Mahatma Gandhi's leadership earned them great respect. By their heroic actions and their self-sacrifice for the national cause, they gained moral clout in the battle to improve the status of women. During the 1920s they won the right to vote in various states. After independence (1947), the constitution guaranteed that there would be no discrimination on the basis of sex with reference to social, political and economic acts. Special provisions were made, moreover, to improve the status of women. Women as well as men now had the right to an adequate livelihood and equal pay for equal work. Jawarhalal Nehru, the first prime minister, even argued for women's economic independence and abolition of the joint family system. Successive laws addressed many other problems faced by women: child marriage, divorce, maternity benefits, sexual harassment, assault, seclusion, cruelty to married women and rape. Although some people today think that laws could still be improved,[28] others conclude that liberal legislation is largely in place and the remaining task is to encourage women to exercise their rights.

Images of Women in the Popular Cinema of India

Indian films have been classified as Popular Cinema (commercial films, usually in Hindi but with regional variants in Tamil, Telugu, Kannada or Bengali) in contrast to New Cinema, also known as Parallel or Art cinema. (The latter often deals with issues of social significance rather than "art for art's sake" as the term "Art Cinema," borrowed from the West, would imply.) To date there is little consensus on the nature of Popular Cinema. It is necessary to understand this genre, however, in order to assess the criticism of the portrayal of women by film reviewers (not to mention the portrayal of women in the films themselves). But to assess the criticism of the portrayal of women, it is also necessary to understand various societal trends. After examining several perspectives on Popular Cinema, I will discuss the relation of genre, criticism, gender and societal change.

A View from *Manushi*

The magazine *Manushi*, from a perspective informed by feminism and socialism, examines issues related to women's employment, domestic life, legal status and political action. It also features poems and short stories written by women. Film reviews by women – Madhu Kishwar, Ruth Vanita, Mukul Kesavan, "Geeta," Bina Agarwal, Harsh Sethi, Prabha Krishnan, "Anjali" and "Ujala"[29] – who work for *Manushi* in Delhi are a staple item of each issue. Though well educated, most of these urban women are not professional academics or film critics; rather, they are social commentators who work for the women's cause as represented by *Manushi*'s mandate to inform Indian women about women's issues, to provide an outlet for their thoughts and to promote a sisterly solidarity. One of the agendas of the modern women's movement (including that in India over the past century) has been to lessen, if not remove, the economic, political and emotional dependence of women on men. This is being done by destroying the dichotomy between private and public realms and by promoting education and jobs for women.[30] For these reasons, a positive assessment of women in the work place and promotion of greater independence should be reflected in Popular Cinema. But is this really the case?

Writing for *Manushi*, Madhu Kishwar and Ruth Vanita observe that women's work is largely ignored in Popular Cinema. Popular films encourage the view that women of all classes work only when it is economically necessary for the survival of their families. Work is viewed as undesirable and to be abandoned as soon as the family's financial position has improved. The films present several specific reasons why a woman goes to work: death or injury of the male income-earner, abandonment, lack of dowry or desire to leave the husband. The overall impression given is that work in the public realm, although sometimes necessary for survival, is viewed as unfeminine by Popular Cinema and to be avoided or discontinued as soon as possible. For example, in a film called *Agreement*, say Kishwar and Vanita, the heroine who dominates her husband, refuses to have children and thrives as a businesswoman is viewed as abnormal. The norms of womanhood are restored, however, by the end of the film. The wife grows her hair (short hair being a sign of Westernization), dons a sari and sexually submits to her husband. And he takes over the business.[31] Similarly, women who have tried to escape bad domestic situations by working and setting up independent households ultimately give up their jobs and return, repentant, to their husbands. Even though a husband's bad behaviour had encouraged a wife to leave him in the first place, she views herself as worthy of blame in the final result.

Kishwar and Vanita conclude that Hindi films portray the working woman ambivalently. She may be viewed with pity if she is forced to work in the public realm in order to fulfill her role of serving her husband and family. This is especially true for a poor woman. But pity turns to hostility when a woman competes with a man in his domain and tries to be independent. Kishwar and Vanita suggest that sexual competition is sometimes related to class competition. The poor woman who does not conform to middle-class patterns of the "self-sacrificing wife" (and may not even want to)[32] symbolizes the constant threat to conservative, middle-class norms. It is for this reason, the reviewers, that films give licence to middle-class men to seduce, rape or kill the lower-caste, working woman. Though she becomes a martyr in moral terms (as a victim of sexual and caste/class abuse), she is no longer a threat. The message is given to all women that safety lies in conformity to the middle-class norms of womanhood (*strīdharma*).[33]

Hindi films, the reviewers for *Manushi* note, portray educated women as too independent and selfish. In the film *Yeh Kaisa Insaaf*, the dilemma of the educated woman is explored. "'I am educated. You are educated. I earn. You earn. If you look after your family, you'll be praised. If I do the same, I'll be condemned. Why these double standards?' asks Madhu of her husband."[34] With these words she leaves her husband. Her only option, however, is to go back to her own family and work for them. The film ends with Madhu returning to her husband. It is she who pleads that he never leave her again!

In the film *Swayamvar*, after Ram, the hero, sings a song in comic vein about women's liberation — including the line "Women are striding ahead so fast that the ground is slipping from under men's feet"[35] — men are reassured: "Don't feel threatened by this idea. It's only an absurd game played by women. They'll come safely back to your feet."[36] And the weapon of rape is used to bring the wife there. Lakshman, the brother of Ram, tells a recalcitrant Rupa: "Remember this, the husband is the only true companion and protector of the wife."[37] To prove this, her husband appears at the right moment to save her from the inevitable stereotyped film rapist. She then succumbs to sexual relations with him that had earlier repulsed her.[38] The reviewer suggests that the reference to "women's armies marching out in every land"[39] alludes to the profound discomfort of feminism experienced by male film-makers who react to feminism by promoting traditional stereotypes of women and by laughing at women's challenges.

Educated women are also portrayed as too Westernized. In *Kalyug Aur?*, for instance, as soon as the god Hanuman descends to earth:

> he encounters a short-haired woman in dress and hat who smokes, drinks and takes part in fancy dress parades. "You should be ashamed," he tells her. "Such clothes are a blot on the name of Indian womanhood...." The hero constantly delivers self-righteous chauvinistic speeches on the need to keep evil women and the evil West at bay.[40]

The words of the title, *Kalyug Aur*, which goes back to a theme of the Purāṇas, refers to the final period of time before the world is destroyed, a time when immorality prevails. Women are causing this immorality by ignoring their traditional norms. In *Kalyug Aur?* the woman eventually conforms to the model of Sītā and demands that all women be accepted as wives, even though she pays homage to modernity by singing a song about how "she will bear no more fire ordeals (as did Sītā to prove her innocence), will burn the veil and put out the sun."[41]

Occasionally a film features a superwoman who seeks revenge when she or others are wronged. Kathryn Hansen[42] notes how the Bombay film industry in the 20s, 30s and 40s borrowed heavily from the genre of folk theatre, including its stories of the *vīrāṅganā*. The *vīrāṅganā* as bandit queen has remained popular in Hindi films. Hansen discusses how one film, *Kahani Phulvati ki*, has its origin in the real life story of Phūlan Devi, a low-caste woman who waged revenge on the high-caste men who had sexually assaulted her. Phūlan Devi has inspired not only many women of her region to become dacoits, but also induced craftsmen to make clay images of her to be sold in the market along with those of deities![43] She is now of international fame, thanks to stories in *Time* and *Esquire*.[44]

In the masculinist press, Phūlan has been portrayed as an irresistible, insatiable man-eater. The image constructed of her combines elements of wild beauty, se-ductiveness, and extraordinary danger. *Esquire* describes her as a "legendary six-foot-tall, raven-haired, one-armed beauty, a beautiful femme fatale who had butchered twice as many men as she had bedded." It ... is noteworthy that Phūlan has also become a symbol of women's liberation, to urban Indians as well as to the rural women who emulate her. Phūlan and her sister-bandits, Kusima Nain, Meera Thakur, and others, have been called a "beacon of hope for countless young women who have a score to settle with society." In Bombay and Delhi, Phūlan "appeared to represent the ideas expressed by such feminists as Kate Millett, Betty Friedan, and Germaine Greer," in her stance as "the new woman ... a brash Amazon who had risen above caste and the traditionally subservient position of the Indian female."[45]

Although the *vīrāṅganā* figure is still found, many such heroines are portrayed today with limited power, say our film reviewers. In *Meri Izzat Bachao*, for instance, the heroine named Durgā, is "the avenging fury, complete with whip, knife, poison, destroying one rapist after another to the claps of the predominantly male audience."[46] But Durgā is far differ-ent from the ideal male hero, comments Vanita. Because she has killed, she herself must ultimately die, unlike the male heroes who triumph and live. Other films that start with the actions of a strong heroine end only with their sanction or approval by male authorities. Some films that fea-ture *vīrāṅganās* today portray them, moreover, not as moral heroines as in the past, but as immoral figures. In short, both the power and the morality of the female heroine have declined.

The reviewers who write for *Manushi* conclude that the traditional norms of Hindu womanhood (*strīdharma*), which have been dramatically reformed in many communities, are endorsed by Hindi films. Even the *vīrāṅganā* figure is being pacified. But what they find more disturbing is the portrayal of rape. Rape, in fact, is extremely common in Popular Cin-ema, note the reviewers. Comment on this phenomenon is a staple fea-ture in most *Manushi* film reviews. The myth that working women will be molested is propagated, Kishwar and Vanita think, to show the woman as victim, the villain as victimizer and the hero as protector. It also serves as a high point of drama. Rape is associated with the boss' treatment of female employees, the landlord's treatment of his female labourers and the upper-caste man's treatment of tribal women. Some films suggest that men will retaliate against the growing independence of women with rape. Kishwar and Vanita find that the theme of rape has the unfortunate result of alienating a woman from the idea of work and depicting her as a "protected and passive being"[47] whose real place is in the home. Too much attention on sexual assault, according to the feminist reviewers, also deflects attention from other important work issues such as low wages, maternity leave, job security and childcare. It communicates that working women are sexually promiscuous. It may also encourage male viewers of the film to think that such molestation is normal behaviour for working men, an attitude that could then be acted out in real life.

One of the most "notorious" rape scenes occurred, we are told, in the film *Red Rose*, portraying a sex maniac who avenges his rejection by some women when he was a young man by raping other women today. According to one critic:

> The film tries to make the audience sympathise with the rapist, and glorifies him as a romantic, lonely figure who pitches himself against an unjust world which has failed to understand him. Do we not need to ask: When a woman is sexually insulted or raped, does she take revenge? No, she is often forced to commit suicide. Such suicides occur very frequently in our society.[48]

It seems that this film actually inspired a rape of two female children by two young men in Bangalore. As a result, The Forum Against Rape in Bombay organized a boycott of the film. The review ends with an impassioned plea to stop glorification of rape as "manly behaviour" and bemoans the fact that the lines between villain and hero in films have been blurred. So this is not simply another story. It is propaganda against women, we are told. It adds to the illusion that all women who are victims of rape and violence, are immoral, provocatively dressed and deserve to be treated with disrespect and cruelty. The film shows virtuous women as immune from atrocities and longing for male domination and protection.[49] The author of the review concludes by crying out: "Ban *Red Rose*."

Not all films reviewed in *Manushi* receive such harsh criticism by the women reviewers. A few are judged to give a realistic portrayal of modern women or raise issues of concern to them. One film that is deemed supportive of women is *Bheegi Palkein*. According to Bina Agarwal, this film is about Shanti, a young woman who is modern (she marries a man of her choice and works full-time outside the house) but also traditional (she performs rituals and is devoted to her husband and child). Bina Agrawal comments: "This characterization successfully challenges and breaks out of the Bombay film caricatures of modern working women as promiscuous, immoral and flirtatious, causing the break-up of marriages by their neglect of husbands and children."[50]

As for rape, there is another film, *Insaaf Katarazu*, that presents it in a more realistic manner, according to one feminist critic writing for *Manushi*. First, the rapist is neither a psychopath nor a criminal but an average man. Second, the act of rape is motivated by the desire to dominate and humiliate the woman. And third, the woman fights back instead of committing suicide. She takes the man to court and makes the crime public. When the court sets the rapist free and he rapes her sister, the heroine is transformed into the goddess Durgā, pursues the villain and kills him. Says Ujala in her review, "Rape is seen throughout the film as a crime against the woman—*she* is the injured party and this is a new thing in films."[51] Usually the topic of rape is explored as a problem between men, one of whom is wronged (because the woman is related to him as wife, mother, sister, friend) and one of whom is the villain. According to the reviewer:

> The court depiction of the rape trial made the two main points very force-fully—one, that it is impossible for a woman to prove that she did not consent and meaningless to ask her to prove this, and two, that the court atmosphere reeks of anti-woman prejudice and the woman's sexual history is dragged out to unjustly defame her and justify the rapist. Though there are many contradictory statements in the film and its overall assumption is that woman's place is in the home as wife and mother, yet it is a step forward as a statement against violence against women.[52]

A presupposition of the women who write film reviews for *Manushi* is that films are to be assessed in sociological terms. Popular Cinema should be an accurate reflection of society; it should be *cinema vérité*. With this criterion in mind, they ask questions such as the following: Is the film an accurate reflection of women's position in society? Does it adequately criticize what is wrong with society's treatment of women? Or, does it create positive images for women which, even if not yet common in society, show what a better world might be in the future?

The reviewers for *Manushi* are not only feminists but also socialists or marxists. They are critical because women are rarely portrayed working and because portrayals of work—when they do occur in Popular Cinema—promote capitalist values. By seductively portraying the attractive materialistic world of yuppies, filmmakers inspire the desire for upward mobility. According to Madhu Kishwar and Ruth Vanita, Hindi films promote the values of the upper middle-class. This is accomplished by portraying the male protagonist as a big businessman in an urban setting or a big landowner in a rural setting. This is also done by presenting even middle-class families as the proud possessors of many material goods who enjoy a range of modern services and an elite lifestyle.[53] Kishwar and Vanita argue that Hindi films do not reflect the lifestyle of the vast majority of Indians. The lives of the poor are virtually invisible and the portrayal of the material prosperity of the middle class is a *yuppified* vision that has no counterpart in reality. "The viewer," Kishwar and Vanita state, "is not led to consider seriously the question of poverty in our society. Nor do everyday problems of the poor, such as squalid living conditions and scarcities of various kinds, have to be dealt with in any detail."[54]

As socialists, the women who write for *Manushi* object to the portrayal of poverty as but a bleak phase—soon to be eliminated—in the history of an otherwise middle-class individual. They are frustrated when socialist sentiments are used to establish a moral claim for the individual who senses injustice in life but does not call for societal transformation to improve material conditions for the poor. Therefore, even when work is portrayed, they think that it is not positively portrayed because it is presented in a capitalist context. In contrast, they approach film from the perspective of the marxist theory of hegemony. Accordingly, they view popular films as a means by which the ruling class propagates a false consciousness, thereby concealing from the masses how they are exploited. They think that the hegemony of elite and middle-class men is also perpetuated by films. According to the *Manushi* reviewers, it is striking that the theme of women's work does not receive a more sympathetic treatment in many Hindi films, given the official endorsement by the government of the importance of women in the labour force. The reviewers suggest that this is because men, including makers of films, want to maintain their male power and privilege by ensuring the dependence of women. But in point of fact, the reviewers argue, there has been tremendous social change. The films do not acknowledge this, just as they do not acknowledge the need for further change to improve the position of women.

Sudhir Kakar's View

According to Sudhir Kakar, a psychoanalyst, Hindi films were never intended to be a reflection of society. He sees them pre-eminently as stories that work out traditional psychological problems. As a psychoanalyst, he looks to the psychic roots of stories in childhood experiences. He approaches the films very differently from the women writing reviews for Manushi who bemoan the films' lack of realism, their use of stereotypes, and above all, their insistence that whatever the trouble between the sexes, happy marriage and the *pativrata* image of womanhood will prevail.

Kakar agrees that this *pativrata* image will prevail but for different reasons. Using the film *Ram Teri Ganga Maili* — "a syrupy tale of the eternally pure woman whose devotion and innocence triumph over the worst efforts of lustful (mostly older) males to enslave and exploit her"[55] — as his example, he observes that the heroine is the perfect embodiment of the *pativrata* ideal: steadfast in her devotion to a hero, which leads to great suffering. Rape scenes, he suggests, are the product of fantasy.

> The question why rape is a staple feature of Indian cinema where otherwise even the kiss is taboo, why the sexual humiliation of the woman plays such a significant role in the fantasy of love, is important. That this rape is invariably a fantasy rape, without the violence and trauma of its real-life counterpart, is evident in the manner of its visual representation. Villains, mustachioed or stubble-chinned, roll their eyes and stalk their female prey around locked rooms. With deep-throated growls of gloating, lasciviously muttering a variant of "Ha! You cannot escape now," they make sharp lunges to tear off the heroine's clothes and each time come away with one more piece of her apparel. The heroine, on the other hand, retreats in pretty terror, her arms folded across her breasts to protect her dishevelled modesty, pleading all the while to be spared from the fate worse than death.[56]

Psychoanalyst that he is, Kakar relates these conventional rape scenes to the problem that every boy must face: separation from Mother and the world of women to achieve masculinity. This separation anxiety is symbolically remembered in scenes of rape that express the humiliation and rejection of his own feminine self to become a man. A woman in the audience, observes Kakar, appropriates the rape scene very differently. For her, it expresses the constant fear that an older, authoritative figure will destroy her virginity. Kakar thinks that behind these figures lurks the image of the father who withdraws from emotional intimacy in her adolescence in recognition of her new womanly status, a status that is to be enjoyed only by another man in marriage. Rape, then, in Kakar's view, is the girl's fantasy that the father is really not rejecting her but rather desires her. Because the identity of the father is disguised by a fearful mask, she can project her own deviant desire yet not feel guilty. So much for rape.

The theme of romance in Hindi films, Kakar says, draws from myths of an "eve-teasing" hero who watches women bathe. This represents the narcissism of the boy at the beginning of the Oedipus stage when he aggressively tries to win, with mounting excitement, the attention of a heroine who is annoyed or recalcitrant. Such a theme, the psychoanalyst comments, is the fantasy of the young man who needs to be reassured by women of his powers and abilities to transform a cool amazon into an aroused, lusting female. The fantasy is also that of the virgin who becomes aware of her sexuality but, after a brief period of spirited play and teasing, reverses the roles. She then is "reduced to a groveling being, full of a moral masochism wherein she revels in her 'stickiness' to the hero."[57]

Kakar also explores how Indian men have a tendency to bifurcate a woman into a good and bad woman: pure mother, impure prostitute. He relates the portrayal of romance in Hindi films to the need for the romantic lover to find a home for his illicit love. This is often split off from his respectable self. The brothel (*kotha*) is:

> Hindi cinema's favourite abode for the denied and discarded sexual impulses, a home for vile bodies. Sometimes replaced by the shady night club, a more directly licentious import from the West, the *kotha* provides the alcohol as well as the rhythmic music and dance associated with these degraded impulses. Enjoyed mostly by others, by the villain or the hero's friends, for the romantic love the sexual pleasures of the *kotha* are generally cloaked in a pall of guilt, to be savored morosely in an alcoholic haze and to the nagging beat of self-recrimination.[58]

And there is also a new lack of romantic interest on the part of the hero in the films of the "good-bad guy" type.[59] Kakar sees in this underworld figure a reaction to the loss, absence or ambivalence of a mother in childhood. But the ambivalent male hero is also an expression of the forces of modernization (overcrowding in slums, dehumanized bureaucracy and loss of traditional skills). He is a kind of transitional person who is culturally confused when the traditional codes of behaviour no longer function. He has lost identity, earning power and social status, and responds aggressively to the many pressures of modern society. Because of the precarious emotional terrain of romance, this kind of hero prefers admiration to a woman's love, and freedom to commitment. The heroine in such films, Kakar observes, is more a sympathetic and undemanding junior comrade or sister, rather than his lover. "She exemplifies the low place of heterosexual love in the life of the transitional man, whose fantasies are absorbed more by visions of violence than of love, more with the redressal of narcissistic injury and rage than with the romantic longing for completion—a gift solely in the power of a woman to bestow."[60] In the final analysis, Kakar thinks that Hindi films express the fantasies of each sex toward the other and in the process explore the realm of the impossible and the forbidden by bridging desire and reality.

Even if the idea that Hindi films reflect a great deal of fantasy (and are closer to folktale and myth than real life) is accepted, an important question here is, whose fantasy? Kakar discusses mainly male fantasies reflected in Hindi films: rape, brothel scenes or macho heroism. Several scholars and film critics have concluded that Hindi films are made for men. In fact, observes the critic Anil Saari, it is mainly men who go to Hindi films; in the villages women are usually not taken by their husbands because of the cost[61] or because their husbands are embarrassed by the immorality of the films and do not want their women folk to see them.[62] According to Beatrix Pfleiderer, films now cater mainly to the growing industrial wage-labourers in urban and semi-urban areas. Thus, they do not reflect the hegemony of upper- and middle-class men (as the *Manushi* reviewers argue). Rather, they appeal primarily to people in transition between agricultural village life and industrial city life. Today, this perspective of the "little person" becomes the quintessentially ideal Indian in comparison to the person corrupted by foreign ways.

Chidananda Das Gupta's View
One of the most comprehensive studies of Hindi cinema to date is the 1991 book *The Painted Face* by Chidananda Das Gupta. Das Gupta introduces himself as a film critic who has extended his interest in New Cinema to Popular Cinema (especially Hindi films). For this task, he has turned to psychoanalysis, although he is not trained in the field. Unlike the other interpretations surveyed here, Das Gupta's is nuanced in its discussion of changes in Indian film, the relation of these changes to social, political and economic developments, and the evolving concepts of genre. His metaphor for the nature of Indian popular cinema is "the painted face." This originated in folk theatre in which the hero's face is painted to give it a fair complexion, symbolizing high status. The painted face, thinks Das Gupta, functions as a mask, even in films, and demonstrates how easy it is for Indian audiences to suspend reality.

Unlike the New Cinema (e.g. Satyajit Ray's films) which portrays women as individuals, Das Gupta argues that Hindi films present women stereotypically. And unlike earlier film images of women as active, strong, virtuous, hardworking and just, contemporary films show women (mothers and wives) as passive. The portrayal of woman as passive, continues Das Gupta, comes not from the Vedas and epics (*Mahābhārata* and Vālmīki's *Rāmāyaṇa*) in which women are comparatively free and strong but from Manu, Islamic influence, Tulsīdās' *Rāmāyaṇa* and today's televison versions of the epics. Das Gupta observes that in today's films there is ambiguity about educating girls. Divorce and widow remarriage, moreover, is not seriously entertained as a genuine option in life — even if it is shown as a possibility, the girl dies before it can occur. Education also falls into disrepute, for schools and universities are depicted as lovers' playgrounds. The virtuous, innocent, shy, home-centred girl is preferred to the better-educated, more independent student. Other films castigate the modern Indian woman for being Westernized and therefore evil:

> Suspicious of modern Western ways, the cinema rates traditonal mores above them. Some films strain to contrast East and West; *Do Raaste, Evening in Paris* and *Purab aur Paschim* declare the East superior and the foreign devil a threat to home and integrity. Others express the same beliefs by implication in an occasional sequence or stretch of dialogue. This often relates to the roles of women. The westernized woman, for instance, is admitted mostly at the margins of society; she is the nightclub singer or bandit, or the golden-hearted prostitute living outside the main stream of society and therefore well accustomed to episodes of sex or violence. Also, a woman who may have consorted with a man other than her husband has forfeited the right to choose her partners in bed; she must accept whoever comes along.[63]

Mothers are glorified in these films:

> As woman is cast in the mould of the absolute mother image, her aspect as wife is attenuated to the point of disappearance.The wife living in a fulfilling relationship with her husband is virtually non-existent in the popular cinema. Being the wife is only the preparatory phase of her graduation, first to mother, and then to mother-in-law.[64]

For Das Gupta, this focus on the mother is new in India; previous texts spoke of wives (Draupadī, Gandharī, Sītā) not mothers. He locates this current mother-fixation in the fact that village men who migrate to the cities are traumatized by their estrangement from the values and rhythms of the village and their marginal life in the cities. The mother represents, then, the security of village life — a meaningful, ordered universe — and the security of childhood. Ultimately, the obsession with the mother, says Das Gupta resorting to a psychoanalytic frame, expresses the unwillingness of the hero (who represents migrant men in the city) to grow up and take charge of his life in his new environment, however difficult that may be. In short, it is the longing for the womb and, for Das Gupta, a regressive force in current Indian society, especially when financed with black money and buttressed by traditional values of womanhood. Despite saying that the mother-fixation is new, Das Gupta also links it to the age-old Oedipus conflict.

Although the mother is glorified in Hindi films of the last several decades, she is not aways the perfect being. She often persuades her son to marry a rich woman or obtain wealth in some manner. This demonstrates that women, too, are supremely greedy in the new capitalist economy, and seek upward mobility through their sons, who are sent off to the cities to make the family's fortune. In actual society, Das Gupta observes, mothers are sometimes implicated in the extraction of more dowry from the family of a new daughter-in-law, which may even lead to a dowry death. Dowry death, however, is not a theme for Hindi films. It represents too much social realism. On the contrary, the mother's greed is cloaked under her affection for her son and her test of his loyalty by requesting him to fulfill the needs and desires of the family. She is also portrayed as the one who requests her son to take illegal revenge when the family's honour is destroyed. In effect, then, she is portrayed as the *deus ex machina* who both orders and legitimizes the Robin Hood-style actions of her son, thereby elevating family over society and a mother's desires over law. (Although Das Gupta does not say so, this transfer of blame to women absolves the male hero of any misdemeanour by suggesting that he is ultimately but the puppet of a woman.)

Das Gupta claims that rape is "an essential ingredient of the popular film and an increasing reality, particularly in north India's Hindi speaking area."[65]

> It is obvious that whenever rape is made attractive, the male audience is being asked to gather vicarious satisfaction. It is analogous to the cry of 'kill him, kill him' at the boxing matches. No revenge device, however inventive, can wipe out the subtext of sexual satisfaction left between the lines of this moralistic tale. In our films, rape alone can provide the opening for the frank and open sexuality that is sublimated by the song in love stories in deference to the squeamishness of the audience and its protectors. Only the rapist, that is, the criminal, is allowed an open expression of the animal in us. It is safe to watch him at the act, because he stands condemned already as an outsider to decent society. If you get a secret, vicarious satisfaction from watching the act, there is no need to talk about it. The chorus of disapproval will drown such talk anyway.[66]

In Indian society, the film critic adds, rape makes the woman polluted; she becomes like *jootha* or polluted food, categorically destroying the purity of the person. When Sītā's purity was challenged by Rāma, Das Gupta reminds the reader, she was tried by entering into fire. In past films, raped women did not fight off their assailants. Now, occasionally, they do, in films such as *Pratighaat* (1987) about a housewife who kills her attacker; *Zaikhmi Aurat* (1988) about a police officer who is raped and seeks revenge through castrating her tormentors; and *Be-Abroo* (1985) in which the woman lures her rapists into a trap and then kills them. "The humiliation of a woman who wields power over men is thus the real event; her revenge is sensational, but not to be taken seriously."[67] Such scenes reflect not so much a position against rape per se, says Das Gupta, but more a renewal of the *vīrāṅganā* theme. Although the rapes are reported to legal authorities, police and courts prove ineffective in prosecuting the crime (an expression of a more general indictment of law that is common in Hindi films). And so personal revenge becomes the order of the day. Das Gupta thinks that this lack of confidence in the law is not only an expression of the producer's own black market, criminal mentality but also "the demise of the sense of hope that imbued the films of the fifties and the early sixties."[68] For a woman, it is a simple confirmation of the fact that she cannot expect justice from the legal system; even when the overt text of films portrays her seeking revenge, the subtext may confirm traditional views of womanhood.

Assuming this discussion accurately reflects the films themselves, we find a refusal to appreciate modern images of woman as educated, working, free both to marry a man of her choice and to divorce him to remarry if she feels this is in her best interest. Also, as the mother-son relationship dominates such films, the father image recedes. Das Gupta suggests that the absent father could reflect the sociological reality of men absent from their families, since they have left the village and gone to the city to work. This would leave female-headed families in the villages and strengthen the mother-son bond, which has always been strong in Indian society (a compensation, some Indian analysts suggest, for the lack of love and husband-wife bonding in some arranged marriages).

Throughout Das Gupta's analysis, his presupposition is apparent. He is a marxist, who is concerned to expose the mask of Popular Cinema in the symbol of the "painted face." The rural migrants are the lumpen proletariat, and the film producers, the bourgeois. Hinduism is the opiate of the masses, obscuring the light of reason, science and technology; in its resurgence it is particularly dangerous for the democratic and intellectual traditions of the country that are needed for progress. Although his judgement can only be labelled biased for its reductionism, in its selection of the most negative aspects of the religion, and in its categorical blame of the religion as if it were the only or even most important source of current problems (Das Gupta's own analysis suggests that a major input into the films is not religion but the anti-social "criminal mentality" of many producers), his study nevertheless points to a trend in current Indian society that may adversely affect women. It is to a more general discussion of genre, gender and social trends that I now turn.

On Gender, Genre and Social Change
When we compare the analysis of the various reviewers, we find some differences. The *Manushi* reviewers analyze the films sociologically; Kakar analyzes them psychoanalytically; and Das Gupta analyzes them

sociologically, psychoanalytically and historically. The *Manushi* reviewers and Das Gupta are socialist and marxist in their perspective; Kakar's political leanings are not evident in his discussion of films.

Aside from these differences, there are many points of agreement. They all observe that there is little positive imaging of modern, educated working women; new legal possibilities such as divorce and remarriage are rarely depicted as real options. Although there is some experimentation with romance and other modern behaviours, ultimately conservative values on the model of Tulsīdās' Sītā are affirmed for women. When the independent woman or *vīrāṅganā* is portrayed, she is a mythic figure, not a sociological reality. Whereas in the older Hindi popular films, good triumphed over evil, now evil triumphs over good. These films split the image of woman into stereotypes of a good and a bad woman; there is no realistic individual who has both virtues and vices. Moreover, male camaraderie is emphasized at the expense of romance with women, and sexual harassment and rape are commonplace.

With these observations in mind, it is timely to return to the question of genre. How is the genre of Popular Cinema best defined? Is it primarily a reflection of reality or fantasy? Is it myth, crypto-myth, or secular myth? How reviewers assess the portrayal of women in Hindi films has a great deal to do with how they understand the genre, and what they think the genre should be. How the genre evolves, though, may also reflect changes in the society.

From the reviews, it seems that most Hindi films of the past several decades are midway on the continuum between a mythological and a sociological treatment (both of which have been popular in the past).[69] There have been various attempts to classify this mix of the mythic and the sociological. Kakar suggests that Hindi films, although ostensibly secular, are close to the religious mentality. The Indian public moves easily in and out of fantasy worlds just as it moves easily in and out of religious ones. If I read his comments correctly, he is suggesting that the deep estrangement of religion and secularity has not yet occurred. Heroines are still the *vīrāṅganās* of folklore or of myth-in-the making such as the tale of Phūlan Devi, or even in the image of the goddess Durgā herself. Thus, even when films are ostensibly about everyday people, they are really modern-day versions of traditional folktales and myths.

Kakar views film as story and fantasy, akin to India's mythic tradition. At its best, he comments, fantasy rebuilds the past, heals trauma, fixes identity and creates a new future.[70] But Hindi films also portray the latest technology, fashions and social trends whether in India or abroad. Anil Saari argues that the Indian popular film mediates tradition and modernity (as defined first by the colonial, British-dominated culture and later by industrialization). It also mediates the "great contradictions of Indian society with one format: the idealistic and the immoral, the ascetic and the hedonistic, the rags and the riches, the brave and the ludicrous."[71]

Like the great oppositions (*dvandvas*) that characterize Indian myth and philosophy, it seems that Hindi films are structured on a fundamental opposition of fear and hope, modernity and tradition, city and village. With Das Gupta, Saari thinks that Hindi films appeal to the desire for change and growth of the personality, but also to the little person's fear that the rapid changes occurring may become a tidal wave that will destroy existence. "A people living on the border of extinction, surviving against odds all the time – they are a people who are too frightened to change, lest they destroy even the little that preserves them presently. Therefore the symbol of change must be one of make-believe."[72]

But Das Gupta is also skeptical. He observes there is now more fear and cynicism than hope and growth expressed in these films. And he comments that the learning experience promoted is not just how to integrate technology, but also how to get ahead through criminal means. A view of film as fantasy, folktale or secular myth does not take account of the fact that such a genre is not always beneficial for society. Reaffirmation of tradition can have negative effects on society or certain groups within it, if they had actually been in need of reform. A secular myth, for instance, could encourage a society to refuse to educate its women, if this had once been religiously endorsed (as was the case with the norm of *pativrata* during some periods of Indian history). But does this imply that society necessarily wants to ignore the reforms of the past century? The reviewers for *Manushi*, even though they are profoundly disturbed by the portrayal of women in many of these films, say "no." So does Das Gupta.

Das Gupta argues that Popular Cinema is powerful because pre-industrial peoples (as represented by the rural migrants to cities or the Indian villagers themselves) have difficulty separating myth from fact. This is one of the reasons why a few young men see harassment or a rape on film and then are inspired to re-enact it in everyday life.

> When some eighty sons of business magnates in Calcutta tried to molest girls coming out of a college, their war cry was *Oye, Oye* – the song from *Tridev* (a movie). Thus the ubiquitous rape scene in popular cinema which Kakar sees as fantasy on the part of both the men and the women in the audience can hardly be seen as a self-contained phenomenon that does not influence reality. Indeed the somewhat indulgent attitude to rape as entertainment and all of popular cinema as self-contained fantasy can be seen as a clear (and very western consumerist-existentialist) refusal to engage the question of value.[73]

Similarly, people have reported in a Hindi newsweekly that they feel guilty for seeing films which are filled with immoral behaviour; nevertheless, young boys confess that they have imitated the manners and attitudes of their film heroes toward girls, and college girls have revealed that they have mimicked their screen heroines when away from the parental eye. Imitation of film figures has also led a young man to molest the girls of his village, others to make vulgar taunts to girls, and still others to turn to crime.[74]

The enormous success of the film *Jai Santoshi Maa* about a goddess, which started a new religious cult throughout the country, is an example of what Das Gupta calls the remythologization of the present. The television serial *Rāmāyaṇa* also reflected the renewed popularity of the mythological formulas:

> "A crowd of over 40,000," reported the *The Times of India*, "waited patiently outside Jaipur's Birla mandir to have a glimpse of Rama (Arun Govil) and Sita (Dipika) who were due to grace. the shrine. Even ministers jostled with mesmerised fans for a *darshan*." Once more, people were taking off their shoes before watching Rama on the screen, and throwing flowers at it.[75]

What does this mean for women — a loss of the liberal laws gained over the past century and a return to conservative images of womanhood represented by Tulsīdās' Sītā or other mythological ideals? Or a selection of old and new roles?

It is difficult to assess the current trends for women in India. Many middle-class and elite women are educated and work. Women are breaking into male professions, as in the West. Some have bona fide careers. Certainly, many urban, educated middle-class women base their identity at least in part on their work and view it positively. Some observers of change in modern India think that Popular Cinema is not just escapist fantasy but is contributing to changing values as urban, middle-class women, especially those who work and have some economic freedom, begin to date and seek romance. Films are playing an important role in this transformation. They comment on new social problems such as arranged versus love marriage; joint-family versus nuclear-family living patterns; family versus work roles for women; divorce and remarriage versus staying within a marriage.

> Less than a decade ago, the middle class contented themselves with soulful, long distance glances. Couples trundling down snowy slopes to Cashier Chamber's music was the stuff dreams were made of. Some of that fantasy has now become flesh. Young people in the cities are dating at every level, especially the middle classes and lower income groups. The virtual apartheid between the two sexes in conservative families has begun to give way. A sexual glasnost is breezing through, sending young clerks, stenographers and receptionists out in pursuit of romance.[76]

Such changes are quite recent and may still be confined to a small circle of people. Nonetheless, films portraying women in these roles — despite their eventual affirmation of traditional values of womanhood — seem to be having an effect on the society. But, as Das Gupta and other observers of recent events in India suggest, the larger direction of change may be different from that predicted by economists and reformers who have argued that greater literacy, education and job training for women will automatically lead to more women working and greater independence. Many women of the urban, lower middle class work to help accumulate dowry before marriage but then give up their jobs afterwards. In rural areas, women's work may be abandoned as soon as their family's overall economic position improves, and it can afford to keep its women at home. It should come as no surprise to find these traditional patterns being repeated in a modern setting, thanks to the new opportunities for upward mobility made possible by new jobs and a changing economy. Although this reaffirmation of female withdrawal from work outside the home (if not actual seclusion) may be initiated by men, it is likely that many women from lower castes who have difficult jobs would also welcome this change due to upward mobility.[77] In any case, women have never been unanimous on the topic of work, since the type and rewards of work have varied enormously. Many Indian women themselves, moreover, still look forward to marriage and motherhood, although on terms somewhat different from the past. The growing religious fundamentalism within the middle classes may appeal to women who still have a traditional orientation towards the family or who think that the model of the independent woman goes too far in the changes that it demands.

In the final analysis, however, one cannot help but think that the insistence of the Hindi films on women's domestic orientation also has something to do with contemporary male psychology (if not exactly the pathologies described by Kakar and Das Gupta). Across cultures, masculine identity has been defined primarily by three roles: being a progenitor, protector and provider.[78] To be a protector, men need someone or something to protect. In paleolithic times, they protected women and children against wild animals. In neolithic times, when warfare became common as horticultural societies fought over land, men protected women against rape or abduction by warriors of other tribes. With the development of despotic chiefdoms and early states, experiments with male power (including power over both men's and women's lives) made the role of protector even more important. The role of protector is now enshrined in masculine identity as the protection of the family's honour; loss of the chastity of the family's women by whatever illicit means is shame. "To rape" in Hindi is, for example, *izzat lutna*, "to steal one's honour." But when society is comparatively safe, the role of protector is no longer necessary. Yet it is possible that it has been such an important part of traditional masculine identity that it cannot be easily abandoned. Consequently, some men may continue to rape the women of another community to define their dominance over the men of that community (who proved incapable of protecting their women), but also with the awareness that this sets up a cycle of revenge (which will ensure their own role as protector of women). The modern counterpart of male dominance may be the rape of the lower-caste or tribal woman by the upper-caste man. Still, such acts are relatively rare. Every man is certainly not a rapist, though he may want to be a protector. Thus, even though the role of protector is no longer necessary for survival, it remains important for the concept of masculine identity. Could it be, then, that Hindi films with their preoccupation with villains (in the form of rapists) and heroes (in the form of protectors and revengers) re-enact a scenario that helps men to fulfill their identity as protectors? Such fantasy is hardly escapism. Rather, to the degree that it is successful, it provides the vicarious experience of manhood as protector. To the degree that it is not successful, of course, it may inspire the real thing, as with the film *Red Roses*. Myths about protectors, then, may become self-fulfilling prophecies in an age when masculine identity is being threatened in many ways.

Rape may have another etiology. Anthropological evidence shows that in some societies men have enforced social norms for women by the threat of rape.[79] If women's changing expectations are sufficiently threatening to men, there may be a tacit understanding to force them into conformity by the threat or act of rape. Thus, if women adopt Western dress, if they date, drink or smoke, this may make them worthy of rape in the eyes of those men who see themselves as protectors of the culture at large, rather than a particular woman. Allusions to the Kali Yuga in current films, in which social instability and miscegenation are blamed on women, may be relevant in this context. Aside from the occasional rape within the extended family by a sexually frustrated man (perhaps because of disappointment in the arranged marriage) or rapes by a disturbed man who feels he has no power and wishes to gain it by the temporary, forced domination of a woman, these other interpretations of rape may help us understand what is going on in Hindi films. Some Indian scholars have argued that a new macho identity emerged after national independence to compensate for the earlier feelings of emasculation experienced by Indian men who felt that they had been stripped of their power and were treated as women under Muslim and then British rule.[80] If so, identification with manly "protectors" in films may be important compensation.

This discussion helps us to understand that there is more to the formation of masculine identity than simply separating from Mother, as Kakar would have us believe. And the changing desires of women may be profounding disturbing to men, if this means a radical loss of masculine identity[81] when women claim that they need neither a protector (thanks to self-defence courses and new inspiration from the *vīrāṅganā* archetype) nor a provider (thanks to the new confidence that they can do everything men can do). Women's new interest in independence may also threaten men's identity as fathers.

The reviews of Hindi cinema suggest that Indian society is at a real crossroads. It is experimenting with new ideas while holding onto images of traditional norms. Under the surface, as women's fantasies and desires expand, men's become more threatened and threatening. In the meantime, the hero, as Kakar says, having lost identity, earning power and social status, is prone to aggressive responses to the many pressures of modern society. As for his relationship with a woman, he still seeks her admiration but is as incapable of love as if he is redressing a narcissistic injury and rage.[82]

If, as Das Gupta suggests, myth slides easily into reality, then the current types of pessimistic film heroes may contribute to the mood of urban pessimism. On the other hand, there may be an attempt to wrest the power of film away from those who have run the industry to date (since, as black marketeers, they have no interest in how women, Hinduism or culture is portrayed except as a means of making money). Whether this will be done by the socialists and marxists (like Das Gupta and the reviewers for *Manushi*) or by the religious fundamentalists remains to be seen. Film in general, and its portrayal of women in particular, is a dynamic medium responding to but also capable of initiating changes in society. If women were portrayed as subservient to men in some Hollywood films of the 1980s despite the success of the American feminist movement — which inspired Susan Faludi's book *Backlash* — this genre did not remain. Many Hollywood films of the early 1990s portrayed women as strong and heroic, virtual *vīrāṅganās*. Who knows, maybe the weak *vīrāṅganā* of current Hindi films will once again become strong. Then again, if Hinduism recovers a sense of selfhood and confidence, perhaps a moral, energetic Hindu woman who selects from both tradition and modernity and avoids the extremes will emerge to replace both the superhuman independent woman and the passive Sītā in films of recent years. In this context we should not forget that female leaders in the recent Hindu resurgence are often married women who have careers, and while they pay lip-service to tradition, they are highly selective in what aspects of tradition they preserve. Some people think, moreover, that some current films are less violent and are becoming more appealing to the middle classes. Since film is a dynamic medium, it is necessary to pay close attention to the presuppositions of the reviewers of these films, to the changing nature of the genre, to social trends and to biases that may cloud a vision of what is going on. Only in this way can we understand the complexities of norms of Hindu womanhood presented in Popular Cinema.

Notes

1 Chidananda Das Gupta, *The Painted Face: Studies in India's Popular Cinema* (New Delhi: Roli Books, 1991), p. 156.
2 Susan Faludi, *Backlash: The Undeclared War Against American Women* (New York: Crown Publishers, 1991).
3 I thank Dr. Paul Nathanson, a Canada Research Fellow at McGill University, for the insight that the enormous cost of each minute of film means that no scene is superfluous.
4 Sudhir Kakar, *Intimate Relations: Exploring Indian Sexuality* (New York: Viking Penguin, 1989), p. 26.
5 Ibid.

6   For an example of how a film may be analyzed according to these formal properties, see Paul Nathanson, *Over the Rainbow: The Wizard of Oz as a Secular Myth of America* (Albany: State University of New York Press, 1991), p. 21-53.

7   In 1772, Warren Hastings requested ten traditional scholars (pandits) from Bengal to compile a digest of Hindu civil law so that they could standardize Indian law and then integrate it with British law. Because the pandits used brahmanical law for this exercise of creating a common Hindu code, they subjected lower-caste women to strictures such as no divorce and no remarriage which had not governed their lives up to that time.

8   There are many regional variations and historical changes that cannot be addressed here; the inadequacies are painfully apparent to any scholar.

9   Whereas Sītā in the original Vālmīki *Rāmāyaṇa* is supportive of her husband, Rāma, she is by no means his mere servant or follower. She even abandons him, withdrawing to the forest and raising her sons by herself when he refuses to believe that she remained chaste when abducted by Rāvaṇa. Tulsīdās, by contrast, ignores the view of the Hindu wife as complement to her husband (*sahadharmiṇī*), which was popular in some historical periods or with some authors. He accepts a more conservative role for Sītā, making her subservient and dependent on her husband.

10 A brahmin woman had to marry within her subcaste (*jāti*) and be monogamous; an upper-caste man, however, could be polygamous and take one or more wives (even from a lower *jāti* — a practice called *anuloma*, literally going with the hair or grain, therefore in a natural direction, in contrast to the forbidden practice, *pratiloma*, a woman marrying down and therefore going against the hair or grain).

11 Manu, *The Laws of Manu*, Georg Bühler, trans., 5:147-48 (Dover: New Jersey, 1979), p. 195.

12 From other perspectives, however, he was the protected, she the protector of his health, life and destiny; she was the actual power or Śakti, he but the controller of it or its passive foundation. This view appears not only in texts influenced by Tantra but also in the ideology of the *satī* as the "good wife" who makes possible her husband's longevity and — if she performs the act of *sati* (self-immolation on his funeral pyre) — his attainment of heaven (as well as her own).

13 In Vedic religion of the ancient period, women remarried; it is only in the later period that remarriage was forbidden for upper-caste women. The early period was pronatal and wanted to maximize a woman's reproductive role for the extended family (which is why she was allowed to marry her dead husband's brother, a custom called *niyoga*). When population expanded in the Gangetic plain, leading to a demographic crisis, however, remarriage and *niyoga* were forbidden, since it was no longer desirable to have many children.

14 In point of fact, *Sati* was the conservative Hindu woman's equivalent of other forms of religious self-willed death, such as the Jain monk or nun fasting to death; the Hindu yogi burying himself alive; or the Buddhist *bodhisattva* sacrificing his body to feed a hungry animal. See Alaka Hejib and Katherine K. Young, "Sati, Widowhood and Yoga," in Arvind Sharma et al., *Sati: Historical and Phenomenological Essays* (Delhi: Motilal Banarsidass, 1988), p. 73-85.

15 Hindu women in the past used the term *śakti* to refer to goddesses but not to human women. The term *abalā* was used for the latter; it was a discrete power attained through ascetic regimens (*tapas*) for the welfare of husband and family.

16 Sātī and her later incarnation Pārvatī subdue, for instance, the wild Śiva. This is not unlike the image of American pioneer women who bring culture to the west, taming the wild frontier men.

17 The esoteric Tantric tradition from about the 6th century CE went about the business of promoting the salvation of women in an even more radical fashion; in this case, all norms were reversed, and women (though rarely of the upper castes) were the spiritual partners of men or even their guides.

18 It was considered inferior, though, to other forms of marriage practised by brahmins and other high castes, such as the gift of a daughter (*kanyādāna*).

19 See, for example, Śūdraka's *The Little Clay Cart*. This Sanskrit drama is about Vasantasenā, a courtesan, who tries to escape the unwelcome advances of the king's cronies, takes refuge with the Brahmin Cārudatta, and then falls in love with him. The play is filled with passages expressing a delicate but passionate love: "Let the clouds pile high; let the rain fall; let the rain pour down unintermittently! My heart yearns for the one whom I love, and I shall not stop for any obstacle" (quoted in Farley P. Richmond et al., eds., *Indian Theatre: Traditions of Performance* [Honolulu: University of Hawaii Press, 1990], p. 60).

20 Whereas the upper-caste woman came to be considered *avaidika* (without knowledge of the Veda) and therefore uneducated, the *gaṇikā*, a courtesan who specialized in worldly knowledge such as music, poetry and dance was considered educated, although by a different standard.

21 Leslie C. Orr, "Hindu Temple Women of the Chola Period in South India" (Ph.D. diss., Faculty of Religious Studies, McGill University, September 1993).

22 See A.K. Ramanujan, "On Women Saints" in J.S. Hawley and D.M. Wulff, eds., *The Divine Consort* (Berkley: Berkley Religious Studies Series, 1982).

23 Kathryn Hansen, "Heroic Modes of Women in Indian Myth, Ritual and History: The *Tapasvinī* and the *Vīrāṅganā*," in Arvind Sharma and Katherine K. Young, eds., *The Annual Review of Women in World Religions* (Albany: State University of New York Press), Vol. 2, *Heroic Women*, p. 22.

24 During the independence movement, both Durgā and Kālī became even more popular, thanks to their symbolism of independence. Nalini Devdas, "Mother India, Mother Goddess and Militancy in Neo-Hinduism: The Role of Sister Nivedita," in Sharma and Young, eds., *The Annual Review of Women in World Religions*, p. 63-91.

25 Hansen, "Heroic Modes," p. 26-34. The real warrior women were certainly heroic but not as fierce as their mythic counterparts.

26 This de facto acknowledgement functioned to maintain norms for upper-caste women but also to recognize women who, because of caste or choice, acted independently. It also legitimized men's relationships with multiple women as in the case of the *veśyas*, *gaṇikās* and *devadāsīs*.

27 This had the reverse effect of extending brahmanical norms of womanhood to lower castes and thereby dramatically curtailing the freedom of many groups of women.

28 See Madhu Kishwar and Ruth Vanita, *In Search of Answers: Indian Women's Voices From Manushi* (New Delhi: Horizon India Books, 1991).

29 The full names of the film reviewers are sometimes not given.

30 Women have also tried to prevent exploitation of those lower-class women who have had to work for survival or their family's welfare. This has involved an effort to open all jobs to women (so that they are not relegated to the menial ones that men do not want) and equal pay for equal work. The constitution has also prohibited discrimination on the basis of sex. In addition, development schemes have begun to support the participation of women in new industrial and agricultural jobs.

31 Madhu Kishwar and Ruth Vanita, "Films: The Labouring Woman in Hindi Films," *Manushi*, 42-43 (1987): 63.

32 The life of the upper-caste woman, after all, was much more restrictive regarding marriage, divorce, remarriage, work and power to make decisions.

33 Kishwar and Vanita, "The Labouring Woman," p. 63.
34 Anjali, review of *Yeh Kaisa Insaaf* in "Films: Oppressors as Heroes," *Manushi*, 6 (1980): 58.
35 "Geeta," review of *Swayamwar* in ibid.
36 Ibid.
37 Ibid.
38 Ibid.
39 Ibid.
40 Ruth Vanita, *Film Reviews: Kalyug Aur?*, *Manushi*, 44 (1987): 44.
41 Ibid.
42 Hansen, "Heroic Modes."
43 Ibid., p. 49.
44 Ibid.
45 Ibid., p. 51-52.
46 Prabha Krishnan, "Films: *Meri Izzat Bachao*," *Manushi*, 27 (1985): 47.
47 Kishwar and Vanita, "The Labouring Woman," p. 71.
48 Anjali, review of *Yeh Kaisa Insaaf*, p. 57.
49 Ibid.
50 Bina Agarwal, "Film: *Bheegi Palkein* — A Convincing Portrayal," *Manushi*, 2 (1983): 48.
51 Ujala, "Films: *Insaaf Ka Tarazu*," *Manushi*, 7 (1981): 58.
52 Ibid., p. 59.
53 Kishwar and Vanita, "The Labouring Woman," p. 62.
54 Ibid.
55 Kakar, *Intimate Relations*, p. 32.
56 Ibid., p. 33-34.
57 Ibid., p. 37.
58 Ibid., p. 36.
59 In the 70s and 80s, Hindi films increasingly blurred the distinction between good and evil. The hero of a number of films was the actor Amitabh Bachchan, ostensibly a Robin Hood figure but in reality more like a common criminal. Such films, says Kishwar ("Mythic Saviours Lumpenising Social Protest," *Manushi*, 37 [1986]), promote a kind of cathartic but harmless release by allowing the exploited to vicariously experience revenge. This is depicted as occurring at the lower rungs of the system. At the top, waiting in the wings, is a good guy (a judge, minister, or other authority figure). This gives the message that the industry or institution is corrupt only at the local or lower levels. This safety valve, she concludes, may serve to pre-empt real political action, for ordinary people are portrayed as passive individuals who must await a godlike hero to help them and initiate a new world order. Such a figure is like the avatāra, the Lord who descends to earth whenever there is a decline of righteousness in order to save people. Kishwar, in fact, alludes to this in the title of her review called "Mythic Saviours . . . " and in her comment "The belief in a superhero who descends in people's midst to release them from bondage, also strengthens self contempt among people" (ibid., p. 44). Although this theme is an old one for Hindi films, she thinks that it has recently undergone a change: "In the 1950s and 1960s, films often ended with the villains undergoing a change of heart. The films of the 1980s insist on exterminating the 'bad guys' " (ibid.). In recent versions, the notion that the means justify the ends is promoted; the hero uses the same immoral and expedient tactics as the villain to pursue his cause. This approach, notes Kishwar, may breed cynicism, but it may also breed more gangsters. In any case, it keeps protest at the level of the individual rather than the level of society.

60 Ibid., p. 41.
61 Anil Saari, "A Critic's Notes," in Beatrix Pfleiderer and Lothar Lutze, eds., *The Hindi Film: Agent and Re-agent of Cultural Change* (New Delhi: Manohar, 1985), p. 47.
62 Vishnu Khare, "The Dinman Hindi Film Inquiry: A Summary," in Pfleiderer and Lutze, eds., *The Hindi Film*, p. 144.
63 Das Gupta, *The Painted Face*, p. 157.
64 Ibid., p. 159.
65 Ibid., p. 160.
66 Ibid., p. 163.
67 Ibid., p. 162.
68 Ibid., p. 161.
69 Mythological films proper were once common (in fact, seventy percent of films were about deities and saints between 1910 and 1925). Not only was film technology appropriate for giving "a direct glimpse of God," (Das Gupta, *The Painted Face*, p. 36), it could also promote a common religious identity at a time when the Indian independence movement needed to forge various castes and regions into a common group to oppose the British. From 1925, social films dealing with the need to reform Hindu society so that it could remove the yoke of colonization began to displace the "mythologicals." These films, made by and for the middle class, were the vehicle for social criticism of practices that affected (1) the lives of women (widowhood, *sati*, polygamy, dowry, arranged marriage, lack of divorce and remarriage) and (2) the lives of outcasts, bonded labourers and other disadvantaged groups in the society. During the war years and through the fifties, says Das Gupta, the spirit of social reform continued with its message of greater justice and its hope for a better future. But the clientele began to shift to the now-burgeoning working class consisting of migrants (often single men) from the rural areas to the cities, just as financing and production shifted to the traditional mercantile castes and an underground economy based on black money. In the sixties, these changes affected the very genre and clientele of the films. The portrayal of social reform and genuine love stories gave way to a new machismo reflected in car chases, gun fights and liaisons with cabaret women. By the seventies, the seductive machismo of the actor Dharmendra had changed to the vindictive machismo of Amitabh Bachchan who, like Robin Hood, operated outside the law, stealing from the rich and giving to the poor. The role played by Amitabh Bachchan in *Zanjeer* inspired a number of films: *Sholay, Aj ki Awaaz, Insaaf ka Tarazu, Bahu ki Awaaz, Mard, Coolie*, and *Kanoon Meri Mutthi Mein*. As its Western counterpart — "cops and robbers" or "cowboys and Indians" — such films used violence as entertainment. The final scene was often a massive final fight. Das Gupta analyzes gender in this last genre, which continues to the present. The genre of the vindictive hero reveals a loss of the romantic view of women, an increasing obsession with the mother, attenuation of the father and the emergence of a misogynic male *camaraderie*.
70 Kakar, *Intimate Relations*, p. 27.
71 Saari, "Concepts of Aesthetics," p. 22.
72 Ibid., p. 23.
73 Das Gupta, *The Painted Face*, p. 294-95.
74 Khare, "The Dinman Hindi Film Inquiry," p. 146-48.
75 Das Gupta, *The Painted Face*, p. 166-71.
76 Madhu Jain and M. Rahman, "Dating: An Open Embrace," *India Today* (15 May 1991): 73-75.

77 In this context, we should remember that views of work even in the West have been closely related to social class. During the Industrial Revolution in the nineteenth century, the goal of most working-class women was to achieve middle-class status and get out of the factories and sweatshops with their deplorable working conditions that made it difficult to raise children.

78 See David Gilmore, *Manhood in the Making: Cultural Concepts of Masculinity* (New Haven, Co.: Yale University Press, 1990). For an historical overview of these masculine roles as mentioned in this paragraph see Paul Nathanson and Katherine K. Young, *Beyond the Fall of Man: From Ideology to Dialogue in the Conflict Over Masculine Identity* (forthcoming).

79 See, for instance, the use of gang rape by the Mundurucu of Brazil's Amazon Valley. Yolande Murphy and Robert F. Murphy, *Women of the Forest* (New York: Columbia University Press, 1974), p. 101.

80 Joanna Liddle and Rama Joshi, "Gender and Imperialism in British India," *Economic and Political Weekly*, 20/43 (26 October 1985). See also Amrita Chhachhi, "The State, Religious Fundamentalism and Women: Trends in South Asia," *Economic and Political Weekly* (18 March 1989): 571.

81 For a general discussion of the radical loss of masculine identity (provider, protector, progenitor) in modern societies, see Paul Nathanson and Katherine K. Young, *Beyond the Fall of Man: From Ideology to Dialogue in the Conflict Over Masculine Identity* (forthcoming).

82 Kakar, *Intimate Relations*, p. 41. Since the women's movement has affected many societies, it should not surprise us to find that this narcissistic injury and rage is found elsewhere where there is breakdown of family life and urban alienation among youth. As a recent *New York Times* article bemoans: "James Faunleroy, 15, says the teenagers in his circle either don't date or don't admit to it. 'Nobody wants a relationship except the girls,' he said. . . . 'The guys don't want to look soft to their friends.' That fear, and the desire of boys to demonstrate their manhood by abusing or showing disrespect to girls, was repeated time and again in more that 50 interviews with teen-agers across the region last week after a series of reported sexual assaults by groups of teen-agers in a Bronx swimming pool, a Montclair, N.J. school stairwell and a Yonkers playground.

While it is impossible to quantify the attitudes and alienation expressed by the inner-city and suburban teen-agers—white, black, Hispanic and Asian, from both middle-class and low-income families—sociologists and psychologists are concerned about the apparent increase of abuse as a group activity. . . .

'What school do you go to' and she'd say something like: 'Are you a virgin? Who was the last girl you were with? How was your relationship?' She'd be like, 'Did you ever hit skins'—have sex?'" (Melinda Henneberger with Michel Marriott, "For Some, Youthful Courting Has Become a Game of Abuse," *The New York Times*, [11 July 1993], 1, 33).

Chapter 11

PROTECTION AND HUMANITY:
A CASE STUDY OF FEMININE SPIRITUALITY IN
THIRTEENTH-CENTURY MARSEILLES

Francine Michaud

Admittedly limited by an interest focussed primarily on male spirituality, the attention given to women's spirituality in the Middle Ages has always shed a lot more light on "religious" women rather than lay women. So far, in looking at the period from early Christianity to the eve of the Reformation, historians have been entranced by institutionalized communities of women, such as traditional Benedictines or those associated with the reform movement (Cistercians and Gilbertines), or with the Mendicant movement (Clarisses, Dominicans and Beguines), or else with the voices of dissent (Waldensians, Cathars and Lollards).[1] It is true that quite a few mystic figures, anchoresses or recluses, from Marie of Oignies to Margery Kempe, have been objects of research by prominent scholars in recent years. Nevertheless, women who remained in the secular world and who qualified as *lay* figures[2] have been neglected as a definite group within their own community.[3]

For the last 30 years, studies conducted on lay spirituality and religious behaviour (especially through canonization inquiries and wills) have at best given women only incidental attention, for they were seen rarely as specific religious souls, but rather as a subdivision of other social groupings, i.e., socio-economic, professional, ethnic, religious, geographic or age. At best, lay women's attitudes toward spiritual matters have so far been analyzed only insofar as they relate to the attitudes of their male counterparts—fathers, brothers, husbands, etc. In short, the concept of "feminine spirituality" has been largely ignored or oversimplified in traditional historiography. It is partly due to the fact that its definition lies in preconceived or impressionistic beliefs, whether they carry positive or negative value, and more importantly, because of the scarcity of direct historical evidence.[4]

The purpose of this paper is not to define what "feminine piety" means, but rather to draw the contours of lay women's religious attitudes in thirteenth-century Marseilles. This study is based on a comparative analysis of male and female wills.

Marseilles truly presents itself as a privileged environment for this sort of enquiry. Since the late twelfth century, mercantile functions based on long-distance trade made it possible for the middle classes to take charge of the town's destiny.[5] Moreover, commercial endeavours created a need for notarial records, which in turn instilled amongst the urban population a taste for notarial assistance. By the end of the thirteenth century, the presence of the public notary (*publicus notarius*) was increasingly required for family and personal deeds, such as the writing of a will. Above all, Massilian wills belong to the most ancient and abundant archival series in existence in the French territory. Therefore, notarial evidence allows the recovery of both the nature and the form of popular devotions and, consequently, gives access to an unparalleled knowledge of the spirituality of women taken as a collectivity, and this as early as the thirteenth century.[6]

In a period when virginity was still highly praised (much more than marriage — despite its recent sacralisation), the demands on women were even more stringent than those imposed on men, for their sex determined their very place in society, while altogether justifying their exclusion from the sacred orders.[7] Even during the evangelical movement of the twelfth and thirteenth centuries (an era of very intense lay spirituality illustrated by the elevation of non-religious figures to holiness), virginity remained the cornerstone of salvation and sanctification, especially for women.[8] In this context, there is very little doubt that lay women perceived themselves as second-best in the Christian scale of value, far behind nuns and recluses.

While the Virgin Mary was, of course, proposed as the traditional model of piety, other models of sanctity were offered in the formidable wake of lay spirituality in the twelfth and thirteenth centuries. The Friars, and more particularly the Franciscans, were keen to stress fundamental qualities that women should acquire on their path to perfection:

- preservation of virginity (or, at least, the recovery of chastity),
- renunciation of worldly goods,
- association with the Mendicants' third ordeer, and
- a life exclusively religious, wholly dedicated to prayers and meditation.

By the end of the thirteenth century, the route to sanctification for lay women had progressively shifted away from a genuine interest in the alleviation of human suffering through charitable works. The contemplative life, leading to states of ecstasy, as well as such spiritual activities as prayer and meditation, came to be emphasized. On the eve of the following century, the search for mystic union with God virtually became the only true goal for women seeking sanctification.[9] We must not ignore this subtle shift in the clerical conception of female holiness in our examination of ordinary lay women's attitudes toward piety.

It is important to remember that during the period under study, the overwhelming majority of nuns and holy women came from the upper classes, whereas female willmakers belonged to a broader spectrum of

society, which includes the middle classes and, sometimes, the lower arti-
san milieu.[10] One might argue that, for this reason, the primary sources
upon which the present study is based are not totally reliable in assessing
feminine spirituality as a whole. Nevertheless, the unprecedented evolution in the economic context of the twelfth and thirteenth centuries, especially in Mediterranean societies, allows a reasonable cross-section of
the social fabric.

The rise of the money economy, which progressively supplanted the
traditional Germanic gift economy, contributed to the social and political
promotion of the middle classes in a still very feudal civilization.[11] As a
direct consequence of these fundamental changes, new needs and forms
of expression of lay spirituality emerged. The faithful of the twelfth and
thirteenth centuries came to express their spiritual feelings in three basic
ways: (i) literary expression, (ii) artistic depiction, and (iii) performance.[12] Aspects of the practical side of devotion are what we will be
emphasizing here, thanks to the study of wills.

The expansion of commerce from the twelfth century onwards facili-
tated access to property for those below the ranks of nobility. It also led
to the "democratization" of the instruments of trade, including
widespread use of the notarial service. By the end of the thirteenth century, notarial records were produced by the hundreds. Not surprisingly,
this trend coincided with the diffusion of paper mills in Latin Christendom and the progress of Roman Law from Italy to Provençe and from
there to points further north.[13] The registers contain a variety of private
acts, such as transaction sales, dowry contracts, and wills that allowed the
free disposition of one's goods through bequests.

Massilian Willmakers, 1277-1320

The purpose of the medieval will was twofold: it made provision both for
spiritual and for family concerns. However, it is often difficult to differentiate these functions. The expression *"pro amore Dei et anima mea"* ("for
the love of God and the salvation of my soul") incorporates gestures of
human solidarity as well as family piety. We shall therefore select a series
of criteria enabling us to evaluate and compare religious behaviour toward Church institutions and representations as well as toward fellow
Christians.

Let us first consider the primary sources. The wills span the years
1277 to 1320, i.e., from the date of the earliest extant registers up to the
eve of one of the worst community crises in the history of Marseilles, the
Great Famine of 1323.[14] The corpus consists of 293 wills: 150 produced
by 137 men, and 143 by 141 women.[15] It is important to stress the equality
of number between men and women testators, which is in itself exceptional, for in other areas of Christendom wills produced by men usually
outnumbered those of women by a third.

Who were the Massilian willmakers? They were mostly from the upper and middle classes, although women generally came from a slightly higher level on the social scale (Table 1). In effect, women belonged to the urban elite, including the families of nobles and magistrates. It is possible that since upper-class women enjoyed a greater disposable income, they could bequest in greater proportion than women from more modest backgrounds. Indeed, as well we shall see, this phenomenon can also be explained through the particularly close bonds existing between well-to-do women and clerics, especially the Friars. This also can be further substantiated by two complementary factors: the willmakers' matrimonial status and the sizes of their families. A greater proportion of women than men were unmarried or widowed at the time they wrote their wills (Table 2). Furthermore, they also had half as many living children (1.2) as their male counterparts (2.02). Under these conditions, women could enjoy a greater legal and economic freedom than men.

TABLE 1

Social Origin of Male and Female Willmakers in Marseilles, 1277-1320

Social Categories	Men	Women
Nobles	4	6
Religious people	11	4
"Domini" (magnates)	19	24
Business people	8	7
Jurists	2	3
Notaries	4	6
Craftsmen	24	15
Peasants	14	10
Villagers	7	5
Unknown	44	61
Total	137	141

Predictably, in a God-fearing society, what people fear most is to be struck by a sudden death that will prevent them from adequately preparing their soul for salvation. Massilian testators did in fact vividly express this fear as an open statement at the beginning of their will. Approximately 75 per cent of all willmakers acknowledged that they were ill when they called upon the public notary to record their last wishes. Before organizing the general distribution of their goods, they first made sure of the disposal of their soul by recommending it to Jesus, His mother Mary and the court of all saints. The cult of one given patron saint was virtually absent from this nomenclature. However, by the beginning of the fourteenth century, the devotion to the eucharist appears timidly and progressively in the wills of well-to-do citizens, men and women alike, presumably people of a certain literary culture.[16]

Before bequesting their property for family (if not lineage) purposes, willmakers set apart a fixed amount of money for the redemption of their soul. In this era, the new concept of purgatory, intertwined with a deeper sense of spiritual introspection, increased eschatological anxiety.[17] In order to appease their "unquiet souls," the faithful distributed alms more or less generously to both ecclesiastical institutions and to their fellow Christians.

TABLE 2

Marital Status of Male and Female Willmakers in Marseilles, 1277-1320

	Married	Widowed	Married* or Widowed	Single	Clerics	Unknown	Total
Men	88	6	19	15	7	2	137
Women	56	67	2	13	-	3	141
Total	144	73	21	28	7	5	278

*The name of the spouse is not revealed, but that of the children is. This could be caused either by the negligence of the scribe, or simply by the fact that the spouse is already dead – and not worth mentioning.

Alms to the Church and its Servants

The average Christian rarely gave without expecting some spiritual benefit in return. The first concern was to choose the burial site. Massilian people generally preferred to be buried in their own parish cemetery (men 64% vs. women 57%), whereas more women than men favoured the Friar's graveyards (women 23% vs. men 15%; Table 3a). The reasons for a particular choice could be linked to tradition or to genuine spiritual attachment to a given institution. The latter reason seems to have had particular significance for women. However, the most striking gender difference was in the motivational expressions behind the choice. Twice as many women indicated a determination to be buried with a family member (37 w/19 m), with their father foremost (19) but also with their mother (7), or even with their spouse (6). Men, for their part, preferred almost exclusively their father (13/19) (Table 3b). This may be an indication of a greater capacity for women to bond with their relatives and in a more diverse fashion than men, who mostly focussed on the memory of the *paterfamilias* (or father figure).

Very few testators designated the Church as their universal heir: the ones who did, specified that their bequest should be distributed as alms to the poor. However, most Massilians left a minimum sum of money, generally a customary amount to the local parish church, in exchange for community prayers and the celebration of masses:[18] one on the day of their death, and another three days later. Sometimes a third mass was held a year later, once (it was understood) the soul had forever departed from the living.[19] But more substantial were the gifts bestowed on the newcomers in the religious landscape of thirteenth-century Marseilles: the Friars. In fact, among the 98 willmakers who generously ascribed money to the forerunners of the ideal of voluntary poverty, 59 were women.

TABLE 3

Burial Sites: Institutional Preference and Family Bonds

	Men	(%)	Women	(%)	Total
a) Chosen Burial Sites by Male and Female Willmakers in Marseilles, 1277-1320					
Parish Church	87	(63.5)	80	(56.7)	167
Mendicant Church	20	(14.6)	32	(22.7)	52
Monastic Church	11	(8.0)	15	(10.6)	26
Unknown	19	(13.9)	14	(10.0)	33
Total	137		141		278

	Men		Women		Total
b) Chosen Beloved Ones to be Buried with, by Male and Female Willmakers, 1277-1320					
Father	13		19		32
Mother	2		7		9
Both Parents	2		2		4
Spouse	1		6		7
Kinfolk*	1		2		3
In-Laws	-		1		1
Total	19		37		56

* Brothers, sisters, uncles and aunts

More than men, women also had the inclination to indulge in personal offerings to religious people, especially the Mendicants: 64 per cent of these gifts were made by female testators (Table 4). After all, not only had the Fourth Lateran Council of 1215 relaxed the canonical restrictions on clerical acceptance of lay gifts, but two pontifical bulls[20] issued by Gregory IX (*Quo Elongati*, 1230) and Nicholas III (*Exiit qui seminat*, 1279) had allowed the more ascetic Franciscans to enjoy (if not own) material goods, including real estate.[21] Members of the order in late thirteenth-century Marseilles enjoyed a fervent popularity, particularly, it seems, among women. It is noteworthy that, of the 60 female benefactors who made these personal clerical offerings, two-thirds were unmarried (widows or single women).

TABLE 4

Distribution of Personal Gifts to Clerics by Male and Female Willmakers in Marseilles, 1277-1320

	Men (41)		Women (60)	
	Number of bequests	Number of testators	Number of bequests	Number of testators
Mendicants (Friars)	52	23	125	45
Franciscans	11	5	62	23
Dominicans	12	3	19	12
Servites	13	12	21	13
Others	16	12	23	12
Secular Priests	34	24	23	12
Monks/Nuns	23	9	12	8
Total	161	88	285	125

One should not underestimate the confession of one woman testator who eloquently admitted her affection toward her *amicus* (friend), the Franciscan Bernard Dangier, when she left him 20 shillings.[22] By the end of the period under consideration, one should also point out the increasing presence of personal confessors as beneficiaries in wills, who were mostly Friars, twice as many appearing in female testaments. Furthermore, twice as many women appointed ecclesiastics — here again Mendicants in majority — as executors of their wills. Here too these women were almost exclusively unmarried or widowed.[23] Loneliness, calling for friendship and spiritual guidance, could well underline personal forms of generosity.

Conversely, men tended to save a larger portion of their pious bequests for the foundation of perpetual anniversaries (37m/26w), i.e., commissioning the local Church authorities to appoint a chaplain whose duty it was to celebrate an annual mass for the redemption of the deceased soul and this, of course, for eternity (Table 5a). In order to guarantee its performance, a portion of the testator's real estate was set aside, thus allowing an annual rent to be collected for that purpose. Indeed, the spiritual provision for one's own salvation was costly. Considerably more modest, although more frequent, were alms made for charities, friends and acquaintances in need.

TABLE 5

a)   Chronological Distribution of Perpetual Anniversaries between Male and Female Willmakers in Marseilles, 1277-1320

	Men	Women	Total
1277-1280	-	-	-
1281-1285	1	-	1
1286-1290	4	2	6
1291-1295	5	4	9
1296-1300	10	5	15
1301-1305	4	3	7
1306-1310	2	3	5
1311-1315	6	5	11
1316-1320	5	4	9
Total	37	26	63

b)   Chronological Distribution of Alms to Charities between Male and Female Willmakers in Marseilles, 1277-1320

	Men		Women	
	Number of bequests	Number of testators	Number of bequests	Number of testators
1277-1280	25	11	26	11
1281-1285	31	10	18	6
1286-1290	22	12	44	16
1291-1295	11	4	15	7
1296-1300	18	9	14	6
1301-1305	8	3	8	3
1306-1310	-	-	12	7
1311-1315	11	6	5	3
1316-1320	8	4	14	8
Total	134	59	156	67

Medieval Christians had traditionally been encouraged to provide for the needy throughout their sojourn on earth. Giving to the poor of Christ increased one's chances of being saved. In this golden age of evangelical poverty, magnified by the relative enrichment of urban middle classes, burgesses were repeatedly reminded by local preachers of Matthew's exhortation to give away one's wealth for "it is easier for a camel to go through the eye of a needle, than for a rich man to enter the kingdom of God."[24] Consequently, wills allow only a quick glance at a fraction of a presumed lifetime practice of good works. Longtime habits had no doubt shaped the testator's ways of expressing their compassion toward the poor, the disabled, poor unmarried girls, orphans, widows and so forth. That is why a common pattern is noticeable in the bequests of men and women as far as institutional gifts are concerned (especially to hospitals, charities and confraternities). Nonetheless, female testators were slightly more numerous when considering this particular religious gesture (67w/59m, Table 5b). But interestingly enough, between 1277 and 1320, charitable bequests (i.e., what historian Jacques Chiffoleau calls "ancient forms of charity"[25]) declined as requests for perpetual anniversaries rose (Table 5a and b). This may show the emergence of a new sensitivity toward the self, or self-concerned spiritual values, at the expense of more humanitarian feelings toward the suffering masses.

TABLE 6

Distribution of Alms to Individuals *Pro Amore Dei* between Male and Female Willmakers in Marseilles, 1277-1320

	Men		Women	
	Number of bequests	Number of testators	Number of bequests	Number of testators
Beneficiaries				
Godsons	35	20	22	18
Goddaughters	33	20	40	26
Total	68	(26)	62	(38)
Servants (m)	5	4	-	-
Servants (w)	17	15	27	23
Total	22	(19)	27	(23)
"Friends" (m)	50	24	47	23
"Friends" (w)	94	33	165	57
Total	144	(41)	212	(61)

N.B. Figures within parentheses are the total number of testators who have bequeathed gifts to one or more beneficiaries.

At a different level, however, we see an ongoing preoccupation with individuals beyond the family circle, for whom willmakers provided a very symbolic sum of money *pro amore Dei* (for the love of God): godchildren, servants and "friends."[26] Here again, women distinguished themselves among all testators. They were consistently more numerous in bestowing gifts on their godchildren (38w/26m), servants (23w/19m)[27] and acquaintances (61w/41m), particularly if the beneficiaries were female. Men who bestowed gifts on individuals beyond the family circle also were more inclined to favour females over males (Table 6). In medieval society, unmarried girls were undoubtedly seen as being more needy than boys, not only because their sex was perceived as a fundamental weakness (*propter fragilitatem sui sexus*), but also because the only acceptable status for honest lay women was matrimonial and this required the provision of a dowry. Clerics reminded their parishioners that without a dowry, there could not be a decent marriage for a girl.[28] In fact, this frame of mind was so deeply rooted that even the municipal legal code of Marseilles echoed the canonical principle in this matter.[29] So it was necessarily seen as a pious gesture to provide for a girl's dowry, which was indeed her economic contribution to the marriage (and very often her single and only inheritance).

Conclusion

There is very little doubt that social pressures influenced the way in which medieval women expressed specific spiritual characteristics. In the context of the thirteenth-century evangelical movement, especially when they belonged to a commercial urban community, women testators revealed an inclination to care for others within (reunion with a beloved one in the burial site) and beyond the family unit (distribution of bequests). Humanitarian concerns were still very much present when they bestowed their wealth on their deathbed.

But it is also very clear that female willmakers sought the personal assistance of clergymen in spiritual matters, especially the Friars who were viewed as the "New Poor of Christ."[30] It is possible that women were more receptive to the Mendicant preaching than men.[31] Nonetheless, I should stress that these women, mostly freed from marital bonds, probably needed a special, honest, and presumably chaste masculine companionship. In doing so, they maintained the established order in the eyes of society, for they moved from their father's or husband's physical and economic protection to the Friar's spiritual protection.

It seems that these "competing" beneficiaries, whether true poor or Mendicants, were both fulfilling the spiritual needs of late thirteenth-century women in Marseilles. The more introspective values that were manifest through the assistance of a confessor, for instance, had not yet replaced feelings toward "suffering humanity" as it has been proposed by André Vauchez. Perhaps, so far as ordinary lay people were concerned, women's religious behaviour was undergoing a phase of transition. Self-concerned spiritual pursuit was more obvious among male testators. Did women follow the trend? The progressive decline of institutional (anonymous) charitable bequests in female as well as in male wills could be a sign of this. Further study into the period following the one I have been discussing here (i.e., up to the Black Death, at least) may shed some light on this problem.

I must argue, however, that it is methodologically hazardous to amalgamate personal or even institutionalized spiritual behaviour and values with spiritual behaviour and values of larger groups of people such as ordinary (single, married or widowed) lay women who have not "renounced the world." In other words, the ideas expressed, for instance, in spiritual treatises do not automatically reflect contemporary shifts of collective sensibility and values, as C.W. Bynum has suggested.[32] Ideally, one should attempt to approach lay spirituality in relation to, and not as an extension of, the spiritual "complexities of a few hearts."[33]

Notes

1 Substantial literature exists on the subject that cannot be reproduced here. For a general overview, see: Francis Oakley, *The Medieval Experience: Foundations of Western Cultural Singularity* (Toronto: Medieval Academy of America, 1988), p. 194-96.

2 Yves Congar, "Laïc et laïcat," *Dictionnaire de spiritualité* (1976), coll. p. 79-93. According to the strict Christian definition, all women are lay since they do not have access to the sacerdotal office: Nicolas Huyghebaert, "Les femmes laïques dans la vie religieuse des XIe et XIIe siècles dans la province ecclésiastique de Reims," in *I Laici Nella "Societas Christiana" Dei Secoli XI e XII* (1965): 347.

3 Even Carolyn W. Bynum, who offers a most needed interpretation of female spirituality, limits her inquiry to women mystics and communities of nuns (*Jesus as Mother: Studies in the Spirituality of the High Middle Ages* [Berkeley and Los Angeles: University of California Press, 1982], p. 170 ff.). In her recent book on English nunneries, Sally Thompson also ignores the concept (*Women Religious: The Founding of English Nunneries after the Norman Conquest* [Oxford: Clarendon Press, 1991]).

4 "The question of 'feminine' piety is not entirely extricable from larger questions about the existence and nature of the 'feminine': does it exist, and is it biological, social, or a mysterious and innate 'principle' above and beyond biology, society, or history?" (Clarissa W. Atkinson, *Mystic and Pilgrim: The Book of Margery Kempe* [Ithaca: Cornell University Press, 1983], p. 158 n.2).

5 V.-L. Bourilly, "Marseille: la vie et les institutions municipales," chap. 8 in *Des origines à 1348*, in *Les Bouches-du-Rhône. Encyclopédie départementale*, 3e partie. *Le sol et les habitants*. T. 14. *Marseille-Aix-Arles*, ed. P. Masson (Paris: Champion, 1935), p. 171-95.

6 The paucity of notarial archives in part explains why contemporary studies of women's spirituality based on wills are virtually non-existent in other areas of Latin Christendom. Even where notarial collections are available (e.g., in the Northern Italian peninsula) twelfth- and thirteenth-century wills have yet to be examined from a perspective of feminine piety. Indeed, most scholars who have worked with Italian notarial archives of the Middle Ages (e.g., Eleanor Riemer for Siena, *Women in the Medieval City: Sources and Uses of Wealth by Sienese Women in the Thirteenth Century* [Ph.D.diss., University of New York, 1975]; Diane O. Hughes, "Towards Growth

and Family Structure in Medieval Genoa," *Past and Present*, 66 [1975]: 3-28; and Stephen Epstein, *Wills and Wealth in Medieval Genoa, 1150-1250* [Cambridge, MA.: Harvard University Press, 1984]), have been concerned with family matters, and have virtually ignored spiritual questions concerning women).

7 In the eyes of the Church, it even kept them from attaining the state of holiness to a large extent: "Un double handicap pesait sur les femmes, leur interdisant en règle générale l'accès à la sainteté: leur faiblesse physique et morale qui, aux yeux des hommes de ce temps, ne faisait pas de doute, et leur statut dans l'Eglise qui les condamnait à n'y jouer qu'un rôle passif, sauf dans les cas exceptionnels où la naissance et le mariage leur conféraient des moyens d'action dont elles pouvaient se servir pour favoriser le clergé" (André Vauchez, *La sainteté en Occident aux derniers siècles du Moyen Age, d'après les procès de canonisation et les documents hagiographiques* [Ecole Française de Rome, Palais Farnèse, 1981] p. 428). Joyce E. Salisbury has recently summarized the patristic positions on female virginity and sexuality in *Church Fathers, Independent Virgins* (New York: Verso, 1991).

8 Vauchez, *La sainteté en Occident*, p. 247, 326-27, 442. See also C.W. Bynum, *Jesus as Mother*, p. 15.

9 Vauchez, *La sainteté en Occident*, p. 244-49.

10 Ursmer Berlière, *Le recrutement dans les monastères bénédictins aux XIIIe et XIVe siècles* (Bruxelles: Maurice Lamertin, 1924), p. 16-22; Eileen Power, *Medieval Women*, ed. M.M. Postan (Cambridge: Cambridge University Press, 1975), p. 89, and *Medieval English Nunneries c. 1275 to 1535* (Cambridge: Cambridge University Press, 1922). See also Michael Goodich, "The Contours of Female Piety in later Medieval Hagiography," *Church History*, 50 (1981): 20-32.

11 Following the definitions of Lester K. Little, "in a gift economy, goods and services are exchanged without having specific, calculated values assigned to them," whereas "in a market economy, . . . one expects everything to have an assigned value" (*Religious Poverty and the Profit Economy in Medieval Europe* [Ithaca: Cornell University Press, 1978] p. 4). In Europe, the passage from one form of economy to the other was underway in the eleventh and twelfth centuries (ibid., p. 3-18). On this issue in relation to the evolution of religious trends, see also Barbara H. Rosenwein and L.K. Little, "Social Meaning in the Monastic and Mendicant Spirituality," *Past and Present* 63 (1974): 4-32.

12 Richard Kieckhefer, "Major Currents in Late Medieval Devotion," in Jill Raitt, ed., *Christian Spirituality: High Middle Ages and Reformation* (New York: Crossroad, 1987), p. 77.

13 Jean Irigoin, "Introduction of Paper," *Dictionary of the Middle Ages* 9 (1982): 388-90.

14 The Latin manuscripts that I have consulted are to be found in the Municipal Archives as well as the Departmental Archives of Bouches-du-Rhône in Marseilles.

15 In this age, individuals frequently made more than one will where illness was not immediately followed by death; illness indeed acted as a strong stimulus for one's legal and spiritual preparation for death.

16 It is not possible, so far, to link the findings of C.W. Bynum on women mystics' spirituality and female Massilian testators: "Images of food and drink, of brimming fountains and streams of blood which are used with special intensity by thirteenth-century women, express desire for direct, almost physical contact with Christ in the eucharist and for power to handle this Christ as only the priest is authorized to do" (*Jesus as Mother*, p. 8).

17 Jacques Le Goff, *La naissance du Purgatoire* (Paris: Gallimard, 1981).

18 Only eight per cent of testators bestowed nothing to the Church.

19 In the medieval will, "on parle moins de l"heure de la mort' que du 'temps de la mort,' et ce *tempus* dure et englobe non seulement le moment précis où l'on passe de vie à trépas, mais aussi la veillée, les funérailles, la neuvaine et tout le temps du deuil jusqu'à la messe de bout-de-l'an. Ces pratiques rituelles correspondent à l'idée d'un passage vers l'au-delà qui ne se fait pas d'une seule traite mais qui a une durée propre, des étapes qu'il convient de franchir" (Jacques Chiffoleau, *La comptabilité de l'au-delà, les hommes, la mort et la religion dans la région comtadine à la fin du Moyen Age* [*vers 1330-1480*] [Rome: Ecole Française de Rome, 1981], p. 117).

20 A formal papal decree.

21 Antoine Bernard, *La sépulture en droit canonique, du décret de Gratian au concile de Trente* (Paris: F. Loviton, 1933), p. 141-52; John Moorman, *History of the Franciscan Order: From its Origins to the year 1517* (Oxford: Clarendon Press, 1968), p. 177-81.

22 Will of Huguette Maurelli, widow of Trenquier Genesi: Departmental Archives of Bouches-du-Rhône, Marseilles, 381 E 3, ff. 41v-42, 4 May 1286.

23 In fact, nine out of the ten women who specifically mentioned a confessor were widows; in addition, twenty-two of twenty-five women, including eighteen widows and two single women, chose clerics as executors of their wills.

24 Matthew 19:24.

25 Jacques Chiffoleau, "Pratiques funéraires et images de la mort à Marseille, en Avignon et dans le Comtat Venaissin (vers 1280-vers 1350)," *Cahiers de Fanjeaux*, 11 (1976): 271-303; also, *La comptabilité de l'au-delà*.

26 It is hard to qualify these persons in relation to the testator since the word "friend" (*amicus/amica*) rarely appears in the sources.

27 The discrepancy between men and women is rather slim here. Ancillary loves can explain the incentive that compelled men to make provisions for their maids and possibly their illegitimate children. This issue has been discussed in my dissertation: *Un signe des temps: accroissement des crises familiales autour du patrimoine à Marseille à la fin du XIIIe siècle* (Université Laval, 1990), p. 153 ff.

28 René Metz, "Le statut de la femme en droit canonique médiéval," *Recueil de la Société Jean Bodin*, 12 (1262): 59-113.

29 Régine Pernoud, ed., *Les statuts municipaux de Marseille* (Paris-Monaco: Librairie Auguste-Picard, 1949), p. 122 ff.

30 This "metaphor" is used explicitly by few women testators when favouring the Franciscans. Huga Longa, daughter of an influential magnate, expressed it quite clearly: "Jubeo dari et distribui (XX libras) pauperibus fratribus minoribus Massilie" (Municipal Archives of Marseilles, 1 II 12, f. 26, 9 February 1292).

31 Although it is difficult to assess in those terms, the thirteenth-century preachers were certainly aware of the complexity of the social fabric of their audience. As early as the first half of the thirteenth century, the Dominican Hubert of Romans acknowledged the existence of other categories beyond the socio-professional classes, such as gender, age, moral state, worldly involvement, etc., being specifically targeted by the sermons of the preachers. On this issue, see M. Zinc, *La prédication en langue romane avant 1300*, Nouvelle Bibliothèque du Moyen Age, 4 (Paris 1976): 171.

32 Bynum, *Jesus as Mother*, p. 8.

33 Ibid.

Chapter 12

HSING-SHIH YIN-YUAN:
KARMIC VERSUS PSYCHOLOGICAL VIEWS OF A
MAN'S RELATIONSHIPS WITH HIS WOMEN

Fan Pen Chen

Published works on women and religion in the field of Chinese studies are sparse but cover several approaches and concerns. Kathryn A. Tsai's "The Chinese Buddhist Monastic Order for Women: The First Two Centuries,"[1] for example, is historical and research oriented, while Emily M. Ahern's "The Power and Pollution of Chinese Women"[2] is an anthropological study. A number of articles have treated the question of gender in Chinese philosophical and religious contexts. Roger T. Ames' "Taoism and the Androgynous Ideal,"[3] Richard W. Guisso's "Thunder Over the Lake: The Five Classics and the Perception of Woman in Early China"[4] and Alison H. Black's "Gender and Cosmology in Chinese Correlative Thinking"[5] treat the identification and confounding of gender ideals in ancient Confucian and Taoist texts. Jordan Paper's "The Persistence of Female Deities in Patriarchal China,"[6] on the other hand, suggests a continued existence of female power as reflected by the presence of female deities in China, despite the obvious patriarchal nature of its society. As we can see, the genderedness of texts and contexts has been of much interest. In this paper, rather than discussing the gender constructs in my primary source, the traditional Chinese novel *Hsing-shih yin-yuan*, I would like to deconstruct its male author's use of the basically misogynistic religious concept of karma, in favour of a psychological analysis of the protagonists. The author's point of view, a view inevitably governed by patriarchal values, can, in fact, be seen as a limited construct incapable of applying justice to both genders equally. And, as such, it may be seen as a less valid analysis of its own female characters than a psychological reading of them.

The two works on women and religion in China which I find illuminating for my present study are Ahern's paper on the power and pollution of Chinese women and Paper's article on the persistence of female deities and also his assertion of female power. That female power existed in China is not surprising. The consistent and stringent measures taken to ensure patriarchy and perpetuation of the male-dominated concepts of justice, value and virtue must have been a reflection of a considerable amount of male anxiety. From attributions of the downfalls of all dynasties to the evil of women, to exhortations of feminine obedience, Confucian scholars had, since the inception of Chinese civilization, tried to put women in "their place." Their persistence and insistence may well indicate a continued inability to subdue their women.[7]

The men felt threatened and therefore they suppressed and oppressed that which they feared. Despite the lower status and all the Confucian rules to contain the women, however, many of them nevertheless managed to possess power. While the power held by empress dowagers and aging matriarchs has frequently been noted,[8] that of common wives has rarely been discussed. It is possible that women may have been considered to have possessed a certain amount of power by virtue of the evil (the ability to pollute) inherent in them, as shown in Ahern's study. But it seems more likely that they derived most of their power through either ignorance of, or purposefully rejecting, Confucian rules of propriety.

While it was much easier to guide and restrain women in "good" families—families which educated their girls according to Confucian ideals—it must have been a continuous struggle for society to instill patriarchal values in all women. Indeed, we find traditional Chinese novels, including *Hsing-shih yin-yuan*, overflowing with unchaste women, especially from the lower classes. An underpinning of Confucianism is the need for a clearly defined hierarchical order in which the male should dominate. When this order is subverted, chaos is believed to prevail. In the name of preserving stability, therefore, scholars and fiction writers alike have felt it incumbent upon them to subjugate their women and to punish the defiant ones.

Although the novel to be discussed is peopled by Taoist priests and priestesses, Buddhist monks and nuns, and is framed in the Buddhist concept of karmic retribution, the ideals propagated are basically Confucian. *Hsing-shih yin-yuan* (literally meaning karmic marriages to awaken the world) is a didactic work. It aims to censure certain types of behaviour through the use of the concept of karma as its pedagogical tool. According to the karmic law of cause and effect, in the law of retribution,

> meritorious and demeritorious actions, respectively, produce different effects: the former produce pleasurable consequences for the actor; the latter, painful ones. The merit or demerit created by many karmic actions, however, is of a magnitude that retribution cannot be fully worked out in one lifetime. That being the case, for each such action the retributional imbalance requires an additional rebirth—sometimes more than one—so that full retribution might be achieved. . . . In short, rebirth is caused by unfulfilled or incomplete retribution for karmic actions performed in previous rebirths.[9]

Thus, the inexplicable and condemnable power exerted by some women upon their husbands, when viewed karmically, are manifestations of punishment for sins committed by the men during their previous lives.

While the karmic framework is frequently used by traditional fiction writers, it is usually a fairly insignificant structural device, appearing in no more than the first and last few chapters of novels. In *Hsing-shih yin-yuan*, however, the karmic theory ceases to exist as a tacked-on framework. It becomes the raison d'être for the inexplicable behaviour and relationships of the protagonists. Almost a quarter of this 100-chapter book (1,224 pages in the edition used) is devoted to describing the lives and affairs of characters whose relationships will become the basis for those during their future lives.

The didactic intention of the author and his desire to use the concept of karma to demonstrate the reason for marriage to shrews are clearly expounded in his preface to the novel. Everyone knows that marriages are predestined. Once the Old Man Under the Moon has secretly tied together a man and a woman's ankles with a red thread, no matter how far apart they live and how much animosity exists between their families, they will invariably become united in marriage. According to this notion, then, all wives and husbands should presumably be perfectly matched couples. Why is it, however, that eight or nine out of ten marriages are rather incompatible? In some, an intelligent person marries a stupid mate; in some, an ugly person marries a handsome one; in some, the husband loathes the wife; in some, the wife abuses the husband; in some, the husband abandons his wife for a whore; and in others, the wife makes a cuckold of her husband behind his back. Such perversities are too numerous to be cited individually.

> Dear readers, take a guess, how do you think this problem of "cause and effect" is formed? They are all engendered unknowingly by incidents that happened in one's previous life and manifest themselves now without a hitch.... [A good wife] must have been a fast friend, a person indebted to one, or even a spouse or a brother to the person during his previous life.... Similarly, the abused, the cheated and the murdered of a past existence will become wife to the oppressor... [in order to torment him] better than the chopping, smashing and grinding on the mountains of knives and trees of swords of the King of Hades' eighteenth and lowest level of hell....
>
> An avenging wife is like a tumor on one's neck. Removing it would be fatal but what pain it causes if left alone. There is no escape during day time and at night [the torment] becomes even more intolerable. Laws of the officials cannot protect one from it, the powers of one's parents cannot alleviate it! (Preface, 3-4)[10]

Consisting of almost a million character-words in 100 chapters, *Hsing-shih yin-yuan*[11] is one of the longest and most critically controversial traditional Chinese novels. Aside from the enigmas surrounding its date and authorship,[12] critical opinions of the work range from the famous modern writer Chang Ai-ling's acclaim that it should rank as a world-class novel and Hsü Chih-mo, another famous writer's outbursts of admiration,[13] to the Western sinologist, Andrew Plaks' conclusion that in spite of some "potential areas of meaning, we must allow that *Hsing-shih yin-yuan chuan* is not a profound work of literature."[14]

Despite the famous modern scholar Hu Shih's attempts at reintroducing the novel to the public, mainly through his seminal study on its author, *Hsing-shih yin-yuan* has remained largely neglected. Numerous factors seem to account for its lack of popularity. The reasons have been variously attributed to the novel's anonymity and use of the Shantung dialect,[15] and to its crudeness and lack of fast action.[16] While the former problems also exist for the famous *Chin P'ing Mei*, the latter objections may also be construed as a matter of opinion. Indeed, *Hsing-shih yin-yuan* seems more likely a victim of its immense volume,[17] its seeming structural incoherence[18] and its traditional, and hence trite, morality.

As the title of the novel and the author's[19] preface (above) indicate, marriage is the theme of *Hsing-shih yin-yuan*. Based on a patriarchal and fatalistic point of view, bad marriages, which here refer to marriages with terrible wives, are but manifestations of retribution for misdeeds perpetrated during one's previous life. The novel traces the lives of his main characters through two reincarnations and shows how the idiosyncrasies and abusiveness of the wives during the second life can be explained by the wrongs they suffered during their previous lives.[20] Examining this rather realistic novel from a feminist psychological perspective, however, one finds the behaviour of the women understandable without the karmic component. The backgrounds of their relationships during their present reincarnation, when viewed from a non-patriarchal and non-traditional angle, provide adequate explanation for their behaviour.

Karmically speaking, the torment Ti Hsi-ch'en suffers in the hands of his wives is a manifestation of the consequence of crimes perpetrated by him during his previous life against the former beings of these women. In the first part of *Hsing-shih yin-yuan*, the protagonist, Ti Hsi-ch'en's former self, Ch'ao Yuan, is responsible for the deaths of both a fox spirit and his main wife. The fox spirit is a vixen which has lived for so long (more than a thousand years) that it has come to possess special powers and is able to take on human forms. During a hunt, it transforms itself into a ravishing beauty in the hope of seducing Ch'ao Yuan. Ch'ao is readily attracted, but his hunting dogs soon detect her true nature and she is frightened into reverting back into her original form. Having sensed his initial desire for her, she now seeks refuge under his horse. But instead of protecting her, Ch'ao shoots her and has her skinned for her pure, white fur. Psychoanalytically speaking, her position under the hunter/lover's horse places her in a position of potential intercourse. That the lover "shoots" and skins her intimates defloration which also ended her life. In the second and main part of the novel, Ch'ao is reborn as Ti Hsi-ch'en, marries Su-chieh, the reincarnation of the fox spirit, and is tormented most brutally by her.

Ch'ao Yuan's role in the death of his main wife, Chih Shih, is less direct. He favours a newly acquired concubine, Chen-ke so intensely that the main wife is eventually forced into committing suicide.[21] In her reincarnation, she becomes Ti Hsi-ch'en's second wife, Chi-chieh, whom he marries in order to escape the torments of his first wife. But the sweet girl Chi-chieh soon turns into a terrible shrew almost comparable to Su-chieh and eventually forces her maid, Chen-chu (the reincarnation of Ch'ao's concubine, Chen-ke), into committing suicide.

The only real romantic relationship (one not ruined by marriage) ever encountered by Ti Hsi-ch'en is a short-lived affair with a delightful young courtesan, Sun Lan-chi. Their intense mutual attraction and the fact that even his mother cannot help but liking her are explained by predestination. They are fated to have this affair because of a vow made between Ch'ao Yuan and a prostitute during their previous existence.

Let us now examine the backgrounds of the relationships between Ti Hsi-ch'en and these women without the aid of their karmic histories. The romantic affair between Ti Hsi-ch'en and Sun Lan-chi can be understood as a natural sort of mutual attraction between two charming teenagers (they are both about fifteen years of age by Western count[22]) under an unusually free environment. As a courtesan, Sun Lan-chi does not exhibit the usual inhibition and shyness found in traditional girls. It is she, in fact, who introduces Ti to the art of love-making. Their love is characteristically imbued with a sense of innocence, unadulterated by feelings of sinfulness, guilt and possessiveness. And as a student taking his provincial examinations away from home, accompanied only by a couple of servants, Ti steals away easily and spends much of his time with this young mistress of his.

The fact that he is considered a clown at home and that he passes all three provincial examinations through cheating and sheer luck are never made known to Sun Lan-chi. As far as she is concerned, he is an intelligent, handsome young scholar. Even when they meet again three years later, at the residence of her husband, the pawnbroker, he presents himself as a dashing young gentleman. In order to meet her without the husband, he purposely makes an appointment to meet the pawnbroker at his shop and then visits his home instead. They manage to steal a kiss and exchange some tokens of love in the maid's absence. Ti never sees her again but the handkerchief and shoes[23] she slipped him, which he always carried with him, gave him much solace until they were discovered by Su-chieh. Thus this romance is maintained by virtue of its short duration, unusual circumstances, and the glorified image that Ti was able to present.

The relationship between Ti and Su-chieh, the worst marital relationship depicted in Chinese literature, never had the benefit of such a blissful ignorance. Su-chieh is betrothed to Ti before birth. The families are very close and her brothers are Ti's classmates. Hence, Su-chieh grows up with full knowledge of the stupidity and mischievousness of her betrothed. From the beginning, Su-chieh has felt an intense dislike for Ti. Even as a child, she tells her mother that she cannot stand the sight of him and does not want to marry him.

An intelligent,[24] ravishing beauty fully aware of the fact that her brother wrote the answers for Ti during his examinations, Su-chieh must have felt it a disgrace to be married to such a dunce of a husband. Hence her sudden change into a fierce shrew the moment she enters the Ti household may not have needed the author's supernatural explanation. According to the novelist, she has a nightmare the night before her wedding in which her heart is ripped out and exchanged for an evil one (44:549).

Su-chieh's career as a fierce shrew is unequalled in Chinese literature. She begins by using verbal abuse, clawing, slapping, clubbing and biting; and finally ends her highly eventful career with pouring burning coal from an iron down Ti's back (97:1185) and shooting him with an arrow (100:1218). Her contempt for him, however, doesn't quite explain her cruelty toward him. One finds an explanation for this aspect of her personality in Ti's own cowardly disposition and physical weakness.

Soon after their wedding, they engage in a quarrel that turns into a fight. Ti grabs hold of a whip which is immediately snatched away by Su-chieh who manages to sit on his head and give him a full beating, thus taking control both literally and figuratively. Ever after, Ti seems totally subdued by her. When she imprisons him in the chamber pot area of their bedroom as a punishment for having shown injuries inflicted by her to a cousin, he dutifully stays there for ten days for fear of her wrath (60:755). Hence, his meekness seems to encourage and feed her desire to trample over him.

Her main problem lies, however, in her refusal to accept the Confucian hierarchy, its strictures and the double standards it promotes. She so craves freedom—the ability to leave the inner apartments and visit the sights—that she considers the secluded life of women at an official residence to be imprisonment and would rather die than be cooped up. When she fails to persuade Ti's cousin and his family to let her out of their luxurious residence in Peking, she attempts suicide so that "at least her ghost would be able to roam" (77:951-52).

She fears neither death nor divorce (73:901). Indeed, Su-chieh's disregard for both divine retribution and bad reputation enables her to elude the grip of Confucian ethics. She once yells at Ti, "If you hope to use this to discredit me, you are dreaming! I, Old Su, have no fear of defamation, and I have no desires for having any commemorative steles built for me!" (66:822).

But her lack of restraint and her refusal to accept Confucian values eventually cause her doom. While she could have become a tragic hero ine in a modern novel, there is no place for her in a traditional society; she must be punished and eliminated.[25]

Su-chieh's story without the karmic, retributive element is a tragic tale of a strong female forced into marrying someone she detests; she abuses the power she possesses and has to suffer for her defiance of the accepted norm. Influenced by her birth mother not to submit to the strictures of their patriarchal society, to reject the role of self-abnegation deemed rational for women, she becomes a madwoman. Her story is that of a woman who rebels against patriarchal domination so vehemently that she looses sight of her own humanity. Defiance and deviance are the only means available to Su-chieh to release her pent-up anger and attain freedom and equality, but the price that such a woman must pay in traditional China is insanity, physical and psychological torment and death. Her relationship with Ti never had a chance and it bespeaks the horror of a totally incompatible marriage.

The relationship between Ti and Chi-chieh is slightly more complicated and once again different from the other two. Escaping to Peking to eschew Su-chieh's tortures, Ti falls in love with his landlord's daughter, Chi-chieh, and takes her as wife, guaranteeing her the same status as the first wife. The enigma concerning Chi-chieh is her transformation from a sweet playmate who adores Ti to a jealous shrew after their marriage.

The pretty Chi-chieh before marriage was intensely attracted to the handsome young Ti with a bachelor's degree and from a well-to-do family. She confesses later: "I loved to hear whatever he had to say; even his shadow seemed handsome. Others considered his sweat smelly, but I thought it fragrant. Others considered him muddle-headed, but I thought him gentle. If we hadn't found each other so agreeable, would I have married him?" (80:976-77) Although they never transgress sexually and the games they play are quite innocent, the relationship is intimate and blissful. Like Sun Lan-chi, Chi-chieh is ignorant of Ti's ignominious past. And thus, Chi-chieh's blissful relationship with Ti before their marriage is somewhat similar to the romance he experienced with Sun Lan-chi. But this romance ends soon after their marriage.

Chi-chieh is vehemently jealous and she bears an intense resentment against Ti for either showing interest in other women or not showing enough care for her. While she may have considered it her right to monopolize his favours, especially given the premarital affections they harboured for each other, jealousy is not condoned in this polygamous society. The situation is furthermore complicated by Ti's lack of the will to remain faithful. Being the muddle-headed weakling that Ti is, he never fails to confirm her suspicions and provide her with reasons to be angry. Ti is easily dominated, which Chi-chieh soon discovers, but she is never as abnormally cruel and pent-up with hatred as Su-chieh is towards Ti, and her shrewish behaviour is also of a quite different nature.

The minute Ti and her own mother suggest that Chi-chieh provide the freezing Chen-chu with warmer clothing, Chi-chieh strips off her own padded outfit, hands it to Ti and says, "These are mine. I took them off so that you can give them to her!" Ti becomes so scared and pale that he loses "all semblance of being human." When her mother voices disapproval of her measure, she answers,

> It's nothing really. I'm truly not cold. Right now there really isn't anything available in the house. Where is there any cloth or cotton? Even if there are cloth and cotton, there isn't enough time to get them made right away. If I didn't take mine off for her, his love would freeze, and I'd feel uncomfortable wearing them anyway. I'll bet you, if I were the one without padded clothing, he would have said that he'd never noticed it. (79:969)

When Ti tries to protest, Chi-chieh kowtows exaggeratedly to Chen-chu, begs for her forgiveness, asks to be divorced etc., but maintains that only she or the maid is allowed to wear a padded outfit.

Chi-chieh's jealousy notwithstanding, Ti tries to start an affair with Chen-chu Pearl the first opportunity he gets, without realizing that the girl he believes to be Chen-chu is in fact Chi-chieh in disguise (79:974). Thereafter Chi-chieh stamps his penis with a seal nightly and examines it every morning to ascertain his fidelity. Should the imprint by chance have faded, she would invariably beat and torture him until he suffers almost as badly under her as he did in the hands of Su-chieh.

Chi-chieh's behaviour improves when she becomes pregnant and, later, after Chen-chu dies. She starts a row with Ti again on their boat trip to Szechuan, mainly because he has purchased gifts for everyone but her. She had hoped that he would have inquired of her desires when he disembarked to do shopping at Nanking, or at least he could have bought some wine or pork crackling to show his affections (87:1068-69). It is not until Su-chieh arrives at Ch'eng-tu and tries to kill their husband that Chi-chieh becomes protective of him. The relationship between Chi-chieh and Ti eventually normalizes and the latter finally leads a peaceful life until the ripe age of eighty-seven.

Viewed karmically, Chi-chieh's hatred of Chen-chu and her change in behaviour after marriage are explained through debts owed her from an earlier reincarnation. One sees in this need to justify the possessiveness in Chi-chieh, as well as changes in personality between girlhood and womanhood, some limitations in the perception of traditional authors. Viewed from a feminist psychological perspective, Chi-chieh's intense jealousy and possessiveness are reflections of her love for Ti, coupled with a strong sense of insecurity. The unusual opportunity she had to have been able to fall in love with the person she was to marry must have intensified the feelings of possessiveness. The fact that Ti proves himself to be interested in Chen-chu whenever the occasion arises must have also compounded her sense of insecurity. However, despite Chi-chieh's jealousy (unlike Ti's marriage to Su-chieh), this marriage is founded on love and compatibility. With the arrival of children and the passage of time, it does develop into an ideal marriage relationship.

As for the changes in Chi-chieh before and after marriage, one finds in the traditional authors an inability to accept drastic change in the development of personalities. Theirs is a rational and static universe where characters remain within the confines of their types. Hence characters modelled after real situations, especially women, must have puzzled them.[26] Whereas we might consider Chi-chieh's change in behaviour between being a girl being courted and a wife who is competing for her husband's attention only natural, the author can only explain it karmically.

It is obvious that this novel was written by a male author for a predominantly male audience. The main thrust of its didactic intent is the exhortation for men to treat human beings and animals alike with kindness so as to prevent marriages to shrewish wives in their future lives. As instruments of the karmic law, the right to poetic justice of these women who are supposedly avenging wrongs suffered during their previous lives, is, however, totally ignored. Their unseemly behaviour must be discouraged. Hence, paradoxically, the women who seem to have a right, karmically speaking, to avenge their erstwhile tormentors, must also be punished for their disregard of Confucian propriety in their present lives. They have either to turn over a new leaf or die.

Viewing the marriages from a male point of view in which justice and equality were not universal in their applicability, the novelist was unable to accept and comprehend the insistence on equal treatment by the so-called shrews. He is aware of their reasoning, but the mere fact that he writes them down doesn't signify endorsement. Rather, he must have intended to show how aberrant and unreasonable they were. One might compare the phenomenon to that of a historian who disapproves of Naziism but who nevertheless reports its purported reasons for annihilating the Jewish population. Certainly, awareness of the supposedly "crooked" reasoning of the shrews in *Hsing-shi yin-yuan* does not constitute affirmation on the part of the author. While the modern reader may applaud Su-chieh's rebuttal that she was too smart to be conned into attending a commemoration ceremony for two filial daughters-in-law who fed their own flesh to their ailing mother-in-law, one must assume that the traditional writer and his readers held a very different point of view.

Be that as it may, given that the motivations of the women are painstakingly described so as to elicit a patriarchally conditioned set of reactions, they nevertheless provide modern readers abundant insight into the raison d'être of many of the phenomena. Freed from masculine precepts and worldview, we can today examine the characters psychologically, from a feminist perspective. The three different relationships experienced by the protagonist with his wives and mistress can now be understood without the need for a karmic explanation. Hence, by discarding masculine bias, we are able to understand these characters better than the author did. Rather than an inexplicably amicable prostitute and two condemnable shrewish wives, Ti's three women, when studied in terms of their environments and their own feelings, provide an entirely different reading. He is either blissfully blessed by their ignorance, or direly plagued by their knowledge of him. Although karma may help, through a religious affiliation, to justify the existence of and reinforce stereotypes that are unjust to women, contemporary readings from a female perspective can lead to reinterpretations of such traditional Chinese texts.

Names of the Characters

Previous Incarnation	*Present Incarnation*
Ch'ao Yuan (husband)	Ti Hsi-ch'en (husband)
Chi-shih (wife)	Chi-chieh (wife)
Chen-ko (concubine)	Chen-chu (Pearl) (maid)
The Fox Spirit	Su-chieh (wife)
Pan-chiu (prostitute)	Sun Lan-chi (prostitute)

Notes

1 Kathryn A. Tsai, "The Chinese Buddhist Monastic Order for Women: The First Two Centuries," in Richard W. Guisso and Stanley Johannesen, eds., *Women in China: Current Directions in Historical Scholarship* (Youngstown, NY: Philo Press, 1981), p. 1-20.

2 Emily M. Ahern, "The Power and Pollution of Chinese Women," in Margery Wolf and Roxane Witke, eds., *Women in Chinese Society* (Stanford, CA: Stanford University Press, 1975), p. 193-214.

3 Roger T. Ames, "Taoism and the Androgynous Ideal," in Guisso and Johannesen, eds., *Women in China*, p. 21-46

4 Ibid., p. 47-61.

5 Alison H. Black, "Gender and Cosmology in Chinese Correlative Thinking," in Caroline Walker Bynum et al., eds., *Gender and Religion: On the Complexity of Symbols* (Boston: Beacon Press, 1986), p. 166-95.

6 Jordan Paper, "The Persistence of Female Deities in Patriarchal China," *Journal of Feminist Studies in Religion*, 6/1 (1990): 25-40.

7 In his *Male Anxiety and Female Chastity*, T'ien Ju-k'ang has correlated the anxiety of scholars in specific areas of China during the Ch'ing dynasty to the promulgation of acts of female chastity in forms such as public shows of suicides by widows. The more anxiety-ridden the unsuccessful scholars were, the more they seemed to have tried to exert the influence of patriarchal ideologies upon their women. That the women complied and even initiated these suicides themselves demonstrates not only the profound influence of the patriarchal value system (statistically, the majority of these women came from intellectual families) but also the lack of other avenues for women to distinguish themselves. See T'ien Ju-k'ang, *Male Anxiety and Female Chastity* (Leiden: Brill, 1988).

8 See, for example, Richard Guisso, "Thunder Over the Lake," in Guisso and Johannesen, eds., *Women in China*, p. 60; and Yang Lien-sheng, "Female Rulers in Ancient China," in Yu-ning Li, *Chinese Women Through Chinese Eyes* (Armonk, NY and London: M.E. Sharpe, 1992), p. 29.

9 J. William Angell and E. Pendleton Banks, eds., *Images of Man* (Mercer, GA: Mercer University Press, 1984), p. 47.

10 The numbers refer to chapters and pages of the Lien-ching ch'u-pan shih-yeh kung-ssu edition (Taipei, 1986). All the quotations from this novel are translated by myself.

11 The original title of the book was *O yin-yuan*; it has also appeared under the titles *Ch'ung-ting Ming-ch'ao yuan-yuan ch'uan-chuan* and as *Hsing-shih yin-yuan chuan*. See Yenna Wu, *Marriage Destinies to Awaken the World: A Literary Study of "Xingshi Yinyuan Zhuan"* (Ph.D. diss., Harvard University, 1986), p. 284-96, for the most comprehensive list of the extant and modern editions of the novel. The edition I am using is not listed therein, however.

12 Much controversy beclouds the date and authorship of the novel published under the pseudonym of Hsi-chou Sheng (literally, Man of Western Chou). Hu Shih had advanced a theory which attributed *Yin-yuan chuan* to none other than P'u Sung-ling (1640-1715), author of *Liao-chai chih-i*. See Hu Shih, *"Hsing-shih yin-yuan chuan k'ao-cheng,"* in *Hu Shih lun-hsüeh chin-chu* (Taipei rpt.: Shanghai Shangwu *yin-shu-kuan*, 1935), p. 333-402. Some contemporary scholars still maintain the validity of this hypothesis, including Liu Ts'un-yan in his preface to *Chinese Middle Fiction from the Ch'ing and Early Republican Eras* (Hong Kong: The Chinese University of Hong Kong Press, 1984), p. 6-11. The attribution is largely discredited, however. The most cogent arguments against its weaknesses are presented by Chu Yen-ching *"Hsing-shih yin-yuan" yen-chiu* (M.A. diss., National Taiwan University, 1978), p. 14-61, before the publication of Yenna Wu's even more elaborate discussion of the topic in *Marriage Destinies*, p. 19-86. They both refute the attribution of authorship to P'u as well as to Ting Yao-k'ang, supposed author of a sequel of *Chin P'ing Mei*, and conclude that the author was probably a native of Shantung. While Chu Yen-ching pinpoints *Yin-yuan chuan's* date of publication to 1721, Yenna Wu, however, more cautiously places its later limit at 1728 and earliest limit at 1628, and believes it "probably safe to assume that the novel was written in the early Qing" (p. 85). Chu Yen-ching derives her date by finding the only year *hsin-ch'ou* mentioned in its preface, between 1728 (the date of the Japanese bibliography, *Hakusai shomoku* which lists the novel with its preface) and 1701 (the year, according to the annals of Ching history, that the river god, the Fourth King of the River Dragon, also mentioned in chap. 86 of the novel, was consecrated. Yenna Wu, however, doubts whether the Kang-hsi confermant corresponds to the sacrificial feast described in the novel. According to Hsi-chou Sheng, this particular river god was originally a Jurchen prince, rather than the Sung loyalist described by Chao i (1727-1814), a Ch'ing historian, in his *O-pei ch'uan-chi* (p. 83-84). It seems possible that the Kang-hsi Emperor, himself a Manchu and most likely antagonistic to the ideal of consecrating a Sung loyalist, changed the legend to suit his own inclinations. The Jurchens were relatives of the Manchus but archenemies of the Sung.

13 For a quotation of Chang, see Chu Yen-ching, *"Hsing-shih yin-yuan,"* p. 155. See also Hsu Chih-mo, "Hsu Chih-mo ch'uan-chi" (Taipei: *chuan-chi wen-hsueh ch'u-pan-she*, 1969), p. 454, 458. The famous modern scholar, Hu Shih also maintains that *Yin-yuan chuan* ranks as one of the top five Chinese novels. See Hu Shih, *"Hsing-shih yin-yuan chuan kao-cheng,"* p. 389. The Ch'ing scholar, Hsueh Hung-chi singles *Yin-yuan chuan* out from among Ming and Ch'ing novels for its mimetic

portrayals in "Ming-mo Ch'ing-ch'u hsiao-shuo man-i," in *Ming Ch'ing hsiao-shuo lun-tsung* (Shen-yang: *Ch'un-feng wen-i ch'u-pan-she*, 1984), Vol. 1, p. 22.

14 Andrew Plaks, "After the Fall: *Hsing-shih yin-yuan chuan* and the Seventeenth-Century Chinese Novel," *Harvard Journal of Asian Studies* 45/2 (1985): 580. The Chinese literature department of Peking University which compiled *Chung-kuo hsiao-shuo shih* criticizes *Yin-yuan chuan* for its feudalistic thought content, its exaggerated style and its loose structure. See Pei-ching ta-hsüeh chung-wen hsi, ed., *Chung-kuo hsiao-shuo shih* (Beijing: Beijing daxue, 1983), p. 188-92.

15 Chu Yen-ching, "*Hsing-shih yin-yuan*," p. 1. Chi-chen Wang adds his own testimony to the authenticity of the Shangtung dialect in the book in the preface to his partial translation, "Marriage as Retribution," in Liu Ts'un-yan, ed., *Chinese Middlebrow Fiction from the Ch'ing and Early Republican Eras* (Hong Kong: Chinese University of Hong Kong Press, 1984), p. 45.

16 Ibid., p. 44. Chi-chen Wang states that "the reason for its neglect is that it was too crude for sophisticated readers who preferred *Hung Lou Meng* and *Chin P'ing Mei*, and not exciting enough for the average reader, who preferred more action and faster movement (as provided by *Shui-hu chuan*, *The Romance of the Three Kingdoms*, and many lesser novels.)"

17 Plaks is probably right in asserting that "this is a novel which few modern students have had the patience to read in full, and still fewer have subjected to a thorough critical analysis." See Andrew Plaks, "After the Fall," p. 545. Chi-chen Wang also mentions the book's length as an important reason, noting that "it was too costly to produce and too expensive for most people to buy." See Chi-chen Wang, trans., "Marriage as Retribution," p. 44.

18 See Andrew Plaks, "After the Fall," p. 556-67; Chi-chen Wang trans., "Marriage as Retribution," p. 42; and Pei-ching ta-hsüeh chung-wen hsi, ed., *Chung-kuo hsiao-shuo shih*, p. 191.

19 As the narrator is basically omniscient and does not seem to have been created to express a different point of view from that of the author, the term author is used throughout this chapter for both the narrator and the author.

20 See chart at the end of the paper for a list of the main characters in their two reincarnations.

21 She is not only neglected by him and insulted by the concubine but threatened by divorce. The concubine accused her of keeping a monk after she had been visited by a fat nun. Her only recourse to avenge herself is suicide. Abused wives in this novel are characteristically helpless and neglected by their own families until they kill themselves. Only then do their families gather relatives and converge upon the husbands' residences to wreak havoc and exact revenge for them.

22 Since a newborn is considered one year old by Chinese count, the young couple are a year younger by Western count.

23 Due to the practice of foot-binding, the shoes, of course, must have been tiny. Foot fetishism, especially that for very small feet, has always been a characteristic of the Chinese male culture, and even the shoes were considered highly erotic.

24 Although unschooled, she understands the ribald, unorthodox nuptial songs at her wedding better than Ti (56:710).

25 For a more detailed analysis of Su-chieh, see Fan Pen Chen, "Su-chieh: The Untamed Shrew of *Hsing-shih yin-yuan*," forthcoming in Lena Ross, ed., *To Speak or Be Silent: The Paradox of Disobedience in the Lives of Women* (Chicago: Chiron Publications, 1993).

26 All the writers of fiction of that period, and most likely the majority of the readers as well, were male.

Chapter 13

MULTIDIALOGICAL SPIRALLING FOR HEALING AND JUSTICE

Marilyn J. Legge

Introduction[1]

The work of Christian feminist liberation ethics begins with understanding women's oppression and moral agency as both personal and political. As Beverly Harrison aptly puts it, this critical consciousness involves

> recognition that what we have experienced, in isolation and silence, as private pain is in fact a public, structural dynamic. *My* life is now perceived in a new way in light of *your* stories. Together we slowly revision our reality so that what appeared, originally, to be an individual or personalized "problem" or even a human "failing" is exposed as a basic system or pattern of injustice.[2]

Priority is given to women's empowerment and well-being as involving a full range of issues which include history, religious traditions, sexuality, family, work and homophobia. Women's lives are appreciated as embedded in a matrix of specific political and personal, historical and cultural, physical and economic, social and emotional factors. Because women are differently affected by these realities – by the way power and access to resources can limit or enrich their lives – all of these topics must be read through an understanding of the interstructural oppressions of race, class, gender and compulsory heterosexuality, so as to render visible the particularity of women's experience.

To hold healing and liberation together challenges those working for justice to attend to one's own personal life in ways attentive to the different sufferings and sources of hope among all women. This involves working towards appropriately mutual relations, especially towards the poorest of non-white women. Seeking a dynamic, multidimensional solidarity, Christian feminist liberation ethics must also critically appropriate church scripture and tradition in order to offer a vision of communities of justice and love as promised by Jesus. What resources are available for this task of making the intricate and often obscured connections between personal pain and systemic injustice, between individual stories and social location, between healing and liberation?

First, justice is integral to the Christian tradition. It depicts how Jesus of Nazareth and his followers were people without a place in a world of injustice and misery. Jesus used the word righteousness or justice, the basis of his Jewish tradition, to speak of the nature and will of God. The early Christians lived their faith in Justice/Love, becoming known as "the people of the Way." Standing in this faith-and-justice tradition, feminist liberation theology and ethics employ a discourse of justice as the power of mutual relation or the power to act-each-other-into-well-being.

Power is related to justice and is rooted in feminist thought where power is identified positively with such concepts as physical energy, empowerment, endurance, creative work, enjoying sensual/sexual experience, connection with nature and making meaningful lives out of chaos. Because persons exist as embodied selves-in-relation, shared power enables them to become persons in their own right and to create a space where all can breathe freely. Hence in movements for justice which believe that there is no liberation without community, power — to be authentic and life-giving — must be shared. That is, it will arise from particular lives, in specific social locations and be flexible and dynamic among people in the different domains of nature and history. (Both of these concepts are understood as always and everywhere mediated.)

Given the different domains of ethic of shared power, the central theological claim of justice as mutuality incarnated involves the difficult task of integrating personal healing and liberation with struggles for social transformation. The challenge is to relate brokenness and felt oppression to the structural aspects of social relations that reinforce and reproduce brokenness and oppression according to gender, sexual identity, race, ethnicity, religion, nation, class and so forth. For women, specifically, to seek justice means becoming the subjects of their own lives within a community. Hence, another way of talking about justice is to understand it as the power of shared personhood.

Second, the connection between healing and justice towards human liberation needs to be acknowledged. Beverly Harrison, in a course syllabus, names the necessary elements in this way: Feminist liberation ethics is a praxis (activity and reflection on that activity) of resistance to human oppression and struggle for human solidarity in light of women's concrete experience. Herein lies the vision: to seek healing, be it wholeness or abundant life, is to be part of a process that nurtures justice. A feminist theological approach affirms the experience of struggling for justice as the base for our theological conceptions. I have drawn on the work of Delores Williams to describe this process of keeping healing and justice together as a "multidialogical spiral."[3]

Multidialogical Spiral of Healing and Justice-Making
I will now briefly introduce this heuristic device, and then elaborate on its three constitutive elements or basepoints. The initial basepoint in this spiral involves sharing our stories about suffering and joy. Experience is a primary source for feminist theology and ethics. Although it is sometimes exaggerated within the religious women's movement, so that there is virtually no subsequent reflection on women's stories, experience is fundamental to the critical capacity of women and others who appeal against a

dominant religious tradition, opinion or ideology. For example, because women have taken their own experience seriously, they have discovered that in Christian scripture and tradition there are prescribed ideals which are all too often compromised. Thus there is:

- an ethic of care for strangers that none the less renders precarious the safety and shelter of daughters
- an ethic of chastity so undermined by innuendoes of pleasure, lust and pride that it renders precarious the moral status of women of integrity
- an ethic of Christian duty that can threaten the basic security by the abuse, etc., of women living with men
- an ethic of love, so identified with the privacy of the home and heterosexuality that it renders ambiguous, if not problematic, the basic foundations of justice.[4]

From these examples, it becomes obvious that experience is *not* highly privatized in feminist theological work. Experience indicates the boundary between our own bodyselves and all that exists beyond the stories of our people. Hence when we insist on appeals to experience — and we must in feminist liberationist perspective — we are also insisting on the responsibility to communicate our experience of God in community. This being the case, we ought not be surprised that just as tensions exist within experience, so too will language and images from God witness to both struggle and hope. Be it for example, as the Passion for Justice,[5] Caller to Accountability, Vision Keeper, Challenger of Apathy, Holy Advocate, Bestower of Disturbing Peace, Earth-maker, Companion in Struggle for Life, Pain-bearer and Co-creator, we ourselves are involved in and with diverse aspects of Sacred Power.

The second element in the multidialogical spiral is attention to moral agency — to the conditions and ethos of action for a centred, self-determined existence in community. Theologically, we are co-creators and have been given the gift of life to struggle for, embrace and pass along. We must therefore choose life, take responsibility for our lives-in-relation and discover ourselves, grow in self-knowledge, self-esteem and self-acceptance. Here we need social analysis to see how power and social structures shape our experience. When we connect our lives with others, we will discover realities of unfair advantage as well as brokenness and oppression.[6] So we will attend to the way power and access to resources limit or enable the authentic living of our lives, the creation of our personhood and of moral agency.

Thirdly, in the spiral of action for wholeness and justice, we need to reach out to build community and to be involved in transforming life-denying relations, systems and structures. This spiral step signals that the sum of personal narratives does not, for instance, constitute a unilateral feminist understanding of social life nor insist that all women's experiences of oppression are the same. Our commitment to the discarded, the poor, the suffering, to all those yearning for justice, as well as to our own integrity is rooted in faith in the One who works in, with and through humanity for a healed, whole, full life.

Thus, what this spiral indicates is that healing is not completed for individuals until persons reach out to act, to build community and create a healthy connectedness — as people seek a self-determined social existence. So to heal fully, to recover and to achieve a certain degree of freedom, all need to be able to understand personal oppression in terms of the structures of race, class and gender that contribute to social location and interpersonal patterns of lived-world experience. This then is used as the foundation of awareness from which to strive to heal ourselves and our community. Having introduced this multidialogical spiral, deeper exploration of its three basepoints is required to draw some connections in each between healing and justice.

Who We Are: Reflection on Experience as Relational Selves in Particular Social Locations

If justice is the mainstay of religious faith and reason for being, feminists begin with making connections between their lives and those who are the victims of injustice, those who a treated as "the other." While from a theological perspective accountability must always be to the lives of those who are designated as other if Justice/love is God's name, women need also to admit that they can also objectify and treat themselves as objects, as other. Thus, they can also stand in need of conversion to themselves as the subjects of their own God-given lives, rather than remain the objects of someone else's definition and design. As a result, we also struggle to be self-respecting, to believe in our own worth and dignity, to trust our abilities enough to identify what we truly need and, if need be, be self-assertive.

Those of us who have come to define ourselves as feminist did so because the social situations we continue to experience — including those in the church, of course — call for struggle, analysis and change if we are to become fully human. However, just because we become conscientized and active in struggles for transformation does not imply we automatically eradicate the contradictions of our everyday lives. Instead, we must come to accept the presupposition that our own stance, whatever it is, is not natural or normative, but is itself the product of many complex factors that may heretofore have escaped our notice. Once identified with the shifting, multifaceted terrain of feminist consciousness, one will soon be plagued by what is referred to in feminist theory as "social location" or what Canadian cultural critic Joan Borsa calls "the politics of location":

those places and spaces we inherit and occupy, which frame our lives in very specific and concrete ways, which are as much a part of our psyches as they are a physical or geographical placement. Where we live, how we live, our relation to the social systems and structures that surround us are deeply embedded parts of everything we do and remain integral both to our identity or sense of self and to our position or status within a larger cultural and representational field. While many of us are actively in feminism, [in religious practice], in cultural production and in critical social theory [and theology], our historical, social, political and economic realities vary – there is a great deal of structural difference between us.[7]

Given the historical specificity of any social location, no one is ever "naturally" consigned to a particular space. This is so even if we were otherwise informed by ideologies that systematically utilize difference as a tool for domination and teach that certain groups, by virtue of their difference, naturally have particular power and privilege.[8] It is the awareness of one's particular social location that can liberate one from seeking to exercise over others a kind of theological imperialism. Self-critical awareness and deepened historical understanding of the structures of race, class, culture and gender are enhanced by such attention to difference.

Because "all difference is not the same difference,"[9] a key challenge in the work of feminist theologians and ethicists is to be able to name one's social location, to question where particular experiences of power, unfair advantage, and oppression, as well as specific practices, fit within our current network of social relations. For example: How is the agenda for feminist ethics and theology set? Who is included in this work and to whom is it accountable? How does access to resources for shaping one's own life affect the way one relates to the church and broader context?

In exploring how difference functions to objectify and negate the other, the work of Canadian philosopher Susan Wendell is also particularly helpful. She observes:

When we make people "other," we group them together as the objects of our experience instead of regarding them as fellow subjects of experience with whom we might identify. If you are "other" to me, I see you primarily as symbolic of something else – usually, but not always, something I reject and fear and that I project onto you. We can all do this to each other, but very often the process is not symmetrical, because one group of people may have more power to call itself the paradigm of humanity and to make the world suit its own needs and validate its own experiences. [For example, disabled people are "other" to able-bodied people, and ... the consequences are socially, economically and psychologically oppressive to the disabled and psychologically oppressive to the able-bodied. Able-bodied people may be "other" to disabled people, but the consequences of this for the able-bodied are minor (most able-bodied people can afford not to notice it).[10]

Because the unearned entitlement or conferred dominance that some women have is at the expense of others, it can differently damage both those who have it and those who are deprived. Thus, it is imperative to do much more than simply note the presence of difference[11] – we must study and learn to recognize how it distorts our humanity and struggle to overcome our varied positions of outsiderhood.[12] Women are differently subordinated and yet may have some similar constraints on their moral agency under particular historical conditions – for example, women, despite their differences, are more vulnerable to violence. Yet such a generalization, while a basis for solidarity, cannot provide a universal prescription of response for women in all violent situations. We must resist both a simple acceptance and a rejection of the differences among women. Instead, the aim is to empower each woman to specify the particularities of her own life, to learn the particular causes of her personal sufferings as structurally sustained, and to name the sources of hope required for her well-being.

Each person was created in the image of God, and justice demands all should have access to resources to become whom they were created to be. But misogyny – that reaction of fear and/or hate which occurs when women's concrete power to live and act as full persons in their own right is claimed – limits women's right to this access. In a similar fashion, racism, heterosexism, homophobia and economic exploitation construct a dichotomy between positions of unearned advantage and an otherness that is excluded or even, in extreme cases, erased.

To be created in the image of a God who creates, liberates and sustains the earth and all life opens up immense and sacred possibilities of becoming human by coming to know and keep faith in God by acting as God does. This mystery is the heart of being human. In Jesus, Christians recognize the incarnation as the exemplar of what it means to be human: to love the victim with a strong and a tender love. Jesus' humanity manifests God's presence by the radical transformation of relationships that occcurs when each person is valued as made in the image of God. However, neither Jesus' life nor God's action as creator in any way reduces human responsibility for honouring one's own power as a co-creator. Our task as persons created in the image of God is to make and keep life human. In response to the dehumanization of injustice – of moral evil – I join those who believe we best live our faith as pilgrims inspired by the quest for justice for all.[13] Within the limitations set by our relatedness to others and to our environment, if we are to follow in the example of Christ, people are to be held morally accountable for the state of world.

Choosing Life: Social Analysis and Moral Agency

We become human – that is, we act in the image of God – when we claim our freedom. Freedom is the power to name and shape the world as self-respecting, other-regarding persons. To put it another way, to be like God is to be life-giving. In feminist ethics, the category of full moral agency best describes the work of co-creation. According to Bruce Birch and Larry Rasmussen, moral agency

is a way to name that which is necessary to make sense of ourselves as creatures who act "morally." It is a tag for describing human experience, and especially human action, from a moral point of view. It means we are those kinds of creatures who are able to perceive various courses of action, weigh them with a view to various considerations, and act on the basis of the considerations, and act on the choices. It also means we can be held accountable for our choices and actions. "Agency" encompasses both character and conduct, both our moral "being" and our moral "doing"....[14]

To engage in this historical project of becoming fully human persons, one needs power. For feminists this is often referred to as empowerment, a form of creativity of building up oneself in community. Theologically, power is the capacity to act with God, to fully exercise our moral agency.

Yet it needs to be acknowledged that freedom for responsible self-direction in community also includes the capacity for evil. Traditionally, sin has been defined as alienation from God, the state of being opposed to God, the loss of a bond, a root, which occurs as the result of the misuse of human freedom. In a liberationist understanding, we include alienation from God, self, neighbour and creation itself. Everywhere we look it is plain to see that people are not treated as images of God. Dehumanization and loss of conditions to create full life are evil. In feminist theology and ethics, the critical task is to uncover the massive social denial and distrust of women's moral agency—which is a form of alienation. Such oppression destroys the vocation of being created for freedom and responsibility. And, from a feminist perspective, various forms of interlocking oppressions can be discerned to operate in direct contradiction to a theology of active engagement in creation.

The understanding of the church as a people of the resurrection is shocked by such oppression. Susan Davies defines oppression as "the exercise of authority or power in a burdensome, cruel or unjust manner."[15] Governments are oppressive when they systematically restrict and violate the civil and personal rights of their people. Organizations and social systems are oppressive when they suppress and deny the humanity of individuals simply because they do not fit certain categories.

This collective oppression has two aspects: first, the power to define the norm of personhood and second, the power to enforce it on an institutional, economic and/or individual basis. Oppressed groups are constructed as "other" on the basis of a dominant norm of personhood. Such a norm or standard declares who is the most fully human, the most acceptable kind of person. Oppression is perpetuated when that standard is used to judge all people and to enforce the exclusion or punishment of those who do not meet this standard. Those outside that circle of significance, those who do not fit that norm, are treated as less than fully human.

According to Suzanne Pharr, in the dominant North American culture, the defined norm, as found in its language and laws, businesses and advertisements, churches and synagogues and mosques, schools and clubs, is "male, white, heterosexual, Christian, temporarily able-bodied, youthful, and has access to wealth and resources."[16] This norm, however, does not reflect the majority of people in Canada; instead, it represents those who have the ability and power to exert control over others.

Social analysis is required to challenge the assumed moral standards based on this norm. Critical analysis exposes the way very limited standards are presented as the universal model of being human and full of life. Critical social analysis is also necessary to stay grounded in concrete social realities so that the resultant theo-ethical decisions remain rooted in serving personal and social transformation. One significant result is the ongoing and proper questioning of "the" (white, elite, middle-class, heterosexual, able-bodied, etc.) feminist position. Instead, multicontextual expressions of feminist religious reflection are being recovered and constructed which honour the multifarious particularities of women's experiences of sacred power.

Building Community: Healing and Solidarity
The third crucial element in the multidialogical spiral is community action for authentic healing and liberation. The important point is that "personhood" and "peoplehood" never have, and do not, just happen, even if we share common geography, events or experience. The task is to create communities formed around common commitment to human wholeness and creation's well-being.

An essential aspect of taking responsibility for our own lives as moral agents is battling the oppression which exists under our own skin: How have I internalized a demeaning view of myself? How have I, or do I, oppress others? Audre Lorde encourages a process of accountability to those who do not belong to the white, heterosexual elite. This implies, for many women, reaching down into that deep place of knowledge inside and touching that terror and loathing of any difference that lives there. The result is a recognition of the face it wears, so then the personal as well as the political can begin to illuminate all our choices. Lorde goes on to testify: "Without community there is no liberation." Genuine community involves learning how to take our differences and make them strengths, especially among those who stand outside the circle of society's definitions of acceptable women — poor, lesbian, coloured, older women.[17]

Thus, in community, we are accountable for our actions and lives within a web of relations that includes different resources of power. These resources are available within the particularity of our lives and the ongoing ways we strive for justice and balance with ourselves, our neighbours and God. We are morally creative and responsible when we declare to whom we are accountable and, in this process, assess who is implicated in and who bears the cost of our decisions and actions. If we are to link our lives with those we believe God calls us to be in right relation with — those who are different and despised — it is essential that we make our decisions in solidarity with them. To do so, we must struggle with our own suffering in order to remember how we have been hurt. Then, from this emotional connection, we can begin to identify, understand and act in solidarity with the oppressed, rather than simply maintain any unfair advantage. As a result difference can be a creative spark for dialogue and bridge-building in a movement of resistance against all manner of injustice.

If justice is good news, a contemporary name for grace is solidarity — the cultivation of full humanity through concrete justice, by active recognition of the uniqueness, value and interconnectedness of all the living. We image God most when we claim our own creative power for life; when we learn to recognize each others' problems and possibilities as the interconnecting basis for solidarity; and when we live into a future in which all persons can be whole.

Each community of women and marginalized people that gains its own distinctive voice opens up new wisdom and resources for healing. All engaged in nurturing justice in ourselves and the world are enriched by these insights. This does not mean that each community of justice remains limited to the vantage point of its own reflections. What it means is that each community can learn from others' reflections. Some need to learn from the insights of Aboriginal, Quebeçoises, prairie cooperators, racialized, lesbian and gay liberationists and other struggling communities about the needs that are central to each one's liberation. Different communities have different priorities — work, safe space, housing, lifelong learning, friends, religious practice. Just as feminists demand that male theologians reorient their work when sexism is exposed in religious tradition and culture, once the problems of heterosexism, classism and racism have been identified within feminism itself there needs to be change in the way all (pro) feminists of faith look at their religious practice. The ongoing work of healing ourselves invites us to recognize shared interests in the transformation of dehumanizing social relations in all dimensions of a society which denies the great majority access to creative work and recognition.

Given that the category of experience is fragmented and multiple, how can we hope to work across these differences that concretely divide us and look towards a shared liberation? Fears must be brought out into the open in order to dispel them. Much emotional work is required for a liberative spirituality. Hence, theoretical work must also include reflection on the problems of sustaining our lives — on the drudgery, struggles and celebrations of everyday life. Feminist consciousness must come from bag ladies as well as from farmers, from prostitutes as well as from academics. We can make alliances over common causes if we listen closely to the interpretations and meanings of those with different interests and learn to connect our struggles with those most marginalized.

In theological terms, Dorothee Soelle describes solidarity as related to difference and the everyday work of resurrection, healing and justice. "Where we break the neutrality of silence and abandon our complicity with injustice, the new life begins. People who earlier were invisible and forgotten become self-assured and find their own language. They stand up for their rights and this revolt, this rebellion, is a sign of resurrection."[18] This observation serves also to remind us that there is no such thing as justice in the abstract. Abstract justice is a liberal fallacy that assumes that in the search for human justice the pain of any one group can be ignored. Instead, feminist liberationists insist that to be fully a person is to be deeply related to others in particular, concrete, historical experiences. Thus, feminist liberationists insist that personal struggles for healed and fulfilled existence are neither misguided nor selfish. We also insist that love is not a subjective attitude but an active engagement with life which enables us to remain in the struggle.

If we are to act with the sustained energy and commitment needed to oppose oppression, I hope we will think of ourselves as unfinished, capable of change, and capable of gaining power over our own lives. In other words, theologically God's grace embraces us with co-creative possibilities, as responsible for our own well-being. Initially, we affirm ourselves as women in terms of rescuing specific struggles for freedom from public invisibility. From this concrete engagement with our own agenda, we join with others in common projects in church and society, as for example, organizing for adequate day care and medical coverage, helping survivors of incest, or working to repeal oppressive and unjust policies and laws. The criteria for life in right relation are then — empowerment, the reduction of unearned privilege and the elimination of domination.

Justice, in this perspective, is radical equality and mutuality in community; it is our co-capacity for relationship; it is a quality of humanness that calls us into connection and solidarity. Justice includes the distribution of wealth, income and other material goods and is wider than seeking to liberate an abstract individual or simply to define one's own ends as liberal theory teaches. Instead, justice names the perspectives, principles and procedures for evaluating institutional norms and rules.[19] The idea of justice in a liberationist paradigm shifts from a focus on distributive patterns in an accepted system to procedural issues of participation in both deliberation and decision-making.

For a norm to be just, everyone who follows it must, in principle, have an effective voice and be able to agree to it without coercion. Hence, for a social condition to be just — for right relation — it must enable all to meet their needs and exercise their freedom. Thus justice requires that all be able to express their needs. This means that without the presence of different voices, especially the most silenced and neglected, we cannot shape justice or promote a common vision. The challenge has been well put, in another context, by Delores Williams and her notion of "multidialogics." What she urges is that if we are nurturing justice in ourselves and our world, we will be persons in dialogue across the differences of history, region, race, class, gender and sexual orientation.

Conclusion

Multidialogical spiralling through difference is a way to learn about the way we are, who we are and who we want to be. The aim is to go beyond the fear of difference, beyond the tolerance of injustice, and beyond the dread of displeasing people, so that human beings share relational power as justice/ love.

The affirmation of one's "power-in-mutual-relation" recognizes the finite nature of human existence and underscores that persons are morally accountable for the world even within the limitations set by human relatedness to others, one's social location and to the environment. "From this theological perspective," Beverly Harrison observes:

> faith is understood chiefly as the power (and it is power, a shared and communal power) to live one's life fully, genuinely engaged in receiving and communicating a sense of life's joy and possibility. To live by faith means to accept one's own power, always partial and finite, always power-in-relation, but nonetheless real, to engage with others and to tenderly shape the processes of nature/history for genuine human and cosmic fulfillment. Such faith, according to an ancient Christian theological formula, requires hope as its ground and love as its foundation.[20]

Justice as making right relations incorporates the insight of the Jewish tradition that "doing justice" entails not only advocacy for those marginalized but also solidarity with them by way of mutual accountability. Hence, justice and the struggle for justice are foundational to love itself.

In short, healing and justice are integral to discerning that the theological significance of one's life in relation will be gleaned when one struggles against conditions which crucify and perpetuate injustice. In this process God is known as a liberating, healing and empowering Presence who encourages human cooperation so that each person can become the subject of his/her own destiny. Indeed, people find their way to God by doing justice because it brings us into right relation with God, neighbour, self and nature. God is where the passion for justice is alive and yearning.

Notes

1 A version of this chapter was originally presented at the event "Nurturing Justice in Ourselves and Our World," St. Stephen's College, University of Alberta, Edmonton, May 6-8, 1992. I dedicate it to my sisters with whom I shared leadership, Charlotte Caron and Carter Heyward.

2 Beverly Harrison, *Making the Connections: Essays in Feminist Social Ethics* (Boston: Beacon Press, 1985), p. 243. I am indebted to her wisdom and theological articulation, here and below.

3 Delores Williams names the element of multidialogical intent as the first in a Christian womanist (African American) theological methodology: "A multidialogical intent will allow Christian womanist theologians to advocate and participate in dialogue and action with many diverse social, political, and religious communities concerned about human survival and productive quality of life for the oppressed." See "Womanist Theology: Black Women's Voices," in Judith Plaskow and Carol Christ, eds., *Weaving the Visions: New Patterns in Feminist Spirituality* (New York: Harper and Row, 1989), p. 184.

4 I have adapted this list from Lois Gehr Livezey, "A Christian Vision of Sexual Justice: Theological and Ethical Reflections on Violence Against Women," in *In God's Image*, 10/1 (Spring 1991): 18-32. Available from Asian Women's Resource Centre, 136-46 Younchi-Dong, Chongro-Ku, Seoul, Korea.

5 See for example Carter Heyward, *Our Passion for Justice: Images of Power, Sexuality, and Liberation* (New York: Pilgrim Press, 1984).

6 On this reconceptualization of "privilege" among women, see Delores Williams, "Womanist/Feminist Dialogue," in *Journal of Feminist Studies in Religion*, 9/1-2 (Spring/Fall 1993):70-71; also Peggy McIntosh, "White Privilege and Male Privilege: A Personal Account of Coming to See Correspondences Through Work in Women's Studies," Working Paper No. 189, Wellesley College Center For Research on Women, Wellesley, MA 02181.

7 Joan Borsa, "Towards a Politics of Location: Rethinking Marginality," *Canadian Woman Studies/les cahiers de la femme* 11 (Spring 1990): 36.

8 See Charlotte Bunch, "Making Common Cause: Diversity and Coalitions," in *Passionate Politics: Feminist Theory in Action* (New York: St. Martin's Press, 1987), p. 151.

9 Ruth Smith, "The Evasion of Otherness: A Problem for Feminist Moral Reconstruction," *Union Seminary Quarterly Review* 43 (1990): 151.

10 Susan Wendell, "Towards a Theory of Disability," *Hypatia* 4 (Summer 1989): 112.

11 Feminist theorist Caroline Ramazanoglu fruitfully addresses the complexity of the problem of difference; see her *Feminism and the Contradictions of Oppression* (New York: Routledge, 1989).

12 This term is from Cherrie Moraga, *Loving in the War Years* (Boston: South End Press, 1983).

13 For a most vigourous and salient presentation of a feminist liberative theological approach, see Beverly Harrison, "Theological Reflection in the Struggle for Liberation: A Feminist Perspective," in *Making the Connections: Essays in Feminist Social Ethics* (Boston: Beacon Press, 1985), p. 235-66.

14 Bruce Birch and Larry Rasmussen, *Bible and Ethics in Christian Life*, rev. ed. (Minneapolis: Augsburg Press, 1989), p. 40.

15 Susan Davies, "Oppression and Resurrection Faith," in Letty Russell, ed., *The Church with Aids: Renewal in the Midst of Crisis*, p. 91. I am indebted to her theological analysis of oppression and otherness.

16 Suzanne Pharr, *Homophobia: A Weapon of Sexism* (Point Reyes Station, CA: Chardon Press, 1988), p. 53. I strongly recommend her book for the ongoing work of fighting and understanding interlocking oppression. It is available from The Women's Project, 2224 Main St,. Little Rock, AR 72206, USA.

17 Audre Lorde, "The Master's Tools Will Never Dismantle the Master's House," *Sister Outsider* (Trumansburg, NY: The Crossing Press, 1984), p. 112.

18 Dorothee Soelle, *Choosing Life* (Philadelphia: Fortress Press, 1981), p. 88-89.
19 See Iris Marion Young, *Justice and the Politics of Difference* (Princeton: Princeton University Press, 1990), p. 33-34.
20 Beverly W. Harrison, *Our Right to Choose* (Boston: Beacon Press, 1983), p. 92-93.

Chapter 14

A RELIGIOUS PHILOSOPHY OF SELF[1]

Winnie Tomm

In this paper, the self is assumed to be a composition that is constructed not by a single composer but by interacting participants within local community conditions. The paper is divided into five parts. In Part 1, I attempt to establish a rationale for positing the existence of a self, in the face of postmodern efforts to deconstruct it. Deconstructing the self (taking away the essence of the self) is problematic for both a feminist and a religious view of self. If one wishes to maintain the category of self, as I do, it is important to show the limitations of postmodern attempts to decentre it. It is necessary to reconcile social constructionism with some form of essentialism. I aim to show that essentialism and constructionism are contiguous rather than oppositional. Belief in the mutually influential relation between essentialism and constructionism shapes the discussion throughout the paper with respect to language (Part 2), body (Part 3), and metaphorical expressions of bodied spiritual consciousness (Part 4). The paper concludes (Part 5) with a brief discussion of the social implications of revisioning a religious philosophy of self for women.

1 Self-Definitions
Self-determination as composition
To borrow the title of Mary Catherine Bateson's book, *Composing a Life*, self-determination is about composing a life as a process of improvisation.[2] It is not about the unfolding of fixed essences. Bateson draws an analogy between the relatively unplanned patterns of many women's lives and the improvisational process of jazz musicians. Women's lives, like jazz improvisation, emerge through interaction among participants. The key notion in the analogy is that of interdependency. Life is a process of improvising with others, of creating a rhythm in which each person's contribution is an integral part of the composition. Sometimes there is beautiful music, other times there is dissonance which requires more listening and responsiveness to the interactive process. The metaphor of self as improvisation reflects the Buddhist view of self as it is expressed in the doctrine of *pratītya samutpāda* (interdependent origination). The self, in this view, is essentially participatory. Subjectivity and relationality are two dimensions of the interactive process of epistemology and ontology in which the self continually emerges in new ways of knowing and being.

Decentring a Self

Decentring a self has been an essential component of anti-essentialists' activities, in the interest of spelling out ways in which any self is socially, psychically, politically, linguistically, and historically constructed.[3] By *decentring a self*, I mean deconstructing any assumed essence to which all contingent personal qualities are subordinated. Deconstruction includes exposing hidden assumptions about essences which define natures and purposes in terms of sex-specific qualities, racial characteristics, economic class-related features, and so forth. This has important implications for gendered role prescriptions and social organization. For example, if the capacity to exercise theoretical wisdom (Aristotle, *Nicomachean Ethics*) is taken as the essence of a human being, then the ability to understand abstract mathematics is valued more than child care. When reason is asserted as the essence of human nature, an ethics based on dispassionate reason automatically takes precedence over one in which affiliation is normative. Hierarchies of social relations get established on the basis of one's proximity to assumed essential features of human nature.

The social relations of the sexes are organized around assumptions about the nature and purpose of women and men, according to assertions about different essences. Immanuel Kant, for example, describes the essences of women and men as beauty and reason respectively.[4] He claims that the sexes are "different but equal." Rather than equality, however, the differences between the sexes are associated with the domination of reason and the subordination of beauty. Describing individuals in terms of sex-specific essences within a social context in which only one essence is positively connoted does not amount to equality. Those who are esteemed largely as *environmental decorations* have less value than *sublime* thinkers. The problem does not lie with either beauty or reason but with the assignment of them exclusively to either sex as though they characterize essences which determine psychological attributes and social roles. This view of essences influences expectations with respect to acceptable individual aspirations and social structures which facilitate or impede those expectations. For those who accept their *naturally* inferior status, it would be inappropriate to expect equal pay, equal employment opportunities and equal social authority. In short, current power relations between the sexes are largely determined by essentialist views of human nature. We can see, therefore, that deconstructing traditional essentialism is in the interests of those who claim they have a right to self-determination regardless of their sex. Parallel arguments can be applied to other social issues such as race, class, sexual orientation, ableness and ethnicity.

The act of decentring the subject and focussing on the social construction of the subject, especially through language, undercuts the power of arguments from nature. They are no longer uncritically accepted and freely used to maintain status-quo power dynamics with respect to differences among people. Gender social justice for a greater number of people in families, local communities, nations and the world is a likely consequence of the work of influential social constructionists such as Derrida, Foucault and Spelman. There is little doubt that the deconstruction of exclusionary categories and the dismantling of pernicious arguments from nature is a great service to marginalized individuals and groups.

The actualization of human potential of persons who are positioned differently with respect to social power requires social justice: the protection of rights and possibilities of self-determination for all people. In light of structural imbalances of power, affirmative action is necessary to bring about social justice. From a religious perspective, social justice depends upon spiritual agency, which moves people beyond socially constructed categories based on hegemonic interests, i.e., the interests of those in control. In particular, it is important that God be deconstructed. Women who no longer live according to essentialist interpretations of God, of woman or of self could be expected to eagerly participate in efforts to open spaces for self-determination through deconstruction of exclusive categories such as those in the philosophies of Plato, Aristotle, Aquinas, Descartes and Kant.

It is clear that self-determination for women in a patriarchal culture requires the deconstruction of oppressive concepts. One can ask, however, whether deconstruction of essentialist categories and the construction of self through historical determinism are the only alternatives for a theory of self-determination for women. Is it necessary or even desirable to reject all categories of identity in order to avoid the pitfalls of essentialism? Is there not more to life than socially and culturally constructed realities? From the perspective of a believer in agency of the self, including spiritual agency, I believe that deconstructionism and historical determinism are only partial explanations. When historical determinism disallows for the self as a subject, it becomes *sociological essentialism* and excludes the agency intrinsic to self-determination.

The importance of a category such as *subjective agency* for the purpose of supporting an argument for self-determination is fairly obvious. There is clearly a need for the category of *women*, around which organization for social change can continue to occur. Both these categories (subjective agency and women) require the category of a *self*. It is counterintuitive to deny that there are individuals with specific identities and groups with members who share similar concerns and goals. Nor need one deny individual or group identity in the process of deconstructing exclusive, essentialist categories. The interdependency of egoity and sociality is depicted in the analogy between jazz improvisation and composing an individual life.[5] Jazz musicians can dispense with the score and rely on their sense of what makes good music. Likewise, our sense of humanity develops through listening and responding to others. Individual and group identity emerge through each other. Being at home with oneself includes a *fit* between one's inner self and the image in the mirror as well as through the mirroring of others. Self-determination requires centring the self through both kinds of mirroring. Being at home with oneself is something for which most of us have a great appreciation. What could that mean without some experience of oneself as essentially oneself?

Essentialism

There are various forms of essentialism. As Diana Fuss shows in *Essentially Speaking*, it is possible to retain some senses of essentialism without assuming transhistorical, eternal and immutable essences.[6] She argues that essentialist assumptions lie at the basis of all constructionist arguments. Fuss says, "My position here is that the possibility of any radical constructionism can only be built on the foundations of a hidden essentialism."[7] She refers to Jacques Derrida's critique of the essence of woman as an example of a constructionist's dependence on essentialism. He says "there is no one place for woman" and then goes on to say that "it is without a doubt risky to say that there is no place for woman, but this idea is not anti-feminist."[8] Fuss points out that

> There is an interesting slippage here from the claim that "there is no one place for woman" to the claim that 'there is no place for woman" – two rather different statements indeed. But Derrida's point seems to be simply that "a woman's place," a single place, must necessarily be essentializing. This is doubtless true, but we need to ask whether positing multiple places for women is necessarily any *less* essentializing. Does "woman's *places*" effectively challenge the unitary, metaphysical notion of the subject/woman who presumably fills these particular places and not others?[9]

In Derrida's view, woman has no essence, or at least not one "which is rigorously or properly identifiable."[10] Fuss shows how the ambiguity of Derrida's deconstructionist strategies allows him to slip from saying that woman has no decidable essence to the claim that "the essence of woman is to *be* the undecidable."[11] The ambiguity of the manner of speech in Derrida obscures the subject addressed. It hides the deconstructionist's dependence on a form of essentialism. In this case, it obscures the reliance on the essentialist category of *woman* in positing a plurality of woman's places or identities. "[I]n the end Derrida does not so much challenge that woman has an essence as insist that we can never 'rigorously' or 'properly' identify it."[12] This becomes inverted into the view that woman is the unidentifiable, to which I shall refer later in the paper. I support Fuss' claim that deconstructionism and its positive side, constructionism, depend on some form of essentialism.

Fuss' argument that some form of essentialism is foundational to any constructionist position relies on the claim that essentialisms are themselves socially constructed. She says "Essentialism is embedded in the idea of the social and lodged in the problem of social determination."[13] She takes the category of *the body* as an example of the interweaving of essentialism and constructionism. The two extreme views are that the body is real in a pure way (a strict realist form of essentialism) or that it is always only a product of cultural inscriptions (radical constructionism). Fuss says "To say that the body is ... deeply embedded in the social is not by any sure means to preclude essentialism."[14] It may preclude an essentialism that assumes that nature is unchanging, but that is not the only form of essentialism. One may assume, as Fuss does, that nature is essentially changing. I support Fuss' suggestion that

> If we are to intervene effectively in the impasse created by the essentialist/constructionist divide, it might be necessary to begin questioning the *constructionist* assumption that nature and fixity go together (naturally) just as sociality and change go together (naturally). In other words, it may be time to ask whether essences can change and whether constructions can be normative.[15]

One form of essentialism that has become increasingly widespread is that of *sociological essentialism* which is at odds with any form of ontological essentialism. I assume an ontological essentialism in this paper which is characterized by change. That assumption underlies my discussion of self as a composition which evolves through the process of listening and responding to others as well as to all of nature. What I call a *metaphysics of interrelatedness* situates this discussion of self as composition.[16] I wish to distinguish the kind of ontological essentialism that I assume from one that includes an unchanging essence. I do not support an account of essence as something that can be ascertained with absolute certainty. I, therefore, reject, along with the constructionists, arguments from nature which do not take into consideration the construction of individual natures through social and cultural inscriptions of meaning. Those meanings are invariably subject to hermeneutical analysis. Different interpretations of any phenomena, including the self, mean that knowledge is always more akin to probabilities than to certainties. The sceptic's position that one can never be certain about any aspect of the phenomenal world is in order here. That is not to say, though, that in the face of rejecting reified categories which allegedly transcend diverse interpretations one is required to abandon all forms of essentialism.

Essentialist categories that assume change are necessary for resisting existing patterns of social oppression and for developing strategies for social change. It is, therefore, self-defeating for deconstructionists/constructionists to reject these categories altogether. The claim that any attempt to theorize about constructing a self is totalizing in the transhistorical, hegemonic, ontologically static sense is, itself, a totalizing claim. It is also a confused one. It confuses one form of ontological essentialism, which assumes a fixed essence, with other forms which entail a nominal reality as well as, in some cases, an ontological essence characterized by change. All essentialist categories have a nominal character. They are constitutive of social categories developed through observation of empirical evidence and shared meanings that have been constructed linguistically. Essentialism and constructionism, therefore, interact in the composition of a self located in the larger context of ontological interrelatedness. The ontological self is an essential reality whose presence is always known through structured systems of meaning — the most pervasive being language.

2 Language

Language is "a system of relational signs, where meaning is a product of differences between signs and not an essential property of any fixed sign."[17] It is the map which situates a person in any particular political, religious, social or historical territory. Language inscribes the self, both as objectified and subjectified. It is the reflective component of consciousness which interacts with felt sensations (prereflective consciousness). Language is the major form of semiosis by which self-identity is constructed. Semiosis is the systematic development of meaning through the use of symbols, images and signs. It is about the ways we give coherence to our thoughts and sensations so that we can give meaning to our experiences. It is generally contrasted with the imaginary in which symbolic ordering of meaning has not occurred. The simple distinction is between order and decidability, on the one hand, and chaos and undecidability, on the other.

According to Jacques Derrida, woman is characterized by undecidability because of her location outside male-oriented linguistic symbolism (semiosis).[18] That quality is positively connoted by Derrida. Despite his essentialist view of women as undecided, Derrida claims to reject the notion of essence and says "there is no such thing as a woman, as a truth in itself of woman in itself."[19] The very notion of undecidability for Derrida entails diversity and cannot, therefore, be reduced to an indivisible unity. Moreover, Fuss says that Derrida is engaged in "the redeployment of essentialism."[20] She claims that for Derrida "Woman ... is yet another figure for *différance*, the mechanism which undoes and disables 'ontological decidability.'"[21] His nominal essentialism becomes a real essentialism within his attempt to deconstruct the transcendent subject in the existing symbolic order. His phrase "always already" (*toujours déjà*) indicates an essential underlying script, according to which the construction of a self occurs. It is like a tape playing in the background of our consciousness. In Derrida's view, women are securely relegated to the wilderness, the place of disorder where the imaginary prevails.[22]

Jacques Lacan, like Derrida, emulates woman's place as wilderness dweller and attributes truth to her because of it.[23] He sees woman as "not all," that is, she can not altogether be explained with existing linguistic tools, which are modelled after a singular, unifying signifier (the phallus). The view of woman as the excess factor leads him to suggest that woman is Truth because she necessarily exists partially outside the Symbolic order erected by a restrictive phallocentric mindset. Woman, he says, is closer to the Unconscious and therefore knows more adequately. One can never be sure which implications will be drawn from such a claim. For my part, I do not wish to be either decentred or emulated for it. I might choose to be a wilderness dweller but that is different from being assigned to that place. Furthermore, there is nothing self-evident about language remaining phallocentric, as Luce Irigaray has demonstrated.

Nancy Hartsock claims that it is not in women's interest (or anyone's in a relatively powerless subject position) to accept the decentring of the subject.[24] At the same time, it is worthwhile to criticize pretenders to absolute subject positions which authorize certainty of interpretation and which claim superior disambiguation of the highly ambiguous conditions in which we all live. Resisting totalizing claims to authority is necessary for enunciation from a subject's perspective. For example, romanticising the otherness of women because of their assigned position outside the phallocentric model of discourse does not obviously liberate women from marginalization. Much the same can be said about decentring the subject when a particular subject has never experienced being a subject in her own life. Such help we don't need. It provides neither a source of resistance nor a legitimation strategy for change. Self-determination of women in our society, where structural power imbalances inhibit it, requires a move from the position characterized as *other* to one of *subject*.

Postmodern attempts to deconstruct the subject come out of good intentions. They are motivated largely by the desire to overcome widespread privileging of the few at the expense of the others. Michel Foucault argues that, by decentring the subject, it is possible to resist hegemonic tendencies to dominate from a totalizing position espoused by an alleged transhistorical subject-position.[25] But isn't he re-enacting that same kind of subject-position in his attempts to deconstruct the category of subject? Isn't he assuming the role of Subject in his assumption of what is in everyone's interests, namely their decentring, even if they are marginalized? Isn't he totalizing the category of subject without taking into consideration the desire of the marginalized others who might very well wish to be subjects? To be a subject does not necessarily mean to be a transcendent Subject who can legitimately speak for all people of all time. It is surely possible to be a subject with a lower case "s," indicating one among many variously located subjects. That is a major difference between human beings and God in patriarchal discourse. Or, at least, it is supposed to be. Is it man as Subject or is it God as man who is decentred by deconstructionists?

An interesting question arises here. Who is God in patriarchal discourse? God is usually the reality that is outside historical decidability. For Lacan *woman* is the excess factor which exists beyond the explanatory parameters of patriarchal symbolism. In philosophy of religion, God is typically the excess factor beyond linguistic conceptualization. In deconstructionist theory, does woman become God? There is no need, here, to follow the question further into the wilderness. I only pose it as a possible question that arises within the discussion of the transcendent Subject that is being displaced by mostly male deconstructionists and the identity of woman as Truth because she is more than what can be explained within existing semiotics.

From the standpoint of the dispersed, there is a need to name their collective subjectivities. As Bernice Reagon points out, "At a certain stage, nationalism is crucial to a people if you are ever going to impact as a group in your own interest."[26] This applies to women cross-culturally as well as to culturally specific ethnic groups. The attempt to change structural power relations rather than to merely resist them is a major difference between the feminist focus on systemic change through restructuring and Foucault's emphasis on resistance. Nevertheless it is important to recognize the significance of acts of resistance.

The restriction of self-expression within a network of social/power relations is often manifested through subversive tactics, such as feminine wiles. Using Foucault's discussion of resistance in the face of power, we can see that it may be an unwarranted expectation to get the disempowered to act and speak straightforwardly. It may be more appropriate to work on transforming the power relations first and then to encourage self-revelation and honesty. An interpretation of women's wiles as subversive tactics, used in the interests of self-protection in the context of unjust power relations, might be a more accurate reading of such *feminine* qualities than to attribute them to female nature.

From a feminist standpoint, Hartsock correctly states that "power relations are less visible to those who are in a position to dominate others."[27] It is not helpful to those who have been systematically dominated to be told that their subjectivity cannot be collectively identified and properly used to transform existing power relations. The feminist task is primarily that of transforming power relations, not merely redescribing them. Feminist epistemology assumes the existence of structural power imbalances between categories of diverse people. It is important to acknowledge both the categories and the structural relations among them in order to effect change.

Issues of self-determination are inseparable from issues of power, i.e, bringing about change with regard to individual, collective and/or institutional activities. An important feminist task is to construct theories of power for women that counteract stereotypical discrepancies between femininity and power. Another one is to mitigate fear of women's powers associated with their (our) biology. Theories of power for women are closely related to theories of self. A central issue in both sets of theories is women's bodies. The relation between language and bodies is crucial.

3 Body Consciousness

According to Lacan and Derrida, women's bodies have placed them in the wilderness. Women need to participate fully in the construction of the symbolic process which gives meaning to our experiences. Teresa de Lauretis claims that experience is "an on-going process by which subjectivity is constructed semiotically and historically."[28] In order to give meaning to our experiences, it is important to pay attention not only to women's words but also to their (our) bodies, without sliding into biological determinism.

Women's experiences, which were previously trivialized, are now being regarded as sources of knowledge and serve as bases for new epistemologies.[29] In addition to women's experiences with people and things more or less external to themselves, women's experiences of their (our) bodies are important sources of knowledge. As our bodies speak to us we learn to speak in a new language. In speaking differently, we are different. We thereby construct ourselves and are constructed in new ways through the mutually influential impact of our bodies on our language, and the meaning given to our body experiences through the ways we express ourselves in speech.

The interaction between body and meaning depends on the presence of both felt sensations and cognitive reflections. Consciousness has the two components (sensations and reflections) which are required for self-identity. For many women, the social constructions of patriarchal culture become more normative (i.e., natural) than the non-linguistic, felt sensations of the body. It is precisely because of the normativeness of social and cultural mappings onto women's bodies that it is important to claim one's body as an essential reality which is intrinsic to oneself. For a woman to claim her own body for herself is a revolutionary act in our society. According to Andrea Nye, the flight from women's bodies motivated the patriarchal history of logic.[30] Continuing that flight is not in the interests of women. Saying no to it requires not accepting the present cultural encoding that determines the meanings of women's bodies. Such resistance depends on a sense of self that has the agency to resist normative social prescriptions. Acknowledging the reality of one's body as a site of resistance is a source of agency for women. It creates the possibility for social change. Luce Irigaray, in *This Sex Which Is Not One*, uses the body to demonstrate women's plurality of self. She blows up Lacanian psychoanalysis from the inside.[31] Lacan believes that the production of the subject comes through language. He assigns women to the wilderness because of the impossibility of their (our) being wholly constructed through phallocratic language, developed from a unitive signifier, i.e., the phallus. Women constitute the excess factor. They (we) exist partially outside the symbolic order of meaning. Irigaray subverts the semiotic power structure by attempting to shape a new women's semiosis through attention to the plurality of women's sexual parts. In listening to the "always already" existing meanings, Irigaray says our ears get "closed to what does not in some way echo the already heard."[32] We need to listen without "always already" hearing echoes of disabling discourse. We must "not immobilize ourselves in these borrowed notions" of ourselves."[33]

Mobilization of ourselves as women has, in my view, much to do with situating ourselves lovingly in our bodies. Irigaray emphasizes the notion of "nearness" in women's identity. She draws on women's anatomy to support her theory that women's identity is pluralistic and connected rather than singular and set apart. Her specific focus is the "two lips" which are always near each other and which are mutually stimulating to each other. The disposition toward loving embrace, she says, is part of women's embodied consciousness. The semiosis of the body should, according to Irigaray, infuse itself into linguistic symbolism and vice versa.[34] Luce Irigaray has aroused serious criticism from other feminists because of her focus on the female body as a site for initiating a new kind of semiosis for women. She has been accused of reinforcing the old biological determinism, the form of ontological essentialism that has been so problematic for some feminists and some constructionists. Tension between social determinism and biological determinism is at the heart of the constructionist/essentialist binarism in discussions of self. Issues relating to the body bring out the dichotomy in its sharpest relief.

Materialist anti-essentialists reject the work of Luce Irigaray as an apology for biological determinism. For instance, Monique Wittig[35] claims that the body is materially and culturally constructed. It is, therefore, a mistake to start with a body per se as either a signifier of anything or as a referent to be signified through language. The body can only be known through its cultural inscriptions, according to its importance within the social context in which it is situated. Speaking about the body as a decontextualized reality, for a materialist like Wittig, would be like speaking about the Godhead from a phenomenology of religion perspective. One could only know it as it is represented to us through our interpretive frameworks. There is no possibility, from either perspective, of referring to the referent directly. There is a major difference, of course, between the two objects of reference. The Godhead is allegedly immaterial, while the body is manifestly material.

The awkwardness of Wittig's position is striking. As a materialist, she assumes the existence of a material context in which a self is constructed. The body, however, is a matter she avoids. In her attempt to avoid any form of essentialism, especially one that would entail biological determinism, she denies the materiality of the body de facto: a material thing that acts on culture as well as being acted upon. I do not mean to say that the body is free from cultural inscriptions. Rather, I mean that there is an actual referent that is both a signifier and something signified. It simultaneously provides meaning through its particular form of existence and is given significance through the relations of meanings constructed symbolically. The interplay between body and language composes new meanings and allows us to move beyond old echoes in the construction of ourselves in innovative ways. Irigaray is an important resource for women as we attempt to hear new meanings for ourselves and thereby to listen and to respond differently. Her refusal to abandon her body in the construction of a meaningful semiosis for women contributes to the grounding of theories of a self in lived experience.

An important way in which the body impinges upon our symbolic structuring is through the use of the mirror. Jenijoy La Belle, in *Herself Beheld: The Literature of the Looking Glass*, claims that the looking glass is also the speaking glass.[36] In La Belle's view, "all selves are known to us only through signifying media."[37] A self is not an entity but an activity. There is "a continual process that gives rise to concepts by which an individual both distinguishes herself from others of her species and situates herself in relation to these other 'selves.'"[38] In her view, the mirror is "at a historical focus of female identity and questions dichotomies between self and reflected image, between spirit and flesh, between psychological presence and physical body."[39] Self-conceptions are often subordinated to social categories. The mirror "addresses the issues of self-conception and the recovery of information about how other people have conceived of her."[40] It always involves a paradox. La Belle says that "the image in the glass is always at once a self (at least the visual self) and not a self."[41] Resonance with, and alienation from, the image characterize one's relation to the mirror. Identity and alterity co-exist in the same moment as we look into the mirror, thereby reflecting the paradox of actual self-consciousness. The mirror reflects the composite nature of a self: both objectified and subjectified in an interactive process.

The production of self for many women includes the objectification of self in the mirror as the reflection of the internalized other as well as the reflection of the subjectified identity. The influential social categories externally imposed on oneself are part of the construction of oneself through reflections from the mirror. Those reflections impact on conceptualization to become integral to cognitive objectifications within one's self-consciousness. In La Belle's view, mirroring contributes to self-consciousness through the projection of the subject as object in the mirror, which can then observe the subject and thereby constitute self-consciousness. Mirroring is an important part of self-creation for many women, according to La Belle's study of fictional and actual women in the literature. The process of self-creation is partially the presence of other and ego simultaneously in the construction of self-consciousness. La Belle found that a particularly female gesture was to "transform a self into an object perceived by another."[42] The construction of self, then, often entails "a profound process of negation as a means of creation."[43] The conceptualization of self for many women is closely tied to the mode of projection reflected in the mirror, which depicts their cultural objectification, primarily through the eyes of men. La Belle notes that many of the female characters she studied imagined what certain men would think of them as they studied their own reflections in the mirror. That represents over-identification with the objectified image and includes self-negation through the act of creating ones's self-consciousness. It is a reduction to a reflected presence.

It is precisely such reduction that Irigaray urges us to avoid as we conceptualize ourselves through new sensations of our bodies. Her use of the speculum as a semiotic tool is particularly helpful. Mirroring from inside our bodies is a way of minimizing the objectification of ourselves in the mirror and of maximizing our subjectivity through embodied consciousness. The mirror is a symbol that reminds us of our inner, hidden beauty which can be revealed both to ourselves and others in the process of constructing and representing our realities as subjects with self-determining agency.

4 Symbolizing Bodied Spiritual Consciousness in Metaphor

Expression of the body through language requires metaphor. Generally we use metaphors to indicate meaning beyond linguistic formulation. Through the use of metaphors we attempt to indicate a reality of which we are conscious but which we cannot adequately interpret. Metaphor provides a more fluid form of description than the rigid logos that governs allegedly rational thought. It circumvents static thought and reification of fixed images and concepts. For that reason, it is a welcome mode of conceptualization. Luce Irigaray uses the two lips as a metaphor for an ontology of presence. Jenijoy La Belle uses the mirror as a metaphor for subjective reflection, the external speculum of the unseen self. She evokes Irigaray's discussion of "specular vision" in *Speculum of the Other Woman*.[44] The possibilities for a woman to see herself from within her body is an important starting point for self-knowledge and the construction of a subject position. If the body is taken to be the temple of the spirit, then one's reflections through the looking glass or the speculum are spiritually enlightening. In the beginning of the paper, I said that spiritual agency moves individual agency beyond egocentric boundaries, toward community participation. Body consciousness and spiritual consciousness are captured in the same reflection.

The Buddhist doctrine of *pratītya-samutpāda* provides a context in which the two lips is a metaphor for metaphysics of presence. The presence of the lips to each other is constitutive of their identity. The two lips symbolize contiguity and nearness in the construction of identity. Female morphology provides a bodily basis from which to construct a new language of identity that is different from the perpective of singularity and separateness that characterizes the male-oriented construction of identity, albeit not necessarily.[45] Identity, in this view, is invariably relational.

At the same time, individual self-organization is intrinsic to identity. The mirror is a metaphor for *beholding* the inner self, the subjectivity of personal agency in the process of improvisation. The cultural projections that objectify women in our society lend an urgency to the need for the development of new ways to positively construct women's subjectivity with regard to their bodies.

La Belle claims that time is constructed by men for well-socialized women. The woman who constructs herself with reference to cultural projections in the mirror marks time not chronologically but according to her reflection as men see it. When she is young she thinks of the future taking up residence in her body in so far as it is appealing, or not so, to men. Later she evaluates how she is doing with respect to men's approval of her appearance. Much later she loathes herself because she is past redemption with regard to appeal to men's desires. The relation between *properly* socialized women's identity and their "ocular presence in the mirror is circumscribed by father time."[46] All of this has relevance to representations of men as well. Men, however, have been thought of more in terms of having faces or having bodies; whereas women have been more identified with their faces and bodies. In many stereotypical representations men *have* bodies which reflect various dimensions of power, women *are* bodies which are there in the service of the socially powerfully. Language is written differently by differently sexed bodies which are, in turn, inscribed differently by language. Positive body images which reflect women as subjects are required for an expansion of language that includes expression of female subjectivity.

Earth-based spiritual traditions are sources of helpful imagery for the construction of female agency. As Charlene Spretnak points out, native spirituality shows us the intimacy of human nature with all of nature, while goddess spirituality focusses on the personal body as the locus of spiritual energy.[47] Both of these wisdom traditions support Irigaray's discussion of the "sensible transcendental," a bodily-based subjectivity that transcends individuality through participatory improvisation. Imagery from these traditions connects subjective consciousness with intersubjective, community, global or cosmic consciousness. A metaphysics of presence, such as that entailed in the Buddhist doctrine of *pratītya-samutpāda*, is intrinsic to earth-based spirituality and is effectively depicted through metaphor. Images of the self as a flame, a tree, a cougar, a wolf, for instance, alter the interpretation of identity from a framework of fixed boundaries to one of shifting boundaries. Identity is experienced more in terms of fluidity. Shape shifting between a human form and another form is not extraordinary from this perspective. Similarly with goddess imagery, identification with various imaged realities such as Kali, Athena, Artemis, the crone, the mother or daughter provides new dimensions for self-identity. Being present to oneself while in the presence of the other is part of the metaphysics of presence in which the self is constructed. The metaphysics of presence of Buddhism, native spirituality and goddess spirituality is compatible with the metaphysics of presence that is evoked in Irigaray's emphasis on "nearness" in her metaphor of the two lips. Using female-defined body images, within an interpretive framework of a metaphysics of presence, helps women to conceptualize their own subjectivity as ontologically legitimate and epistemologically sound. This kind of centring of the self in the body might allow for greater possibility for a woman to use the mirror as a constructive semiotic tool as she reflects on herself. It might be possible then to celebrate with La Belle "Herself Beheld." The mirror is an ancient sacred symbol associated with goddess power to see the self from within.[48] In this view of reality as a process of interdependent origination, the inner self is invariably an agent in the determination of social organization. Using body-based images to reflect female power is an important way to depict women's agency. Grounding agency in female-imaged, bodied, spiritual consciousness opens space for an expanded semiosis in which women can conceptualize new possibilities with regard to their own plural idenities. Spiritual images which directly impact on women's bodies contribute significantly to personal coherence. "Father time" disappears into the mist, the mirror becomes an affirmation of one's inner strength, and cultural reflections change to be more inclusive of spirit, mind and body in its representations of women.

5 Social Implications

As mentioned earlier, a theory of self-determination for women needs to take into account the power relations of the sexes. A theory of power for women, in light of the structural imbalances of power between women and men, is supported by women's spiritual agency that is experienced and described in women-friendly language. Constructive epistemologies are inseparable from life-affirming ontologies in this body-based religious philosophy of self. At the same time, such ontologies require corresponding epistemologies to bring about social change.

Traditional social and cultural constructs have confined women. Examples are: social categories which shape identities according to material conditions, such as disproportionately low salaries for the majority of women; sexual, physical, emotional, intellectual bullying and violence against women; and general dependency associated with femininity. All impinge on women's self-determination. It is of little value to develop a religious theory of self without taking such social realities into consideration. Restrictive social realities and social injustice exists more or less in every corner of women's lives: in the family, the community, the schools at all levels, religious places and the diverse paid labour force. The restrictions are more severe within communities of aboriginal people, those who have moved here from other countries (with the exception of Britain and the United States); the variously abled, those with same-sex orientations, the elderly and various groups that are not reflections of the culturally privileged. Structural changes are required for categories of disadvantaged people to benefit from theories of self-determination.

Social structures rest on cultural assumptions and projections. Language and the mirror are two important reflectors of cultural assumptions as well as creators of them. They are semiotic constructors of our identity. Irigaray urges us especially to hear differently through a new language constructed in relation to our body, while La Belle reminds us that it is possible to look subjectively and objectively without being influenced exclusively by the internalization of men's objectifying desires.

I am suggesting that hearing and seeing in ways that are not governed by echoes of "always already" existing sounds and sights are assisted by the construction of new linguistic symbolizing that represents positive body knowledge. A bodied spiritual consciousness, imaged metaphorically, that affirms individual agency for women, facilitates constructive participation in the construction of social idenities. Irigaray says "Let our imperatives be only appeals to move, to be moved, together."[49] Her commitment to the expansiveness of self is captured in her sentence "I—continue."[50] The construction of a positive self-consciousness through bodied spiritual agency that is symbolized in La Belle's phrase "herself beheld" is one dimension of the composition of the self. Another dimension is the construction of an integrative social order. Restructuring social power relations is intrinsic to the task of constructing a new symbolic order in which women are ontological and epistemological subjects.

Notes

1 I wish to express my appreciation to Claire McMordie (lawyer, Calgary), Peter Schouls (Philosophy Department, University of Alberta, Edmonton) and Karl Tomm (Psychiatry Department, University of Calgary) for their careful and helpful reading of earlier drafts of this paper.

2 Mary Catherine Bateson, *Composing a Life* (New York: A Plume Book, 1989).

3 For example, see Jacques Derrida, "Women in the Beehive: A seminar with Jaques Derrida," *Subjects/Objects* (Spring). Reprinted in Alice Jardine and Paul Smith, eds., *Men in Feminism* (New York: Methune, 1984); Michel Foucault, *The Archeology of Knowledge and the Discourse on Language*, trans. A.M. Sheridan Smith (New York: Pantheon Books, 1972); Jacques Lacan, *Écrits*, trans. Alan Sheridan (New York: W.W. Norton & Company, 1977); Richard Rorty, *Philosophy and the Mirror of Nature* (Princeton: Princeton University Press, 1979); Elisabeth Spelman, *Inessential Woman: Problems of Exclusion in Feminist Thought* (Boston: Beacon Press, 1988); and Monique Wittig, "The Mark of Gender," Nancy K. Miller, ed., *The Poetics of Gender* (New York: Columbia University Press, 1986).

4 For a lengthy discussion of Kant's account of the differences between the natures of women and men see my "Spirituality, Rationality, and Sexuality," *Zygon*, 25/2 (June 1990).

5 The terms "egoity" and "sociality" are borrowed from John Macquarrie, *In Search of Humanity: A Theological and Philosophical Approach* (New York: Crossroad, 1983). He distinguishes between egoity and egoism. Egoity refers to the self as centred in one's own power. Centredness allows for creative contributions to social relations.

Egoism, by contrast, is egocentricity or self-centredness. An egocentric person enters into relations from the standpoint of neediness rather than strength.

6 Diana Fuss, *Essentially Speaking: Feminism Nature and Difference* (New York: Routledge, 1989).

7 Ibid., p. 12-13.

8 Jacques Derrida, "Choreographies," interview with Christie V. McDonald, *Diacritics*, 12/2 (Summer 1982): 66-76. Quoted by Fuss, *Essentially Speaking*, p. 14.

9 Ibid.

10 Ibid.

11 Ibid.

12 Ibid.

13 Ibid., p. 9.

14 Ibid., p. 6.

15 Ibid., p. 15.

16 I discuss a metaphysics of interrelatedness at length in "Gender Factor or Metaphysics in a Discussion of Ethics," *Explorations*, 6 (Fall 1987): 5-24 and in "Spinoza, Hume, and Vasubandhu: The Relation between Reason and Emotion in Self-Development" (Ph.D. diss., The University of Calgary, 1984).

17 Fuss, *Essentially Speaking*, p. 9. Fuss is drawing on Lacan, who claims that speech and language constitute the subject, which is partially the view in this paper. The rest of the constituted subject, which signifies language in part, is the body. I do not take the body to be totally inscribed by language, but rather, as with la Belle (1988), that there is a reflexive relation between language and body. Her word is "reflective" rather than "reflexive" because she is concerned centrally with the reflectivity of the mirror.

18 Jacques Derrida, *Spurs: Nietzsche's Styles* (Chicago: University of Chicago Press, 1979).

19 Ibid., p. 101.

20 Fuss, *Essentially Speaking*, p. 13.

21 Ibid.

22 See Carole Pateman, *The Disorderly Woman*, for an eloquent critique of the Freudian viewpoint about women as disorderly and, therefore, subversive of civilization.

23 Lacan, *Écrits*, p. 121-23.

24 Nancy Hartsock, "Foucault on Power: A Theory for Women?" in Linda J. Nicholson, ed., *Feminism/Postmodernism* (New York: Routledge, 1990), p. 157-75.

25 Foucault, *The Archaeology of Knowledge*; Colin Gordon, ed., *Power/Knowledge: Selected Interviews and Other Writings 1972-77*, trans. Colin Gordon et al. (Brighton: The Harvester Press, 1980).

26 Hartsock, "Foucault on Power," p. 163.

27 Ibid., p. 165.

28 Teresa de Lauretis, *Alice Doesn't: Feminism, Semiotics, Cinema* (Bloomington: Indiana University Press, 1984), p. 182.

29 Mary F. Beleny et al., *Women's Ways of Knowing* (New York: Basic Books, 1986).

30 Andrea Nye, *Words of Power: A Feminist Reading of the History of Logic* (New York: Routledge, 1990).

31 *This Sex Which Is Not One*, trans. Catherine Porter (New York: Cornell University Press, 1985).

32 Ibid., p. 113.

33 Ibid., p. 217.

34 Jane Gallop's *Thinking Through the Body* (New York: Columbia University Press, 1988), is an excellent development out of Roland Barthe's semiotics, which can be used in conjunction with Irigaray's attempts to map out a female-based linguistic model.

35 "The Category of Sex," *Feminist Issues* (Fall 1982): 63-68; "The Mark of Gender," in Miller, ed., *The Poetics of Gender*, p. 63-73.

36 (New York: Cornell University Press, 1988).

37 Ibid., p. 12.

38 Ibid., p. 3.

39 Ibid., p. 2.

40 Ibid., p. 15.

41 Ibid., p. 42.

42 Ibid., p. 53.

43 Ibid.

44 Luce Irigaray, *Speculum of the Other Woman*, trans. Gillian C. Gill (Ithaca: Cornell University Press, 1985).

45 A case could be made as well for a pluralistic view of identity associated with male morphology. It is arbitrary to select only the penis as the signifier of masculine identity. The "nearness" of the scrotum and penis might be used as a morphological basis for a metaphorical depiction of the plurality of masculine identity.

46 La Belle, *Herself Beheld*, p. 63-64.

47 Charlene Spretnak, *States of Grace: The Recovery of Meaning in the Postmodern Age* (San Francisco: Harper, 1991).

48 Rita Nakashima Brock, "On Mirrors, Mists and Murmurs," in *Weaving the Visions: New Patterns in Feminist Spirituality* (San Francisco: Harper, 1989), p. 235-43.

49 Irigaray, *This Sex*, p. 217.

50 Ibid.

Chapter 15

THE NEGATIVE POWER OF "THE FEMININE": HERBERT MARCUSE, MARY DALY AND GYNOCENTRIC FEMINISM

Marsha Hewitt

Although feminism is neither a monolithic theory nor unitary political practice (nor aspires to be such), feminism does have a central preoccupation that is common to all its variations: domination. As a critique of the oppression of women, feminism is, at its root, a critique of domination. Any attempt at a feminist rethinking of the dynamics of power, and the hierarchical social relations that render women as its objects, must ultimately account for domination in all its forms. Feminist critical theory, then, seeks to comprehend the phenomenon of domination and its integral role in the development of Western civilization, as well as to conceptualize strategies for overcoming it. Most important of all, feminist critical theory must seek to penetrate and expose the hidden, invisible workings of domination that twist and distort our most private experience, resulting in alienated relationships and social structures.

Feminist critical theory begins with the assumption that there is no standpoint outside of domination and alienation from which to theorize, but rather that we ourselves speak from within the conditions of alienation that are already given to us, mediating our critical knowledge. If we accept this premise as constituting the ground from which we begin to construct feminist critique, we must accept that we must work with what is, while struggling to transform what is into what could be, under current conditions. If what is, is understood as historically and culturally constituted, then this hope for transformation is rooted in concrete possibility, rather than in metaphysics and ontology.

A comprehensive feminist critical theory of domination is, in part, an immanent critique of distortion, alienation, suffering and injustice, the explicit goal of which is to bring about their end. Such a task was described by Max Horkheimer as the insistence on the "negative side" of the historical process, "the gruesomeness and injustice of it all. . . . It cannot prescribe how people are to escape from the charmed circle of the status quo; it can only give the charm a name."[1]

Negative critique is central to critical theory, finding expression in Adorno's philosophy of *negative dialectics*, an extended critique of Hegel and the Western philosophical tradition that insists upon the correspondence between concepts and reality. For Adorno, the true philosophical task was to expose this "untruth of identity," shifting philosophy's focus to reveal and sustain non-conceptuality, individuality and particularity, which all previous philosophy had considered as transitory and insignificant.[2] The theme of negativity, however, was strongest in the work of Herbert Marcuse, for whom "the battle between negativity and positivity is the most consequential and decisive battle in the world."[3]

For Marcuse, negativity reveals the hidden truth of things, dissolving and penetrating beneath their alienated, distorted surface to discover and release their inner authenticity. Every particularity contains within it a contradiction, in that it is constituted by what it is and is not. For something to be what it really or authentically is, it must become what it is not, through the process of negation of its given state of alienation leading toward the realization of its potentialities. All things must be grasped as transcending their appearance as "common sense," as "mere facticity," as containing the negation of their own negativity. While Marcuse derived his concept of negativity from Hegel, he concentrated on the realization of potentiality within the historical, rather than the ontological, realm of existence. The progress of freedom out of unfreedom demanded, in Marcuse's view, that thought, or reason, be understood as political, as "the shape of a theory which demonstrates negation as a political alternative implicit in the historical situation."[4]

Marcuse's version of critical theory stresses that historical negation takes place through political opposition, no matter how "fragmented, distorted, or hopeless"[5] social forms of opposition might appear at any given moment. Critical theory's role is to expose the unrealized possibilities contained within the social structure, "potentialities created by a gulf between prevailing human existence and human essence (the unfulfilled historically constituted abilities and capacities of human beings)."[6] Marcuse's stress upon potentialities and the possibility of their realization was not shared by Horkheimer and Adorno, whose critical theory did not venture far beyond "the gruesomeness of it all."

For Marcuse, Reason, as "the power of negative thinking"[7] was capable of generating its opposite, that is, reason as domination, or instrumentality; on the other hand, reason could overcome this tendency, since "reason alone, contains its own corrective."[8] The dialectical structure of reason allows for the possibility of freedom to emerge as an explosive shattering of the existent, since "unfreedom is so much at the core of things ... the development of their internal contradictions leads necessarily to qualitative change: the explosion and catastrophe of the established state of affairs."[9] The history of reason in Western civilization in the form of domination could be overcome in a kind of apocalyptic negation that would unleash a new rationality of liberation and happiness that Marcuse came to identify with the *feminine*.

Marcuse understood domination as assuming different forms in different historical periods; in advanced capitalist societies, domination "congeals into a system of objective administration"[10] that structures social institutions and systems of distribution in ways that appear to provide and preserve "the good life of the whole"[11] so that maintaining the status quo becomes widely perceived as necessary, and with the vast increase of cheap consumer goods, even desirable. As near-total administration, domination becomes internalized within individuals, resulting in the repression of "natural" human aspirations for freedom and happiness deep within the psyche. Drawing upon and reinterpreting Freud's theory of instincts, Marcuse differentiated psychic repression as that which is necessary for the preservation of the achieved level of material conditions and "surplus repression," which functions to sustain social domination beyond the modifications of the instincts necessary for the continued life of the society.

Surplus repression functions in the service of domination *for its own sake,* and is so strongly entrenched throughout society that its complete negation can appear to be the "only truly revolutionary exigency"[12] open to humanity. Marcuse was well aware that the perception of domination as a unified totality was illusory, and that the demand for its absolute dissolution could only produce an equally abstract, reified "revolutionary" negation incapable of changing "the Establishment."

At this point I wish to introduce an important distinction between *determinate negativity* and *reified* negativity, because both exist in an unresolved tension in Marcuse's work, and, at times, weaken the emancipatory intent in his thought. Although Marcuse repeatedly insisted on the possibility of liberation as determinate negation of the existent, he also succumbed to a more reified, ideal (and, I believe, ultimately metaphysical) notion of negativity, which becomes most apparent when he explicitly associates it with a particular agent—*woman.* Marcuse's reified concept of *woman* occupies an important place in his critical theory, constituting an irrational moment that tends to weaken both the critical nature and emancipatory potential of his social philosophy.

At the same time, the theme of the transformative power of *the feminine* is integral to a deeper, more crucial insight into the necessity of human self-transformation as a non-negotiable prerequisite for a liberated human future. For Marcuse, liberation included both social transformation as well as transformations in the psychic and emotional "infrastructure"[13] of human beings, since the possibility of a free society depended upon the formation of "a new sensibility [as] the medium in which social change becomes an individual need, the mediation between the political practice of 'changing the world' and the drive for personal liberation."[14]

Unlike Horkheimer and Adorno, Marcuse still believed in the possibility that such comprehensive transformation could be brought about through the actions of particular historical agents. Marcuse addressed his critical theory to concrete subjects, which tended to distinguish him from his Frankfurt colleagues, who long abandoned any hope in the revolutionary potential of the industrial working class or of any other social group. Marcuse addressed his critical theory to those diverse, often isolated "militant minorities"[15] whose varied practices of political resistance against 'the Establishment' represented what he called the "Great Refusal to accept the rules of a game in which the dice are loaded."[16] In a later essay, Marcuse most strongly identified the politics of resistance and potential transformation with a single movement, socialist feminism, and, in so doing, reduced feminism to a form of reified negativity which is the inevitable result of locating the role of revolutionary agency in any particular group or individual. Marcuse's hope in the promise of socialist feminism as a *gravedigger* of *patricentric-acquisitive* societies was based upon the dubious notion of a *female counterforce* as the negative power of historical transformation.

Marcuse visualizes this *female counterforce* in the image of Delacroix's *Liberty*, the bare-breasted woman who leads the people on the barricades, rifle in hand, promising to abolish unfreedom and inauthenticity through violent struggle.[17] Marcuse's imaging of *woman* in this way is indicative of a progressive reification in his thought that conceptualizes *woman* as an abstract category who is *naturally* linked with Eros, long repressed in Western civilization by the hegemony of distorted Reason that Marcuse associated with patriarchal domination and destructive productivity. Female-Eros represents the power of negativity that threatens the continued mastery of Male-Thanatos, promising the ascendency of a new rationality and the emergence of a new sensibility with its corresponding values and ethics of receptivity, peace, and justice that would generate qualitatively new interpersonal relationships and social structures. There is something of an eschatological dimension to this vision of liberation that counters the subversive element of determinate negation by giving way to a more reified negativity that is both socially and politically ineffective.

However Marcuse images *woman* at any point in his work, she is always symbolic of that apocalyptic, negative power that can shatter *mere factuality*, breaking open the unalienated, transcendent possibilities that exist within present conditions. At the same time, Marcuse expresses a lingering ambivalence concerning possibilities of transformation that causes him to vacillate between determinate negation, on the one hand, and reified negation, on the other. He expresses this ambiguity in the contradictory thesis that, "advanced industrial society is capable of containing qualitative change for the foreseeable future," and that "forces and tendencies exist which may break this containment and explode the society."[18] When Marcuse attempts to theorize those explosive forces of transformation by identifying them with *the feminine*, determinate negation as an historical and political process dissolves into reified negation. When this happens, theory totters on the brink of the ideology of messianism, which can only result in a cult form of political action that hypostatizes praxis and strengthens domination.

The theoretical ground for the reification of *woman* as feminine negativity was already laid in *Eros and Civilization*, Marcuse's philosophical reconstruction of Freud's theory of instincts. In Marcuse's historical account of the conflictual drama between Eros and Thanatos, the distortions they undergo as a result of psychic repression are not irreversible, nor are they intrinsic to the process of repression itself, but are rather historically and culturally determined, and so open to change. In the course of civilization, Eros and Thanatos split into mutually antagonistic forces, which resulted in the ascendency of patriarchal Reason over repressed Eros. In advanced capitalist societies, the rule of Thanatos takes the form of the Performance Principle, which is the guarantor of alienated labour in class society.

Prior to their fragmentation, Eros and Thanatos existed in immediate, natural union in the Mother, in whom the son (the daughter's experience is not considered by Marcuse) experienced "Nirvana before birth," the "integral peace" of complete gratification and the absence of all need, desire and want. This primal memory of security and peace experienced with the Woman-as-Mother represents an alternative rationality to the domineering rationality associated with the Father. As the embodied, "libidinal energy" of Eros,[19] the Woman-Mother is identified with an alternative, "pre-genital," "libidinal morality"[20] in which reason and sensuousness are reconciled, as was their original state prior to their violent separation that resulted in the rule of the Male-Performance Principle.

Marcuse reinterprets the Oedipal drama as the son's "sexual craving" for the Mother not simply *qua* Mother, but for the Mother "*qua* woman — female principle of gratification."[21] According to this reading, the incest taboo is erected by the Father to ensure against the son's achieving the total gratification he once experienced in the womb. If satisfied, the son's sexual craving for the Woman-Mother "threatens the psychical basis of civilization,"[22] the preservation of which depends upon the continued hegemony of the Performance Principle. Marcuse's account of the history of the instincts is the story of two realities, of two rationalities structured around the polarities of domination (Performance Principle) and freedom (Pleasure Principle). The "return of the repressed" takes place through the release of critical remembrance, the mover of Eros: "Remembrance retrieves the *temps perdu*, which was the time of gratification and fulfilment."[23] Here, one cannot help but recall Lukacs' critique of Hegel's philosophy, as "driven inexorably into the arms of mythology,"[24] which accurately describes this aspect of Marcuse's thought.

In his later work, Marcuse distanced himself somewhat from the Woman-as-Mother concept, realizing that such an identification is itself repressive, in that it translates "biological fact into an ethical and cultural value and thus ... [it] supports and justifies social repression."[25] Yet instead of following through on his own logic and repudiating the Woman-Mother paradigm altogether, Marcuse rather intensifies the reification of *woman* with the substitution of a revolutionary "female principle," whose "natural" characteristics promise social and individual liberation through the "femalization" of the male, a necessary precondition of a future socialist society.[26] "The faculty of being *receptive, passive*, is a precondition of freedom: it is the ability to see things in their own right, to experience the joy enclosed in them, the erotic energy of nature — an energy which is there to be liberated."[27]

The unfortunate history of women's oppression, due to the imposition of feminine attributes onto women as a means of regulating their lives, is not given sufficient critical attention by Marcuse, and indeed cannot be, because of his idealization of women. At times, he celebrates *feminine* characteristics as if they possess a life of their own that resides beyond historical and political reality. However, the qualities of *receptivity* and *passivity* belong to the aesthetic realm as well, and underscore the unreality he inadvertently ascribes to women. Art and *the feminine* are treated in almost identical fashion by Marcuse as negative counterforces to both the status quo and the continued hegemony of the [male] Performance Principle. According to Marcuse, the beauty of woman and art, along with the happiness and reconciliation they promise in a future liberated society, is "fatal in the work-world of civilization."[28]

Marcuse describes the "radical qualities of art" as

> grounded precisely in the dimensions where art *transcends* its social determination and emancipates itself from the given universe of discourse and behaviour while preserving its overwhelming presence.... The world formed by art is recognized as a reality which is suppressed and distorted in the given reality. This experience culminates in extreme situations ... which explode the given reality in the name of a truth normally denied or even unheard. The inner logic of the work of art terminates in the emergence of another reason, another sensibility, which defy the rationality and sensibility incorporated in the dominant social institutions.[29]

Art unleashes the power of the imagination to glimpse the possibility of a new world, with a new social morality and new institutions of freedom within a "culture of receptivity," a "sensuous culture."[30] Here Eros finds expression in both the aesthetic and the feminine, combined in a utopian vision of a liberated society where beauty, pleasure, joy and *nonrepressive, desublimated* sexuality (no longer trapped within genitality as a form of sexuality most suited to alienated labour) mediate all human relations, including work. In a direct reversal of Freud, Marcuse sees *polymorphous* sexuality as authentic to liberated human beings — the negation of the alienated sexuality of genital fixation which is co-opted in the service of maintaining exploited labour, oppressive bureaucracy and technocratic control.

This rather schematic paradigm of the new society displaces the struggle for historical transformation from the actions of human beings to a mythic world of higher forces locked in an epic struggle for control over the universe. As far as feminism is concerned, it is not living, suffering, women who work for their liberation, but their surrogate, the revolutionary *female principle*, the vehicle of the ascending Eros. Although Marcuse acknowledged the struggle for equality as an important goal in the women's movement, he emphasized the necessity to go "beyond equality" on the grounds that "equality is not yet freedom . . . beyond equality, liberation subverts the established hierarchy of needs. . . . And this, in my view, is the radical potential of *feminist socialism*."[31]

Marcuse's insistence on going *beyond equality* is to some extent understandable and reasonable, on the grounds that equality within alienation is another form of it, not freedom from it. Many feminists are too well aware that the full liberation of women is not to be found in mere equality, but in the complete transformation of all aspects of human existence and its underlying logic of binary opposition and domination. At the same time, equality is a necessary and unavoidable stage in the process of women's liberation, as Marx fully recognized. Full equality with men in all aspects of life will require changes in social structures, which will in turn effect the transformation of human relationships. A *transvaluation of values* cannot take place without changes in the existing social and political structures as well. In the words of Emma Goldman, "all existing systems of political power are absurd, and are completely inadequate to meet the pressing issues of life."[32] Marcuse's enthusiasm for the *radical potential* of feminist socialism undermines that same potential by formulating it ultimately not in political terms, but in the reified terms of ontological negativity.

Marcuse, in his valorization of traditional feminine attributes and their power to negate their masculine counterpart, understood as aggression, violence, competitiveness, brutal ambition and so on, along with his claim that feminine-specific characteristics are rooted in the *natural* difference[33] between women and men, contradicts his earlier repudiation of equating *biological fact* with *ethical and cultural value*. With this apparent reversal of his previous view, Marcuse justifies a politics of biology that reifies gender difference into hypostatized categories in which no historical woman could possibly recognize herself, nor find political solutions adequate to address her situation. Marcuse's grounding of the ethical values of receptivity and non-violence, etc., in the female, who " 'embodies' them in a *literal* sense"[34] (emphasis added) drives women back to the state of natural immediacy described by Hegel's philosophy.[35] At such points, Marcuse forgets his Marxian roots. For Marx, and for Marcuse, part of being human involves the necessary freedom from enslavement by unconscious natural forces. In the dialectic of history and nature, human beings surpass the condition of struggle for mere survival, which is a necessary part of the development of full human potentialities. Yet Marcuse could not quite include women in this process because of his inability to see them as historical agents, thus perpetuating the Hegelian view of women's close association with nature. Although Marcuse recognizes that women's confinement to family and home was an important factor in their historical oppression, he claims that their isolation from civil society and paid work also functioned as a protection from the alienating effects of the Performance Principle, which was more destructive to the male.[36]

Marcuse's thesis concerning *natural* female specificity as an adequate basis for political praxis anticipates a theoretical expression in contemporary feminism that can be most accurately described as *gynocentrism*.[37] Although gynocentric feminism is differently nuanced in the work of various feminist authors, it can be described according to certain common features. In part, gynocentric feminism accounts for women's oppression in terms of the historical denial and exclusion of values, ways of thinking and relating that are traditionally defined as feminine. More significantly, gynocentric feminism presumes a "stable subject of feminism"[38] which exists behind the socio-cultural category of gender. The premise of a *stable subject, woman*, provides the basis for the formulation of the notion of *universal patriarchy*[39] that is the source and sustainer of women's oppression. The notion of *woman* as the stable subject of feminine gender constructions functions as an underlying unity of all cultural, racial, class and linguistic difference between women, which in turn provides a basis for solidarity by virtue of the universal commonality of being female. This is a position closely related to Marcuse's. Further, the presumption of a stable subject allows for the designation of a set of characteristics or attributes that are sex-specific as well as possessing a corresponding ethics. According to this theory, patriarchal societies value and promote male-specific qualities such as aggressiveness, assertiveness, con-trol, etc. at the expense of female-associated values, which are their potential negation and must therefore be repressed.

One of the most important theorists of contemporary gynocentric feminism is Mary Daly. However, hers was not always a gynocentric feminist approach. Daly's first book, *The Church and the Second Sex*, is a feminist critique of the treatment of women in the Catholic theological and ecclesiastical tradition. At the same time, the tone of this book is strongly marked by the liberal spirit of the second Vatican council, which Daly briefly attended. In this work, Daly seeks to reclaim and articulate the more promising elements in Christianity that could be "sources of further development toward a more personalist conception of the man-woman relationship on all levels."[40] In this respect, she is very close to the feminist perspectives of theologians such as Rosemary Radford Ruether and Elisabeth Schüssler Fiorenza, although *The Church and the Second Sex* predates their major feminist work. Daly called for a "real partnership" between men and women, in which they would work together in order to

> at last see each other's faces, and in so doing, come to know themselves.... Men and women, using their best talents, forgetful of self and intent upon the work, will with God's help mount together toward a higher order of consciousness and being, in which the alienating projections will have been defeated and wholeness, psychic integrity, achieved.[41]

Although in her next book, *Beyond God the Father,* Daly's religious vision moved beyond Christianity to embrace a Tillichian *theism above theism* or *ground of being* in a supercession of God reformulated by Daly as the "Verb of Verbs, Be-ing,"[42] including her displacement of Jesus with the Goddess, Daly could still express the hope of human beings "becoming ... androgynous human persons."[43] Later, Daly repudiated her view of androgyny as an adequate model of human wholeness, on the grounds that it conveys "something like the images of Ronald and Nancy Reagan scotch-taped together."[44] Her feminist critique and rejection of Christianity as one of the sources of the oppression of women had not yet taken the complete gynocentric turn that was to surface in *Gyn/Ecology* and *Pure Lust.* The perspective in these works, although anticipated in the previous books, marks a radical shift in Daly's thinking in her move toward a militant gynocentric philosophy of women's liberation.

Daly is far better understood as a philosopher than as a theologian. The feminist critical philosophy advanced in her later works has its roots in the post-Enlightenment intellectual traditions of the West. Daly's thought resonates with Marcusian and Hegelian themes of being, negativity and reconciliation. Her treatment of these themes shows a strong Hegelian influence that is similar to Marcuse's reading of Hegel, particularly in relation to the notion of negativity, which permeates all of Marcuse's thought and runs throughout Daly's. For example, the identity between negativity and the *feminine principle* in Marcuse also occurs, in highly metaphoric fashion, in Daly's later work. Daly is certainly familiar with Marcuse, and refers to him several times in *Beyond God the Father,* and *Pure Lust.* The similarities between Marcuse and Daly are deeper than scattered citations might indicate. There is a profound affinity with Marcuse that is apparent in many of Daly's themes, and if rendered explicit, helps to make her thought more intelligible than it often is on first reading.

Daly's ideal philosophical vision postulates a world of alienation against which women struggle in order to realize their inner psychic and spiritual creativity and integrity, described by Daly as a journey or quest toward "Elemental participation in Be-ing. Our passion is for ... recalling original wholeness."[45] As an integral part of this journey, and as the condition of the possibility of "biophilic participation in Be-ing," women must negate or "transcend" the "forces of necrophilic negation" that make up patriarchy, "the perverted paradigm and source" of all social evil.[46] Against the negative force of "Phallic lust" that spawns pseudo/sado-societies whose aim is to contain and control women's striving for the abundance of be-ing, Daly counterposes Elemental female Lust, the negation of phallic negation, an "intense longing/craving for the cosmic concrescence that is creation."[47] Women who consciously embark upon this quest are blazing pathways to a "Background/homeland" from which they have been cut off, but dimly remember. In overcoming the alienation of forgetting the source and end of their Elemental be-ing, women move, or "race" toward an ontological state of reconciliation, where female inner essence finally comes into unity with its original integrity, or Self. In achieving this ultimate reconciliation, women negate those forces that negated their potentialities, thus coming into their *truth*, finding groundedness and oneness in "Metabeing."[48]

Daly's discussion of the journey to the Background/homeland that leads away from the alienated "foreground" to participation in Metabeing parallels Hegel's idea of the movement of Absolute Spirit toward unity with itself, after having overcome and negated all previous forms of alienation. Hegel describes this movement, or "Becoming of Spirit," as a "coming-to-be of the whole": "It is in itself the movement which is cognition — the transforming of that *in-itself* into that which is *for itself*, of Substance into Subject, of the object of *consciousness* into an object of *self-consciousness* . . . or into the *Notion*."[49] Spirit, or Being, for Hegel is Subject, whose "negativity" unfolds in Spirit's "own restless process of superseding itself."[50] As all being is movement for Hegel, determinate being is not a separate metaphysical entity but part of the process through which all particular beings unfold into what they really are. Being-itself is the ground or substratum of all particular beings. According to Marcuse's reading of Hegel, "From this point, it was comparatively easy to take this most universal being as 'the essence of all being,' 'divine substance,' 'the most real,' and thus to combine ontology with theology. This tradition is operative in Hegel's *Logic*."[51]

This tradition is operative in Daly's logic as well, in her repeated claim to women's inherent capacity for biophilic participation in Be-ing that occurs in the form of a restless negativity through and beyond progressive forms of alienation (both internal and external) that will culminate in the reconciliation of existence and Notion, of determinate female be-ing and cosmic Be-ing. Daly's dialectic of the "male-centred and monodimensional" world of alienation, or "foreground"[52] must be negated, overcome and superseded in the process of women's movement to the Background, the state of complete reconciliation of women's being with Elemental Be-ing. As Hegelian philosophy posits a universal structure of all being, so does Daly, but whereas with Hegel, all forms of particularity will be reconciled into Absolute Spirit, for Daly, female particularity attains a similar ontological reconciliation through the negation and exclusion of male particularity in all its manifestations. In order to come into their ontological and existential truth in the fulfilment of their inner potentialities, women must exorcise the male-identified characteristics within, such as "male approval desire," ("MAD"), as well as aspirations toward "femininity" – a "man-made construct" and "quintessentially" male attribute.[53] Daly's uncompromising analysis of atrocities enacted against women in history, such as Chinese footbinding practices, the Indian rite of "Suttee" or widow-burning, the horrors of the gynecological profession and the burning of large numbers of women in the European witch-hunts is an attempt to demonstrate beyond all doubt the gynocidal intent of patriarchy. The concept of negativity functions in Daly's work much as it does in Marcuse and Hegel, that is, as a means for uncovering the latent truth implicit in forms of determinate being which could then be released and actualized. This movement of women to wholeness and authenticity is contingent upon the negation of the male both within the female self and in external phallicist social forms, described by Daly in terms such as "phallocracy," "cockocracy," "bore-ocracy," "sadosociety," "Vapor State," "jockdom," "Daddydom" and so on. Daly's conceptualization of reconciliation departs from Marcuse and Hegel in the very significant respect that it is not inclusive of all humanity since all authentic being, including Be-ing,[54] is identified exclusively with the female element.

Despite the flamboyant and intensely metaphoric language used by Daly in her later work, her underlying philosophical theory is steeped in the Western intellectual tradition in which she was formed. In like fashion with Hegel and critical theory, Daly too sustains the reified, idealized concept of *woman* that marks most of this philosophical tradition. In Daly's work, not women, but *woman* functions as the underlying subject to which individual women must correspond if they are to realize their Elemental Selves. Daly is theorizing within an identity logic that postulates authentic female-identified be-ing as the standard or measure against which alienation on the particular level of concrete existence is defined. Daly refers to "fembots" and "totaled women" who unconsciously enact the socialized roles constructed for them by patriarchy and thereby participate in their own servitude.[55] Such women are dislocated from their inner essence, which can only be realized in the negative process of dissolving the patriarchy within. Daly herself uses the language of identity in writing of a "correspondence between the minds of Musing women and the intelligible structures of reality," and of the "process of Realizing Elemental ontological reason" that can actualize the "natural, elemental relation between women's minds and the structures of our own reality."[56] The reality to which she refers evokes that reality spoken of by Hegel and taken up by Marcuse, that is, the hidden, latent truth of all things contained within the external forms of alienation from which they strive for release. She celebrates Elemental female capacity "to receive inspiration, truth from the elements of the natural world, the Wild, to which our Wild reason corresponds."[57] There are the "Metamorphosing women" who are committed to the "consciously willed and continual affirmation of Ongoing Life that is Pure Lust."[58] For Daly, women's yearning "for experiencing our ontological connectedness with all that is Elemental implies a longing to mend, to weave together the Elemental realities that have been severed from consciousness."[59]

Daly's metaphoric descriptions of Elemental female being, along with its power and desire for experiencing and enhancing "ontological connectedness" – "gynergy" – is the equivalent of Marcuse's concept of female-identified Eros, discussed above. As we have seen, Marcuse associates Eros with creativity and life forces, describing it as "the builder of culture."[60] We have also seen that Marcuse counterpoints Eros with the Performance Principle, identified with male-specific attributes which must be negated and transcended if society and individuals are to come into their own freedom and truth. Daly expresses a similar view in her dichotomy of Pure Lust and "Pure Thrust," the latter understood as "phallicism," or "phallocracy," "the basic structure underlying the various forms of oppression,"[61] in which all forms of domination are rooted. Daly cautions women not to forget that "racial and ethnic oppression, like the sexual oppression which is the primary and universal model of . . . victimization, is a male invention."[62] Here we see a serious contradiction in Daly's thought, which claims reconciliation and participation in the flow of Be-ing as its goal but which at the same time is rooted in the antagonistic dichotomy of woman against man that is both ontological and existential, and is a significant reversal of her earlier position of partnership and androgyny.

Daly directly acknowledges Marcuse's influence on her thought by referring, for example, to his "useful concept of *repressive desublimation*"[63] which she already found *useful* in *Beyond God the Father*. Daly agreed with Marcuse's insight that a "relaxed sexual morality within the firmly entrenched system of monopolistic controls itself serves the system. The negation is co-ordinated with 'the positive.'"[64] Following Marcuse, Daly cautions women that lesbian sexuality by itself, under the oppressive conditions of patriarchy is not any kind of authentic freedom, but requires a more profound expansion of "gynergizing connections between women" that has the power to negate the patriarchal status quo. Applying Marcuse's concept of "repressive desublimation," to lesbianism, she writes,

> *Liberated* women who are merely *gay* remain bound libidinally to the institutionalized fathers. But if violation of the Total Taboo encompasses and transcends the sexual sphere and leads to *refusal and rebellion* that is holistic and

Elemental, guilt is indeed transferred to the fathers, and women can Touch and Move.[65]

Daly also cites Marcuse's critique of Erich Fromm in *Eros and Civilization*, in which he objects to Fromm's articulated "goal of therapy" as the "optimal development of a person's potentialities and the realization of his individuality." For Marcuse, this goal is unrealistic insofar as the "very structure" of the "established civilization" denies it.[66] For Daly, "Radical feminism, insofar as it is true to itself, is the Denial of this denial."[67]

Daly's only criticism of Marcuse is that he fails to direct his critique "*directly* and *essentially*" at sexual oppression."[68] While she agrees generally with his view that the "liberalization of sexuality provided an instinctual basis for the repressive and aggressive power *of the affluent society*," she argues that it is "*the sexist society*,"[69] and not the *affluent society* that is aggressive and repressive. Daly charges that Marcuse's "social criticism does not go far enough" because he locates the "radical source" of social and individual alienation in capitalism,[70] whereas for her, its real source is in sexism. However, by replacing capitalism with sexism as the focus of critical social theory, Daly narrows the scope of domination and simplifies its dynamics, reducing it to a basic antagonism between male and female. In doing this she dismisses—without serious consideration—Marcuse's critical insights into the subtle and intangible workings of domination that have become so sophisticated in late twentieth-century industrial-technological societies as to be nearly invisible. It is as if in eradicating male power over women, or at least rendering it ineffectual, women will have no problems whatsoever and will encounter no barriers on their journey to the Background/homeland of Elemental Be-ing.

What Daly never addresses is the question of the context of this journey; where does it take place, in history or in some other realm to which only women have access? She writes of living "on the boundary," and of "creative boundary-living" that is "expressed and symbolized" by "whales and dolphins", the "tortoise" and "the hermit crab" whose main virtue is that she is "at home on the road."[71] Daly's description of the hermit crab's "resourcefulness of . . . moving into the discarded shells of other animals . . . in which she comfortably travels while seeking larger shells to occupy as she increases in size" is a metaphoric expression of the Hegelian concept of negativity, where Spirit, in the process of congealing into external forms that are momentarily adequate to its unfolding, must also continuously negate, discard and finally supersede them. Daly's theorizing is here similarly vulnerable to Marx's critique of Hegel which objected that the moving, creative force of history was not Spirit but human beings in their concrete labouring activity. As Hegel displaced human beings as the subjects of history, Daly also exhibits a tendency in the same direction as she ontologizes femaleness and thus objectifies and reifies it with the result that living individual women all but disappear.

Concerning Daly's exhortation for boundary living, most women already live on the boundary of social existence and do not find it a poetic experience. However heightened many women's ecological consciousness may have become, it is both sentimental and absurd to offer hermit crabs and tortoises as models for how women might live alternative lives away from patriarchal oppression. What Daly proposes here is little more than a form of romantic escapism by driving women's revolutionary energy for social and personal transformation into esoteric realms of privatized experience. Her extended essays and detailed passages outlining the specific atrocities committed against women in various cultures and historical periods are actually lists of horrors devoid of social analysis which would expand her theoretically inadequate assertions of male perversity, evil, and gynocidal intent. The value of Marcuse's social theory is that it offers profound and relevant insights into the complex dynamics of domination by examining its social and psychological mediations. Moreover, Marcuse's vision of a liberated, transformed humanity is profoundly humanist and inclusive. Daly's religio-philosophical vision is structured in terms of exclusivism and is anti-humanist. Not only does her philosophy exclude all men, it implicitly excludes heterosexual women as stamped with the alienation of patriarchy.

Gynocentric feminism, as represented by Daly and as a general theory of women's liberation, is aporetic in that it rests upon a logic of identity that generates a regulatory fiction, by imposing a compulsory correspondence between a transcendental female subject and individual women. Daly's Elemental, Lusty, Racing Race of Women, Crones, Hags, Archelogians, Hag-Gnostics, Spinners, Websters, etc., say little to women who daily struggle against domination in its nearly infinite variety of forms. Daly's A-mazing Amazons are mythological figures with which no woman can identify in ways that can open insights into oppression that may further lead to practical, emancipatory action. Daly is spinning new reifications of female nature, and her exhortations for living on the boundary drives revolutionary activity into imaginary esoteric realms that are severed from concrete reality. In this, she shares in Marcuse's failure to adequately address women's oppression and construct an effective theory and practice of liberation. But Marcuse at least connected feminism with socialism, recognizing the need for a comprehensive feminist social theory that directly addressed women's condition in a way that opened up emancipatory possibilities for all humanity. Daly simply dismisses socialism and "its by-product, *socialist feminism*" as nothing more than a "bombardment of verbiage which often replaces/displaces any signs or acts of genuine biophilic concern."[72] Daly's feminist philosophy at best is capable of providing only an abstract unity *among* women at the expense of the concrete differences that exist *between* women. Efforts to realize abstract unity not only dissipate and atrophy revolutionary energy, they all too easily result in an oppressive politics of regulatory practices that exclude difference in the name of an illusory reconciliation only possible in a mythic utopia.[73]

A major problem with most gynocentric approaches to feminism concerns the elusive quest for a feminine essence that is so prominent in Daly. I have in mind here Monique Plaza's critique of Luce Irigaray as an illustration of this point.[74] It should be noted that Daly has much in common with some forms of French feminism, especially in her creative use of language, which she describes as "gynocentric writing,"[75] but this is a theme to be explored elsewhere. The critique above of Daly's concept of Elemental female can as well be made in relation to some of the leading theorists of French feminism, such as Luce Irigaray, although the emphasis on female bodily existence is far stronger there than in Daly. Against Irigaray's theory of feminine sexuality as a basis for a different rationality, discourse and way of relating, Plaza argues that a feminist theory rooted in women's bodily experience traps women once more within the parameters of their sexuality and physicality, reinstating sexual difference with all the old stereotypes left intact. Andrea Nye comments that the kind of feminist approach advocated by Irigaray deflects women "from their real struggle in the world for justice (by engaging) in a marginal and essentially illusory search for a feminine essence."[76] Notions of a feminine essence can easily assume the negative function of pure antithesis to its male counter-image, leading inevitably to reification and ineffectual politics. The social institutions, economic and political structures of domination that produce and maintain the subordination of women remain untouched, while *touching* women profoundly, in all aspects of their lives.

For all the unreality and mythic quality to Marcuse's utopian vision of a pacified, liberated society governed by the new rationality of female-Eros, he did not propose that the feminist movement (or any other oppositional minority) merely reject the patriarchal *status quo* without first confronting it in a political praxis of determinate negation.[77] Marcuse claimed consistently that the possibilities for future liberation are contained in the present, and he even developed a set of criteria by which the rationality of a given historical effort for change could be evaluated. These are:

> (a) the transcendent project ... must demonstrate its own *higher* rationality [in that] it offers the prospect of preserving and improving the productive achievements of civilization; (b) it defines the established totality in its very structure, basic tendencies, and relations; (c) its realization offers a greater chance for the pacification of existence, within the framework of institutions which offer a greater chance for the free development of human needs and faculties.[78]

Thus we can see in both Marcuse's critical theory and in feminist theory two somewhat contradictory concepts of negativity, one determinate and dialectical, the other abstract and reified. I would associate humanist feminism with the former, and gynocentric feminism with the latter. Determinate negation was for Marcuse and must be for feminist theory a political, subversive power rooted in the concrete actions of real historical subjects—human beings opposed to suffering and injustice, and who refuse to accept the existent state of affairs as well as refusing to relinquish their right to transcendence, "which is part of the very existence of [human beings] in history: the right to insist on a less compromised, less guilty, less exploited humanity."[79]

That Marcuse's notion of determinate negation collapses into utter reification when identified with *the feminine*, attests to the general incapacity of the tradition of critical theory to conceptualize women as historical agents, and thus as full human beings.[80] Because of critical theory's failure to account for women as subjects of history, it could not articulate a theory of difference adequate to women's experience. This led to a further inability to formulate an ethics of intersubjectivity that is necessary for a reconstructed theory and practice of inclusive, pluralistic and fully democratic politics. This failure of critical theory is reproduced in gynocentric feminist theory. Because of their inability to comprehend women in human terms, the Frankfurt school thinkers could not theorize difference, they could only romanticize it. The following statement by Marcuse is perhaps the most moving illustration of the way in which critical theory understood relations between men and women: "All joy, and all sorrow are rooted in this difference, in this relation to the other, of whom you want to become part, and who you want to become part of yourself, and who never can and never will become such a part of yourself."[81]

It is ironic that Marcuse could not sustain his analysis of the dynamics of alienation and domination within advanced capitalist societies when it came to understanding the oppression of women and the task of feminist politics. His concept of the negative power of the feminine prevented him from fully accounting for the historical forms and specific dynamics of the domination of women so that he could do no more than celebrate the women's movement as the vehicle of Eros triumphant and the new humanity, rather than formulate possible strategies for overcoming the negative condition of women in society.

I will conclude this essay with the suggestion that Marcuse could not sustain his theory of determinate negativity for two major reasons: (1) his inability to comprehend women in any other terms than those of romanticized reification, and (2) his recurring emphasis on the future. Marcuse returned repeatedly to the theme of the "ingression" of the future into the present as the "depth dimension of rebellion,"[82] and the redemptive power of the present. Marcuse's stress on the future and the possibility of reconciliation of human beings with their potentialities, including his attempt to picture what a liberated humanity in unalienated society could be like, lends a religious dimension to his critical theory.

If it is to retain its negative power over against the present, the future can only be conceptualized in terms of absence, for that is where the truth lies. As Adorno wrote, the truth is the "unwhole." Efforts to conceptualize the future beyond this can only produce more alienation, because our ability to think and even imagine, is necessarily mediated by what is. Our commitment to a liberated future empowers our efforts to negate the present in the name of unrealized possibility, because we know that what is—the suffering, injustice, and misery experienced by most of humanity, and especially women—must be brought to an end in the name of a just humanity that could, and should be. The power of subversive negativity is located exactly there, in concrete struggles against the existent, against domination in all its manifestations. As domination congeals into ever more remote, and less tangible forms, it becomes ever more the task of critical theory to expose them. As for the future, it must take care of itself. The closing statement of *One-Dimensional Man* expresses what can only be the task of critical theory under the current state of affairs: "The critical theory of society possesses no concepts which could bridge the gap between the present and its future; holding no promise and showing no success, it remains negative. Thus it wants to remain loyal to those who, without hope, have given and give their life to the Great Refusal."[83]

Notes

1 Max Horkheimer, *Critique of Instrumental Reason* (New York: Seabury Press, 1974), p. 32.
2 Theodor W. Adorno, *Negative Dialectics* (New York: Continuum, 1973), p. 5-8.
3 Richard J. Bernstein, "Negativity: Theme and Variations," *Praxis International*, 1 (April 1981): 87-100.
4 Herbert Marcuse, *Reason and Revolution: Hegel and the Rise of Social Theory* (Boston: Beacon Press, 1969), p. xiii.
5 William Leiss, quoted by David Held, *Introduction to Critical Theory* (Berkeley: University of California Press, 1980), p. 224.
6 Ibid., p. 225.
7 Marcuse, *Reason and Revolution*, p. vii.
8 Ibid., p. xiii.
9 Ibid., p. ix.
10 Herbert Marcuse, *Eros and Civilization* (New York: Vintage Books, 1962), p. 89.
11 Herbert Marcuse, *One Dimensional Man* (Boston: Beacon Press, 1968), p. 255.
12 Ibid.
13 Herbert Marcuse, *An Essay on Liberation* (Boston: Beacon Press, 1969), p. 4.
14 Herbert Marcuse, *Counterrevolution and Revolt* (Boston: Beacon Press, 1972), p. 59.
15 Marcuse, *An Essay on Liberation*, p. 52.
16 Marcuse, *Reason and Revolution*, p. x.
17 Marcuse, *Counterrevolution and Revolt*, p. 78.
18 Marcuse, *One-Dimensional Man*, p. xv.
19 Herbert Marcuse, "Marxism and Feminism," *Women's Studies*, 2 (1974): 279-88.
20 Marcuse, *Eros and Civilization*, p. 208.
21 Ibid., p. 247.

22 Ibid.

23 Ibid., p. 213.

24 Georg Lukacs, *History and Class Consciousness* (London: Merlin Press, 1971), p. 146-47.

25 Marcuse, *Counterrevolution and Revolt*, p. 75.

26 Ibid.

27 Ibid., p. 74.

28 Marcuse, *Eros and Civilization*, p. 146.

29 Herbert Marcuse, *The Aesthetic Dimension* (Boston: Beacon Press, 1978), p. 6-7.

30 Marcuse, *An Essay on Liberation*, p. 89-90.

31 Marcuse, "Marxism and Feminism," p. 285-86.

32 Emma Goldman, *Anarchism and other Essays* (New York: Dover Publications, 1969), p. 199.

33 Marcuse, *Counterrevolution and Revolt*, p. 77.

34 Ibid.

35 G.W.F. Hegel, *Hegel's Philosophy of Right*, trans. T.M. Knox (London: Oxford University Press, 1967), p. 114, par. 165, 166.

36 Ibid.

37 For a clear, concise and fairly accurate description of gynocentrism, along with examples of feminist writers who are identified with it, see Iris Marion Young, "Humanism, Gynocentrism and Feminist Politics," *Women's Studies International Forum*, 8/3 (1985): 173-83.

38 See Judith Butler, *Gender Trouble: Feminism and the Subversion of Identity* (New York: Routledge, 1990) for an interesting critique of the "stable subject" of feminism.

39 Ibid., p. 3.

40 Mary Daly, *The Church and the Second Sex* (New York: Harper Colophon Books, 1975), p. 73.

41 Ibid., p. 79, 223.

42 Mary Daly, *Websters' First New Intergalactic Wickedary of the English Language* (London: The Women's Press Ltd., 1988), p. 64.

43 Mary Daly, *Beyond God the Father: Toward a Philosophy of Women's Liberation* (Boston: Beacon Press, 1973), p. 15.

44 Mary Daly, *Pure Lust: Elemental Feminist Philosophy* (Boston: Beacon Press, 1984), p. 341.

45 Ibid., p. ix.

46 Ibid., p. xi, xii.

47 Ibid., p. 1-3. Since Daly uses such language over and over throughout this book, I will not note each reference when it is a matter of a phrase or term denoting either female power or male perversity.

48 Ibid., p. 61.

49 G.W.F. Hegel, *Phenomenology of Spirit*, trans. A.V. Miller (Oxford: Oxford University Press, 1977), p. 487, 488, 492.

50 Ibid., p. 491.

51 Marcuse, *Reason and Revolution*, p. 40.

52 Daly, *Wickedary*, p. 76.

53 Mary Daly, *Gyn/Ecology: The Metaethics of Radical Feminism* (Boston: Beacon Press, 1978), p. 68, 69, 72.

54 Daly writes "on some level we have known with profound certainty that this has not always been 'a man's world,' and that reality in the deep sense—Elemental being—has never been such. For the man's world, patriarchy, is the Foreground" (*Pure*

Lust, p. 138). Daly is referring to the theories of matriarchy put forward by writers such as Elizabeth Gould Davis and Matilda Joslyn Gage.

55 Daly, *Wickedary*, p. 198, 232.

56 Daly, *Pure Lust*, p. 163, 165.

57 Ibid.

58 Ibid., p. 347, 352.

59 Ibid., p. 354.

60 Marcuse, *Eros and Civilization*, p. 76.

61 Daly, *Pure Lust*, p. 320.

62 Ibid., p. 381.

63 Ibid., p. 252.

64 Marcuse, *Eros and Civilization*, p. 86.

65 Ibid., p. 253.

66 Ibid., p. 235.

67 Daly, *Pure Lust*, p. 359.

68 Daly, *Beyond God the Father*, p. 176.

69 Ibid., p. 176.

70 Ibid., p. 175-76.

71 Daly, *Gyn/Ecology*, p. 394-95.

72 Daly, *Pure Lust*, p. 326.

73 For example, see Audre Lorde's "An Open Ltter to Mary Daly." While I agree with Lorde's main argument that Daly implies that by virtue of being women, all women suffer the same forms of oppression, I do not think that Daly's theory would be any more adequate if she also referred to African myths and legends in a search for "the true nature of old demale power." In making such a statement, Lorde indulges in a similar kind of reifying of women as Daly.

74 Cited in Andrea Nye, *Feminist Theory and the Philosophies of Man* (London: Croom Helm Ltd., 1988), p. 153-54.

75 See the "New Intergalactic Introduction" to *Gyn/Ecology* (Boston: Beacon Press, 1990), p. xix.

76 Ibid., p. 154.

77 Richard Bernstein cautions that in Marcuse's thinking there is a certain lack of "determinate negation" insofar as "What always seems to be missing in Marcuse is not 'Man' or 'human potentialities,' but men — or better, human beings in their plurality who only achieve *their* humanity in and through each other" ("Negativity: Theme and Variations," *Praxis International*, 1 [April 1981]: 87-100). Bernstein makes this critique in part as a privileging of Jurgen Habermas' theory of communicative ethics over Marcuse's theory of social and individual transformation. While I think Bernstein has a point, my argument is that the real weakness of Marcuse's concept of determinate negation is linked to his incapacity to theorize women as concrete, historical agents of social and self-transformation. In Bernstein's critique, it might be noted, there are only references to men.

78 Marcuse, *One-Dimensional Man*, p. 220. See also p. xi, n. 1, for Marcuse's definition of 'transcendence,' which he uses in the "empirical, critical sense," as "overshooting" the "established universe of discourse and action toward its historical alternatives (real possibilities)."

79 Marcuse, *An Essay on Liberation*, p. 71.

80 For a fuller account of the notion of "woman" in critical theory, see my "The Politics of Empowerment: Ethical Paradigms in a Feminist Critique of Critical Social Theory," The *Annual of the Society of Christian Ethics* (November 1991).

81 Marcuse, "Marxism and Feminism," p. 287.

82 Marcuse, *An Essay on Liberation*, p. 89.

83 Marcuse, *One-Dimensional Man*, p. 257.

Chapter 16

And What if Truth Were a Woman?

Morny Joy

Nietzsche begins his preface to *Beyond Good and Evil* with the ironic statement "Supposing that Truth is a Woman."[1] This affords him the opportunity to reflect in his enigmatic fashion about the nature of both truth and women. Now Nietzsche hadn't heard about the present-day distinction between sex and gender. As a result, he involves himself in a series of conundrums, which, at first reading, appear to be largely deprecations about the nature of women.

Have men attempted to capture truth, assaulting her with obtuse and dogmatically awkward overtures? Truth, on this reading, is elusive, alluring, a tantalizing chimera that can never be captured by such boorish behaviour. In this sense, woman as truth remains the eternal seductress: a wily antagonist and heretical nemesis of men's most exalted endeavours. As such she is denigrated and despised by men.

But another reading is possible. What if truth itself is an illusion? What if the very tenuous and makeshift categories invoked as truth are revealed in all their vapid and naive posturings. In this other sense women represent a discredited position. Their non-intellectual and superficial situation reveals the paucity and pretensions of any claims to certainty. Women and truth both lack substance. Woman is, in fact, a lie.

Yet, there is a third possible reading, and one that Nietzsche seemed unable to resolve. It involves Nietzsche's own disaffection with truth and his search for new modalities of expression. In trying to move beyond traditional forms of rationality that he characterizes as "masculine," Nietzsche appropriates a "feminine" disposition—creative, capricious, perspectival, metaphoric. Such a movement of dissociation puts into question the usual binary and hierarchical points of reference. Instead of formal classifications, all is now flux and abandonment, willful indulgence in Dionysiac revels and reversals. But Nietzsche cannot associate this "feminine" style with flesh and blood women; and this is where his own ambivalences and blindspots become obvious.

Nietzsche was highly critical of the women of his time who were seeking emancipation. He interpreted this as their wanting to become like men—thus they would be additional and identical perpetrators of the very system he was trying to dismantle. At heart, Nietzsche remained a captive of the mystique that romanticized women as supporters and inspirators, never executors in their own right. As a result, his subversive "feminine" enthusiasm was not to become the province of women; they remained confined to the stereotypical distinctions that Nietzsche was, somewhat inconsistently, trying to sabotage.

Yet, out of this "feminine" style with its sceptical attitude and irreverent exposures of all that is held sacred — in form or deed — could come another interpretation of woman and truth. This would be of a woman who is not dependent on any formulations made by others. As her own agent, in iconoclastic fashion, she interrogates whatever has been held as an absolute or ideal. She submits it to her own radical examination which holds in abeyance all appeals to truth. For this woman knows there is no truth — specifically as it has been articulated in conventional models.

It is this figure of woman that Derrida co-opts and exploits in his own discussion of Nietzsche and women. In his book *Spurs: Nietzsche's Styles*, the Dionysiac woman becomes the exemplar of the deconstructive interventions.

> There is no such thing as the essence of woman because woman averts, she is averted of herself. Out of the depths, endless and unfathomable, she engulfs and distorts all vestige of essentiality, of identity, of property.... There is no such thing as the truth of woman, but it is because of that abyssal divergence of the truth, because that untruth is "truth." Woman is but one name for that untruth of truth.[2]

Despite his excesses and idiosyncrasies, Derrida here is issuing a reminder of an important proviso. All this talk of "woman" has been conducted in a generalized and even "essentialized" fashion. Just as there is no such thing as "truth" in a deconstructive dispensation, so there can be no such thing as "woman." Idealized generalizations no longer hold. So woman and truth cannot be compared, for the basis of any such resemblance has been demonstrated as fictitious.

But this then leads to a question that is particularly troubling both in religious and philosophical circles. How can a woman define herself today, assuming she avoids the trap of presuming to speak on behalf of all women? And what claims can be made with regard to truth? Have we moved to a postmodern paradigm where any assertion must at the same time be subject to ingenious disclaimers?

There are many feminists who subscribe to the postmodern paradigm, finding in its polyvalent tendencies and marginal discourse a sympathetic affiliation with their own revolt against the monolithic impositions of male-dominated systems of knowledge and power. Just as deconstruction displaces traditional ideas of truth, identity and subjectivity, so, such feminists argue, do contemporary feminists strive to formulate a new way of ordering their descriptions of the self and of the world in ways that are multiple, interconnected and non-oppositional.

Susan Hekman is an articulate proponent of this relationship.

> The two movements [feminism and postmodernism] are by no means identical.... The similarities between the two movements, however, are striking.

Feminism and postmodernism are the only contemporary theories that present a truly radical critique of the Enlightenment legacy of modernism. No other approaches on the contemporary intellectual scene offer a means of displacing and transforming the masculinist epistemology of modernity.[3]

In this scenario, truth can no longer be located according to abstract and absolute principles. Often this stance is interpreted as nihilism or relativism, where truth as a concept is totally banished from the scene. But perhaps what is at stake is a clearer distinction between Truth and those truths that are representative of values and modalities of self-definition which no longer reflect univocal forms of dogmatism.

Hekman appeals to Foucault's model of contextual, historical, "local" discourses as an example of such a modality which disrupts universal structures. At the same time, these modalities seek to articulate "the formulation of a feminist discourse that constitutes the feminine, the masculine and sexuality in a different way."[4] These alternate forms of truth do not subscribe to traditional formats, but seek to describe ways of thinking and acting that are appropriate to the circumstances. Yet how can such a limited position be considered as pertaining to any form of truth? And what does this approach offer for the specific needs of women today?

Questioning this approach, there are some feminists who wonder if such pluralistic and heterogeneous extravagances have anything at all to do with a feminist agenda. Linda Kintz, who acknowledges the brilliance of Derrida's disruption of white, male, European presumptions, wonders whether Derrida's proclaimed impartial posture is not just one more male autograph in this magisterial tradition.[5] It seems that women are either still being told what to do, or, even in trying to find their own voice, still taking their lead from the dominant and fashionable male-determined theories of the day.

Kintz is particularly suspicious of Derrida's warning women against formulating a position for a female subject. On his reading, to do this would be to fall prey to the old system of dichotomized thought and its metaphysical presuppositions that both deconstruction and feminism wish to repudiate. But Kintz argues that such theoretical admonitions are made in the absence of any context and could be interpreted as just another instance of abstract paternalism at work. For Kintz, what is particularly necessary for women today is to emphasize "the differences that gender always introduces into the situation of reader and writer."[6] This will mean that each woman, as she reads and writes, needs to take into consideration the presuppositions that influence any subjective discourse, specifically the effects of culturally determined gender differentiation. As Kintz so eloquently queries:

If we do not try to work out a theoretical position from which we can analyze how men and women read and write differently, not because of any essence that either gender somehow possesses which would make their readings "truer" but because they enter with a different historical relation to language, in what way can women claim the right to speak at all as women in a system of deconstruction?[7]

Another feminist scholar, Leslie Wahl Rabine, is also wary of adopting deconstructive manoeuvres wholesale.[8] Instead, she advocates a strategic adaption, rather than being caught up in deconstruction's interminable, indeterminate ploys. Rabine understands that it is impossible for women to abandon concrete action on specific issues, and that in such instances, there is no room for ambiguity or irresolution. Such activity will always require a degree of complicity with the very frameworks that are being contested—be they metaphysical categories or political organizations.[9] But though such conduct is imperative, women need to become aware that no particular form of behaviour need be endorsed as demarcating the truth. As Rabine suggests: "every position can be analyzed as lacking a full truth or a fully correct politics."[10]

And so, while women may be constrained by circumstances to make a yes/no decision—this need not indicate that such a response is the ideal to be replicated unquestioningly in all similar situations. No single formulation is adequate to account for the complex variations that can occur in women's lives. In this connection, any unilateral pronouncement will always be inadequate. Thus, Rabine states that a feminist strategy should not be considered "in terms of a stable opposition but in terms of an oscillation between several positions, in which the necessity of adopting a position in a given situation would include simultaneously calling it into question."[11]

But this "calling into question" of the very grounds on which any decision is made, any procedure undertaken, can, in Rabine's account only occur within specific historical or institutional contexts. Thus, both Kintz and Rabine, while cautious concerning the wholesale incorporation of deconstructive tactics into a feminist agenda, nevertheless agree that, as a qualification, it can check any impulses ready to seize upon a certain frame of reference and to label it unequivocally as "truth." Crucial to such an awareness is the distinction between sex and gender, i.e., the understanding "that gender is not an innate feature (as sex may be) but a sociocultural construction."[12] In a way, this separation between biological and cultural aspects should further mitigate the tendency to make truth claims as regards women, either in terms of physiological determinations or of alleged eternal feminine attributes. Yet that has not stopped such a clarification from leading to a certain impasse between various persuasions in recent feminist discussions.

While not rejecting this view, Susan Bordo is troubled by the apparent presumption on the part of certain proponents of postmodernism that their theoretical orientation provides *"the* authoritative insight" into issues of gender. Gender, however, in this perspective is viewed as "only one axis of a complex, heterogeneous construction, constantly interpenetrating, in historically specific ways, with other multiple axes of identity."[13]

Bordo worries that this theoretical emphasis on diversity and mutability dismisses any generalizations regarding gender "as *in principle* essentialist or totalizing."[14] This exclusive attitude, she believes, overlooks the inevitable partiality and limitation of any position, for which we should take responsibility. It is a complex argument, for what she is protesting is not so much the indecisiveness and whimsicality of the postmodernist approach, but rather its insistence on theory at the expense of the concrete. The concrete itself is infinitely various on Bordo's reading, but what is needed is contextual evaluations of each situation, rather than a predetermined methodological appropriateness. Bordo is thus herself a supporter of gender plurality, as are the postmodernists, but she baulks at what appears to her to be a presupposition on their part that no generalizations whatever can be based on this fact. For her, the abstract heterogeneity of certain postmodern feminists assumes a dismissive stance of other positions in a manner similar to traditional philosophic truth claims.

Another variant of the dissatisfaction with the appeal to ahistorical postulates is the fear that their diffuse and constantly shifting grounds prevent the organization and implementation of practical endeavours to reform the societal abuses of patriarchy. Teresa L. Ebert focusses on this aspect of the debate in a recent review in *The Woman's Review of Books*.[15] Her concern is voiced in describing what she views as a conflict between localizing and totalizing theories. She believes that the systems and structures as they exist have to be named, which inevitably will result in some form of totalization. But this undertaking is necessary, she believes, to understand how such totalities as patriarchy operate. Such generalizations need not result in any irrevocable definitions; in fact, they need to take into account that definitions of patriarchy should be seen as an "ongoing, historically contingent and differentiated system of relations of exploitation."[16]

What is apparent in both Bordo and Ebert's objections to aspects of postmodern theory is their concern that the practical dimension of the struggle that marks feminism will be forgotten. It is not as if they are unwilling to admit the contingency of any political position or even of definitions, but they believe that this must be negotiated in an on-going process of interaction between the particular and the universal. Their objections are to a theory that, in the name of irreducibility and discontinuity, prevents a provisional generalization (that acts as a guiding principle) from being effective. If this happens, they imply, feminism loses all credibility as a movement that is dedicated to changing the structural distortions and omissions that regulate women's lives.

This is not a quarrel over truth in the sense of a competition between types of valid arguments. Nor is it a debate as to which theory more faithfully (or truly) reflects women's lives. Instead, it is a disagreement about tactics and consequences, about which option is of most benefit to women. Neither position has a vested interest in asserting that there is still a "truth" that pertains to women as such. But the apprehension that some feminists feel is that postmodern theory, in the hands of some adherents, adopts an attitude of theoretical correctness.

Teresa de Lauretis worries that these examples of polarization within the feminist camp may be detrimental to the movement. Her concern is not specifically with the controversy of theory versus practice, or the universal versus the particular, but rather with its manifestation in the guise of essentialism versus anti-essentialism, which appears in a variety of expressions.[17] In an earlier volume, de Lauretis had expressed her own preference on the question of biological essentialism and social constructivism.

> For the understanding of one's personal condition as a woman in terms of social and political, and the constant revision, reevaluation, and reconceptualization of that condition in relation to other women's understanding of their sociosexual positions, generate a mode of apprehension of all social reality that derives from the consciousness of gender. And from that apprehension, from that personal intimate, analytical, and political knowledge of the pervasiveness of gender, there is no going back to the innocence of "biology."[18]

In that same work, de Lauretis carefully delineated her own understanding of feminism as intricately involved in an ambiguous situation that she describes as both "within and without gender."[19] This is to say that women are caught in the tension between forms of representation (usually within compromised constructs) and actual historical contingencies. This tension need not be construed as a contradiction, or as an irreconcilable conflict between paradigms. Instead, de Lauretis locates feminism in the very dynamism generated by these seemingly anomalous stances.

> The condition of feminism here and now [is] the tension of a twofold pull in contrary directions – the critical negativity of its theory, and the affirmative positivity of its politics – [this] is both the historical condition of existence of feminism and its theoretical condition of possibility.[20]

In a recent article, de Lauretis expands this model of interaction between seemingly antithetical positions. She laments the adoption by certain feminists of the term "essentialism" as a scapegoat to discredit positions deemed inferior. This oppositional trend has unfortunate consequences in that it does not remain an internal dispute within feminism, but diminishes the impact of feminism on the wider socio-cultural horizon.

While de Lauretis acknowledges that feminism is concerned with difference, and with the difference that being a woman can signify, she does not wish the discussion of that difference to be confined to disagreements about its theoretical versus practical implications. What de Lauretis would prefer to acknowledge is a less absolute or rarefied conception of the term "essential" which indicates the specific difference between a feminist and a non-feminist orientation.

> That difference is essential in that it is constitutive of feminist thinking and thus of feminism: it is what makes the thinking feminist, and what constitutes certain ways of thinking, certain practices of writing, reading, imaging, relating, acting, etc., into the historically diverse and culturally heterogeneous social movement which, qualifiers and distinctions notwithstanding, we continue with good reason to call feminism.[21]

Inherent in this understanding of feminism and its difference from other positions is the notion of the clash of different approaches within feminism that de Lauretis regards as virtually "essential" (in the sense of necessary) to feminism. For feminism cannot be allowed to rest complacent with either its definitions or practices; each element should in some way challenge or check the stance of the other in an ongoing process of insight and development. It is this particular system of checks and balances, with its paradoxes and contradictions, "that constitutes the effective history, the essential difference of feminist thought."[22] Thus, the emphasis is on the permutations and combinations of difference rather than essentialism. The consequence of this position is that, if there is any truth that is pertinent to feminism, it lies in the agonistic relation of the demands of theory and practice that is virtually endemic to these procedures. De Lauretis thus strives to avoid unnecessary polarization and infighting within feminism so as to incorporate disparate and even dissonant voices within its multifaceted boundaries.[23] So truth, in the sense of the ideologically pure, is thus dispatched in favour of a type of truth that reflects and responds to the manifold elements of women's lives and their consequent thematizations.

What is perhaps most intriguing about de Lauretis' model is her further naming of these two discordant inclinations in feminism as an "erotic, narcissistic drive" and an "ethical drive" respectively. From this perspective, it is the erotic, with its destabilizing differentials of excess and confrontation, that is in conflict with the more communal and conciliatory bonds of the ethical in feminism's encounter with the socio-cultural system. But it is the process of their exchange that is especially significant. There is no dialectical synthesis, but instead an ongoing reciprocal interrogation by which each side contests the other's premises. This critical reinforcement is not destructive, but inculcates creative regeneration. In fact, what is thereby established is a cycle or spiral of accumulated knowledge (both personal and social) that constantly checks its presuppositions before diving once more into the fray of divergent directions that constitutes the hurly-burly of existence.

Could it be said that this acknowledgement of the variegated, inconsistent and even refractory patterns of our living and thinking is a "truer" version of the way things are? And, concomitantly, could it be argued that in taking these considerations into account, feminist theory could be more true as an authentic evaluation of "reality" than former abstract theories of correspondence, coherence, etc.?

It is at this juncture that an intimation of similarity comes to mind of another current form of philosophy that also looks to alternate ways of substantiating truth—specifically truth as it resonates with our experience of the lifeworld. This approach (which is not without its problems) is termed "hermeneutics." Its problematic nature stems from the fact that, by and large, hermeneutics has been employed by men to describe their insights and perceptions. So the aim of this comparative exercise would not be to see how feminist modes of enquiry and formulation fit into any established hermeneutical categories, but how feminist orderings might inform/transform hermeneutics.

What is appealing about a hermeneutic approach is its emphasis on the situatedness of all knowledge. Its specific challenge to traditional forms of knowledge is that all knowing is contextual, i.e., we are marked by the presuppositions that we bring to any act of knowing, while at the same time any other person/text we encounter also brings certain qualifications to the encounter. To acknowledge these predispositions as "prejudices" in a non-pejorative way is, in Gadamer's eyes, to reject the established criterion of truth as purely objective.[24]

Yet just to concede the impact of such presuppositions in any act of knowing does not seem sufficient, for there is no implication involved as to their legitimacy (or lack thereof). In fact, Habermas has criticized Gadamer for what could be interpreted as simply an endorsement of tradition.[25] Though Gadamer responded to the effect that any involvement with tradition needs to be critical, I do not feel that this qualification meets the demand of a feminist scrutiny as regards the distortions and omissions that have permeated the Western mindset.

Paul Ricoeur's "hermeneutics of suspicion" would seem to be a further step in the right direction. Insofar as the masters of suspicion, Nietzsche, Marx and Freud, were sufficiently observant to detect that we may not always mean what we say, or be in control of what we do, they encourage a radical critique of seemingly secure and impartial pronouncements. This indeed is exactly what a feminist hermeneutics of suspicion would undertake and has indeed been undertaken in the work of women scholars in religion, Rosemary Ruether and Elisabeth Schüssler Fiorenza. Their research has exposed the virtual exclusion or erasure of women's personal experiences and reflections in the Western biblical and theological heritage. Where de Lauretis' position expands their discriminating exercise is in its insistence on self-examination—not simply in the service of disclosing duplicity—but in the interests of openness and non-adherence to any solution as definitive for all women.

What is perhaps most appealing in the hermeneutic model of knowing is its abolition of the subject/object dichotomy. Instead, there is the notorious "hermeneutic circle" in which all knowing is a constant process of movement between understanding and explanation. This duality encompasses a project of coming to know an object or a text wherein the person involved does not make a discrete differentiation between the two phases. While alleged objective findings of the hard sciences are not rejected as irrelevant, their conclusions are taken into consideration from a hermeneutic perspective, which will always acknowledge that they are not final, and that the historical location of any act of knowing is also relevant. But this deference to the personal situation must not be understood as the final imposition of meaning by a self on the flux of experience. Hermeneutics supports instead the abdication of any legislative activity on the part of a knowing subject in favour of a non-imperial or non-egoistic self who receives from the process both insight into the world as well as further self-understanding. In fact, insofar as a self can even be deciphered, it is a strategic or thematic self, unburdened by previous constraints as regards mastery and control of the procedure.

Such a description, in fact, reflects the continuous interpretive activity de Lauretis describes as the way subjectivity is constructed. Though she understands this as a "semiotics of experience" where it is the interpretation of cultural signs that is stressed, nonetheless it is the reciprocity of subjectivity and the social practices/structures in this process that is crucial. De Lauretis expands:

> Semiosis specifies the mutual over-determination of meaning, perception, and experience, a complex nexus of reciprocally constitutive effects between the subject and social reality, which, in the subject entails a continual modification of consciousness, that consciousness in turn being the condition of social change.[26]

However, de Lauretis radicalizes the hermeneutics project in two ways. Firstly, she does this by her emphasis upon social practices as opposed to simply the interpretation of texts. The interaction is nonetheless similar to that with a text (as in traditional hermeneutics), but it is in the very exercise of the critique that a hermeneutic circle can be deciphered whereby a change in consciousness instigates changes in social practice and vice versa. Now, while this mirrors the hermeneutic circle and a model of creative, progressive insight into self and world as advocated by the hermeneutic philosophy of Paul Ricoeur,[27] it is the focus on the social context and the accompanying imperative for change that distinguishes de Lauretis. For while Ricoeur may nod in the general direction of a poetic and practical merger (in contrast to de Lauretis' erotic and ethical categories) with admonitions that the implementation of new insights is desirable, his work does not have the intensity and specificity for women's situations of de Lauretis.[28] To meet her requirements, the dynamics of creation/discovery of the hermeneutical circle needs to be extended to encompass not simply new insights into the world of text and self-understanding, but also the radical re-evaluation of the very fabric of the social constructs that inform our lives.

This leads to the second emendation that de Lauretis' thought brings to hermeneutics which gives it a strong feminist flavour (and this is where her approach is similar to Ruether and Schüssler Fiorenza). This is the recognition that all learning/thinking is through the lens of gender, and so this awareness of "engendered thinking" and "embodied situated knowledge" must permeate all feminist discourse.[29] So then, if a feminist hermeneutics is to be entertained at all, both its critical and creative components need to reflect the actual experience of women, mediated through language and socio-political institutions. Provision must be made, however, for the fact that all of these elements are constantly in process, constantly subject to review, so that an ultimate definition is not to be desired or achieved. So feminist theory/practice is never complete. But this open-ended and productive endeavour should never be construed as an uninhibited eclecticism or indeterminate relativism. It is a conversation grounded in the actualities that circumscribe our existence, which nonetheless lends itself to observant and careful revision. For these moorings to the "social construction of reality" can never be entirely cast off. The commitment to changing them in the name of equality and justice is the indispensable requisite of a feminist orientation. They also constitute the constraints that prevent rampant relativism.

Thus, the static and eternal prescriptions used to mould and control women no longer exact their dominating influence. And perhaps this is Nietzsche's nightmare come true. Women no longer want to be truth, either in terms of Nietzsche's bewitching disembodied ideal or according to the capricious and aberrant ways that flout this truth. It is no longer the prerogative of men—be it Nietzsche or Derrida—to decide the appropriate demeanour of women, no matter how ironic their depictions. Truth, in this sense, has had its day. As women explore their new options, truth, or tying things down, seems the last thing needed. In time, it will be up to women to determine what truths, if any, they wish to appropriate.[30]

This process has been particularly interesting to observe in the domain of theology or, more specifically, God-talk. Women have rejected the traditional formulations of theology, most specifically its prescriptions of timeless designations of truth as absolute and as having a distinct male flavour. What is emerging from feminist investigations in theology is a move to reformulate the task of theology itself, rather than just reinterpret the old formulas along more egalitarian lines. As Rosemary Ruether envisages the task: "This means that feminist theology cannot just rely on exegesis of past tradition, however ingeniously redefined to appear inclusive. It is engaged in a primal re-encounter with divine reality and, in this encounter, new stories will grow and be told as new foundations of our identity."[31]

Though it is still too early to nominate these new foundations, as such explorations are still in their infancy, certain tendencies can be detected that characterize feminist theology. Perhaps, most importantly, there is open acknowledgement of the pluralistic nature of theology itself. Instead of the proclaiming that any theological enterprise is a facet of one, univocal discipline, that can summarily assess the legitimacy of truth claims, feminist scholars allow that there are many diverse currents in theology.

> There exists not one feminist theology or the feminist theology but many different expressions and articulations of feminist theology. These articulations not only share in diverse presuppositions and perspectives of feminist studies but also function within the frameworks of divergent theological perspectives, such as neo-orthodoxy, evangelical theology, liberal theology, process theology, and various confessional theological perspectives.[32]

Undoubtedly each of these divisions may still proffer criteria for assessing the content of their respective assertions, but this negotiation tends to be conducted more along consensual lines than according to the rubrics of instrumental reason. This does not forego contention and debate as to what are the standards of adequacy for a particular case, and, in this connection, disputes are bound to occur. But, as with de Lauretis' attitude in feminist theory, many scholars are concerned that the long-term efficacy of the feminist endeavour and its practical agenda are more important than short-term, and often short-sighted, theoretical impasses. So it is that Ruether endorses a plurality of approaches as the basis of feminist theology.

> Feminist theology needs to be seen as a network of solidarity between many feminist communities engaged in the critique of patriarchalism in distinct cultural and religious milieux, rather than one dominant form of feminism that claims to speak for the whole of womankind. So I state that it is from a Western Christian context that I speak of patriarchal and feminist theologies.[33]

Central to Ruether's statement is the awareness that each feminist theology is a response to a particular context and historical position — a hermeneutical disposition, if you will. But such a situation does not endorse an abandonment to relativism. And it is in this connection that de Lauretis' depiction of the ongoing interrelation of the social context and personal participation, with the consequent amendment of either party in the procedure, is relevant. Reflections regarding traditional God imagery by women theologians is beginning to flourish along such lines.

In her work *Models of God: Theology for an Ecological, Nuclear Age*, Sallie McFague proposes a metaphorical theology.[34] In advancing this model, McFague acknowledges that it is pluralistic in two ways. Firstly, she understands all theological models as attempts to capture that which escapes encapsulation. Thus, all such undertakings need to be regarded as illuminating some aspects of a divine/human inter-relationship. Inevitably, they are partial and contextual. Her second concession to pluralism is that such a metaphorical approach is "but one kind of theology, not the only or proper kind."[35]

Thus qualified, metaphorical theology can then be viewed as a heuristic endeavour that allows for experimental excursions into the way God might be conceived as inherent within a changing context. The resultant interpretations would naturally mirror the concerns of a particular era. So it is that McFague advances models of God as mother, lover, friend, in an attempt to depict the divine in ways that have relevance for an "ecological and nuclear age."[36] Her intention is to try and convey images that emphasize a "destabilizing, inclusive, non-hierarchical vision of fulfillment," which is how she understands the Christian message can have relevance for the world today. In this light, I would see her project as akin to those of other feminists in theology who wish to revamp the monolithic and authoritarian figure of God that has dominated theological truth declarations for too long. At the same time, cognizance is registered of the particular historical and personal contingencies that foster such revised speculations.

Such a move is also apparent in the reflections of women from other monotheistic traditions who are representative of other belief systems, geographical locales or ethnic identities. In *Standing Again at Sinai*, Judith Plaskow discusses the pervasive masculinity that has been evident in traditional Jewish discussions of God.[37] In the chapter, "Reimaging the Unimaginable," Plaskow investigates new images of God that resonate with women's experience, and that tend towards expressions of fluidity and pluralism.[38] She also wishes to move away from hierarchical and separatist models of God to ones that are more consonant with the natural world and its energies. Crucial to this process are reclamations of imagery that have connotations of God's presence as indwelling and diffusion, such as *makom* and *Shekinah*.[39] Such intimations of an all-pervasive, animating spirit also discourage anthropomorphic rigidities. In the same fashion as McFague, Plaskow views these searchings as in their formative stage, but nonetheless a necessary propaedeutic to more developed explications in the future.

Chung Hyun Kyung, in *Struggle to be the Sun Again: Introducing Asian Women's Theology*, presents graphic portraits of Asian women's attempt to discern God in their struggles not only against patriarchal domination, but also against forms of colonial oppression.[40] In their reflections, they tend toward envisioning God as a life-giving spirit that permeates their personal and communal activities in the name of deliverance from unjust structures.

In womanist theology, the emphasis is much more centred on the figure of Jesus, the incarnate form of God, as liberator and inspiration in the struggle of Afro-American women to find legitimation for portrayals of their experience. To achieve this, they must be able to recognize and name the interweaving and often undifferentiated structural oppressions of race, class, sex and imperialism. Many of these womanist theologians, such as LaTaunya Marie Bynum, Katie Cannon, Jacquelyn Grant, Pauli Murray and Dolores Williams are critical regarding the applicability of white women's visions of God to their burdens and their battles for emancipation.[41]

In addition to these explorations, there are many other forms of feminist theology also emerging at the present time, such as that in Hispanic (*mujerista*) and African contexts, that contribute to the richness of this multifaceted development — Pamela Dickey Young's chapter elaborates these in more detail.[42]

There are other feminists, however, who would claim that Christian and Judaic-influenced models of God, however modified, are intrinsically unacceptable because of their past patriarchal affiliations. Feminists such as Carol Christ, Naomi Goldenberg, Carlene Spretnak and Merlin Stone believe that women with religious inclinations should take their allegiance elsewhere.[43] Such pagan feminists find inspiration in evocations of ancient goddesses, with either psychic connections and/or cosmically attuned patterns of religious practice. The post-Christian, Mary Daly, who is wary of any anthropomorphisms, either male or female, prefers to locate the divine within the energies of being — whose affirmation of life finds its most graphic expressions at this juncture in the dynamic and debunking of traditional conceptual formulas by hags, witches, crones and other wily reprobate females. In *Pure Lust*, Daly's metaphorical depictions of female-identified life forces of the Arch-images indicate that their source of Meta-Being is a verb rather than a reified noun.[44]

Such pagan and post-Christian forms, for the moment however, are not concerned with undertaking any major exercise of self-critique — defending such unequivocal affirmation by reference to the previous absence of women from forms of self-determination. In their eyes, any excess is justified in the name of exploration. On this score, their seeming "erotic" indulgences clash with more "ethical" and theoretical explorations of those who reconstruct philosophic and theological abstractions on their own ground.

The question of past oppression looms large in any debates between those women who wish to stay within religious traditions that have a history of prejudice against women and those who believe in revitalized female-identified religious forms. Thus far, however, all of these challenges have been presented within modernist conventions. It is the content, rather than the structures or the forms themselves, that have been called into question. As yet the radical questioning of such thinkers as the French iconoclast, Luce Irigaray, has not had a marked impact on women's reflections in religious studies in North America. And perhaps this reflects the distinction made by Arleen Dallery between American academic feminism and post-modernist French feminism: "one emphasises the empirical, the irreducible reality of woman's experience; the other emphasizes the primacy of discourse, woman's discourse, without which there is no experience to speak of."[45]

Influenced principally by psychoanalytic thought, though Derrida's deconstructive wiles also come into play, the work of the French women thinkers such as Hélène Cixous, Luce Irigaray and Julia Kristeva aims to recuperate the dimension of the feminine — that differential aspect which is posited as the repressed of all Western thought.[46] This approach posits that it is not sufficient simply to rearrange the existing categories in the light of feminist claims to equal, compensatory or even superior status.

> Although contemporary feminists can launch their critiques of autonomy and individualism, they do not question the linguistic categories and symbolic codes they employ. French feminists, however, have unearthed the deep structures of feminine repression in the symbolic suppression of women's subjectivity, body and desire in the logocentrism of western knowledge.[47]

This "feminine" symbolic would not seek to valorize women at the expense of men. Instead, it would seek to reformulate the dualist and dialectic paradigms that have governed all Western symbolic formations. One recent collective publication begins to examine the possibilities of this development in religion.[48] How the resultant new insights and representations will be articulated still remains somewhat speculative, but is it perhaps Luce Irigaray who comes closest to formulating a position in her depiction of women as divine.[49] Irigaray proposes that unless women can conceive of themselves as divine (which has always been a male prerogative) they will lack the integrity and the confidence to challenge the dominant mindset which has kept them in subjection. Social equality is one thing, but a changed dynamic of inner valuation that effects a transformative vision of self in relation to the world is, for Irigaray, even more necessary. Irigaray's notion of a divine principle that contests the dominant symbolic register should not be confused, however, with an incarnated goddess. It demarcates instead a process of destablization of established conventions, both concrete and abstract. This occurs in the name of a realization of a reciprocity that can only result from a dismantling of all hierarchies — political, social, philosophical. But the most important domain that needs repealing, according to Irigaray, is that which has been imprinted on all our cultural practices by way of language and its symbolic associations.[50]

The two very disparate programs of North American feminist theologians and the French women thinkers could be conceived as modalities that echo the divergence described by de Lauretis in her depiction of the ethical and the erotic tendencies in contemporary feminism. Instead of confrontation, then, the best strategy would seem to be to acknowledge the necessity of both movements. Though disagreement regarding priorities is inevitable, it is not to anyone's advantage to disparage one option in favour of the other which is then advanced as being the sole agency of truth—let alone as the new manifestation of the ultimate (whatever that might be) for all women. As de Lauretis has observed, much energy is wasted in fruitless conflict. But constant evaluation, within the format of a hermeneutics of suspicion, of all designations regarding personal and theoretical insights and formulations could safeguard any admonition from becoming prematurely prescriptive. Such a dynamic dialectic allows for innovative insights to emerge from the inevitable interchange between the ideals of universalism and the exigencies of context. This will not eradicate controversy and debate, but it may keep it healthy and productive.[51]

God-talk does not occur in a vacuum. It mirrors the hopes, visions, aspirations and fears of a particular era. The past, for better or worse, is a compendium of our attempts to relate these deepest longings to words and images, which, in spite of revelatory import, are encapsulated in historically limited frameworks. Feminists feel a need to burst from such confinements, but the question that remains regarding God-talk is whether it is the fact of revelation itself that is being challenged, or simply its modes of disclosure and reception. The matter of faith is obviously of central concern here, but the God involved is no longer one of grammar, nor of dogma. The intricate problems involved are still in their embryonic stage of investigation and clarification as women begin to find their voices and articulate their intuitions. Women are being allowed to discover and express for the first time their yearnings and aspirations, and to test how and where they might entrust their deepest loyalties. Continuous dialogue and critique are necessary as different options are explored—but the constant perspective must remain one of a vibrant pluralism that reflects the diversity of women's experiences and expressions. What is striking about these new experiments and hypotheses, nonetheless, is the sensitization of women to the hermeneutic issues involved. Truth is no longer proclaimed magisterially from on high in non-equivocal terminology, but is understood to reside in the attempts of women to formulate models of God that have more resonance with their own experiences.

These epistemological adventures, for I believe they are more in the realm of speculative philosophy than of foundational theology for the moment, refute the idea that truth is any longer one and immutable. They also disturb Nietzsche's versions of women and truth as evocative of either deception or illusion. Instead, they bring us face to face with the idea that truth, as a heuristic notion, marks the boundaries of our attempts to define reality. Insofar as people understood reality as an ideal world or a materialistic set of conventions and standards, truth had been prescribed accordingly. Traditionally women were excluded from any such deliberations. But now, as women question these structures and conventions, perhaps a more modest and less pretentious awareness of our own limits, and what we can accomplish by way of definition, may be admitted. Perhaps, it could also be argued, it is contemporary women's disregard for the proprieties in the way that truth has been pursued and imposed that has brought us closer to an acknowledgement of the all-too-circumscribed conditions that constitute the "truth" of the human condition and its infinite ambitions.

Notes

1 Friedrich Nietzsche, *Beyond Good and Evil* (New York: Henry Regnery, 1955), p. xi.
2 Jaques Derrida, *Spurs: Nietzsche's Styles*, trans. B. Harlow (Chicago: University of Chicago Press, 1979), p. 51.
3 Susan J. Hekman, *Gender and Knowledge: Elements of a Postmodern Feminism* (Boston: Northeastern University Press, 1990), p. 189.
4 Ibid., p. 187.
5 Linda Kintz, "In-different Criticism: The Deconstructive Parole," in J. Allen and I. Marion Young, eds., *The Thinking Muse* (Bloomington: Indiana University Press, 1989), p. 113-35.
6 Ibid., p. 132.
7 Ibid., p. 130.
8 Leslie Wahl Rabine, "A Feminist Politics of Non-Identity," in *Feminist Studies*, 14/1 (Spring 1988): 11-31.
9 Even Derrida himself realizes the impossibility of escaping from the metaphysical format. See "Différance," *Margins of Philosophy* (Chicago: University of Chicago Press, 1982), p. 26.
10 Rabine, "A Feminist Politics of Non-Identity," p. 26.
11 Ibid., p. 27.
12 Teresa de Lauretis, "Upping the Anti (*sic*) in Feminist Theory," in M. Hirsch and E. Fox Keller, eds., *Conflicts in Feminism* (New York: Routledge, 1990), p. 257.
13 Susan Bordo, "Feminism, Postmodernism and Gender-Scepticism," in Nancy Fraser and L. Nicholson, eds., *Feminism/Postmodernism* (New York: Routledge, 1990), p. 139.
14 Ibid.
15 Teresa Ebert, "Postmodernism's Infinite Variety," *Women's Review of Books* (January 1991), plus a response in Letters, *Women's Review of Books*, 8/6 (March 1991): 5.
16 Ibid.
17 de Lauretis, "Upping the Anti," p. 255-70.
18 de Lauretis, *Technologies of Gender* (Bloomington: Indiana University Press, 1987), p. 20.
19 Ibid., p. 11.
20 Ibid., p. 26.
21 de Lauretis, "Upping the Anti," p. 256.
22 Ibid., p. 264.
23 In presenting this theoretical interpretation, de Lauretis refrains from any specific definition of what feminism is. In "Semiotics and Experience," de Lauretis had ventured that: "Feminist theory constitutes itself as a reflection on practice and experience: an experience to which sexuality must be seen as central in that it determines, through gender identification, the social dimension of female subjectivity, one's personal experience of femaleness; and a practice aimed at confronting that experience and changing women's lives concretely, materially, and through consciousness" *Alice Doesn't* (Bloomington: Indiana University Press, 1984), p. 184.

24 Hans-Georg Gadamer, *Truth and Method* (New York: Crossroad, 1982), p. 235-74.

25 Jürgen Habermas, "A Review of Gadamer's *Truth and Method*," in *Hermeneutics and Critical Theory* (Cambridge, MA.: MIT Press, 1980), p. 335-63.

26 de Lauretis, *Alice Doesn't*, p. 184.

27 Paul Ricoeur, "Appropriation," in John B. Thompson, ed., *Hermeneutics and the Human Sciences* (Cambridge: Cambridge University Press, 1981), p. 182-93.

28 Paul Ricoeur, *The Rule of Metaphor* (Toronto: University of Toronto Press, 1977), 306-309.

29 de Lauretis, "Upping the Anti," p. 263.

30 In writing these reflections on Nietzsche I have benefited from the insights of contemporary feminist scholars who have pondered Nietzsche's rhetorical insights. These works are: Christine Garside Allen, "Nietzsche's Ambivalence About Women," in L. Clark and L. Lange, eds., *The Sexism of Social and Political Theory: Women and Reproduction from Plato to Nietzsche* (Toronto: University of Toronto Press, 1979), p. 117-33; Debra B. Bergoffen, "On the Advantage and Disadvantage of Nietzsche for Women," in A. Dallery, ed., *The Question of the Other* (Albany: SUNY, 1989), p. 77-88; Jean Graybeal, *Language and the "Feminine" in Nietzsche and Heidegger* (Bloomington: Northeastern University Press, 1990), p. 26-30, 167-68; Ellen Kennedy, "Nietzsche: Women as *Untermensch*," in E. Kennedy and S. Mendus, eds., *Women in West Political Philosophy: Kant to Nietzsche* (New York: St. Martin's, 1987), p. 179-201; Tamsin Lorraine, *Gender, Identity and the Production of Meaning* (Boulder CO.: Westview, 1990), p. 11-12, 134-50; Gayatri Chakravorty Spivak, "Displacement and the Discourse of Woman," in *Displacement: Derrida and After* (Bloomington: Indiana University Press, 1983), p. 169-95.

31 Rosemary Ruether, "The Future of Feminist Theology in the Academy," *Journal of the American Academy of Religion*, 53/4 (December 1985): 703.

32 Elisabeth Schüssler Fiorenza, *Bread Not Stone* (Boston: Beacon, 1984), p. 3.

33 Ruether, "The Future of Feminist Theology," p. 704.

34 Sally McFague, *Models of God* (Philadelphia: Fortress Press, 1987).

35 Ibid., p. 40.

36 Ibid.

37 Judith Plaskow, *Standing Again at Sinai* (San Francisco: Harper & Row, 1991).

38 Ibid., p. 121-69.

39 Ibid., p. 163.

40 Chung Hyun Kyung, *Struggle to be the Sun Again: Introducing Asian Women's Theology* (Maryknoll, NY: Orbis, 1990), p. 45-52.

41 See Pamela Dickey Young's chapter on theology in this volume for further discussion of these aspects of theology.

42 Elsa Tamez, ed., *Through Her Eyes: Women's Theology from Latin America* (Maryknoll, NY: Orbis, 1989); Virginia Fabella and Mercy Amba Oduyoye, eds., *With Passion and Compassion: Third World Women Doing Theology* (Maryknoll, NY: Orbis, 1988).

43 Carol Christ, *The Laughter of Aphrodite* (San Francisco: Harper & Row, 1987); Naomi Goldenberg, *Changing of the Gods* (Boston: Beacon, 1979); Charlene Spretnak, *Lost Goddesses of Early Greece* (Boston: Beacon, 1987); Merlin Stone, *The Paradise Papers: When God was a Woman* (London: Virago, 1976).

44 Mary Daly, *Pure Lust* (Boston: Beacon, 1984), p. 24-30.

45 Arleen Dallery, "The Politics of Writing (the) Body: *Écriture Féminine*," in A. Jaggar and S. Bordo, eds., *Gender/Body/Knowledge* (New Brunswick, NJ: Rutgers University Press, 1989), p. 52-53.

INDEX

Also published by Wilfrid Laurier University Press
for The Calgary Institute for the Humanities

GENDER, GENRE AND RELIGION
Feminist Reflections
Edited by Morny Joy and Eva K. Neumaier-Dargyay
Essays by: Mary Gerhart, Eileen Schuller, Norma Baumel Joseph, Pamela Dickey Young, Monique Dumais, Naomi R. Goldenberg, Doreen Spence, Sheila McDonough, Eva K. Neumaier-Dargyay, Katherine K. Young, Francine Michaud, Fan Pen Chen, Marilyn J. Legge, Winnie Tomm, Marsha Hewitt, Morny Joy
1995 / pp. xiv + 304 / ISBN 0-88920-253-2

ETHICS AND CLIMATE CHANGE
The Greenhouse Effect
Edited by Harold Coward and Thomas Hurka
Essays by: F. Kenneth Hare, Thomas Hurka, Harold Coward, Harvey A. Buckmaster, Peter Danielson, Wayne Stewart and Peter Dickey, Nigel Bankes, G. Cornelis van Kooten, Kerri R. Blair and William A. Ross
1993 / pp. xii + 199 / ISBN 0-88920-233-8

REFLECTIONS ON CULTURAL POLICY
Past, Present and Future
Edited by Evan Alderson, Robin Blaser and Harold Coward
Essays by: Robin Blaser, John Humphrey, Haijo Westra, Jonathan Bordo, Steven E. Cole, Hazard Adams, Gordon Fearn, Anthony Welch, Barry Cooper, Robert Kroetsch
1993 / pp. xii + 194 / ISBN 0-88920-215-X

BAPTISM, PEACE AND THE STATE IN THE REFORMED AND MENNONITE TRADITIONS
Edited by Ross T. Bender and Alan P. F. Sell
Essays by: Alan P. F. Sell, Charles C. West, Marlin E. Miller, Max L. Stackhouse, Howard John Loewen, Iain G. Nicol, Harry Loewen, Hugo Meynell, Harry H. Hiller, Andrew D. MacRae, Tom Sinclair-Faulkner
1991 / pp. xii + 248 / ISBN 0-88920-204-4

THE EDUCATIONAL LEGACY OF ROMANTICISM
Edited by John Willinsky
Essays by: Aubrey Rosenberg, Ann E. Berthoff, Clarence J. Karier, Diana Korzenik, Edgar Z. Friedenberg, Johan Lyall Aitken, Richard L. Butt, John Willinsky, Anne McWhir, Max van Manen, Jane Roland Martin, Madeleine R. Grumet, Deborah A. Dooley, Kieran Egan
1990 / pp. xiv + 310 / ISBN 0-88920-996-0

SILENCE, THE WORD AND THE SACRED
Edited by E. D. Blodgett and H. G. Coward
Essays by: David Atkinson, Robin Blaser, E. D. Blodgett, Ronald Bond, Joseph Epes Brown, Harold Coward, Monique Dumais, David Goa, Stanley Hopper, Doug Jones, Smaro Kamboureli, Rudy Wiebe
1989 / pp. xii + 226 / ISBN 0-88920-981-2

RUPERT'S LAND
A Cultural Tapestry
Edited by Richard C. Davis
Essays by: Richard I. Ruggles, Olive P. Dickason, John L. Allen, Clive Holland, Sylvia Van Kirk, James G. E. Smith, Robert Stacey, Irene Spry, Fred Crabb, Edward Cavell, R. Douglas Francis, Robert H. Cockburn
1988 / pp. xii + 323 / ISBN 0-88920-976-6

.983)

His Craft and Thought
Edited by **Roman Struc and J. C. Yardley**
Essays by: Charles Bernheimer, James Rolleston, Patrick O'Neill, Egon Schwarz, Ernst Loeb, Mark Harman, Ruth Gross, W. G. Kudszus
1986 / pp. viii + 160 / ISBN 0-88920-187-0

ANCIENT COINS OF THE GRAECO-ROMAN WORLD
The Nickle Numismatic Papers
Edited by **Waldemar Heckel and Richard Sullivan**
Essays by: C. M. Kraay, M. B. Wallace, Nancy Moore, Stanley M. Burstein, Frank Holt, Otto Mørkholm, Bluma Trell, Richard Sullivan, Duncan Fishwick, B. Levy, Richard Weigel, Frances Van Keuren, P. Visonà, Alexander G. McKay, Robert L. Hohlfelder
1984 / pp. xii + 310 / ISBN 0-88920-130-7

DRIVING HOME
A Dialogue Between Writers and Readers
Edited by **Barbara Belyea and Estelle Dansereau**
Essays by: E. D. Blodgett, Christopher Wiseman, D. G. Jones, Myrna Kostash, Richard Giguère, Aritha van Herk, Peter Stevens, Jacques Brault
1984 / pp. xiv + 98 / ISBN 0-88920-148-X

DOCTORS, PATIENTS, AND SOCIETY
Power and Authority in Medical Care
Edited by **Martin S. Staum and Donald E. Larsen**
Essays by: David J. Roy, John C. Moskop, Ellen Picard, Robert E. Hatfield, Harvey Mitchell, Toby Gelfand, Hazel Weidman, Anthony K. S. Lam, Carol Herbert, Josephine Flaherty, Benjamin Freedman, Lionel E. McLeod, Janice P. Dickin McGinnis, Anne Crichton, Malcolm C. Brown, Thomas McKeown, Cathy Charles
1981 / pp. xiv + 290 / ISBN 0-88920-111-0

SCIENCE, PSEUDO-SCIENCE AND SOCIETY
Edited by **Marsha P. Hanen, Margaret J. Osler, and Robert G. Weyant**
Essays by: Paul Thagard, Adolf Grünbaum, Antony Flew, Robert G. Weyant, Marsha P. Hanen, Richard S. Westfall, Trevor H. Levere, A. B. McKillop, James R. Jacob, Roger Cooter, Margaret J. Osler, Marx W. Wartofsky
1980 / pp. x + 303 / ISBN 0-88920-100-5

THE NEW LAND
Studies in a Literary Theme
Edited by **Richard Chadbourne and Hallvard Dahlie**
Essays by: Richard Chadbourne, Hallvard Dahlie, Naïm Kattan, Roger Motut, Peter Stevens, Ronald Sutherland, Richard Switzer, Clara Thomas, Jack Warwick, Rudy Wiebe
1978 / pp. viii + 160 / ISBN 0-88920-065-3

RELIGION AND ETHNICITY
Edited by **Harold Coward and Leslie Kawamura**
Essays by: Harold Barclay, Harold Coward, Frank Epp, David Goa, Yvonne Yazbeck Haddad, Gordon Hirabayashi, Roger Hutchinson, Leslie Kawamura, Grant Maxwell, Cyril Williams
1978 / pp. x + 181 / ISBN 0-88920-064-5